现代传记研究

Journal of Modern Life Writing Studies

第 11 辑

2018 年秋季号

No. 11, Autumn 2018

上海交通大学传记中心主办

图书在版编目(CIP)数据

现代传记研究.第11辑/杨正润主编.—北京:商务印书馆,2018
ISBN 978-7-100-16779-6
Ⅰ.①现… Ⅱ.①杨… Ⅲ.①传记—研究 Ⅳ.①K810
中国版本图书馆CIP数据核字(2018)第245196号

Journal of Modern Life Writing Studies XI / Yang Zhengrun

本刊出版得到上海交通大学专项经费的资助,谨致谢忱。
The *Journal of Modern Life Writing Studies* gratefully acknowledges the special financial support received from Shanghai Jiao Tong University.

现代传记研究
第11辑
杨正润 主编

商 务 印 书 馆 出 版
(北京王府井大街36号 邮政编码100710)
商 务 印 书 馆 发 行
苏州市越洋印刷有限公司印刷
ISBN 978-7-100-16779-6

2018年11月第1版　开本710×1000 1/16
2018年11月第1次印刷　印张17.75
定价:52.00元

联系方式

地　址：上海市东川路800号，上海交通大学人文楼209室
邮　编：200240
电　话：86－21－34204579
电　邮：sclw209@ sina. com
网　址：http://www. sclw. sjtu. edu. cn

Contact
Address: Room 209, Building of Humanities,
800 Dongchuan Road,
Shanghai, 200240, P. R. China
Telephone: 86 - 21 - 34204579
E-mail: sclw209@sina.com
Website: www.sclw.sjtu.edu.cn

卷 首 语

传记（1ife writing）是人类的纪念碑。文化的起源中就包含着传记的因素，记载孔子言行的《论语》、柏拉图的苏格拉底回忆录和四福音书为传记树立了不朽的经典。其他文学和文化的文本形式，大都随着时代的变迁而消亡，成为历史的陈迹，只有传记以顽强的生命力绵延不绝；到了21世纪更是超过曾经盛极一时的小说，成为文化文本中的最大类别。传统的他传、自传、回忆录、书信、日记、游记等继续繁荣，新兴的口述历史、群体传记又异军突起。传记还超越了文字的媒介，同电影、电视以及互联网和自媒体结缘，开拓出广阔的新空间，拥有难以计量的读者。越来越多的人为自己、为亲爱者写作传记，以保留一份纪念。21世纪是属于传记的时代。

传记的发展，提出了许许多多的问题，需要研究和讨论；本刊是中国境内第一个专门研究传记的刊物，创办本刊的目的就是提供一个发表和交流的园地，为中国传记的发展聊尽绵薄之力。

在一个全球化的时代，《现代传记研究》是一个开放性的刊物。它向中外传记界开放，它发表对各种传记类型的问题，包括历史的、现实的和理论的问题，所进行的不同角度的研究和探讨；它鼓励和欢迎专家、作者和读者之间的交流和互动；它提倡视角和方法与时俱进、不断创新，同时也倡导严谨、求实的文风。它的目的只有一个，促进传记学术的繁荣，推动传记的发展。

办好一份刊物是一件艰苦的事，我们会不断学习、不断反思、不断改善以求进步。我们也吁求国内外传记界的朋友们、传记爱好者的支持，你们的关注和参与，你们的能力和智慧，是办好这份刊物最有力的保证，期待着你们！

《现代传记研究》编辑部

Editor's Note

As a monument to honor human beings, life writing has permeated culture since its origin. *Analects of Confucius* by Confucius, Plato's *Apology of Socrates*, and *The Four Gospels* are immortal classics in the history of life writing. Despite the fact that many genres of literature and culture perish over time, life writing has persisted in a tenacious manner, and the twenty-first century is witnessing a golden age of life writing, which even surpasses the novel, the once-dominating genre. Life writing now is among the most esteemed of cultural texts. Such traditional forms as biography, autobiography, memoirs, letters, diary and travel writing still maintain prominence and the emerging oral history and collective lives demonstrate great momentum. Simultaneously, life writing, having crossed the border of textual medium into the domain of movies, TV, Internet and We Media, claims an ever new and extensive space with the potential for innumerable readers. An increasing number of people have taken to life wiring for themselves or for their loved ones, aspiring to erect an everlasting monument. In brief, the twenty-first century is an era of life writing.

Life writing as a genre of discourse has posed a great number of questions, requiring energies devoted to deeper studies and thorough scholarly discussions. The *Journal of Modern Life Writing Studies* takes the initiative in China as the first journal exclusively devoted to life writing studies. It aims to make a distinctive contribution to the development of Chinese life writing by providing a forum for publication and exchange of views in scholarship.

In the context of globalization, the *Journal of Modern Life Writing Studies* is an open journal, accessible to the life writing community home and abroad, publishing research and explorations on all kinds of life writing issues (historical, practical and theoretical) from various perspectives, encouraging and welcoming communication and interaction among scholars, authors and readers, and highlighting innovative perspectives and methodologies as well as rigorous and realistic style. Our over-arching commitment is to facilitate the development of life writing and to bring it to a new level of excellence.

A full-fledged journal requires arduous and painstaking efforts. We pledge to consistently aim for progress through consistent learning, reflection, and improvement. We also appeal to dear friends in the life writing community at home and abroad and devotees of life writing for your support, attention and participation. Your talents and wisdom are the most powerful assurance of our success. We are looking forward to your help!

The Editorial Board of *Journal of Modern Life Writing Studies*

目　录

Contents

Reflections on Biography and Its Theory: An Interview with Joanny Anne Moulin

Tang Xiumin

Interviewee: Joanny Anne Moulin is Professor of English Studies at Aix-Marseille Université, and a Senior Member of the Institut Universitaire de France. He is President of the Biography Society (http://biographysociety.org), founded in 2015 to foster the development of the theory and practice of biography, as well as to promote academic research and teaching in biography studies. He is also a biographer, having published five biographies with several French publishers. His current research project is available on "HAL Archives ouvertes": it aims to produce a contribution to the theory of biography based on the critical analysis of a corpus of contemporary biographers' works.

Interviewer: Tang Xiumin is Professor of English in School of Libral Arts at Nanjing University of Information Engineering, China, Editor on the *Journal of Modern Life Writing Studies*, Adjunct Senior Researcher at SJTU Center for Life Writing, and Deputy Secretary General of the Biography Society of China. She is the author of *Lytton Strachey and "the New Biography": A Historical-Cultural Study* (2010) and the major author of *The Development of British Biography* (2012). She is currently working on a critical book on biography.

标题：传记及其理论的反思：乔安尼·安·穆兰教授访谈

受访者：乔安尼·安·穆兰，现任法国艾克斯·马赛大学英文教授，法兰西大学研究院院士，欧洲传记学会（http：//biographysociety.org）会长。该学会成立于 2015 年，旨在促进传记理论与实践的发展和传记学领域的学术研究与教学工作。穆兰也是传记作家，曾在法国多家出版社出版过五部传记。在研项目："HAL Archives ouvertes"，旨在对当代传记作家的作品语料库批判分析的基础上研究传记理论。

采访者：唐岫敏，南京信息工程大学英语教授，《现代传记研究》编辑，上海交通大学传记中心兼职研究员，中国传记文学学会副秘书长。著有《斯特拉奇与“新传记”》（2010），《英国传记发展史》（2012）的第一作者。

Joanny Anne Moulin is the fourth French scholar that the *Journal of Modern Life Writing Studies* welcomes. While Philippe Lejeune and the other two scholars address autobiography, diary and literary biography in their articles, Moulin, in the interview, gives a comprehensive and seminal reflection on biography and the theory, insightful especially with his own life writing experience. The email interview was conducted in April 2018.

Tang Xiumin(TX): *Biographers usually don't talk much about theories. They prefer to talk about influence. As a biographer and as a biography scholar, what do you think of theories in regard to life writing?*

Joanny Anne Moulin(JM): Biographers, like most writers, are not generally fond of literary theory and literary criticism, which can all too easily make them feel like pigs in a bacon factory. Besides, some people repeatedly argue, especially in Great Britain and the United States, that the current demands for a theory of biography are misconceived, as if biography was essentially incompatible with theory, and therefore should be left untheorized. This sort of argument is really a vestige of the so-called "theory wars" of the 1970s and 1980s, and it rests on a confusion between literary theory, which is, with literary history and literary criticism, one of the three modes of expression of literary science, and "French theory", which has been a moment and a current in the history of ideas, quasi-synonymous with "post-structuralism" in the English-speaking world. It can also be roughly equated with what Richard Rorty has called the "linguistic turn" in the humanities, from Jacques Derrida's philosophy of deconstruction that challenges the notion of transcendence as "logocentric", to Jacques Lacan's contention that "the unconscious is structured like a language", to Michel Foucault's demonstration that political power is fundamentally "discourse". In many universities around the world, this has led to a radically decontextualized and text-centred approach to literature, based on the idea that language alienates us from the real. Because of this historical situation in literary studies, and also because at the same time history as an academic discipline favoured the "long duration", with the social historians and the Annales school, biography remained very much outside the field of vision of academic research. It returned by the back door, if I may say, with the Italian school of *microstoria* around Carlo Ginzburg, and the rise of autobiography studies after Philippe Lejeune's 1975 *Autobiographical Pact*, and the development, especially in the USA to begin with, of life writing as an academic discipline. The theory of autobiography and autofiction has been abundantly developed in the last decades of the twentieth century, but we keep feeling that it does not satisfactorily account for biography. As a biography scholar, I have tried to understand why. As a biographer, I have acquired the conviction that to write about oneself and to write about some other person are two very different forms of writing. Besides, I am certain that the development of relevant biography theory and serious biography criticism are not only unavoidable, but also that they will be beneficial to biography.

TX: *Speaking of Michel Foucault, you mentioned in your essay "The Life Effect" that he made clear the idea for his anthology "La vie des hommes infâmes" that "this is not a book of history". Then what is it? Could you elaborate on it? What made him turn to portraiture writing, or* "nouvelles" *writing?*

JM: That is true. Foucault explains that his "Lives of Infamous Men"(1977, reprinted in *Dits et Écrits* vol.III in 1994) is not a book of history, and he adds that it is "an anthology of lives". I think that, to begin with, he is saying the same thing as Plutarch, in the preface to his "Life of Alexander": "we are not writing histories, but lives", thus insisting on the difference between biography and history. Furthermore, Foucault says that the best term he can think of for his "lives" is "*nouvelles*", which in French means both "short stories" and "news" (in the journalistic sense: "*lire les nouvelles*" means to read the newspapers), and Foucault insists on this "double reference": "to the brevity of the narrative and to the reality of the events related". He goes on to say that, although these lives are different from history, they are also different from literature, saying: "they have stricken more chords in me than what is usually called literature". Foucault's criteria are (1) that these are personages who have really existed, (2) that their lives were obscure and unfortunate (therefore both "*infâme*" or infamous and not famous), (3) told as briefly as possible, (4) in narratives that are not pathetic anecdotes, but "which have really been part of" these existences, and(5) that these related lives produce once again "a certain effect of beauty mixed with terror"(which incidentally is not very far from Burke's sublime). Therefore, says Foucault, he has "banished anything like imagination or literature" from his writing, he "has taken care that" these texts "be always in the greatest possible number of rapports with reality, not only by referring to it, but by playing a part in it"—that they "participate to a staging of the real" ("*une dramaturgie du réel*"). What I find extremely interesting in this text is that Foucault is defining the writing of biographies as *the writing of the lives of real human beings other than himself*, and he is saying that it is *not history*, that it is *not literature*, and even more importantly that it is *not imagination*, that is to say *not fiction*. Like Gérard Genette in *Fiction and Diction* (1991), Michel Foucault is insisting that there exists such a thing as a non-fictional mode of writing, and he is explaining that biography, the writing of lives as he conceives of it here, is an example of such non-fictional writing. These texts are *not fiction* primarily because it was *not the intention of the author to use his imagination*, but on the contrary the author "*has taken care that*"("*j'ai tenu à ce que ...*") these texts be oriented towards *reality* in every possible way. That is where I think that Foucault is crucial for the theory of biography. It seems paradoxical, because some of those who have taken him as a figurehead, and also some of his detractors, see him as the paragon of so-called "post-structuralism" and "French theory". However, in a 1982 conference entitled "*La parrêsia*", he returns once again to several authors among the ancient Greeks, and especially the Cynics, to study this concept of *parrêsia*: an action by which "one makes certain verifications to be very sure that one is able to *alêtheuein*, to say the truth". Therefore "*parrêsia* is the necessary instrument, which, in the other, enables me to know myself". In other words, the Socratic "*gnôti seauton*", or "to know who you are, demands that there be some other one, someone else who has *parrêsia*, who uses *parrêsia* to say in fact in what order of the world one finds oneself placed". This is a central preoccupation in Foucault's philosophy, especially in his last lectures at the Collège de France, published posthumously in *Le courage de la vérité*, and more particularly his "Leçon du 29 février 1984", where he speaks of "the theme of life as the scandal of truth, or of the style of life, of the form of life as the place of emergence of truth(the *bios* as *alethurgia*)". The concept of "*alethurgia*", related to "*parrêsia*", designates "the production of truth, the act by which truth manifests itself".

TX: *It seems that the concept of "literary truth" is somewhat tricky. Some auto/biographers make use of it for neglecting authenticity. What do you think of literary truth, literal truth and biographical truth in life writing?*

JM: I would say that it is not just the concept of "literary truth", but the concept of "truth", which is tricky indeed. Moreover, it is especially tricky for us today, because we are living in a period of the history of ideas when the concept of truth is particularly problematic. It is a central issue in biography studies, in so far as many of those who work on autobiography and memoirs or on biofiction will argue that there is no such thing as literal truth, biographical truth, or even factual truth, because all human experience is mediatized by language, and therefore every expression of "truth" or "fact" is always already fiction. That is a sterile debate. It amounts to a variant on the liar's paradox, well-known in all undergraduate philosophy classes. If the statement "every text is fiction" is true, then it is a fiction and therefore not true, but if it is false, then it is true. It is a piece of nonsense, but it is very hard-nosed nonsense, and I would add that it is dangerous nonsense, because it amounts to a belief that there is no such thing as scientific or historical truth, and therefore it means to grant absolute primacy to opinion over critical judgement. Taken at face value, this would spell the end of philosophy, the end of science, and the end of justice. Incidentally, this is the more or less explicit position of some of the voices against the theory of biography, the argument being that, indeed, if there is no difference between facts and fiction, then biography is a form of fiction, therefore there is no need for a specific theory of biography. The denial of any difference between facts and fiction is an absolute form of negationism, which I understand as "*négationnisme*", defined by the French historian Henri Rousso in 1987, and again in 2007 in the Faurisson vs. Badinter trial, as the denial of historical facts, and in particular facts related to crimes against humanity in World War II. In France, this is made an offence by several laws, the latest being the Gayssot Act of 1990, which in turn is criticized as an encroachment upon the freedom of opinion and the freedom of speech. Currently, the French Assemblée Nationale is preparing to vote a "law relative to the fight against false news" ("*propositon de loi relative à la lutte contre les fausses informations*"), revisiting a law of 1881 on the freedom of the press, already modified several times since the beginning of the century, to repress the propagation of fake news. From negationism as the negation of *some facts*, to negationism as the negation of *facts*, there is only one little step, which has the glitter of intellectual hype. But here we are caught in a dangerous confusion. On the one hand, we have a purely epistemological position claiming that absolute truth is at best an idealistic delusion, therefore it is impossible to establish any "fact" with absolute objectivity, and there is always an element of fiction in our perception of facts. Granted. But on the other hand, we have ideologues and political activists who are using this philosophical position as intellectual validation to practise "post-truth politics", contending that there is nothing but "alternative facts", since every statement is always already "discourse". In other words, once it is admitted that there is no difference between fact and fiction, then all human knowledge is always the provisional result of an endless battle of opinions. In these matters, we are witnessing a paradoxical convergence of highbrow and lowbrow negationists: apologists of the anti-logocentric paradigm and cynical demagogues of all trades—although these two sets of relativists are sometimes poles apart in the ideological landscape—agree that so-called "truth" is always already a construct. But you ask me what I think of biographical truth in life writing. Let me give you an example. The English writer Peter Ackroyd, recognized for his fiction and non-fiction alike, asserts that "there has never been any distinction between 'fiction' and 'fact'." If this is not post-factual discourse, then what is? True, this is what Ackroyd says, not what he does: his biographies have nothing to do with fiction as such. To answer your question on "literary truth", I would say that one good example of literary truth is Ackroyd's notion of "Englishness", as well as the "geniuses" or great men that his biographies celebrate in neo-vintage Romantic fashion. In other words, these literary truths can be understood as "the products of the human mind", which people Karl Popper's "world 3", or the "noosphere" of Vernadsky and Teilhard de Chardin. They are "fictions", but these fictions, these ideas, these myths have a real life of their own, as French anthropologist Edgar Morin maintains in his six-volume opus *La méthode*. Like Foucault's "lives" they play a part in reality: they "retro-act" on it in a loop. But the fact that man-made myths have an impact on reality does not mean that real human beings exist only on the same "noological" or fictional plane as these myths.

TX: *Can forms realize the genuine portrait of the subject?*

JM: The simple answer to this question is no, of course. A form, or a portrait, whether it is painted, written, photographed or filmed, is always necessarily a representation, and cannot be a genuine, that is to say an exact, likeness of a human being. But I would like to respond to your choice of the word "subject". Back in the 1920s, in the Soviet Union, a group of avant-garde writers formed the *Novyi Levy Front*

Iskusstv (New LEF, or New Left Front of the Art), and among them Sergei Tretyakov, theorized the "biographies of things", writing "biographies" of non-human objects like raw materials or manufactured objects. These "factographists", as they called themselves, may be seen as precursors of the biographers of cities, for example. This had something to do with Marx's reversal of Hegel's dialectic, which considered history as a "process without a subject". In this perspective, while the "sciences of man" became the "social sciences", any human subject tended to be perceived as an object, more or less representative of a category or a class, entirely determined by social and cultural forces. That was still the outlook of the French sociologist Pierre Bourdieu, for whom to write a biography partook of an "illusion", as preposterous as to describe a journey on the underground without taking the whole map into account. The problem with Bourdieu's "biographical illusion" is that its radical anti-individualism is fundamentally mistaken: his metaphor is a fiction that warps the facts. We human being do not live our lives merely as bodies transported in a train—the automatic, driverless train of social history. We are subjects. Human beings are "living subjects", not only passively produced by their world—their *Lebenswelt* as Husserl used to say, their milieu, their *oikos* (which is not at all like a railway network to which the train passengers can change nothing)—but also actively co-producing it, in a recursive interactive loop that runs on, like an engine or a vortex, as long as the subject is alive. I think that a biography, rather than trying to make a "portrait"—because the metaphor of painting or photography implies a motionless image—is attempting to capture something of the active-passive process by which human beings interact with their milieus: this dynamic co-producing process, unfolding in time, that is what we call *a life*. So, I suspect that the primary reason why we write and why we read biographies is not so much to have a plausibly authentic finished image of the subject, but rather to find inspiration by dialectical comparison with our own lives, and to derive both "delight" and "instruction", as Samuel Johnson used to say in a 1750 essay for *The Rambler* (No.60), by studying "those parallel circumstances and kindred images, to which we readily conform our minds", which "are, above all other writings, to be found in narratives of the lives of particular persons".

TX: Roland Barthes par Roland Barthes *is a text that autobiography studies cannot avoid. The form is quite innovative. Though in a way it resembles life itself, do you think an autobiography can be deconstructively structured* *like that? Don't you think that the form is too fragmented regarding the presentation of the self?*

JM: Yes indeed, it is too fragmented to make what you would call a "genuine portrait" of the self, but I am convinced that Barthes did it on purpose, precisely to avoid the closure that a narrative biography implies. Closure must be understood both as limitation and as construction. In 2015, Tiphaine Samoyault published a biography of Roland Barthes: a big book, commissioned by Barthes's publishers, Éditions du Seuil, who own the writer's archives. It is very well documented, beautifully written, full of illustrations, exhaustive—but the exhaustiveness is precisely what Barthes did not want, because, if I may put it that way, it encloses him in a *self*, which is a "construct", that is to say an *object*, rather than a *subject*: a *finished object*, rather than a *living subject*. It is well known that the key to what Barthes did in his 1975 *Roland Barthes par Roland Barthes* is to be found in the preface of a book he had published four years before, in 1971: *Sade, Fourier, Loyola*. The book is a little like Plutarch's *Parallel Lives*, and in a seminal preface Barthes explains that "the Text"(with a capital T, meaning any text, the text *qua* text) is "destroyer of all subject". The Text, says Barthes, "contains a subject", but "that subject is dispersed, somewhat like the ashes we strew into the wind after death". And he contrasts "the urn and the stone, strong closed objects", with "the bursts of memory", and "a few furrows of past life". The problem is that the "strong closed objects", like the continuous narrative of a book, or a portrait, are images, representations, portraits of the self, that displace, and in fact replace the subject. To put it differently, the subject is "a truth" that the text hides, although it is still possible, by reading and rereading the texts, to catch some glimpses, to guess some disparate aspects of what the subject must have been, through "a few details, a few preferences, a few inflections", which Barthes proposes to call "biographemes"("*biographèmes*"). The neologism is coined on "grapheme", a concept which, in linguistics, designates the smallest component of a writing system. It implies that a life(whether it is a life being lived or a life being written) is a *writing*, or what Derrida called "*une écriture*", that is to say basically a process, or a *trace*. Barthes continues by saying that it is essentially mobile and "beyond any fate", never circumscribed to any "*fatum*" or entirely enclosed in any destiny. He then compares these *biographemes* to the atoms in the philosophy of Epicurus: minute components of all matter that move constantly in one direction or another, and sometimes swerve, in sudden "hiccoughs", etc. This constant movement, this flux, is an implicit metaphor of the *subject* (as distinct from the *self*). A biography is then ideally a "flow of images" that strive to give some idea of what the subject must have been. Clearly, in *Roland Barthes par Roland Barthes*, this is what he has been trying to put into practice, writing his autobiography as a collection of fragments, pictures, small paragraphs, which do not add up to an overall portrait. But you are right: it is "too fragmented", that is to say that we are under the impression that it is a smoke screen; that it is in fact a non-autobiography, like the non-anniversaries in *Alice in Wonderland*. Many writers, like Barthes, refuse to have their lives written. Some, like T.S. Eliot, leave a last will and testament forbidding anyone to write their biography. Others, like Dickens, destroy their correspondence. Others still, like Barthes, write autobiographies or memoirs in an attempt to retain mastery over their own life story, and some of them theorize the impossibility, and even the iniquity of biography, like Freud, for instance, or like Proust in his *Contre Sainte Beuve*, claiming that it made no sense to attempt to write the biography of writers, or to turn to their lives the better to understand their works, because, said Proust, "a book is the produce of another me than the one we manifest in our habits, in society, in our lives".

TX: *The concept of "life writing" is controversial. Historians prefer to use "biography" instead. What is your stand?*

JM: How am I to avoid entering the controversy? I do not forget that this is the *Journal of Modern Life Writing Studies*. How could I criticize life writing here without breaking the rules of hospitality? Allow me to play my joker by saying that I am French. For, in France, "life writing" does not exist as such, or rather it is circumscribed to the study of "*récits de vie*" in certain social sciences, especially in sociology, and it is not at all the same thing, and anyway it is not much done any more. Likewise, we do have some "*études culturelles*", but that is nothing like "cultural studies". The fact is, "life writing" is very much an American thing, it is an invention of "*les anglo-saxons*", and as such we make it a point of honour not to take it too seriously, because, you know how the saying goes: "the British and the American think the whole world speaks English, but the French think the whole world *should* speak French". More seriously, if I may, some time ago in a conference in Britain, an American interlocutor said to me that life-writing was the Trojan horse that had reintroduced biography in academia. I replied that I think it is rather the Jonas whale that swallowed it up in the process. On the face of it, as "life" is "*bios*" and as "writing" means "*graphein*", "life-writing" is the English for "biography". But when life writing institutionalized itself as an academic specialty, it defined its field of research very broadly as encompassing biography together with autobiography, and memoirs and all that sort of thing. One quick look around at the various websites of most life-writing centres, especially in the English-speaking world, shows that "life writing" designates alternately the method and the object of research, and that the definition of this object is such that it makes no clear epistemological distinction either between biography and autobiography, or between fiction and non-fiction. Moreover, any suggestion that one should distinguish between self and other, or between fact and fiction, is bound, more often than not, to trigger off a controversy, which is always a sure sign that we are crossing the boundary between reason and passion, or between scientific debate and ideological polemic. It is my conviction that the refusal of most "life writers" to take this distinction into serious consideration constitutes a scientific problem—what we call "*un verrou scientifique*"—to the theorization of biography.

TX: *Three of your ideas or biographical visions are striking. One, about transnational biography. You have touched upon such an issue as the reception of a biography in another national community. You think for the sake of readership a biography for one nation should have different narratives for another. This has something to do not only with life writing but also with life translating, I think. Could you elaborate on this notion?*

JM: At one level, the idea of transnational biography is related to the concept of "transnational history", which has been the object of debates among historians, who question the way in which it foregrounds and rehabilitates the nation as a legitimate perimeter of historical studies, whereas "world history" or "global history" would seem to offer a more scientifically neutral approach. Firstly, "transnational biography" may simply mean the writing of transnational lives (*Lebensläufe*), that is to say the history of individuals who spent a long span of their lives in a country different from their fatherland. The adoption of a foreign *Lebenswelt* poses a number of specific problems, which are far from being limited to questions of language, or of translation of one code into another. Secondly, "transnational biography" is therefore closely related to the theory of cultural transfers, first developed, in the wake of the reconciliation between

France and Germany after World War II, by Michel Espagne and Michael Werner, although their first anthology entitled *Transferts culturels franco-allemands* was published in 1988. The most interesting point for biography studies is that these transnational migrants bring with them different cultural *habiti* that convey potentials of innovation for their adopted country. When the graft is successful, the transnational lives may be said to have been the vectors of cultural transfers. It is a particular case of the retroactive loop by which individuals and their milieus mutually co-produce one another. Writing the biography of such individuals or groups of individuals (like the Servan-Schreiber family, for instance), has got very little to do with fiction, but everything with social and anthropological investigation. Thirdly, as you rightly pointed out, "transnational biography" can also simply refer to biographies that are translated into foreign languages, but it is generally the subjects of such biographies that are not so much "transnational" as internationally famous, and in such cases their compatriots are naturally considered the most expert biographers. For instance, Rüdiger Safranski, wrote his life of Goethe in German for the German-speaking world, and then it was translated into several languages: that is all the same thing because Goethe is a *Weltliteratur* superstar. The case is different with biographers who are trying to arouse their compatriots' interest in foreign subjects, whose culture they will have to explain to try and create connections. That is, for instance, Jean-Noël Liaut, writing the parallel lives of Elsa Triolet and Lili Brik, two Russian sisters that were literary Egeriae in the days of the Soviet Revolution, the one being Aragon's mistress, the other Mayakovsky's. But perhaps, after all, the difference is much the same between different countries and between different periods of history, for, as L.P. Hartley famously said, "the past is a foreign country: they do things differently there".

TX: *Two, about comparative biography. You defined the concept in your essay "Two Biographers of François Mitterrand: Pierre Péan and Jean Lacouture." What do you hope such a research will arrive at?*

JM: I have proposed this concept of comparative biography studies, not in the sense of Plutarch's *Parallel Lives* or Suetonius' *Lives of the Twelve Caesars*, where the same author compares different subjects with one another more or less explicitly, but in the sense of studying biographies of one and the same subject by different biographers. The notion should be related to comparative history, which compares elements of the past: that is roughly Plutarch's parallel lives, comparing illustrious

Greeks and Romans. It should also be related to "*histoire croisée*", developed by Michael Werner from the notion of cultural transfer, which, a little like "shared" or "connected" history, concentrates on zones of contact between different cultures, societies or groups. Comparative literature compares literary works from different cultural areas, or works of literature with works of other arts. *Comparative biography* is unique in the sense that it compares biographies of the same subject by different biographers. It could be seen simply as an exercise in historiography, or philosophy of history, if biography was history. However, the referent, being a single life, is relatively well circumscribed, and it turns out to be distinctive of biography also because such an approach would be relevant neither to autobiography, nor to fiction. Besides, it is a distinctive characteristic of a certain biography readership, for there are readers who will read several biographies of the same historical personage, and sometimes as many as they can find. Most of the time, before biographers start writing, they begin by reading all the previous biographies and the biographical documents in existence, and when they write, they do so for readers who also have a preexisting knowledge of the subject, or who have at least some idea of the story line. Moreover, a life has a referent—that is the flesh and blood human being who lived and died sometime in the past—but in most cases a life also has *a complex signifier*, *an eidolon*, *a collective construct*, that is not transcendental, but "superstructural," or "noological": that has an existence in Popper's "world 3" as a myth, an idea, a construct, or in any case a "*pre-notion*", as Émile Durkheim would say after Francis Bacon. Take the author of an autobiography, the author of a memoir, or an author of fiction: they all have an *authority* over their text, relatively to their readers, that a biographer has not. Biographers write under the control of their readers, not just in terms of aesthetic judgement (the biography is more or less pleasant to read), and ethic judgement (it can be fair or unfair, honest or dishonest), but also in terms of epistemic judgement, both categorical (it is true, or false: factual, or fictional) and conditional (it is more or less well informed, more or less verified).

TX: *Three, about the biographical perspectives. Your thesis "The Life Effect: Literature Studies and the Biographical Perspective" gives quite a substantial survey of various theories in spite of the widely accepted idea that biography has no theory. What is the connection between perspectives and theory in terms of life writing?*

JM: The article you are referring to is a chapter I wrote for the 2016 anthology *The Biographical Turn: Lives in History* edited by Pr. Hans Renders, chair of history and biography at the University of Groningen, in the Netherlands. Renders's "biographical turn" thesis is that we are currently witnessing a change of paradigm in the humanities comparable to the one described in 1967 by Richard Rorty in *The Linguistic Turn: Essays in Philosophical Method*. My argument in this paper is that there is indeed a recognizable paradigmatic shift of perspective, in literary science, away from the text-centred perspective of the structuralist and post-structuralist generation, who, by radically turning to linguistics in search of methodical models, had imposed a linguistic modelization on literary studies. This has gone so deep that today "theory" is often understood to be synonymous with this linguistic modelization of literary science and the humanities in general. But theory *per se* is not paradigmatic. It is an optical illusion, just as at the end of the eighteenth century it was easy to think that philosophy was materialistic, but at the end of the nineteenth century it could be viewed as intrinsically idealistic, and at the end of the twentieth century it could easily be confused with deconstruction. Likewise, in physics there have been paradigmatic shifts in the days of Copernic, and then with Newton, and again with Einstein. In the nineteenth century, literary science—what the Germans call *Literaturwissenschaft*—was conceived on a philological model, that is to say on the model of the evolutionary history of languages, with Taine, Lanson and Brunetière in France, and for instance in Spain today it is still called *filología*; in the early twentieth century literary science was modelled on history, with a premium on the biographical knowledge of the author under the influence of Sainte-Beuve, and Carlyle, and Emerson; after World War II, with John Crow Ransom and American New Criticism, then with Roland Barthes and French *Nouvelle critique*, it "killed the author", turned to linguistics for a new paradigm, and started worshipping the text. Today this linguistic modelization is exhausted. It has become a hindrance to the further advancement of knowledge. It has become necessary to admit, once again, that literature is related to reality—that, contrary to the gospel formerly preached by Jacques Lacan, the real is not at all impossible.

TX: *You published biography studies as well as biographies. Do your reflections on biography guide your biographical writing? To be specific?*

JM: Certainly, but I would say it was first the other way around: to have written biographies, to have published biographies with publishing houses of different levels, and to have practiced not just the craft, but also the "trade" of the biographer—all the interaction with publishers, editors, series directors, interviews with printed press, radio and TV journalists, invitations to bookshop events, book fairs, public readings, etc. —these experiences and practices are crucial prerequisites to serious theoretical reflections on biography. One must first learn to know what one is talking about. True, George Bernard Shaw played the part of a musical critic although he was not a musician, but that was purely histrionic. John Ruskin was first a painter, and he could not have become such an important critic otherwise. For institutional reasons, at some point I have had to make a choice between theory and practice. It would be possible for a researcher historian to write biographies as research, but for a literature scholar it is hardly feasible. That is because biography is *referential* literature: it is absolutely reality-oriented. In other words, it is impossible to explain why research on this particular biographical subject, rather than any other one, is particularly relevant to the general study of biography as a genre. It simply is not. This being said, I am convinced that, when I start writing biographies again, it will be in an entirely different way. I also think that the development of biography theory will have an impact on the genre, because theory goes hand in hand with criticism, and therefore provokes an evolution of the general aesthetic judgement. At the beginning of the twentieth century, Mikhail Bakhtin remarked that the theorization of the novel was almost non-existent relatively to the other genres, but the prodigious development of the theory of the novel over the last hundred years has obviously impacted the genre itself, and vice versa, be it only because it has modified the conditions of its reception, to such an extent that when we say "literature" today we tend to hear "fiction".

TX: *An interesting thing is that your diction, whether in biography study or in biographical writing, is often noted for witty metaphors. You used a metaphor, say "the game of musical chairs", to criticize the reviewed textbook for failing to include some heavyweight theorists. You compared an author's awkward imitation of Stracheyan style to "a ventriloquist's show". Georges Clemenceau's character in your eye is something of "a knot, a link, a* hyphen *of sorts", to name a few. Such a feature reminds us of Paul de Man's remark that "metaphors are much more tenacious than facts". Do you take metaphor as a powerful device in Biography poetics?*

JM: Yes, that is a well-known citation from his *Allegories of Reading*, but De Man belonged to that generation of the "linguistic turn", who convinced themselves that there existed nothing but text, and that words were more powerful than deeds. I beg to disagree. In the case of De Man, some facts of his life, his past life in Belgium during World War II—although indeed these facts were essentially publications, and therefore texts—are very tenacious too, certainly much more so than many of his metaphors. But *Allegories of Reading* dates back to 1979, eight years before the revelations came out in a 1987 *New York Times* article entitled "Yale Scholar Wrote for Pro-Nazi Newspaper". However, let us beware of Godwin's law, and leave De Man's not so secret anti-Semitic past aside for the moment: that is biography, and here we are discussing theory. You have done me too much honour indeed, reading my texts so closely as to single out some metaphorical phrases. Thank you very much. However, these quotations are taken from critical and theoretical texts, not from biographies. The "game of musical chairs" image I used in a critical review of a biography theory textbook, whose editors had to make rather unfortunate arbitrary choices in the second edition. The "ventriloquist's show" simile comes from a review of a biography of Darwin, in which the biographer constantly transgresses one of the rules of the art by shifting into a shrill anti-Darwinian preacher's voice, which gives the same effect as a ventriloquist being regularly interrupted by his puppet. The "knot, link, hyphen" metaphor comes from a conference paper in which I was discussing the possibility of writing a biography of Clemenceau for American readers. I was trying to say that "*le Tigre*" was the most American of French leaders, because he had lived in the US in his youth, and married an American, and also because of many aspects of his character. At the same time, Clemenceau was an intermediary figure between two periods: before and after the cult of great men was possible, so that he is perceived as a very important political leader, but perhaps not exactly as a "great man" in Carlyle's sense. So, he was a hyphen with the past; but he was also a hyphen with the future, because his intransigence towards Germany in the negotiations of the Treaty of Versailles had terrible consequences in paving the way for World War II. More generally, metaphors are unavoidable in any writing. In fact, language is essentially metaphorical: using words for things, signs for referents, etc. In a sense, a biography is a complex metaphor for the subject. More importantly, the *self*, which is always a fiction, is itself a metaphor for the subject. I think there is a well-known Chinese proverb that says: "when the sage points at the moon, the fool looks at the finger." Well, in biography, the moon is the fact of life—the subject—and the finger is the fiction.

TX: *What is the purpose of a biography from the biographer's point of view?*

JM: I would like to answer this question by quoting the Irish poet Seamus Heaney: "I rhyme to see myself, to set the darkness echoing." This is what I think is the purpose of biographers when they write biographies. I also think this is the purpose of biography readers. The poem is entitled "Personal Helicon", and a helicon is also a musical instrument, but it is primarily a mountain in Greece, Mount Helicon, reputed to have been one of the residences of the Muses, with Mount Parnassus. On Mount Helicon can be found the Hippocrene spring, were Narcissus fell in love with his own imagewith his own *self* and a temple to the Muses, a *museion*, which is the etymological ancestor of our museums. I would like to return very briefly to Foucault's work on the notion of *parrêsia*, which is a practice to cultivate *alethurgia*, or the manifestation of the truth, and in the philosophical quest to "know yourself" *gnôthi seauton* it stands for the necessity of someone else, an "other", which is the *parrésiaste*. The *parrêsia*, Foucault says, is the "degree zero of rhetoric", or if you like the degree zero of metaphor: a mathematical limit to which biography tends asymptotically. This other one, this *parresiast* is distinctive of biography relatively to autobiography and to fiction. To explain the same thing more concretely, when we read fiction we relate to the "implied author", the author as we figure it out just as the writer relates to what Wolfgang Iser has called the "implied reader". In biography, there is a third one: *the "implied subject" that the biographer is reading by his writing, and that the reader is also reading through the biography*. In this relation, I suspect from experience that both the biographer and the reader are involved in a question, or a questioning, of themselves as subjects, as in most reading situations. This describes the distinctive reading situation of biography as a *ternary relationship between reader, subject, and biographer*, because in biography the personage is real too, whereas in fiction the main character is not, and in autobiography the personage is by definition no other than the implied author.

TX: *Interpretations are crucial in life writing. What is the criterion for the biographer to rely on for his interpretation?*

JM: I think that there is hardly ever only one criterion of interpretation, and I am not sure interpretation is exclusively the biographer's job. When we read an autobiography or a memoir, the interpretative situation is not very different from what it is when we read fiction. It is a dual relationship. In the case of a biography it is different: the relationship is ternary, and the interpretation is dual. In biography, reading is *en abyme*, because a biography is already a reading, so that the biography reader is reading a reading. Furthermore, a biographer is most of the time reading a life through primary and secondary sources. Reader, biographer, secondary sources, primary sources (already used before by the authors of the secondary ones): that is already four times removed reading. Interpretation is indeed a complicated affair in biography. That is easy to realize, especially when one reads several biographies on the same subject, even more so when these biographies were written at different periods of history or in different countries: before long one finds oneself, as a reader, in disagreement with this or that biographer, as one advances in knowledge. This poses the question of the "readability" of the biographical subjects, which varies with time. By contrast, at this point it is interesting to mention the Spanish thinker Gregorio Marañon y Posadillo (1887–1960), a writer of the so-called *generación de 1914*, who developed the notion of "*biografía total*". Marañon was a physician, as well as a biographer, and he can be said to have advocated a scientistic or positivistic approach to biography: he believed that by a thorough clinical and psychological analysis, it was possible to construct a complete interpretation, a "*biografía total*", of the subject. Conversely, another Spanish biographer and theoretician of biography, his contemporary Ramón Gómez de la Serna (1888–1963) preferred to speak of "*biografía integral*", a radically different concept, which he envisaged as a "*resurrección*" and a "*renovación*": a much more empathic, more literary than scientific, conception of biography, which implies the necessity of a constant rewriting of the life of a given subject, as long as the personage continues to have relevance for one generation after the other. Interpretation, for him, was a never-ending process, a continual miracle, "*el milagro de la renovación biográfica*". Personally, I feel more sympathy for Ramón than for Marañon.

TX: *Perhaps from Lytton Strachey on, biographers tend to borrow some novelistic techniques largely. For instance,* The Return, *last year's Pulitzer Prize winner, reads very much like a riveting first-person novel with names of real people and real places. I mention this from the perspective of its composition, writing techniques, and artistic design. Postmodernism has the idea that even language itself cannot give a genuine picture of the contents. What do you think of the novelistic crafts in biography in a broad sense?*

JM: Yes, but Hisham Matar's *The Return* is a memoir, and it is typically an example of what the Americans call "narrative nonfiction", and even brilliant "creative nonfiction" in this case. In terms of poetics, it is not intrinsically different from fiction. Allow me, therefore, to leave the critical commentary of *The Return* to genuine memoir specialists. However, you mentioned this by way of introduction to the question of the use of novelistic techniques, or crafts, in biography. You are right to mention Lytton Strachey as an exemplar. At the same time, in the 1920s, Mikhail Bakhtin called this phenomenon "novelization"—"*romanisation*" in French. André Maurois, before he made an important contribution to biography theory in his 1928 Clarke lectures at Trinity College, Cambridge, which were published as *Aspects of Biography*, to echo E.M. Forster's *Aspects of the Novel*, had published in 1923 a "novelized" biography of P.B. Shelley that received mixed criticism, on the ground that it was "*biographie romancée*". Maurois and Strachey belonged, with Harold Nicolson, to the movement of the "The New Biography": the appellation comes from the title of an essay by Virginia Woolf, published in a posthumous collection under the title *Granite & Rainbow*. It is a beautiful essay, in which Virginia Woolf says that the aim of biography is to "weld seamlessly" the "granite of truth" and the "rainbow of personality", that is to say the "self", of which she had the genius to perceive very early that it is made of the same stuff as fiction. She says that "the truth of fact and the truth of fiction are incompatible", but the art of the biographer nevertheless consists in "that perpetual marriage of granite and rainbow". The two writers she had in mind more particularly were indeed Strachey and Maurois taken as two representatives of the same sort of "novelizing" biographers. But I would like to underline two crucial differences between them: Strachey mixes fictions with facts, which Maurois refuses to do, and Strachey is obtrusive, insisting to foreground his own point of view and to impose it upon his readers, whereas Maurois always strives to remain as self-effacing as he can, leaving as much of the interpretation as possible over to the readers.

TX: *What is a good biography? What are the major qualities for a good biography?*

JM: My personal preference goes to biographies by elegantly self-effacing biographers. When we read a biography, we are interested in the subject, not in the biographer, and above all we do not want the biographer to lecture to us and to tell us what to think. That is only a personal opinion, but your question is interesting also because it poses the problem of the critical judgement of biography. The issue of novelization is again determinant, for just as in biographical films we have, on the one hand, documentaries, on the other hand, fictionalized "biopics", and in-between the abominable mixture of "docufiction", so print biographies tend either to the novelized form of the "*biographie romancée*", or to a more or less academic form of the essay, and between these generic categories run-of-the-mill biographers churn out their industrial potpourris. For reasons that would be too long to explain, in cinema the preference of the public and the critics goes rather to the fictionalized "biopics", whereas in literature the novelized style of biography remains suspect. The main reason for this state of things is that, in addition to the aesthetic and the ethic criteria of critical appreciation that apply to all other literary genres, the critical reception of biography has an additional epistemic criterion. The problem is on the whole that John Keats's slogan, "Beauty is Truth, Truth, Beauty, that is all/Ye know on earth and all ye need to know", is beautiful, but not true. Whether we like or not, the aesthetic criteria by which a book is recognized as good fiction remain contradictory with the criteria by which a book is recognized as good science. As a result, the critical reception of biography will have to develop specific criteria by which to evaluate a genre whose existence is demonstrated by the fact that it fits in none of the Procrustean beds of its neighbours.

TX: *What do you think is the function of literary awards? Are they significant in promoting the development of biography?*

JM: Since the last decades of the previous century, there has been a growing number of literary awards devoted to biography. That is true in most countries, and particularly so in France, where several very significant prizes have been created over the last fourty years, some of which by the most prestigious institutions, like the "*Prix Goncourt de la biographie*", awarded yearly by the *Académie Goncourt* since 1980, or the "*Prix de la Biographie*" of the *Académie française*, since 1987. That is very important, and for several reasons. Firstly, it is an indubitable sign that the status of biography has been changing over a recent period of cultural history. It will always remain a popular genre par excellence, but it is no longer viewed as "low" culture: these prestigious awards are institutionalizing biography, and they are contributing to generating a canon for the genre. Secondly, it creates emulation, and a category of highly recognized biographers, so that biography can no longer seriously be viewed as *only* a form of what Sainte-Beuve called "industrial literature" ("*la littérature industrielle*"), published for strictly mercenary motives: the awards are contributing to give biography its "*lettres de noblesse*". Thirdly, in the long term they are having a beneficial impact on the taste of the public as far as biography is concerned, be it only by establishing an "*académisme*" of the genre, in response to which a dissident, innovative avant-garde can one day re-emerge, as it has tentatively done in the past, in some rare cases, but also by fostering and nourishing a critical discourse in the literary press and academic journals, and a theoretical discourse in the universities. To this, we can only hope that we may have modestly contributed by this conversation of ours, for which I would like once again to thank you very much indeed.

Acknowledgement

I am very grateful to Prof. Joanny Anne Moulin who allowed me to interview him at length.

城市传记的书写实践研究

芦坚强

内容提要： 近年来以城市为书写对象的作品成果丰硕，可将其界定为城市传记。追根溯源，《诗经》中的城市书写、汉代京都赋、魏晋志记、宋代《东京梦华录》及后世“梦华体”作品等皆属于城市传记。新近大量涌现的城市传记是这一传统书写的继续，也是对当下全球化、城市化发展状况的回应，是社会变迁的文化表征。城市传记基于地方性文化精神和城市文化认同的书写城市，具有显明的怀旧气质和认同诉求。

关键词： 城市传记　书写实践　怀旧　认同

作者简介： 芦坚强，文学博士，昆明理工大学人文素质教育中心讲师，主要从事城市传记、影视文化研究。近期发表论文《昆明形象的文学书写》《仙侠玄幻剧之审美批判》等。

Title： Writing “Dreams of Splendor”：City Biography in China

Abstract： In recent years，works on cities have yielded fruitful results that can be defined as city biographies. The writing a city can be traced to the *Book of Songs*，capital odes of the Han Dynasty，chorography of the Wei and Jin Dynasties，*The Eastern Capital* of the Song Dynasty and the Menghua style of the later ages，etc. All of them fall into the category of city biography. The emergence of abundant city biographies in recent years continues this writing tradition. It is also a response to the current milieu of globalization and urbanization and is a cultural representation of social vicissitude. City Biography is a writing based on the local cultural spirit and the urban cultural identification，and has a palpable nostalgic temperament and identity appeal.

Keywords： city biography，writing practice，nostalgia，identification

Lu Jianqiang is Lecturer at Kunming University of Science and Technology. His research interests include city biography and studies of movie & TV culture. His recent publications include "Literary Writing of the Kunming's Image" [*Academic Exploration* 2 (2015)] and "Looking at XianXia Fantasy TV Play Aesthetically: A Critical Study" [*Contemporary TV* 11(2017)]. E-mail: 418070597@qq.com.

随着全球化、城市化发展，近年书写城市的作品如雨后春笋般涌现。它们以历史真实性与文学艺术性书写城市，是将"传记与方志的写法结合起来，以传记方式书写方志对象由此为城市纪史写传，这样的书写是对城市进行的一种文学性、记传性写作"（芦坚强 140）。书写者也以传记命名其城市书写，如安东篱（Antonia Finnane）认为："为一个城市写一本书，某种程度上就相当于撰写一部人物传记。一个地方可以获得某种想象出来的人格特征，乃至获得某种性别，并成为自身历史中的一个角色。"（1）英国传记作家、小说家彼得·阿克罗伊德（Peter Ackroyd）认为伦敦形象就是人体形象，"我们都必须把它看作一具人体，自有其生命和成长的法则。那么，这就是它的传记"（5）。另外，英国文学家西蒙·蒙蒂菲奥里（Simon Sebag Montefiore）主持拍摄纪录片《耶路撒冷：一座圣城的诞生》之后书写了《耶路撒冷三千年》（*Jerusalem: the Biography*, 2011）；英国传记作家克里斯托弗·希伯特（Christopher Hibbert）也以传记命名其伦敦和罗马城市史书写（*London: the Biography of a City*, 1969；*Rome: the Biography of a City*, 2013）。因此，本文认为可将此类作品界定为城市传记，它是与人物传记并列的一种传记类型，是隶属传记文学的一种类型化书写。

作为传记文学的一种，城市传记有着怎样的书写实践和特点？为何新近大量涌现？它有着怎样的书写诉求？本文尝试就以上问题进行相应思考，并对城市传记的书写实践、书写特点等进行探析。

一、书写实践

中国古代有许多作品以城市为书写对象，或书写城市繁盛之貌，或追述城市前世今生，文体样式有诗、辞、赋、志、记等。审视其书写特点会发现，这些作品与传记文学以某人为书写对象相似，且注意书写内容的真实性与书写技巧的文学性。下面将简要梳理可被视为城市传记的主要作品，一方面希望简要追溯城市传记的文学史线索，另一方面希望引起更多学者对城市传记的关注并开展相应研究。

我国先秦时期已有书写城市的作品。《诗经》中有不少描写商周都城的诗作：《商颂·殷武》描绘商代都城的雄伟气概；《大雅·文王有声》记载文王"作邑于丰"；《小雅·斯干》详述周王建筑都城、庆祝宫室落成；《公刘》写公刘率民筑城；《绵》记述古公亶父迁国开基，授田筑室等。楚辞中亦有对都城的描写，宋玉《招魂》曾描写都城的壮丽雄伟。

汉代文人形成专写京殿苑猎的"京都赋"传统，赋作"体国经野，义尚光大"（周振甫 79），多为鸿篇巨制之大赋。汉代班固《两都赋》、张衡《二京赋》、西晋左思《三都赋》、唐代李庾《两都赋》等是其中佼佼者。"京都赋"多书写都城壮丽堂皇，亦有少数赋作如阮籍《东平赋》等书写城市建设混乱、民风险恶等状况。"京都赋"书写盛况延续至北魏和唐代。

魏晋南北朝是地志、地记的繁荣时期，其时的志记是城市传记典范之作。志记以一州一地之山川地理、风俗物产为志书对象，注重对地方的纪实书写并逐渐融入文学性手法。西晋潘岳《关中记》、陆机《洛阳记》、葛洪《西京杂记》、杨衒之《洛阳迦蓝记》等是城市传记的滥觞之作。尤其《洛阳伽蓝记》以洛阳城内寺庙描写为纲，辅以史实典故、人物传说、风俗物产等，通过对洛阳全方位记述反映北魏洛阳城兴衰，以笔记小说继承京都赋书写特点，将京都赋与地志相结合，兼具书写的文学性与历史性。魏晋南北朝乐府诗也多有书写城市，曹植《名都篇》、南朝乐府吴歌、西曲等是城市繁荣的产物，多书写城市生活场景，展现冶艳浮华的社会风气。

宋代孟元老汲取魏晋以来笔记、传奇、小说等志人志事纪物特点，创作《东京梦华录》，其书写脱离志书按城市空间格局书写的特点，以文学手法写人、状物与叙事由此书写城市日常生活，开辟出一条书写城市生活、追忆昔日繁华的笔记小说创作道路。《东京梦华录》与耐得翁《都城纪胜》、西湖老人《繁胜录》、周密《武林旧事》、吴自牧《梦粱录》、袁褧《枫窗小牍》等作品既缅怀繁华又记录风土，开创“梦华体”书写传统，后世多效仿之作。

民国时期即有作家以“梦华体”追忆北平之繁华。夏仁虎《旧京琐记》、穆儒丐题为“北京梦华录”的系列随笔、《宇宙风》期刊社编辑出版的《北平一顾》和纪果庵以北平生活为题材的散文等以怀旧心理书写北京，呈现了“现代性条件下，民国北京的‘梦华体’文化心理和精神内涵”（季剑青 40）。另外，林语堂以英语写就的《大城北京》、齐如山的《北京杂忆》等亦属于“北京梦华录”作品。20 世纪 70 年代，台湾一些文人也书写了“北京梦华录”，如唐鲁孙、夏元瑜、陈纪滢、梁实秋、喜乐、小民夫妇等人的文字与绘画等（王德威：《北京梦华录》 24—25）。香港作家董启章以长篇小说《V 城系列四部曲》书写香港之“梦华体”，王德威认为这是一种后遗民写作，美学特点是推陈出新的“过时的美学”，是将“梦华体”嫁接到后遗民小说的书写（王德威：《千年华胥之梦》 15）。

如果说中国作家书写北京是缅怀京都繁华的话，那么国外学者书写北京则或是受好奇心驱使，着迷于千年帝都文化的庄严与绚烂，或是因学术研究需要而进行的历史文化梳理。林语堂《大城北京》的参考文献中列出一系列国外学者书写北京的作品，其中既有对北京社会生活的描绘，又不乏图文并茂记录北京的杰作（234—237）。

还有一些国外学者以研究方式书写中国城市。施坚雅（G. William Skinner）《中华帝国晚期的城市》中论及上海、南京、广州、宁波以及台湾台北诸城市的历史文化变迁；日本学者斯波义信（Yoshinobu Shiba）《中国都市史》对汉口、上海、宁波、台湾台北、新化等城市发展历史进行相应书写；澳大利亚人安东篱《说扬州：1550—1850 年的一座中国城市》从历史与文化角度书写 16 世纪中期到 18 世纪中期的扬州，并将书写界定为城市传记而非城市研究；迈克尔·麦尔（Michael Meyer）《再会，老北京》以笔记小说形式书写 2008 年奥运会前后北京城市变化，结合亲身生活经历书写北京现代化转型的困境。

新时期以来书写城市的传记作品如雨后春笋般涌现。据笔者粗略统计，以北京、上海为书写对象的城市传记各在60种以上，书写广州的城市传记在30种以上，南京、西安、洛阳、成都、武汉、昆明等城市的传记在10种以上。如果说小说、诗歌等书写城市是一种无意识行为的话，那么近年文人学者书写城市和出版社出版城市传记则是一种有着清醒意识的写作与出版行为。首先，文人学者有意识地进行城市传记书写。各城各地作家以怀旧方式书写属于自己的城市，如洪烛《北京：皇城往事》、宁肯《北京：城与年》、滕肖澜《上海底片》、薛理勇《被误读的上海老照片》、于坚《昆明记》等，这种书写数量更为丰富、形式更加多样，且书写模式与数量随时间推移不断丰富增长。其次，近年各大出版社不约而同地出版城市传记系列丛书：同济大学出版社不断推出与上海建筑文化有关的作品；2010—2012年花城出版社出版12个城市的“名城往事”；2010年广西师范大学出版社出版“广西城市传记”丛书；2011年南京大学出版社出版9个城市的“都市地理小丛书”；2012年中国地图出版社出版8个民国城市的“‘在民国’城市地图皮藏系列”；2014年商务印书馆推出“城市家园读本·寻城记”，寻访6个城市；2014年重庆大学出版社推出6个城市的“老城影像丛书”；上海文艺出版社推出“读城”系列图书；译林出版社推出“译林·城市故事”系列图书；上海人民出版社推出“城市画记”系列作品；部分网站、报纸正不断推出“读城”或品读城市系列文章……

近年西方城市传记书写逐渐丰富并引发关注。彼得·阿克罗伊德《伦敦传》(2000年)、奥尔罕·帕慕克（Orhan Pamuk）《伊斯坦布尔：一座城市的记忆》(2005年)、埃布鲁·宝雅（Ebru Boyar）和凯特·弗利特（Kate Fleet）《伊斯坦布尔的社会历史》(2010年)、穆拉里·阮加纳桑（Murali Ranganathan）《葛文德·那拉扬的孟买：1863年以来的一个城市传记》(2009年)、西蒙·蒙蒂菲奥里《耶路撒冷三千年》(2011年)、克里斯托弗·希伯特《伦敦传》(1969年)、《罗马城市史》(2013年)、若昂·德让（Joan Dejean）《巴黎：现代城市的发明》(2014年)、罗里·麦克林（Rory Maclean）《柏林：一座城市的肖像》(2015年）等是西方城市传记代表作品。西方书写城市传记作家中，英国传记作家相对较多，一方面与作家们的人物传记作者身份有关，如阿克罗伊德、希伯特都是英国著名传记作家，故而作家们也乐意以传记命名其城市书写；另一方面也与英国丰富、悠久的传记文学传统密不可分，在城市化、空间转向背景下，作家们将写作兴趣与学术目光转向城市传记书写也就水到渠成。

二、概念特点

通过以上梳理可以看出城市传记有丰富的实践，学界研究多集中于具体作品，缺乏相对宏观的研究视角。本文认为若将其界定为城市传记并以传记文学特征审视，则可利用传记文学特点将其作为明确研究对象，为这类文本找到学科归属。研究价值与意义在于：一方面可以使对它们的研究合法化又可以扩展传记文学研究范围，为传记文学研究增添活力；另一方面能使传记文学研究紧紧把握当下文学艺术创作状况，达成研究与创作的同步性。因此，城市传记不会导致传记文学研究的危机，反而是人物传记研究的补充与延伸，如果说人物传记是个人出于自我认同完整性需要而进行的书写，那么城市传记则是自我认同的延伸，是自我将认同范畴化至城市及城市文化的结果，城市文化认同是自我认同的变形。

综合书写实践与传记文学特点，本文就城市传记做出如下界定：作为传记的一种，城市传记以城市为书写对象，叙述较为完整的城市历史，在城与人、城市与文化的双向动态影响中注重书写城市地方性精神，城市传记书写的情感基础是对城市记忆的怀旧，心理需求是对城市文化的认同。就内涵而言，城市传记以方志与传记结合方式书写城市，注重在城与人、城市与文化的双向动态影响中书写城市历史文化与地方性精神。就外延而言，城市传记是个“家族相似”的概念。其文体形式是诗、辞、赋、志、记等的综合，多呈现为散文体、小说体或笔记体，甚至城市旅游手册之类的书籍和文章也可归为城市传记，也有部分城市传记以影像方式呈现；城市传记的出现具有较强的现实诉求，是基于城市记忆怀旧而进行的城市文化认同书写，对城市记忆的怀旧指向时间上的过去，对城市文化的认同指向时间上的未来；从篇幅上讲，城市传记多为长篇大著，数量庞大的短篇文章虽在书写城市的完整性方面欠佳，但也属于宽泛意义上的城市传记；在图文关系方面，在城市传记中图像记录历史和叙事的意义更为突出。

城市传记定义具有以下理论内涵与价值特点。

第一，城市传记是传记文学的一种，具备传记文学的共性特点，强调书写的真实性、艺术性和动态发展观。

城市传记具有真实性。传记文学的真实性含义涉及客观性与完整性（杨正润 27），一方面须是真实存在过的事实，不能歪曲和杜撰，另一方面则注重书写的完整性，须有一定长度才能反映出被书写对象的"情理与意义"（杨正润 89），不能有意忽略或隐瞒相对重要的内容。城市传记书写与城市有关的事件、人物、历史也须具备真实性。真实性一方面指历史要求的客观性，即对城市的书写不能违背历史，不能任意扭曲或隐瞒城市历史事实，需书写符合历史要求的客观真实，相比于人物传记，城市传记更多使用照片或绘画等图像，就是希望通过照片记录历史的功能增强城市传记的历史真实性；另一方面指文学艺术体现的真实性，这种真实性指向的是具有普遍、本质意义的真实。亚里士多德认为"诗人的职责不在于描述已经发生的事，而在于描述可能发生的事，即根据可然或必然的原则可能发生的事。……诗倾向于表现带普遍性的事，而历史却倾向于记载具体事件"（81）。诗比历史更富有哲学意味，其所描述的事也就具有普遍意义的真实性。因此在耶路撒冷，某种程度上神话远比真相重要：

> "在耶路撒冷，不要问我真相的历史，"著名的巴勒斯坦历史学家纳兹米·朱贝（Nazmi al-Jubeh）博士如此说，"若拿走虚构的故事，耶路撒冷就一无所有了。"在这里，历史的影响如此强大有力，以至于它一再被扭曲……一部耶路撒冷的历史既是真相的历史，也是传说的历史。（蒙蒂菲奥里 7）

城市传记的真实性还要求书写完整的城市历史或城市断代史，被书写内容需具有一定完整性。如《大城北京》是一部荟萃北京700年文化精髓的城市传记；《说扬州》展现300年间的扬州风貌；《伦敦传》呈现2 000年的伦敦的发展变迁；《耶路撒冷三千年》叙述耶路撒冷3 000年的城市历史；《柏林：一座城市的肖像》想象柏林500年的城市历史；《巴黎，现代性城市的发明》则重点书写巴黎现代性诞生以来的历史，如果说17世纪以前欧洲最负盛名的城市如罗马等以其悠久的历史著称，那么17世纪一种新的都市空间和生活模式在巴黎诞生并被其他城市广泛效仿。

城市传记要求具有一定艺术性。如同人物传记书写，城市传记面对纷繁复杂的写作素材，不能简单地罗列事实，须运用一定艺术手法对相关事实、材料进行艺术加工。城市传记所要求的艺术性主要通过文学表达技巧完成，不同城市传记所运用的艺术表现手法不同：《伦敦传》面对2 000年伦敦历史，采取既非时间线性叙事也非与人物传记结合的方式进行书写，而是以空间、时间、事件、人物相结合的方式切入伦敦，带领读者去体验、求索伦敦历史文化，“伦敦是一座迷宫，半为砖石，半为血肉，我们无法窥见全部，而只能把无尽的小巷和过道、庭院和大街当作一片荒野去体验……本书的叙述本身也是一座迷宫，在时间里纵横驰骋，唯意所之”（彼得·阿克罗伊德 5—6）；《柏林：一座城市的肖像》采取以人物传记与城市传记相结合的方式书写城市传记，选取并书写与柏林有关的21个柏林人传记，以事件与情节将人物互相串联、交织在一起，形成柏林发展变迁的城市风貌；《昆明记》从作者视角出发，将于坚本人的生活经验、存在状态与昆明结合，书写带有个人色彩的昆明传记，“这是任何人都可以写的城市。我的写作不同的是，我写下的是我的生命和记忆之城，我的故乡，我的城市”（于坚 192）。无论采取何种艺术手法，作者都希望将他们心目中真实的城市传记呈现出来，其中可能有虚构甚至想象，但这都是他们理解的城市，罗里·麦克林的说法具有一定代表性：

> 与其他众人一样，我住在柏林，柏林也住在我心里。
>
> 我们的记忆并非固定不变，也并非需要重新拼凑的无序碎片，更不是图书馆中积满灰尘的书籍。相反，记忆促使我们不断地在过去与现在

之间对话。我们的整个历史记忆，个人的或是集体的，都在想象中重新建构，成为不断延伸发展的故事。通过这些故事，我们得以理解眼前的新生事件。（415）

城市传记注重以发展眼光对待书写对象。如同城市发展经历无数摧毁、分裂与重建，城市传记也在城市一次次转型发展中寻找城市的一致性、延续性，因此城市传记书写不能也无法固守关于城市的某种观念，而是以一种动态发展眼光看待与城市有关的一切，发掘、组织并建构城市文化历史。尽管可能存在选择性书写甚至“发明”城市历史文化传统，但关于城市的文化记忆与集体记忆框架是传记书写城市一致性与延续性的有利凭借。城市传记书写者依据城市文化记忆与集体记忆框架并以自己的理解进行书写，因此，不同作者笔下就呈现出不同的城市传记文本，不同传记文本与其他文本一道加入关于城市书写的“家族”中，形成城市传记书写“家族相似”现象。城市传记书写的动态发展观与人物传记书写要求以辩证眼光对待传主一致。

第二，城市传记以历史时间为经线，以影响城市发展的人物、事件等为纬线，书写城市空间布局、建筑风貌、人物情状、民风习俗等，注重城与人、城市与文化的双向动态影响，并努力挖掘城市的地方性精神。

从城市传记注重城与人、城市与文化的双向动态影响角度来看，城市传记亦是一种人物传记，或者城市传记是人物传记的延伸。在书写者看来书写城市如同为人物书写传记，二者没有太大不同。比如《伊斯坦布尔：一座城市的记忆》，与其说奥尔罕·帕慕克书写的是伊斯坦布尔历史，毋宁说他书写的是个人忧伤记忆的自传，“伊斯坦布尔的命运就是我的命运：我依附于这个城市，只因她造就了今天的我”（2）；《柏林：一座城市的肖像》以想象的方式书写不同时期柏林人的生活，将他们相互联结起来共同建构柏林城市历史，“本书通过缅怀那些男人、女人以及无数默默无闻的人来刻画这座城市”（麦克林 8），柏林有德国人也有外国人，有政客也有画家，有建筑师也有妓女，有心碎的国王也有重生的歌星，有恶魔也有天使，他们的众生相构成了作者理解 500 年柏林图景。纵观此书，与其说它是柏林城市传记，毋宁说它是一部关于柏林人物的传记。在《耶路撒冷三千年》中，作者也以人物为线索书写城市历史："我将按时间顺序，通过男男女女——士兵和先知、诗人和国王、农民和乐师——还有塑造耶路撒冷的那些家族的生活来讲述这个故事。我觉得这是把这座城市写活并展示其复杂的、意想不到的真相怎样成为这段历史之结果的最好方法。"（蒙蒂菲奥里 7—8）《新昆明传》重点书写庄蹻、阎逻凤、赛典赤等建造昆明城的人和在城内进行日常生活的人，以与城市有关两种不同的人为两条线索结构作品。

城市传记将人物命运嵌入城市历史发展，通过勾勒人物一生传记展现城市精神，又通过城市变迁表现人物命运无常。这种书写方式并非城市传记开创，人物传记在书写中将人物与时代精神相结合，通过人物命运展现时代精神，又通过时代变迁表现人物命运，这是人物传记书写人物的恰当方式，也是传记文学特征的最佳体现。

从城市传记书写城市地方性精神角度看，城市建筑形态、日常生活方式等的书写是为了刻画城市内在精神意蕴。美国人类学家格尔茨认为："地方性不仅指地方、时间、阶级和其他各种问题，更在于它的腔调——所发生事情的地方特色，并将其与什么能够发生的当地想象联系起来。"（Geertz 215）事情发生的地方特色就是地方性精神。地方性精神在文化观念和思维方式影响下形成同时又反过来影响二者。英国地理学家迈克·克朗理解的地方性是"一个地方特殊的精神。这个词告诉人们的是人们体验到一个地方那些超出物质的和感官上的特征的东西，并且能够感受到对这个地区精神的依恋"（101）。他不仅强调地方性的精神特质，更强调文学与艺术表现地方性精神的独特作用。挪威建筑学家诺伯格-舒尔茨认为地方性精神就是"场所精神"："根据古罗马的信仰，每一个'独立的'存在都具有自己的精神特色，它的守护神。这种神使人和地方具有生命，伴随着它们从出生到死亡，并决定着它们的个性或本质……因此，精神表明一个东西是什么，或者它'想成为'什么。"（Norberg-Schulz 18）每个场所都有自己的精神，应该重视人与场所在物质和精神上保持一种良好的关系，场所精神就是"由地方集合起来的意义"（Norberg-Schulz 19）。华裔地理学家段义孚认为"当地方性能满足人们的生存需要，人们停留在那里，地方性就成为感觉价值中心”（Yi-Fu Tuan 138）。地方性凝聚了人们的价值观念并且能够成为栖居的对象，人与地方之间形成一种美学意义的、情感层面的联系。

城市地方性精神就是人们在城市中形成的思维方式和文化观念，是城与人双向动态影响的结果与体现。地方性精神产生于复杂交织的互动影响，是某一城市区别于其他城市的核心所在。林语堂认为老北京的精神“是许多世纪以来形成的不可名状的魅力。或许有一天，基于零碎的认识，人民认为那是一种生活方式。那种方式属于整个世界，千年万代。它是成熟的，异教的，欢快的，强大的，预示着对所有价值的重新估价——是出自人类灵魂的一种独特创造”（14）。

需要注意的是，城市传记对地方性文化、精神的书写具有选择性。为了突出城市地方性精神，城市传记会有意识地选择书写材料与内容，在城市发展中具有独特意义的事件、人物、建筑等会成为重点书写对象。通过选择性与目的性书写，城市集体记忆与文化记忆框架被建构，城市文化传统与地方性精神被有意“发明”，城市历史文化的合法性也由此形成。

第三，城市传记的文体形式相对自由，可以是诗、辞、赋、志、记等，也可以是它们的综合，多呈现为散文体、小说体或笔记体。从文学书写城市出发，城市传记文体以诗、辞、赋为主；从历史书写城市出发，城市传记文体以志、记为主；以《洛阳伽蓝记》《东京梦华录》为代表的城市传记则呈现为多种文体的综合，文体形式相对自由。

城市传记文体形式的自由与其保留方志书写历史的真实性、抛弃书写形式的严肃性，将笔记小说的活泼性融入城市书写有关。如“梦华体”就形成独具一格的城市传记书写传统，既追求城市历史书写的真实，又以文学方式缅怀城市生活繁华，“《东京梦华录》抛弃了正史官样文章的途径，在宋代文学丛林里开辟出了一条以上下通晓的语言记述市民日常生活，回忆都市繁华的笔记小说的创作道路”（伊永文 117）。“梦华体”叙事“艳说旧事，神游故地，形成正史以外重要的叙事传统”（王德威：《千年华胥之梦》12—13）。

第四，城市传记具有浓郁的怀旧气质。首先，古代城市传记从京都赋开始就具有怀旧气质，如《两都赋》《二京赋》虽颂扬东都之恢宏壮阔，却也回顾了西都之富丽繁华；杨衒之则以“麦秀之感，黍离之悲”（杨衒之 2）写下《洛阳伽蓝记》；《东京梦华录》及梦华体作品更以“缅怀繁华，排遣惆怅，记录风土，细述街市”（伊永文 118）为主旨。其次，近年来的城市传记与怀旧思潮密切相关。怀旧思潮的兴起与现代性、城市化相伴而生。现代性进程导致时空与社会关系重组，现代社会文化转型势不可挡，“怀旧不仅是现代文化转型的表征，还是现代文化转型的后果”（赵静蓉：《怀旧》 424）。城市化加快发展，不少城市建筑被拆除或重建，人们对城市文化、古老建筑的怀旧成为寻找自身认同、应对社会转型的一剂良药。近年风靡一时的“城市老照片”“寻访老城市”等系列图书出版并受追捧，即是受怀旧思潮影响希望还原城市记忆的一种方式，在这些作品中，与城市历史相关的各种照片被重新审视，图像与文字以“图文互现”方式不断激发人们的怀旧情感，人们也以此回顾消逝了的城市生活以及自身记忆。城市传记成为包裹着怀旧思潮面貌的审美现代性表征，是中国社会快速发展过程中进行的“一种独特的表意实践，它不断反思着社会现代化本身，并不停地为急剧变化的社会生活提供重要的意义”（周宪 71）。

第五，城市传记书写与文化认同需求密不可分。现代性使传统时间观发展为一种线性时间，在线性时间的过去、现在和未来三个维度中，过去美好的逝去和现在转型的难以把握使人们对未来充满想象，在怀旧氛围中形成对连续性、同一性和完整性的追求，在重新体验时间中形成自我认同需求。身份认同需从两个层面确认，“从历时性的层面来看，身份认同的过程其实就是一个个体历史建立的过程，过去、现在和未来三个时间维度共同作用这一过程，而个体的身体性以及与其关联的感性感知世界的方式是认同的核心。……从共时性的层面来看，身份认同又是一个社会建构的过程”（赵静蓉：《文化记忆与身份认同》 20—21）。城市传记从历时、共时两个层面将个人认同与城市认同缝合并完成对自我认同的确认：历时性层面，城市传记以个人焦虑为起点追寻城市历史，目的是确定可知的未来，城市传统的同一和未来的可知有助于自我认同确认；共时性层面，自我认同的同一性需求被建构为城市文化认同，个人认同需求被城市传记缝合至城市文化的同一性书写。从认同意义上讲，如果说自传是将自我作为一个有意义的整体来把握，是一个有意识地自我理解、自我塑造的过程（梁庆标 65），那么城市传记就是自传的延续和另一种形式，在城市传记中个人将自我焦虑转化至对城市发展变迁的关注、将自我认同延伸至城市认同。因此，城市传记是基于认同焦虑进行的城市文化认同书写，是现代社会转型的文化表征。

三、结　语

城市传记有着悠久传统和丰富书写实践，就文体形式与书写特点看，城市传记与人物传记极为相似，某种程度上而言城市传记是人物传记的变形与延伸。然而城市传记也有着自身特点，它以城市为书写对象，书写完整城市历史，展现城市地方性精神，以“家族相似”的文体形式涵盖无数作品。

在全球化、现代性、城市化与地方性背景下，城市传记书写具有较强的现实诉求。对昔日生活、城市记忆的怀旧和对个人认同的未来需求，使人们将个人书写与个人认同延伸至城市书写与城市认同。在城市传记中，城市不只是人们生活的环境空间，它更是人们的故乡、精神家园与精神维系所在。注重书写地方性、强调怀旧意义与认同诉求，使城市传记成为社会变迁的文化表征和文学艺术对社会发展转型进行的审美表意实践。

致谢【Acknowledgment】

本文为昆明理工大学人文社科培育项目“城市传记的地方性书写研究”（SKPYYB201624）成果，得到昆明理工大学人文社科研究院的经费支持，作者谨致谢忱！本文写作受到《现代传记研究》编辑委员会各位编辑的肯定与鼓励，且受益于《现代传记研究》匿名评审人多次提出的修改意见，作者谨致谢忱！

My acknowledgement and gratitude go to the research project “Locality Writing of Urban Biography” sponsored by the Academy of Humanities and Social Sciences of Kunming University of Science and Technology. I am grateful to the editors of the *Journal of Modern Life Writing Studies*. Their approval and suggestions enhance my understanding of the concept of city biography. I am also grateful to the anonymous reviewers for their suggestions and comments.

引用文献【Works Cited】

彼得·阿克罗伊德：《伦敦传》，翁海贞等译。南京：译林出版社，2016年。

[Ackroyd, Peter. *London: The Biography*. Trans. Weng Haizhen etc. Nanjing: Yilin Press. 2016.]

安东篱：《说扬州：1550—1850年的一座中国城市》，李霞译，李恭忠校。北京：中华书局，2007年。

[Finnane, Antonia. *Speaking of Yangzhou: A Chinese City, 1550-1850*, Trans. Li Xia. Beijing: Zhonghua Book Company, 2007.]

亚里士多德：《诗学》，陈中梅译。北京：商务印书馆，1996年。

[Aristotle. *Poetics*. Trans. Chen Zhongmei. Beijing: The Commercial Press, 1996.]

Geertz, Clifford. *Local Knowledge: Further Essays in Interpretive Anthropology*. New York: Basic Books, 1983.

季剑青：《追忆逝去的北京——民国时期北京的"梦华体"著述》，《山东师范大学学报》（人文社会科学版）2016年第4期，第38—49页。

[Ji Jianqing. "In Search of the Lost Beijing: The 'Deam-of-Splendor' Writings in Republican Beijing." *Journal of Shandong Normal University* (Humanities and Social Sciences) 4(2016):38-49.]

迈克·克朗：《文化地理学》，杨淑华、宋慧敏译。南京：南京大学出版社，2005年。

[Krone, Mike. *Cultural Geography*. Trans. Yang Shuhua & Song Huimin. Nanjing: Nanjing University Press, 2005.]

梁庆标：《自传研究的萌生与发展：早期西方自传批评史述》，《现代传记研究》（第8辑）。北京：商务印书馆，2017年，第58—69页。

[Liang Qingbiao. "The Origin and Development of Autobiography Research: A Comment on the Brief History of Western Autobiography Criticism before the 20th Century." *Journal of Modern Life Writing* 8(2017):58-69.]

林语堂：《大城北京》。西安：陕西师范大学出版社，2008年。

[Lin Yutang. *Imperial Peking: Seven Centuries of China*. Xi'an, China: Shaanxi Normal University Press, 2008.]

芦坚强：《昆明形象的文学书写》，《学术探索》2015年第2期，第136—142页。

[Lu Jianqiang. "Literary Writing of the City Kunming's Image." *Academic Exploration* 2 (2015):136-142.]

罗里·麦克林：《柏林：一座城市的肖像》，傅敬民译。上海：上海文艺出版社，2017年。

[Maclean, Rory. *Berlin: Portrait of a City Through the Centuries*. Trans. Fu Jingmin. Shanghai: Shanghai Literature & Art Publishing House. 2017.]

西蒙·蒙蒂菲奥里：《耶路撒冷三千年》，张倩红等译。北京：民主与建设出版社，2014年。

[Montefiore, Simon Sebag. *Jerusalem: The Biography*. Trans. Zhang Qianhong & etc. Beijing: Democracy and Construction Press, 2014.]

Norberg-Schulz, Christian. *Genius Loci: Towards A Phenomenology of Architecture*. New York: Rizzoli, 1980.

奥尔罕·帕慕克：《伊斯坦布尔：一座城市的记忆》，何佩桦译。上海：上海人民出版社，2007年。

[Pamuk, Orhan. *Istanbul*: *Memories and the City*. Trans. He Peihua. Shanghai: Shanghai People's Press. 2007]

Tuan, Yi-Fu. *Space and Place*: *The Perspectives of Experience*. Minneapolis: University of Minnesota Press, 2001.

王德威:《北京梦华录:北京人到台湾》,《读书》2004 年第 1 期,第 24—30 页。

[Wang Dewei. "Peking: A Dream of Splendor-Peking Man to Taiwan." *Reading* 1(2004): 24-30.]

——:《千年华胥之梦:董启章孟元老"梦华体"叙事》,《汉语言文学研究》2012 年第 1 期,第 11—18 页。

[——. "A Thousand Year of Hua Xu's Dream: The Narratives in the 'Dream-of-Splendor Style' by Dong Qizhang and Meng Yuanlao." *Journal for the Study of Chinese Language and Literature* 1(2012):11-18.]

杨衒之撰、周祖谟校释:《洛阳迦蓝记校释》。北京:中华书局,2013 年。

[Yang Xuanzhi. *Monasteries in the Capital Luoyang*. 547. Ed. and ann. Zhou Zumo. Beijing: Zhonghua Book Company, 2013.]

杨正润:《现代传记学》。南京:南京大学出版社,2009 年。

[Yang Zhengrun. *A Modern Poetics of Biography*. Nanjing: Nanjing University Press, 2009.]

伊永文:《以〈东京梦华录〉为中心的"梦华体"文学》,《求是学刊》2009 年第 1 期,第 114—119 页。

[Yi Yongwen. "Centering on the Memoir *The Eastern Capital*: *A Dream of Splendor*: The 'Dream-of-Splendor' Literature." *Seeking Truth* 1(2009):114-119.]

于坚:《昆明记》。重庆:重庆大学出版社,2015 年。

[Yu Jian. *Kunming*: *A Biography*. Chongqing: Chongqing University Press. 2015.]

赵静蓉:《怀旧:永恒的文化乡愁》。北京:商务印书馆,2009 年。

[Zhao Jingrong. *Nostalgia*: *The Eternal Cultural Yearning*. Beijing: The Commercial Press, 2009.]

——:《文化记忆与身份认同》。北京:生活·读书·新知三联书店,2015 年。

[——. *Cultural Memory and Identity*. Beijing: SDX Joint Publishing Company, 2015.]

周宪:《审美现代性批判》。北京:商务印书馆,2005 年。

[Zhou Xian. *Critique of Aesthetic Modernity*. Beijing: The Commercial Press, 2005.]

周振甫:《文心雕龙今译》。北京:中华书局,1986 年。

[Zhou Zhenfu, trans. *The Literary Mind and the Carving of Dragons*. By Liu Xie. Beijing: Zhonghua Book Company, 1986.]

"Help Others Out of a Fellow-Feeling": The Romantic Science of the Pathography

Daniel Vuillermin

Abstract: Over the past fifty years the pathography—auto/biographical accounts of illness—has established itself as a genre that the sick and the healthy alike turn to explore the revelations brought about by illness, pain and suffering. This article will provide a broad overview of the historical development of the pathography as a didactic genre by focusing on three key figures: Robert Burton, Samuel Johnson, and Oliver Sacks. Each of these figures in their own right have contributed to the notion that writing and reading about illness can not only provide guidance and consolation but also edification. In the early modern period Burton contributed to the image of the author as a *suffering healer* who acts as a guide to the reader who, in turn, may find solace, if not a cure in the act of reading. One frequent reader of Burton's magnum opus, *The Anatomy of Melancholy* (1621), was the eighteenth-century writer Samuel Johnson, who according to James Boswell, "was the only book that ever took him out of bed two hours sooner than he wished to rise". For Johnson, the *Anatomy* provided practical guidance on how to cope with his melancholy but also advice to others who were undergoing ordeals such as the loss of a loved one. Since the late twentieth century, pathography has gained a wide readership from health care professionals to literary critics. One of the pioneers of the modern pathography is the neurologist and "romantic scientist" Oliver Sacks who sought to reframe medical discourse to discover and affirm the potential positive dimensions of the illness experience. For writers and readers alike the power of pathography lies in the autobiographical pact, that is, the person writing about his/her illness has a direct personal experience of the catastrophic and the transformative effects of serious illness.

Keywords: pathography, autobiography, biography, didacticism

Dr. Daniel Vuillermin is a lecturer at the Institute for Medical Humanities at Peking University. Vuillermin is an editor of the *Chinese Medical Humanities Review* and the reviews editor of the *Journal of Applied Arts and Health*. His research interests include narrative medicine, using art as research in medical education, Chinese cinemeducation, and the cultural history of diagnosis. Email: dvuillermin@bjmu.edu.cn.

标题:“以同情心去帮助别人”——病患志的浪漫主义科学

内容提要: 在过去50年里，病患志（写病情的自传/他传式叙述）已成为一个文类，无论患者还是健康人都开始借此探索疾病、疼痛、痛苦的表现。本文将从具有教化作用的文类角度，对病患志的历史发展做一考察，并聚焦三位关键人物：罗伯特·伯顿、塞缪尔·约翰生及奥利弗·沙克斯。他们都对病患志的理念做出了贡献，认为描写病情与阅读病情不仅能给人以指引和安慰，而且能对人发挥教化作用。在近代早期，伯顿刻画了“痛苦的治疗者”这一作者形象，他通过为读者担任向导，使读者即便没有治愈，也在阅读中获得了慰藉。18世纪作家塞缪尔·约翰生也对伯顿的《忧郁的解剖》（1621年）爱不释手。用詹姆斯·鲍斯威尔的话说，“这是唯一一本让约翰生心甘情愿早起两小时阅读的书”。对于约翰生来说，这部作品为他与忧郁症做斗争提供了实用的指导。此外，这本书还为饱受痛苦折磨（例如心上人辞世）的其他读者提供了建议。到了20世纪后期，无论是健康保健专业人士，还是文学评论者，都广为阅读病患志。现代病患志的一位先驱是神经学家、浪漫主义科学家奥利弗·沙克斯，他力求重构医疗话语，以探索并确认患病经历中潜在的积极方面。无论对于作者还是读者，病患志的力量都不仅在于其自传契约，作者在描写自身病情时，凭借的是自己对病痛直接的个人经历和严重疾病对人的改变作用。

关键词: 病患志　自传　传记　教化作用

作者简介: 魏莱民，博士，北京大学医学部医学人文研究院讲师，《中国医学人文评论》编辑，《应用艺术与健康》书评编辑。研究方向：叙事医学、医学教育研究中对艺术的运用、中国电影辅助医学教学及诊断的文化史。

> Nothing detains the reader's attention more powerfully than deep involutions of distress or sudden vicissitudes of fortune, and these might be abundantly afforded by memoirs of the sons of literature.
>
> —Samuel Johnson, *The Idler* (29 March 1760)

On an early winter's morning in 1540 candles surrounded a clean, shaven corpse to provide light but also perhaps warmth to the hands of the finest anatomist of the pre-modern medical age, Andreas Vesalius (1514–1564). More than 150 doctors, students, and members of the public came to the University of Bologna to witness Vesalius's first public anatomical demonstration. Vesalius began his lesson by describing the different methods that ancient anatomists used to penetrate the body: the "Egyptians and the Arabs begin with the trunk and the extremities, but Galen, whom also Mundinus has followed, begins with the three venters" (Heseler).① Vesalius, however, broke away from his predecessors by making a simple incision and peeling back a section of skin to demonstrate how the *hide* (epidermis) can not be easily separated from the *cutis* (dermis). He then held a candle to the *cutis* showing that it did not blister as it was "more fleshy and fleshlike" than the *hide*. According to Galenic theory this inner layer of skin not only determined a person's complexion but also the "nature" of one's humours. Vesalius's first demonstration concluded with an examination of the muscles, which, according to Baldasar Heseler, a German doctor who studied theology under Martin Luther at the University of Wittenberg, he "dissected with the utmost diligence". Three years later in his magnum opus *On the Fabric of the Human Body* (1543), Vesalius would encapsulate the practice of directly observing the inner workings of the human body with the precept "the violation of the body would be the revelation of its truth" (Giblett 29). Following Vesalius countless bodies have been opened and mysteries of the body from circulation to cirrhosis were revealed. And while full-length published accounts of illness would not emerge until the mid-twentieth century, the notion that revealing auto/biographical stories about illness is a didactic and therapeutic act for both the writer and the reader is at the crux of the genre of pathography.

This article will examine key didactical pathographical models over three periods: early modern, late modern, and the late twentieth century. One representative pathographer of the early modern is the clergyman and librarian, Robert Burton (1577–1640). Although Burton's *The Anatomy of Melancholy* (1621) may not be strictly considered an autobiographical text, the *Anatomy* establishes the notion of the author as a *suffering healer* who guides the reader through her illness and that, in turn, reading about illness is a therapeutic act. In the late modern period works such as James Boswell's *Life of Johnson* (1791), the biographer conflates Samuel Johnson the great sufferer with Samuel Johnson the great writer, which had the unintended consequences of creating an image of Johnson as both monster and hero. The past 50 years have seen the materialist discourse of medicine with its professional concern with the body and its inner structures and systems supplemented, and critiqued by quite different literary forms; the account of illness and medical intervention from the point of view of the patient and narratives of others' illness by biographers and physicians. Early masterpieces such as Simone de Beauvoir's *A Very Easy Death* (1966) have been complemented by Philip Roth's *Patrimony* (1991), and new forms such as the illness essay have emerged with texts such as Leslie Jamison's *The Empathy Exams* (2014) becoming commercial and critical successes. A key contemporary model is the neurologist and "romantic scientist", Oliver Sacks (1933–2015). Sacks's "clinical tales" sought to realign the medical discourse to focus upon patient experience in a period where the sick person as a writer was emerging as an active agent and to discover and affirm the potential positive dimensions of the illness experience. Today, illness narratives have a wide readership: health care professionals, medical students, literary critics, and increasingly the general reader. The pathography has established itself, at least in the English-speaking world, as a genre that the sick turn to in order to understand the journey of illness, and the healthy explore so as to be illuminated by the revelations brought about by pain and suffering.

The Lexical Poverty of Pain

The illness narrative is a genre without an *Iliad*, a *Robinson Crusoe*, or a *Confessions*, and yet it shares many of the tropes of the epic with its battles against monstrous foes, and the novel taking the reader on journeys to unknown lands, and, like St. Augustine, the ill writer adopts a confessional mode of narration to describe but also instruct others about his or her "conversion" from illness to health. Yet whereas poetry, plays and novels often portray characters who experience pain and illness, in life writing book-length narratives dedicated to sickness are rare until the mid twentieth century. One of the first writers to question why illness—an experience as universal and inexorable as love, desire, anger, and jealousy—was not one of the central themes of literature was Virginia Woolf (1882–1941). In *On Being Ill* (1930), Woolf claims that the literary primacy of the "doings of the mind" over the "daily drama of the body" is due, in part, to the inadequacies of the English language to describe pain and illness; "let a sufferer," writes Woolf "try to describe a pain in his head to a doctor and language at once runs dry" (Woolf). Almost a century later literary critic Christina Crosby echoes Woolf in her quadriplegia memoir *A Body Undone: Living on After Great Pain* (2017) stating, "Pain seems on the other side of language. I feel an unassuageable loneliness, because I will never be able to adequately describe the pain I suffer, nor can anyone accompany me into the realm of pain"(31). Groans, whimpers, sighs, and screams are the lingua franca of pain that most powerfully expresses and connects us with each other. In lieu of this lexical poverty Woolf wryly advocates for neologisms to describe pain yet she overlooks the vast proliferation of biomedical language that had amassed during the nineteenth and early twentieth centuries, signalling the gap between the language of the bio-sciences and of the sick person, if not the poet. Despite the specificity of biomedical terminology it does not bring us any closer to lived experience of the personal, social, and cultural expressions of suffering. Eighteen years after Woolf's death, C.P. Snow would neatly label the schism between science and literature the "two cultures" and it is from the gap between the language of biomedicine and the ill person that the modern illness narrative emerges(16).

In the first critical study of illness narratives *Reconstructing Illness: Studies in Pathography*(1993), Anne Hunsaker Hawkins states that illness narratives are "almost exclusively a modern genre" and that, "book-length personal accounts of illness are uncommon before 1950 and rarely found before 1900"(3). In search of predecessors to the modern form Hawkins identifies autobiographical texts such as John Donne's *Devotions Upon Emergent Occasions, and Several Steps in My Sickness*(1624), Samuel Cole Davis's diary of his illness with cancer of the lip, and Fanny Burney's mastectomy letter as formative texts. More recently Ann Jurecic has pointed to the autobiographical narratives of polio patients, who, secluded in institutions during the height of America's polio epidemic during the 1940s and '50s, produced book-length narratives (many polio narratives were published in the 1960s after the end of the epidemic) and shorter pieces that were published in a range of newspapers and popular magazines such as the *Los Angeles Times* and *Reader's Digest*(4–10).

Nascent testimonial autopathographics of the 1960s and '70s were not intended for literary critics or doctors but for fellow sufferers and their loved ones who were passing through what Susan Sontag famously described as "night-side of life"(3). Such accounts of illness served as maps, manuals or models on "how to" cope not only with the illness but the trials of navigating hospitals, dealing with doctors, adapting to medication regimes as well as undergoing and recovering from surgery or treatment. As Hawkins writes, "in pathography the need to *tell* others so often becomes the wish to *help* others"(*Reconstructing* 25). The desire, if not need to help others may be considered an altruistic act whereby the writer exposes her private feelings, beliefs, relationships, and experiences so as to offer assistance, if not salvation. One model altruistic pathographer is the seventeenth-century clergyman and librarian, Robert Burton. Burton spent his "time and knowledge ... for the common good of all" in service to melancholics; his desire was to "help others out of a fellow-feeling" (Burton). Burton, like many contemporary pathographers have laid claim to the therapeutic benefits of writing and reading about illness, acts that are central to the notion and practice of self care.

A Pathographical Act: *The Anatomy of Melancholy*

Robert Burton's encyclopaedic, idiosyncratic *The Anatomy of Melancholy* originates from his personal experience of what modern psychiatry may diagnose as depression. In the preface—*Democritus Junior to the Reader*—Burton informs the reader that he embarked upon his medical *cento* as a means of warding off his own melancholy: "I write of Melancholy, by being busie to avoid Melancholy." By busying himself with the task of compiling a myriad of ancient and contemporary definitions, causes, and cures of melancholy from the shelves of the Bodleian Library at the University of Oxford, Burton scratched "where it itcheth". Writing about melancholy became the means by which he would attempt to "cure" his disease. Burton describes that when he first "took this task in hand, *et quod ait ille*, *impellents genio negotium suscepi*, this I aimed at; *vel ut lenirem animum scribendo*, to ease my mind by writing; for I had *gravidum cor*, *foetum caput*, a kind of *imposthume* in my head, which I was very desirous to be unladen of, and could imagine no fitter evacuation than this". Through the process of compiling the *Anatomy*, Burton sought "to ease my minde by writing" but he does not explicitly disclose his own melancholy. Unlike modern pathographies such as William Styron's *Darkness Visible: A Memoir of Madness* (1990), Andrew Solomon's *The Noonday Demon: An Anatomy of Depression* (2001) or more recently Jay Griffiths's *Tristimania: A Diary of Manic Depression* (2016), which each use autobiography to chronicle but also meditate on the despair, emptiness, and potential destructiveness of depression, Burton masks his identity and the biography of his melancholy by adopting a satirical persona "Democritus Junior". By recounting the life of the ancient Greek philosopher Democratus (c.460 BCE–c.370) who was a "little wearish old man, very melancholy by nature, averse from company in his latter days, and much given to solitariness ... wholly addicted to his studies at the last, and to a private life", Burton provides his readers with a miniature of his melancholia (Burton). Although Burton offers only occasional autobiographical details, the eighteenth-century melancholic

Samuel Johnson discerned that "there is great spirit and great power in what Burton says when he writes from his own mind"(Boswell, *Life* 690).

The *Anatomy*, however, does not qualify as autobiography according to Phillipe Lejeune's autobiographical schema:

1. The *Anatomy* is not primarily autodiegetic, rather it is an eclectic *cento* comprised of a vast array of classical and contemporary medical, literary, astronomical/astrological, biblical, and historical sources(Lejeune 2). Samuel Johnson considered the *Anatomy* "perhaps overloaded with quotation"(Boswell, *Life* 690).

2. Burton does not focus on his individual life nor the story of his personality and the narrative is not written with a retrospective point of view(Lejeune 5).

3. The situation of the author of the *Anatomy* is complicated by Burton's use of a pseudonym "Democritus Junior". For Lejeune, an author is both a "real person", that is the existence of an individual human being that can be verified by official documents (birth/death certificates and personal items such as letters) is identical to the narrator(11). Lejeune, however, does not distinguish between authors who use their verifiable proper name and pseudonyms. He argues that the "pseudonym is simply a differentiation, a division of the name, which changes nothing in the identity"(12). However, critics such as G. Thomas Couser have contended that "lacking a proper name, a pseudonymous persona has no real history to verify"(11) and that for some readers "an author's pseudonym is virtually a synonym for duplicity"(82).

4. The First Partition (the causes and definitions of melancholy) and the Second Partition(cures for melancholy) and the Third Partition (on the relationship between love and melancholy) of the *Anatomy* do not feature a protagonist and the narrator does not employ a consistent retrospective point of view. In the introductory section *Democritus Junior to the Reader* Burton states that he requires a "favourable ensure of all faults omitted" as well as the "perturbations of tenses".

Although the *Anatomy* cannot be classified as a pathography as it is not a first-person or third-person narrative, however, it may be considered a *pathographical act*, that is, an interpretation of an illness that constructs the meaning of illness by "subjecting raw experience to the powerful impulse to make sense of it all, to bind together the events, feelings, thoughts, and sensations that occur during an illness into an integrated whole"(Hawkins,

Reconstructing 18). In this light the *Anatomy* anticipates many features of the modern illness narrative: the genesis of the account is the author's own experience of illness or perceptions of another person's illness experience, the author serves as a "suffering healer" who guides the reader, and claims that reading is therapeutic act that can "drive away" illness "as much as Zisca's drum could terrify his foes"(Burton).

Following the success of the first edition, Burton spent the remainder of his life supplementing and editing the *Anatomy*, which underwent a further five editions(1624, 1628, 1632, 1638, and 1651). Each edition of the *Anatomy* may be thought of as an "antidote" to the melancholy which was "so common in this crazed age of ours, that scarce one of a thousand is free from it". Among the many cures offered in the *Anatomy*—prayer, diet, taking air, searing with hot irons, sleep, bloodletting, and medicines—reading the book itself may "drive away Melancholy". As Mary Ann Lund shows in *Melancholy, Medicine and Religion in Early Modern Europe* (2010) reading was considered an "active process ... a means of keeping the melancholic active" which in itself was considered a curative (196). Today, people with depression are unlikely to turn to Burton's *Anatomy of Melancholy* for solace, but for seventeenth-century readers and eighteenth-century figures such as Samuel Johnson, the *Anatomy* was one of the main sources that one could discover the causes and cures of the "perturbations of the mind"(Burton).② That the *Anatomy* should serve as a "manual" on how to avoid melancholy is evinced by Johnson who in a letter to Hester Thrale(12 November 1773), following the death of her uncle Sir Thomas Salusbury, advises Thrale in a Burtonian manner to "be alone as little as you can" (390). Johnson concludes his letter by directly citing Burton's "important precept, 'be not solitary; be not idle'"(Johnson and Piozzi 390). For Johnson the *Anatomy*, perhaps more so than the Bible, provided him with practical means of dealing with illness, suffering, and grief.

Warts and All: Portraying Illness in the Long Eighteenth Century

In the late eighteenth century when the novelist and diarist Frances Burney(1752–1840) was chronicling her personal experiences of illness and the madness of King George III there were few pathographical models. Accounts of illness were largely documented in diaries and letters some of which were traded posthumously, quoted in biographies or published as part of complete journals. In the long eighteenth-century private records of illness are often concise and candid. One early pathography *The Author's Case* by the British physician George Cheyne (1671–1743) who in his *The English Malady; or, A Treatise of Nervous Diseases of All Kinds, as Spleen, Vapours, Lowness of Spirits, Hypochondriacal and Hysterical Distempers* (1733) describes the symptoms of many cases, including his own, that result from excessive meat and alcohol consumption. Cheyne's indulgent diet brought his health into "great distress" as he grew "excessively fat, short-breath'd, Lethargic and lifeless" (326). Cheyne's physical ailments were accompanied by a range of "nervous diseases", or what we may now describe as psychological disorders, such as "Head-ach, Giddness, Watchings, Lowness, and Melancholy" (329). In order to treat his melancholy, Cheyne, like Burton, turned to a range of scientific, mathematical, religious and spiritual texts to "cure" his "nervous Diseases" (333) as well as common therapies such as "frequent vomits, and gentle purges (bloodletting)" (328–329). Cheyne's prognostic narrative provides a "method" for readers who may be suffering from a similar condition. One reader was the writer Samuel Johnson (1709–1784).

In conversations, letters as well as his prayers Johnson weaved autobiographical fragments that detailed his physical, psychological and spiritual afflictions. In a prayer on 14 April 1770, Johnson describes his arthritic pain and the treatments he used to relieve the symptoms:

> I have for some weeks past been much afflicted with the Lumbago, or Rheumatism in the Loins, which often passes to the muscles of the belly, where it causes equal, if not greater pain. In the day the sunshine mitigates it, and in cold or cloudy weather such as has for some time past remarkably prevailed the heat of a strong fire suspends it. In the night it is so troublesome, as not very easily to be borne. I lye wrapped in Flannel with a very great fire near my bed, but whether it be that a recumbent posture increases the pain, or that expansion by moderate warmth excites what a great heat dissipates, I can seldom remain in bed two hours at a time without the necessity of rising to heat the parts affected at the fire ... The pain harasses me much, yet many have the disease perhaps in a much higher degree with want of food, fire, and covering, which I find thus grievous with all the succours that riches and kindness can buy and give. (Johnson and Thrale)

As John Wiltshire notes, Johnson frequently prayed for "help with his 'troubles and maladies', his 'diseases of mind and body'" (12). But many of Johnson's autobiographical accounts of illness were private and were not compiled until after his death. Other pathographers of the late eighteenth century similarly kept their accounts about illness private. The novelist and diarist Frances Burney upon first meeting Samuel Johnson noted in her diary:

> He is, indeed, very ill-favoured; is tall and stout; but stoops terribly; he is almost bent double. His mouth is almost [constantly opening and shutting], as if he was chewing. He has a strange method of frequently twirling his fingers, and twisting his Hands. His body is in continual agitation, *see sawing* up and down; his feet are never a moment quiet; and in short, his whole person is in *perpetual motion* ... He is shockingly near-sighted, and did not, till she held out her hand to him, even know Mrs. Thrale ... His attention, however, was not to be diverted five minutes from the books, as we were in the library; he pored over them, [shelf by shelf] almost touching the backs of them with his eye-lashes.(Burney)

Burney's portrait of Johnson the sufferer is more descriptive than analytical. Burney does not offer possible causes of Johnson's "continual agitation[s]" nor does she attempt to identify his physical and psychological peculiarities. Diagnosing Johnson's unusual behaviours would become integral to James Boswell's claims of biographical truth. Throughout the *Life of Johnson*, Boswell chronicles Johnson's many illnesses, complaints, and poor habits: the scrofula Johnson contracted from a wet-nurse, the "immense structure of his bones ... hideously striking to the eye"(68), his nearsightedness and deafness, his idleness and struggles to rise early, his "convulsive starts and odd gesticulations", his "morbid melancholy"(47), to his final paralytic stroke. Yet in many cases Boswell takes the extra step of attempting to determine the aetiology of his conditions and diagnose Johnson's physical ailments and psychological torments; an imperfect science that some modern biographers continue to indulge. In *The Journal of a Tour to the Hebrides* (1785), Boswell's first published biographical accounts of Johnson, he focuses on Johnson's peculiar movements:

> His person was large, robust, I may say approaching to the gigantick, and grown unwieldy from corpulency. His countenance was naturally of the craft of an ancient statue, but somewhat disfigured by the scars of that evil, which, it was formerly imagined, the royal touch could cure. He was now in his sixty-fourth year, and was become a little dull of hearing. His sight had always been somewhat weak; yet, so much does mind govern, and even supply the deficiency of organs, that

> his perceptions were uncommonly quick and accurate. His head, and sometimes also his body, shook with a kind of motion like the effect of a palsy: he appeared to be frequently disturbed by cramps, or convulsive contractions, of the nature of that distemper called St. Vitus's dance.

St. Vitus's Dance, now known as chorea, is a neurological disorder that causes brief, involuntary, irregular movements. In the *Life*, Boswell returns to Johnson's unusual movements and makes use of Thomas Sydenham's definition of the condition to support his diagnosis of Johnson:

> This disorder [St. Vitus's Dance] is a kind of convulsion. It manifests itself by halting or unsteadiness of one of the legs, which the patient draws after him like an ideot[sic]. If the hand of the same side be applied to the breast, or any other part of the body he cannot keep it a moment in the same posture, but it will be drawn into a different one by a convulsion, notwithstanding all his efforts to the contrary.(105)

Boswell's accounts of Johnson's mental and physical illnesses were intended to transform Johnson's "medical history into a metaphor" for his lifetime of physical and emotional struggles, conflating Johnson the great writer with Johnson the great sufferer(Newman 15). If Boswell's portrait of Johnson as great sufferer was to dignify the Johnson's maladies it also had an unintended consequence; to portray Johnson as monstrous. This is exemplified by Macaulay's [in]famous review in the *Edinburgh Review or Critical Journal* (August-December 1831) of John Croker's edition 1831 of Boswell's *Life of Johnson*, where he writes:

> Every thing about him, his coat, his wig, his figure, his face, his scrofula, his St. Vitus's dance, his rolling walk, his blinking eye, the outward signs which too clearly marked his approbation of his dinner, his insatiable appetite for fish-sauce and veal-pie with plums, his inextinguishable thirst for tea, his trick of touching the posts as he walked, his mysterious practice of treasuring up scraps of orange-peel, his morning slumbers, his midnight disputations, his contortions, his mutterings, his gruntings, his puffings, his vigorous, acute and ready eloquence, his sarcastic wit, his vehemence, his insolence, his fits of tempestuous rage, his queer inmates, old Mr. Levett and blind Mrs. Williams, the cat Hodge and the negro Frank all are as familiar to us as the objects by which we have been surrounded from childhood. (Macaulay)

Through Macaulay's gaze, Johnson—diseased, impaired, eccentric, tempestuous—had become a Frankenstein's monster-like caricature. The dignity conferred on Johnson's maladies by Joshua Reynolds in his two early portraits(c.1756 and c.1769) had been supplanted by a Dickensian image of the writer that would endure throughout the nineteenth century and continues to the late twentieth century in his portrayal in the British comedy pseudo-historical comedy television series, *Blackadder* (1987). It was not until the mid-twentieth century that scholars such as Katherine Balderston, under the influence of Freud, began to "diagnose" Johnson, in particular, his "erotic maladjustment" (Porter 71). Johnson, along with Abraham Lincoln, Friedrich Nietzsche, and Vincent van Gogh, has since become the subject of numerous retrospective diagnoses by physicians and literary critics. Yet another stream of critics such as Walter Jackson Bate, Ralph Rader and the physician Ronald MacKeith, consider Johnson's prodigious output as a writer all the more remarkable on account of his many maladies. Such scrutiny not only made Johnson's "more widely known than that of any writer", his physical and psychological suffering has made him an inexhaustible source of interest but also an example to others(Bate 3). As MacKeith writes, Johnson "suffered almost daily ... His disorders were many ... Samuel Johnson suffered a great deal but he remained courageous, and we are greatly in his debt for the example of what he was in health and in sickness"(qtd. Bate 8). Here Johnson is transformed again, in this case the great literary sufferer and becomes an inspirational figure, a model of courage and perseverance in the face of illness. In the ever-changing discourses of illness narratives during the late twentieth century the heroic image of the sick person—crafted by Boswell in the eighteenth century—in is one of the dominant myths. Boswell's journals, *The Journal of a Tour to the Hebrides*, and the *Life of Johnson* can be considered proto-illness narratives that mark a literary and cultural shift where illness—physical and mental—shifts from the private journal to the published biography, where the subject becomes an object of medical inquiry and speculative diagnosis, and where the sick person becomes a heroic instructor on how to live with or overcome illness.

Romantic Science: Oliver Sacks

The neurologist and writer Oliver Sacks—once described by writer, critic, and pathographer Anatole Broyard as a "poet laureate of contemporary medicine"—pioneered the modern medical narrative beginning with his remarkable account of a therapeutic breakthrough in*Awakenings*(1973) and later achieved popular success with his collection of clinical vignettes *The Man Who Mistook His Wife for a Hat* (1986), the more sophisticated and extensive 'paradoxical tales' of *An Anthropologist on Mars*(1995), through to his memoir *On the Move*(2016)(19). Sack's writings have been honoured in an extraordinary range of fields—opera, film, and plays—but also quarried and cited in academia by, among others, linguistics, doctors, sociologists, and philosophers. Famous above all for his sympathetic insights into the condition of people with neurological impairments and for his advocacy of an enhanced form of medical narrative—the *clinical tale* that embodies the knowledge and understanding of a *romantic science*—Sacks sought to realign the medical discourse to focus upon patient experience(ix). Sacks lamented the impoverished forms of official biomedical case-history and argued that an enlarged and more humane medicine must be coupled with an enlarged and deepened medical narrative; an argument that underpins Narrative Medicine, which Rita Charon describes as "medicine practiced with these narrative skills of recognizing, absorbing, interpreting, and being moved by the stories of illness"(4). Under Sacks's gaze the patient is reborn as an active agent, a person whose experience of their condition is attended to with the full force of the writer's imagination, and whose uncovered experience, strange, confronting, and bizarre as it may be, can be made to enlighten or instruct others on the wonders of the brain and the extraordinary possibilities of the human condition.

Sack's rise to fame during the 1970s and '80s was a strand of a larger movement of first-person or autobiographical narratives by patients yet many of these works were devoid of the romantic science that Sacks sought to portray. Broyard compared such pathographies to the "dispatches of war correspondents ... Their books are objective, businesslike"(15). But these accounts, like Sacks's pathographical vignettes, present criticisms of current medicine, or mount an alternative vision of medical practice. Such pathographies offer criticisms of medical epistemology—of medicine's former knowledge of the body, of the confined parameters of this knowledge, of its neglect of the emotional, experiential, and philosophical dimensions of illness.

Coincidentally or not, Sack's rise to fame took place during the same period in which there was a tremendous outpouring of first-person or autobiographical narratives of patients. Like Sack's works, many of these narratives present intense criticism of current medicine, or mount an alternative vision of medical practice. Sometimes they merely include incidental portrayals of inept medical practice or medical practitioners, while others contain a critique of biomedical ethics. Such texts amount to a challenge to medicine's professional control and governance of the illness domain. Some of these narratives by people with neurological impairments parallel those of Sacks's patients, like Robert Murphy's *The Body Silent*

(1987), but, whatever the condition they describe and write from, these stories engage with similar issues as Sack's. This is a doctor who acknowledges patient experience as momentous, who discerns capacities for transformation within loss and disability, and during the same years, for perhaps similar reasons, patients are clamouring to present their experience of the body as significant. The patient narrative and the clinical tale seem to share a common purpose and a common target.

Anatole Broyard's posthumous *Intoxicated by My Illness* (1993) is one well-known critique of medical epistemology in the form of a patient narrative. Oliver Sacks, however, is exempted from the strictures of contemporary medical practice. In the midst of a chapter challengingly entitled *The Patient Examines the Doctor*, Broyard declares that "[m]y ideal doctor would resemble Oliver Sacks"(42). Sacks is the embodiment of this alternative dream of a medicine that is sympathetic, intuitive and authoritative. "I can imagine Dr. Sacks *entering* my condition," Broyard writes, "looking around at it from the inside like a kind of landlord, with a tenant, trying to see how he could make the premises more liveable. He would look around, holding me by the hand, and he would figure out what it feels like to be me. Then he would try to find certain advantages in the situation ... Dr. Sacks would see the genius in my illness. He would mingle his daemon with mine"(42–43). The notion of the patient's experience being like another world, or like a foreign land from which a traveller returns to tell the tale, has become a common one. But the notion of the doctor as a landlord, or as a familiar spirit, mysteriously entering this world and blending his consciousness with the patients' gives this familiar idea an unusual twist and a peculiar appositeness to Oliver Sacks.

Broyard's metaphors create the impression of penetrating into the world of the patient's illness, of an informed and scientific, but also warmly appreciative, sympathetic, and transformative understanding. But, in turn, the patient's body(or brain) becomes not just a foreign land but a form of territory for the doctor. It is the physician, Bryoard implies, who owns the body or has epistemological sovereignty over the body and the emphasis on her ability to enter and guide the patient through the illness amounts here to a granting of power and authority to this medical vision. Coupled with that notion of the illness as a site, a territory for medical perception is the idea that Oliver Sacks—the embodiment of the ideal physician—enjoys an unusually clairvoyant sympathy or empathy, able to grasp and wrestle with this "daemon" of the condition, joining his forces with the powers of mortality and disease. The metaphor of the landlord combines these twin notions of inwardness and power. Sacks is the benevolent possessor of the patient's body and brain and he has access to the patient's experience by imaginative means.

These two themes—of medical power and authority and the connection of that authority with the presumption to write on behalf of the experience of the disabled or damaged patient—run through physicians' biographical narratives. What Broyard's metaphors disclose are the underlying political dimensions of medical experience and medical narrative, and these give rise to several questions. How far is medicine's claim to speak on behalf of the patient a form of imperialism? As the physician-turned-patient Paul Kalanithi in his memoir *When Breath Becomes Air* writes:

> Doctors invade the body in every way imaginable. They see people at their most vulnerable, their most scared, their most private. They escort them into the world, and then back out. Seeing the body as matter and mechanism is the flip side to easing the most profound human suffering.(49)

What kind of "invasion" is it that combines the epistemological perspective of the doctor with the distinctive experience of the patient, and on what grounds should one attribute particular authority to the clinical biographical narrative that results? By positioning himself as a doctor, with the institutional and cultural authority of medical science behind him, Sacks has diminished some of the critical and hence political force of the patient critique. His writings appropriate the patient's confessional prerogative. Sacks stands foremost in the public mind as the embodiment of an ideal clinical relation and thereby keeps alive the fantasy that such a medicine is actually practiced and therefore can actually exist. For Oliver Sacks is, above all, the spokesman for and embodiment of a romantic medicine.

Sacks's writings have been especially attended to and honoured in those branches of medical education that seek to supplement biomedicine's biologistic emphasis with a humanistic component, otherwise known as the health or medical humanities. Hawkins offers a laudatory commentary on Sacks that similarly reflects that of Broyard. She argues that Sacks combines two discourses: "'identification', which concerns diagnostically relevant information about a patient and uses the language of biomedical science, and 'understanding', an empathic knowledge about a patient, which uses descriptive language."("Oliver" 230) Hawkins expands on the notion of the doctor as a traveller into the world of the patient, and celebrates Sacks's empathy and intuition as he explores, in his own phrase, the "landscapes of being in which these patients reside"("Oliver" 237). Trajective discourse "requires that the physician be a kind of ethnographer of the world of illness," writes Hawkins, and here too, there are obvious resonances with Sacks's own self-conception, as (variously) traveller, explorer, and anthropologist("Oliver" 233). Of *Awakenings* Hawkins writes that "Sacks's patients, severely crippled by Parkinsonism, are in many ways analogous to the strange and foreign creatures that the ethnographer studies"("Oliver" 233).

Hawkins demonstrates how very different Oliver Sacks's case-histories in *Awakenings* are from the orthodox model, and that his inclusion of the patient's own voice, his use of metaphor, his presentation of himself as an important actor in the drama of the patient's illness suggest analogies with Clifford Geertz's anthropological notion of "thick description", Eliot Mishler's prescription for a medical discourse that attends to "lifeworld issues", and Mikhail Bakhtin's conception of "dialogism" within narrative. Sacks's texts have certainly modified, perhaps even revolutionised, the conventional case-history, as Hawkins suggests.

Sacks's writing is deeply humanist, resting upon a conviction of the continuous identity of the human self and for many reader its appeal lies in it sympathetic insight into damaged and curtailed lives, as well as the ease, warmth and eloquence of its style. Other readers are, in turn, deeply suspicious of just this insight, which rests upon what they take to be some unexamined assumptions, conceiving the medical writer's claim to penetrate into the patient's mind to be merely an extension of medical power and the claims about human identity rest upon a collection of taken-for-granted notions about the "self" employed without proper scepticism or self-critique. For example, Broyard's metaphor of the doctor and patients wrestling together against illness is framed in masculinist terms, which is a reflection of unexamined gender biases in Sacks's own thinking. Sacks's sympathy for his patients, his endeavour to give the patient's experience a central role in the medical narrative, is seen both as a much-needed contribution to the humanising of medicine, and as a condescending, partial, imperialist gesture. Is it meaningful to speak of a continuous "self"? Might a better term be "identity"? Can there be "a neurology of the soul"? There is a hint of the romantic in the positive bias that Sacks's rhetoric often puts on his material. The claims, so often repeated, that enhancements of experience occur in sickness as well as diminishments, that creative energy is released by neurological impairments; these belong to a benevolist and positivist trait in medical epistemology, but more broadly they belong to an idealist tradition which dreams of finding providential symmetry in the arrangements of the world. The title *Awakenings*, for example, accentuates the positive, but between the covers of this book are many accounts of tragedy and disaster that can be read in an infernal sense, against the will of its author. Much of Sacks's success has come from the skill with which he invests the darker conditions of illness with an apparent triumph, suffusing the broken lives and tragic facts he so often encounters with the charm of his own energy, buoyancy and delight.

Conclusion

The dynamic of concealment, revelation, education, if not edification, is at the heart of medical science—from Vesalius's anatomical demonstrations of the mid-sixteenth century, the invention of instruments such as the stethoscope(1816) and imaging technologies such as the X-ray(1895)—but also narratives about illness. Writing about illness is often motivated by a need to help others. Unlike other forms of auto/biography, pathographical writings are often explicitly or implicitly didactic, in that they serve to instruct, enlighten and possibly offer solace. The pathography in its myriad forms also appears to be more prevalent in Anglo-European cultures. In China, for example, there are few published pathographies but many similarly serve to inspire and educate readers. One notable example is the writer, activist and cultural icon Zhang Haidi(张海迪). In the 1980s, Zhang Haidi, a wheel-chair user, emerged as a model citizen, a figure that embodied new socialist ideals of self reliance, self esteem, self respect and self improvement, which Sarah Dauncey describes as the "Zhang Haidi effect"(189-194). Today, however, many sick people in China make use of online platforms, in particular, WeChat and Weibo to tell stories and learn from other people's illness experiences. The popularity of translated works such as Kalanithi's *When Breath Becomes Air* may be a catalyst for more Chinese physicians to write about the humanistic and ethical aspects of their profession and practice. For pathographers, engaging in illness through writing is, as Arthur Frank describes, a "dangerous opportunity"(1-7). Frank writes, "To seize the opportunities offered by illness, we must live illness actively: we must think about it and talk about it, and some, like me, must write about it"(3). For writers and readers alike the power of pathography lies in the autobiographical pact, that is, that the person writing about their illness—unlike their physician—has direct personal experience of the destructive but often transformational effects of serious illness. By guiding the reader through the journey of the illness and reflecting upon its meanings, both may learn how to, as the Roman poet Ovid(43BC-17/18AD) writes, "Be patient and tough; as someday this pain will be useful to you".

Notes

① Roger French writes the "three venters were dissected in a sequence(abdomen, thorax, head) which avoided the worst effects of putrefaction, but which was also the 'philosophical' sequence of the three fundamental faculties of the body: nutritive, vital, and animal"(82).

② By the late seventeenth-century the *Anatomy* waned in popularity and was considered anachronistic. In the eighteenth century no new editions were published, however, in the nineteenth century it regained interest with no less than fourty-eight editions published.

Works Cited

Bate, Walter Jackson. *The Achievement of Samuel Johnson*. New York: Oxford University Press, 1961.

Boswell, James. *Life of Johnson*. 1791. Ed. R.W.Chapman. Cor. J.D.Fleeman. Intro. Pat Rogers. Oxford: Oxford University Press, 2008.

——. *A Journey to the Western Islands of Scotland and the The Journal of a Tour to the Hebrides*, with Samuel Johnson, LLD.. 1785. Web. 7 July 2018. 〈http://www.gutenberg.org/cache/epub/6018/pg6018-images.html〉.

Broyard, Anatole. *Intoxicated by My Illness and Other Writings on Life and Death*. New York: Fawcett Columbine, 1993.

Burney, Frances. *The Diary and Letters of Madame D'Arblay*. Notes by W.C.Ward. 1890. Web. 24 April 2018. 〈https://ebooks. adelaide. edu. au/b/burney/fanny/diary-and-letters-of-madame-darblay/complete.html〉.

Burton, Robert. *The Anatomy of Melancholy*. 1832. Web. 24 April 2018. 〈https://ebooks.adelaide.edu.au/b/burton/robert/melancholy/〉.

Charon, Rita. *Narrative Medicine: Honoring the Stories of Illness*. Oxford: Oxford University Press, 2008.

Cheyne, George. *The English Malady; or, A Treatise of Nervous Diseases of All Kinds, as Spleen, Vapours, Lowness of Spirits, Hypochondriacal and Hysterical Distempers*. London: G Strahan, 1733.

Couser, G. Thomas. *Altered Egos: Authority in American Autobiography*. New York: Oxford University Press, 1989.

Crosby, Christina. *A Body, Undone: Living On After Great Pain*. New York: NYU Press, 2017.

Dauncey, Sarah. "Whose Life Is It Anyway? Disabled Life Stories in Post-Reform China." *Writing Lives in China, 1600–2010: Histories of the Elusive Self*. Eds. Marjorie Dryburgh and Sarah Dauncey. New York: Palgrave, 2013.

De Beauvoir, Simone. *A Very Easy Death*. New York: Putnam, 1966.

Frank, Arthur. *At the Will of the Body: Reflections on Illness*. New York: Houghton Mifflin, 2002.

French, Roger. "The Anatomical Tradition." *Companion Encyclopedia of the History of Medicine*. Vol.1. Eds. William F.Bynum and Roy Porter. London: Routledge, 1993.

Giblett, Rodney. *The Body of Nature and Culture*. New York: Palgrave Macmillan, 2008.

Griffiths, Jay. *Tristimania: A Diary of Manic Depression*. London: Penguin Books, 2016.

Hawkins, Anne Hunsaker. "Oliver Sacks's Awakenings: Reshaping Clinical Discourse." *Configurations* 1.2(1993):229-245.

——. *Reconstructing Illness: Studies in Pathography*. Indiana: Purdue University Press, 1999.

Heseler, Baldasar. *Andreas Vesalius' First Public Anatomy at Bologna, 1540: An Eyewitness Report*. Web. 24 April 2018. 〈https://web.stanford.edu/class/history13/Readings/vesalius.htm〉.

Jamison, Leslie. *The Empathy Exams: Essays*. London: Granta, 2014.

Johnson, Samuel. "No. 102. Authors Inattentive to Themselves." *The Idler*, 29 March 1760. Web. 24 April 2018. 〈http://www.johnsonessays.com/the-idler/no-102-authors-inattentive-to-themselves/〉.

Johnson, Samuel and Hester Lynch Piozzi. *The Letters of Samuel Johnson with Mrs. Thrale's Genuine Letters to Him*. Ed. R.W.Chapman. Oxford: Clarendon Press, 1952.

Jurecic, Ann. *Illness as Narrative*. Pittsburgh: University of Pittsburgh Press, 2012.

Kalanithi, Paul. *When Breath Becomes Air*. New York: Random House, 2016.

Lejeune, Philippe. *On Autobiography*. Minneapolis: University of Minnesota Press, 1989.

Lund, Mary Ann. *Melancholy, Medicine and Religion in Early Modern England: Reading "The Anatomy of Melancholy"*. Cambridge: Cambridge University Press, 2010.

Macaulay, Thomas. *Macaulay's Review of Croker's Boswell*. 1831. Ed. Jack Lynch, 1898. Web. 24 April 2018. (https://andromeda.rutgers.edu/~jlynch/Texts/macaulay.html).

Murphy, Robert. *The Body Silent*. 1987. New York: Norton, 2001.

Newman, Donald J. "Disability, Disease, and the 'Philosophick Heroism' of Samuel Johnson in Boswell's *Life of Johnson*." *a/b: Auto/Biography Studies*, 6.1(2001):8-16.

Porter, Roy. "'The Hunger of the Imagination': Approaching Samuel Johnson's Melancholy." *The Anatomy of Madness: Essays in the History of Psychiatry, Vol.1: People and Ideas*. 1985. Eds. William F. Bynum, Roy Porter, Michael Shepherd. London: Routledge, 2004.

Roth, Philip. *Patrimony: A True Story*. New York: Simon and Schuster, 1991.

Sacks, Oliver. *Awakening*. London: Duckworth, 1973.

——. *The Man Who Mistook His Wife for a Hat*. London: Duckworth, 1986.

——. *An Anthropologist on Mars*. London: Picador, 1955.

——. *On the Move: A Life*. New York: Vintage Books, 2016.

Snow, C.P.. *The Two Cultures*. Cambridge: Cambridge University Press, 2012.

Solomon, Andrew. *The Noonday Demon: An Anatomy of Depression*. London: Vintage, 2001.

Sontag, Susan. *Illness as Metaphor*. New Oyrk: Farrar, Straus and Giroux, 1978.

Vesalius, Andreas. *De Humani Corporis Fabrica* (On the Fabric of the Human Body). Web. 24 April 2018. 〈http://www.bl.uk/turning-the-pages/?id=69a49930-a67d-11db-873d-0050c2490048&type=book〉.

Wiltshire, John. *Samuel Johnson in the Medical World: The Doctor and the Patient*. Cambridge: Cambridge University Press, 1991.

Woolf, Virginia. *On Being Ill*. Web. 24 April 2018. 〈http://www.woolfonline.com/?node=content/contextual/transcriptions&project=1&parent=56&taxa=45&content=6225&pos=13〉.

传记中文本主体的可变性

——以弥尔顿早期传记为例

孙勇彬

内容提要： 约翰·弥尔顿是英国第一位有同代人为其作传的伟大诗人。在萨缪尔·约翰生的《弥尔顿传》之前，有关他的传记有十多篇。然而，同样一位传主弥尔顿，由于传记作家的个性、需求和动机的不同，其气质、习惯和性格也出现了差异，甚至存在截然相反的情形，由此充分证实了传记中文本主体的可变性。这就要求读者应该依据自己的学识和鉴赏能力，抽丝剥茧，去伪存真，多维度理解传主。

关键词： 传记　文本主体　《约翰·弥尔顿传》　萨缪尔·约翰生

作者简介： 孙勇彬，文学博士，南京财经大学外国语学院教授，主要研究领域为英国文学，近期代表性成果是《约翰生〈诗人传〉：博雅教育的典范之作》（《临沂大学学报》）。

Title: The Changeability of Textual Subjects in Biography—The Example of Early Lives of Milton

Abstract: John Milton is the first great English poet who has biographies written by his contemporaries. Before Samuel Johnson's *Life of Milton*, there are more than 10 biographies about him. However, the same biographee Milton appears different or even contradictory in temperament, habits and personalities because of different characters, needs and motivations of his biographers. It sufficiently proves that the textual subjects of biographies have changeability, which requires readers to make a painstaking examination, tell the true from the false and interpret the biographee multi-dimensionally.

Keywords: Biography, Textual Subject, *Life of John Milton*, Samuel Johnson

Sun Yongbin is Professor of English in the School of Foreign Languages at Nanjing University of Finance and Economics. His research area is English literature. His recent article "Samuel Johnson's *Lives of the English Poets*: A Canon for Liberal Arts Education" was published in *Linyi University Journal*. E-mail: syongbin@njue.edu.cn.

杨正润曾提出传记存在书写主体、历史主体、文本主体和阅读主体，并以瑞士精神分析学家赫尔曼·罗尔沙赫（Hermann Rorschach，1884—1922）的墨迹测验原理来类比传记中书写主体的个性、需求和动机的投射机制，认为"同一个历史主体，在不同的传记家笔下出现的文本传主可能有所不同，经历和性格都会有不同程度的差异"（180）。而英国伟大诗人约翰·弥尔顿的早期传记正好可以印证该观点。

选择弥尔顿，不仅因为他是英国第一位有同代人为其作传的伟大诗人，更重要的是有关他的传记材料要比 18 世纪之前任何其他一位有影响的英国诗人都更加完备。萨缪尔·约翰生的《弥尔顿传》之前，有关弥尔顿的传记有十多篇，其中 5 篇出现在 17 世纪，次序为 1681 年约翰·奥伯雷（John Aubrey）的《约翰·弥尔顿先生：生活细节》、匿名的《约翰·弥尔顿传》手稿、1691 年安东尼·伍德（Anthony Wood）的《约翰·弥尔顿，文学硕士》（系选自《牛津大学年鉴》）、1694 年爱德华·菲利普斯的《约翰·弥尔顿先生传》（系弥尔顿《国务信札》的引言）、1698 年约翰·托兰德（John Toland）的《约翰·弥尔顿传》。到了 18 世纪，值得提及的弥尔顿传记有 1734 年乔纳森·理查生（Jonathan Richardson）的《弥尔顿传和一篇评〈失乐园〉的论文》和 1779 年萨缪尔·约翰生的《弥尔顿传》。其中前四篇作者奥伯雷、匿名者、伍德和菲利普斯与弥尔顿关系较近。约翰生曾说过："只有那些和他一起吃饭、喝酒，和他有社会交往的人才能够写有关他的传记。"（Hill 166）确实，他们四位留下的有关弥尔顿生平和性格的记载是无可取代的。而托兰德、理查生和约翰生的《弥尔顿传》也都提供了弥尔顿个性的新材料，与前面四位一起形成了弥尔顿早期传记的权威版本。

在此需要特别说明，那篇匿名《约翰·弥尔顿传》的作者到底是谁，学术界存在着争议：1902 年帕森斯先生（Mr. Parsons）在编辑该手稿时未能发现真正的作者，只是猜测极有可能是熟悉弥尔顿的帕杰特医生（Dr. Nathan Paget）（Darbishire ix）；1932 年海伦·达彼赦根据手稿中某些单词拼写习惯推测该作者是弥尔顿的另一位亲外甥约翰·菲利普斯；1957 年威廉·拉雷·帕克根据弥尔顿第 21 和第 22 首十四行诗的抄写版手稿与斯金纳（Cyriack Skinner）在 1668—1669 年 3 月 23 日的一封信的手稿，推断匿名者为斯金纳（Parker 527）。而此人也是弥尔顿的学生之一。尽管匿名者的身份存疑，但从手稿中可以推断他是一位重视道德、尊重事实真相之人，且与弥尔顿私交甚好。该作品的首段包含一种吁求，要写作好人的传记。很明显他写作的目的是通过弥尔顿的公共生活和私生活，来美化其性格。公共生活方面，他称颂弥尔顿政治原则高尚，并以天主教徒斯宾塞的孙子和保皇党派威廉·戴夫南特爵士从监狱获释的事例证明弥尔顿能够公正对待不同教派和党派人士，并慷慨给予帮助。“他没有因为自我利益而加入任何党派，因此也没有被任何党派作为敌人而加以分离。”（Darbishire 30）在私生活方面，匿名者提及弥尔顿尽管平时很节俭，但喜欢买书，对待朋友也非常慷慨并经常接济他们。也正是在公共生活和私生活方面，不同的传记家对弥尔顿有着不尽相同的叙述和阐释。

弥尔顿的首位传记作家奥伯雷是英国文物学家，有着很强的社交能力。他对伍德的传记词典工程很感兴趣，并醉心于收集名人的趣闻轶事。他对弥尔顿生活细节的叙述为后来者提供了素材。同时，他收集传记材料的方法和执着精神也值得后人效仿。他笔下的弥尔顿，是非常熟悉和了解弥尔顿的人眼中的形象，而且他本人与弥尔顿也相识，这可以从作品中的行文得到印证：“他的个头几乎和我一样高。”（Darbishire 3）奥伯雷作为文物学家的身份，使其长于认真负责、严谨准确的考据。他曾经多次拜访诗人的弟弟克里斯托弗·弥尔顿、诗人的遗孀和外甥爱德华·菲利普斯，向他们求证日期、事实和诗人的生活细节，并仔细标注其权威性。他也会在文中坦率地告知读者某些可疑或不太确切的信息来源，甚至对存在争议的史实也将相应的各个版本的叙述均收入传记中。即便无法获取的事实也在传记中毫不隐瞒而非刻意掩饰或只字不提。因此他的弥尔顿传记中提供了烦琐而详尽的注释，达彼赦称“他是费尽了心血从最好的资料来源获取了事实”（Darbishire xxxv）。从他的手稿中，可以了解到弥尔顿早期学习情况：平时非常努力，经常熬夜至夜间12点，或是凌晨1点；也提及弥尔顿的大学生活和第一任导师的关系，指出在剑桥，弥尔顿也是非常刻苦的学生，所有的功课都获得了好评，但他的第一任导师查普尔（Chapell）先生对他并不友好。可见，在奥伯雷看来，或是奥伯雷从弥尔顿亲属那里听来，错误是在导师。这也为后来者约翰生刻意强化他与导师之间的关系埋下了伏笔。关于弥尔顿的性格和爱好，奥伯雷认为，“他谈话的时候心情非常愉快，在晚餐或是正餐的时候，有时也会嘲讽，也会讲些令人开心的幽默”（Darbishire 6），“甚至他在痛风发作的时候也非常快乐，还唱歌”（Darbishire 5）。从奥伯雷那里，还可以了解到弥尔顿名声很大：他被热情邀请去法国和意大利，外国很多人崇拜他，给他提供升职机会；而且一些外国人来到英国的目的只是想一睹约翰·弥尔顿先生的风采，常常会去参观他出生时的房子和房间。弥尔顿与朋友的交往也非常频繁，“常常有人拜访他，比他期望的要多”（Darbishire 6）。

奥伯雷和匿名者有关弥尔顿的传记手稿虽然都没有正式出版，但两者相对独立，并为伍德完成第一部正式出版的弥尔顿传记作品提供了基础。根据海伦·达彼赦所说，伍德的作品“将近1/2是从匿名者手稿中逐字逐句抄来的，大约1/10是从奥伯雷的手稿中润色而来”（Darbishire ix）。尽管如此，作为一位牛津学者，伍德有着自己的优势和主见。优势体现在他比其他传记作家拥有更加完整的弥尔顿作品列表，而且他自己可以从作品中进行归纳。对于弥尔顿的政治观，伍德也有着自己的主见。与奥伯雷和匿名者不同，他公然控诉弥尔顿与派系结盟。尽管，奥伯雷已经写道：“弥尔顿反对君主独裁，无论他写了什么，并不是出自他对国王本人或是某个派系的仇恨和敌意，而是出自他对人类自由的纯粹热情。”（Darbishire 13—14）然而，由于伍德与弥尔顿分属不同党派，他开始歪曲事实，并错误地阐释动机，认为弥尔顿“做伟大的事情是为了获得名声和财富”（Darbishire 27）。那位匿名者也坚持认为弥尔顿的“付出是为了上帝的荣耀和公众的一些福利”，而伍德对这些不感兴趣。伍德告诉我们，在辩论中“萨尔马修斯受到了极高的赞扬，而弥尔顿则表现出自己的本色”——这句话是伍德恶意篡改了匿名传记作家的句子：“萨尔马修斯在这里得到了极力称赞，而弥尔顿先生则错误地受到了诽谤和中伤。”（Darbishire 27）正如我们所见，伍德的省略如他的修改一样可以说明问题。伍德的政治偏见使得他对弥尔顿的评价有失公允，也给弥尔顿的声誉带来了负面的影响。

爱德华·菲利普斯是弥尔顿的外甥，也是他的学生。他的《约翰·弥尔顿先生传》作为《国务信札》的前言部分，在长度上是两倍于匿名者的，匿名者的又比伍德的长，而奥伯雷的最为简短，所以爱德华的传记比前面三者都要完整和详细。尽管有些日期不值得信赖——他把弥尔顿的出生年份写错了，把1608年写成了1606年，死亡年份1674写成了1673——但是，他对地点的记忆非常好。约翰生评论道：“他的传记作家们非常尊敬弥尔顿，他住过的每一处住宅都有提及。”（Darbishire xiii）这是爱德华·菲利普斯的功劳，使得后来的传记家们能够挖掘弥尔顿在不同地方的事迹。他也介绍了弥尔顿经常与朋友阿尔弗雷先生和米勒先生一起聚会。也是他无意中向我们透露弥尔顿无与伦比的勤奋、慷慨的气质、节俭和有节制的生活。可以理解，外甥为舅舅作传，尊重和赞颂是该传记的基调。

诗人的下一位传记家是约翰·托兰德。他与弥尔顿并不相识，但是他紧紧沿着前面传记家的足迹前行。他认识奥伯雷，他通读爱德华·菲利普斯的作品，与约翰·菲利普斯交谈，从弥尔顿的抄写员之一和他的遗孀那里了解到一些细微之处。托兰德是《基督教并不神秘》的作者、自然神论信仰者和自由思想家。他也是弥尔顿政治作品的热情崇拜者。在去世之前，他在自己的墓碑上称自己是“真理的捍卫者、自由的维护者，这里有一位追随者或践行人”（Darbishire xxviii）。托兰德发现弥尔顿有着类似的精神。他的《约翰·弥尔顿传》作为诗人首部散文作品集的前言于1698年出版。他的叙述主线是沿着爱德华·菲利普斯的作品，也偶尔参考一下伍德的作品，但是他把更多的空间留给了政治事件。托兰德通过这些事件来显示他喜爱的弥尔顿是一位自由和自由思想的捍卫者。他也带着自己的偏见来判断，“显示自由和暴政的不同效果是他《失乐园》的主要计划”（Darbishire 182）。另外，他也提及弥尔顿给予其他作家的慷慨指导和帮助。

18 世纪前半叶，弥尔顿的名声越来越大，他的作品不断有新的版本出现，他的生平也是经常被人撰写。其中有些充斥着溢美之词，没有提及什么新的信息。但值得提及的是画家理查生。他能够竭尽全力询问弥尔顿的后人和相识之人，提供了一些新的细节。因为理查生是画家的缘故，他在人物描写过程中，喜欢用画家的笔法通过色彩、运动、线条等手段来勾勒人物形象，他甚至注意到弥尔顿眼睛的颜色倾向于蓝色，而不是深色。他对弥尔顿姿态以及一些生活场景的描述惟妙惟肖，近乎传神：“我听到有关他口述时候的姿势——他身体向后斜坐在一张舒适的椅子上，一条腿悬在椅子扶手上。”（Darbishire 291）他虽然不认识或没见过弥尔顿，但幸运的是，他认识几位与弥尔顿熟识的人。由于个人对于弥尔顿的崇拜和尊敬，他记录了许多生动的场景和微小的细节，为我们呈现了一位鲜活的人物。通过理查生的眼睛——一位画家的眼睛，我们看到由于失明，“弥尔顿由经营不列颠旧书店的书商梅林顿（Millington）带领着在街上走路”（Darbishire 203）。那个时候，这位书商给弥尔顿提供了住宿。我们也看到“弥尔顿在寒冷天气下穿着灰色驼毛呢上衣”，“在阳光明媚的时候会穿着灰色粗布上衣坐在邦希田园（Bun-hill Fields）附近的房子外面呼吸新鲜空气”（Darbishire 203）。

然而，18 世纪下半叶文坛领袖约翰生的《弥尔顿传》中所描述的弥尔顿在气质、习惯和性情上都不同于其他早期传记家。海伦·达彼赦曾经对此前弥尔顿的传记作了归纳，认为这些作品中弥尔顿形象要和蔼可亲得多：“在公共辩论的时候他可能是严厉的、粗俗的和冷酷的，但是在私生活中，他的朋友和亲戚所知道的是一个不同的人——一个文化人，有教养、慷慨、适合做朋友、言辞诙谐、性情温和、爱好音乐和安静、喜欢与感情深厚的聪明同伴交往。”（Darbishire lxi）然而，在约翰生所作的《弥尔顿传》开篇，作者就不遗余力地显示年轻的弥尔顿作为一个“异化了”的人物，一位“流浪者”的形象。约翰生首先在弥尔顿的大学时代发现影响他一生的非常重要的线索，就是“弥尔顿没有多少朋友”（Johnson 88）。虽然对于大学这段时间，约翰生知之甚少，只有少数有事实依据的传记材料。实际上，约翰生的措辞暗示了他只是推测：有理由怀疑他在学院里面不太受人喜欢。约翰生把这种“不太受人喜欢”戏剧化。根据伯根·伊万斯的研究，约翰生可获得的传记材料很少：“弥尔顿就像其他先前的同学一样，挑起一位老师的不愉快，真的被抽了鞭子。”（Evans 62—63）但是，约翰生以戏剧表演的语气故意拉长：“我羞于讲述恐怕是一件真实的事，就是弥尔顿在大学是排名靠后的学生之一，曾经当众受到过体罚。”（Johnson 88）接着，约翰生讲述了弥尔顿下乡生活的故事。对此，对他充满敌意的人提出他是被学校开除的，在这一点上，弥尔顿持续否认，很明显这不是真的。但是从弥尔顿写给迪奥达提（Diodati）的诗歌来看，很明显他离开学校到乡下去耽误了一个学期时间。约翰生引用弥尔顿关于下乡这个主题的诗句：他厌倦于忍受“一位严厉老师的威胁，以及其他一些事情，如像他这样的脾气”（Johnson 89）。约翰生据此推测，比威胁更甚的可能就是体罚了。这首提及他流放的诗同样可以证明下乡不是长久的事情，因为它的结尾是决定在某个时间会回到剑桥。这里，约翰生通过引用弥尔顿的诗歌，把下乡（rustication）升格为流放（exile），并以此推断弥尔顿有以自我为中心并且喜欢与他人孤立的意识。

对于约翰生来说，友谊是年轻人与社会融合最确定也是最自然的标记。约翰生在后文中非常仔细地暗示了弥尔顿的朋友很少。例如，约翰生有关弥尔顿材料来源之一约翰·托兰德曾经谈到查尔斯·迪奥达提是弥尔顿“亲密的朋友”（Darbishire 88），并说弥尔顿“因为失去最亲密的朋友和校友而悲痛了很长时间”（Darbishire 96）。然而，约翰生对他们之间的友谊到底有多深并未作说明，只是简单介绍了弥尔顿欧洲旅行回来之后听到朋友查尔斯的死讯，为他写了一首题为《达蒙的葬礼》（*Epitaphium Damonis*）的诗歌，并评价这是一首“孩子气的模仿田园生活”的诗歌。弥尔顿另外一首写给一位被淹死的朋友的诗《利西达斯》，也遭到约翰生的批评，认为该诗既没有自然，也没有真理，更没有艺术，因为没有什么是新颖的。该诗的形式是田园诗，简单、粗俗，因此令人厌恶。同时，该诗也未能够作为特殊友谊或是亲密关系的证明。约翰生很少描写弥尔顿与其他人在一起的情形，传中只有一处，还是“在一位隐士的陪伴下，他从罗马来到那不勒斯”（Darbishire 96）。约翰生笔下成年的弥尔顿也有同样的习惯。他几乎没有朋友，实际上，他与别人打交道就是反对他们。传记的中间部分主要列举了他所反对的人和机构：1641 年，他出版了有关改革宗教的两卷本书，反对英国国教。同年，弥尔顿发表《高位圣职的主教制度》来反对五位牧师，他们的名字首字母构成一个单词 Smectymnuus。1642 年，他发表《教会政府鼓励反对高级教士的理由》。同年，他发表了两部小册子，就同样问题，回击他的反对者之一。

弥尔顿作为一个有意识与他人孤立并自认为理直气壮的形象在传中普遍存在。约翰生不遗余力地详细叙述传主这一形象。例如在讲到弥尔顿开始教育他两个外甥的时候，先在圣布莱德教堂庭院内一位裁缝家里租了一个住处。后来他发现房间太小，又在阿尔德盖特街找了一处带有花园的房子。那时候这条街道还是比较热闹的，他就在通道的最末端选择了自己的住处，如此一来他就可以远离街道的喧嚣。可以看出，约翰生浓墨重彩，目的是证明弥尔顿试图尽可能地与外界隔离，而这一形象与前面提及的六部弥尔顿传记存在很大不同。

弥尔顿这样的性格深刻影响了他的婚姻观、政治观和宗教观。约翰生在布道词（1）中说道，婚姻是友谊的永恒形式。他认为弥尔顿在婚姻问题上所经历的困难显示他不能够享受生活中最亲密关系所带来的快乐，而且婚姻并没有给他带来多少幸福。在他 35 岁那年，他和牛津郡和平法官帕尔（Powel）先生的女儿玛丽结婚。他把她带到镇上，期望婚姻带来美好生活。后来约翰生很确定地解释弥尔顿可能并不非常爱她，或是弥尔顿这个人在性情上就不适合结婚。他对婚姻，特别是有关离婚的观点充分说明他是一位以自我为中心的人，一位总是轻视他人的人。关于婚姻，约翰生还有一个观点也是针对弥尔顿的：他前后三位妻子都是处女，“因为他认为成为第二任丈夫会使自己感到不快和尴尬”（Darbishire 131）。约翰生自己和一位布商遗孀结婚，对于弥尔顿结婚对象的选择原则持反对态度，这也是弥尔顿不愿意与他人交往的一个例证：甚至连那些已经离世的人（前夫），也会令他感到不安全。

约翰生相信，弥尔顿的政治观也是一样，对于他人的权利和期望注意很少，反映了他自己高傲自大的优越感："我恐怕弥尔顿的共和主义是建立在如下基础之上的，那是对伟大带有妒忌心的憎恨，对独立持有不温不火的欲望，对控制拥有不可忍耐的烦躁，以及对优越又有轻蔑的傲慢。"（Darbishire 157）在政治社会中，他憎恨国内的僧人和教会里的教士，因为他憎恨所有他需要服从的人。约翰生进一步暗示弥尔顿就像所有的共和党人一样，他们提倡普通大众的自由，但是他们很少在意普通民众的需求和观点。例如，在为处死查理一世辩解时，弥尔顿并没有和普通民众的步调一致。行刑"毫无疑问并没有征得人民的同意，"约翰生告诉鲍斯威尔，"我们知道当查理二世复辟的时候人们快乐的程度有多高。"（Hill 370）

约翰生以同样的方式描述弥尔顿的宗教观点和实践。弥尔顿从来不在公共场合祷告。尽管他经常表达神学观点，但是他自己从不完全参与任何一个教派："他的神学观据说先是加尔文教派；后来，也许在他憎恨长老会成员的时候，他开始转向亚米念主义。"（Darbishire 155）弥尔顿总是反对，很少同意的倾向不仅限于神学辩论。对约翰生来说，弥尔顿从来不通过赞扬的方式把自己与他人联系起来："很少有人写了这么多，但其中的赞扬却如此少。"（Darbishire 94）弥尔顿逃避任何联系，包括教堂、学院和婚姻，他把自己排除在所有这些把人集合在一起的机构和制度之外。

通篇来看，与早期传记家笔下"适合做朋友的、和蔼可亲的"弥尔顿相比，约翰生笔下出现的文本传主迥然不同：弥尔顿俨然是一位异化了的、游离于人间世态之外的孤独者，而他的诗歌在选材、风格、措辞和主题方面与他的特立独行的个性息息相关。约翰生对于弥尔顿诗作的评价与早期传记家相比也存在不同程度的差异，除了所见资料不一致的原因之外，更主要的还是因为传记家约翰生与众不同的眼光和他注重诗人性格与其作品之间关系的批评方式。

综上所述，同一历史主体弥尔顿，在不同的传记家笔下出现了不一样的文本主体，这充分证实了文本主体的可变性。这是传记家的权力体现之一，也要求读者应该依据自己的学识和鉴赏能力，抽丝剥茧，去伪存真，多维度来了解历史主体。

致谢【Acknowledgement】

本文系国家社科基金项目“萨缪尔·约翰生《诗人传》研究”（编号：15BWW041）的阶段性成果，得到全国哲学社会科学规划办公室的经费支持，作者谨致谢忱！

My acknowledgement and gratitude go to the National Social Science Fund of China, for the sponsorship of the project, "The Study of Samuel Johnson's *Lives of the English Poets*"(IC. 15BWW041).

引用文献【Works Cited】

Darbishire, Helen, ed. *The Early Lives of Milton*. London: Constable & Co. Ltd., 1932.

Evans, Bergen. "Dr. Johnson as a Biographer." PhD. Diss. Harvard University, 1932.

Hill, George Birkbeck, ed. *Boswell's Life of Johnson*. Vol. 2. Oxford: The Clarendon Press, 1934.

Johnson, Samuel. *Lives of the English Poets*. Vol.1. Ed. G.B.Hill. Oxford: The Clarendon Press, 1905.

Parker, William Riley. "The 'Anonymous Life' of Milton." *TLS*, 13 Sept. 1957, 527.

杨正润：《现代传记学》。南京：南京大学出版社，2009.

[Yang Zhengrun. *A Modern Poetics of Biography*. Nanjing: Nanjing University Press, 2009.]

知识女性自我塑造中的喜乐与哀愁

——《往事》与《我的人生苦旅》比较谈

刘 萍

内容提要：毛彦文和柳溪的自传《往事》与《我的人生苦旅》以普通人物视角反映复杂、动荡的历史变迁，具有独特而珍贵的史料价值。与此同时，身为女性，毛彦文和柳溪也以自己的婚姻、事业等经历展示出她们隐忍与反抗兼具的品格，尤其凸显出她们作为现代知识女性的成长。纵然两部自传叙事风格不尽相同，但无论冷淡还是热烈，均为现代女性的自我塑造提供了真实而生动的范例。

关键词：毛彦文　柳溪　自传　女性　自我塑造

作者简介：刘萍，文学博士，安徽师范大学副教授，研究方向是欧美文学、中西文学比较，近期发表论文《论〈小团圆〉中九莉的“笑”：兼与简·爱比较》（2018 年）、《惋惜·庆幸·怨忿：关于张爱玲多角恋传记叙述的比较阅读》（2018 年）等。

Title: The Happiness and Sadness in the Self-fashioning of Intellectual Women: A Comparative Study of *The Past* and *My Miserable Life*

Abstract: *The Past* and *My Miserable Life*, the two autobiographies written by Mao Yanwen and Liu Xi, reflect the complex and turbulent history from the perspective of ordinary people, and possess unique and precious historical value. Simultaneously, being women, Mao Yanwen and Li Xi display their characters with endurance and rebellion by their own marriages and careers, especially highlighting their growth as modern intellectual women. In spite of the disparate narrative styles, whether cold or enthusiastic, the two autobiographies provide real and vivid models for modern female self-fashioning.

Keywords: Mao Yanwen, Liu Xi, autobiography, female, self-fashioning

Liu Ping is Associate Professor at Anhui Normal University. Her research interests are western literature, literary theory and comparative literature. She is the author of "On Jiuli's 'Smile' in *Little Reunion*: and Comparing with Jane Eyre"(2018) and "Regretful, Fortunate, Resentful: A Comparative Reading of Zhang Ailing's Multiple Love Narration in the Biographies". E-mail: lp99w@163.com.

《往事》[1]与《我的人生苦旅》[2]分别出自两位女士毛彦文和柳溪之手，是她们的自传。诚然，无论毛彦文还是柳溪都并非声名显赫之人，但在其堪称漫长的人生之旅中[3]，她们都无可避免地被卷入浩大的历史洪流，经历一次又一次无情的冲撞和洗礼。比较阅读《往事》与《我的人生苦旅》可见，作为一代知识女性，由于身处乱世，毛彦文和柳溪都饱受社会动荡之苦，而她们既非一味地怨天尤人，也不盲目地自怨自艾，表现出鲜明的不入俗流的反叛性，同时又自觉不自觉地与传统相归依，在"新"与"旧"的冲突、融合中，建构起自己日益健全的人生品格。为此，她们的所作所为固然谈不上丰功伟业，却无疑值得尊重、钦佩。正所谓"大事件中的小人物，小人物的大命运，……生活的原生态，常常更能反映出历史的本相"（李辉 2），毛彦文与柳溪女士的这两部自传便以独特的视角展示历史的真相，尤其是在婚姻与事业当中的喜乐与哀愁，更为现代女性的自我塑造提供了有意义的参照。

婚姻自古被视为"大事"，在旧社会，能否嫁得如意郎君更是成为女性幸福抑或不幸的一个决定性因素。毛彦文和柳溪一波三折的婚姻同样给她们的生活带来直接而重大的影响：一方面，身为弱女子，她们不得不承受各种各样的压力；另一方面，作为有能力、有主见的知识女性，面对自己的婚姻大事，她们亦曾积极主动地进行抗争或者加以调适。为此，固然由于种种外在条件所限，她们均未能享受持久安宁的婚姻幸福，却也终究没有沦为婚姻的附庸。正是这样，两人不寻常的婚姻经历既透露出身为女性的普遍的悲哀，同时也见证着女性的成长。

说起毛彦文的婚恋往事，一代学者吴宓的大名时常被提及，甚至很多人其实是因为吴宓而知道毛彦文。吴宓是个多情才子，其生平经历原本不乏风花雪月之事——有论者甚至直言这成为吴宓后期学术著作乏善可陈的主要原因之一（余斌 56），说到毛彦文，更是明确表示："真正让他魂牵梦绕的只有一个毛彦文。"（余斌 56）以吴宓当时的才华、声名、气度和痴情，默默无闻的毛彦文似乎只有受宠若惊、欣然接受的道理，然而，毛彦文却毅然决然地拒绝了吴宓一而再、再而三的追求，为此她难以摆脱"无情"抑或"矫情"的骂名而长期以来饱受困扰。回顾这段往事，毛彦文难掩心中的不平："关于吴宓先生追求我的事，不知内情的人都责我寡情，而且不了解为何吴君对我如此热情而我无动于衷，半世纪以来，备受责骂与误解。"（53）究其实情可见，"在吴、毛的这场感情纠葛中，毛始终是一个被动者、勉强接受者，而吴在对毛的追求过程中，不只感情动荡不稳，且有强加对方的意味"（金梅 90）。问题的关键其实并不在于吴宓对毛彦文专情与否，而在于吴宓的苦苦追求终究不过是"单相思"，就诸多看客而言，归根结底只能算是揣测，于毛彦文自己，则关系不大或者说牵强附会了。这里，值得深究的是，毛彦文对吴宓的拒绝本身，显示出知识女性的冷静自持，尽管她很欣赏吴宓的为人，声称："吴君是一位文人学者，心地善良，为人拘谨，有正义感，有浓厚的书生气质而兼有几分浪漫气息，他离婚后对于前妻仍倍加关切，不仅负担她及他们女儿的生活费及教育费，传闻有时还去探望陈女士[④]。他绝不是一个薄情者……"（55）然而，毛彦文深知自己与吴宓的性格完全不同，坦言若两人勉强结合，不仅"不会幸福，说不定会再闹仳离"（55）。于是，面对因吴宓的一意孤行而导致的这段感情纠葛，毛彦文始终保持清醒的判断力，她冷静而果断地消除对方的痴心妄想，不曾刻意迁就，亦没有忘乎所以。

撇开吴宓不论，毛彦文的婚史依然一波三折、颇不寻常，正如有论者评价："毛彦文的一生，可谓现代婚姻史上具有代表性的个案。先是为反父母包办而逃婚，后又与自由恋爱的对象协议解除婚约，再是这次老夫少妻的婚姻，每一回都闹得满城风雨。"（桑农 60）只不过，最初的逃婚多半归功于外力的作用，如老师的教育、亲友的协助等，就毛彦文自己而言，当时固然有明确的反抗意识，面对突如其来的婚事其实还是茫然无措的。好在尽管如此，结果却堪称圆满，毛彦文不仅成功解除包办婚约，还在此事的直接推动下，得以与表哥朱君毅缔结新的婚约。毛彦文与朱君毅属于“青梅竹马、两小无猜”之类，对于这段感情，毛彦文可谓刻骨铭心，直言：“君毅是我初恋的对象，一生命运完全受他的影响。”（36）后来在惊闻对方去世的噩耗后，年逾花甲的毛彦文特意撰长文《悼君毅》，以写信的口吻，直接向对方倾诉：“其实我自情窦初开，以迄于彼此决裂时，二十余年来，全部精神与爱都为你一人所占有，换言之，我二十余年来只认识一个男人，我的青春是在你占有期间消逝的！……你在我幼稚心灵中播下初恋种子，生根滋长，永不萎枯。你我虽形体上决绝四十年，但你有时仍在我梦中出现，梦中的你我依然那样年轻，那样深爱，你仍为我梦里的心上人。”（51—52）因为对朱君毅怀有如此深挚的感情，后来面对对方的移情别恋，毛彦文的痛苦可想而知，但眼看心上人去意已决，毛彦文亦不再强求，特意发起一场颇为正式的解除婚约的仪式，干脆、利落地终止了这段感情纠葛。面对突如其来的情变，毛彦文表现得不卑不亢，她固然对朱君毅用情至深，却终究没有唯感情至上而走极端——顺便说一下，传统女性因受“男尊女卑”思想的影响，对于爱人常常表现出无可掩饰的依附性，其具体表现便是“爱情至上”。换言之，即视爱情为“唯一”和“最高”，其多情可嘉，但终究爱得太过卑微，乃至失却爱情便仿佛失却了全部，终于走向无可挽回的悲剧结局。毛彦文则不然，她为情所扰却并不唯情至上，因此而虽遭背叛，却以自己坦然“放手”的勇气和决心赢得了世人的尊重，与此同时，也在客观上为此后她与熊希龄的一段奇缘创造了条件。

无独有偶，柳溪亦曾遭遇类似情变，且性质更为恶劣。柳溪与陈毓森作为地下革命工作的战友而日久生情、结为夫妻，并且育有一子。五妹清傧因不堪忍受继母的虐待来投奔二姐柳溪，柳溪好意收留妹妹，没想到五妹与陈毓森却在其眼皮子底下发生私情，后来居然在柳溪坐月子期间、连吃饭都成问题的情况之下，采用欺骗的手段抛弃无依无靠的柳溪母子，回老家大摆订婚宴席。柳溪了解到真相后，固然伤心、愤怒，却终究不失理智，她清醒地认识到自己与陈毓森的婚姻已无法挽回，主动提出成全清傧和陈毓森。更难能可贵的是，她没有像传统的弃妇那样一蹶不振或者自暴自弃，而是以大局为重，继续不辞辛劳地开展地下工作，后来又机智勇敢地躲过敌人的追捕，成功从沦陷区撤退到解放区，从而开辟出自己的一片人生新天地。总之，面对爱人的移情别恋，倾情付出的毛彦文和柳溪痛心疾首、备受打击，但悲愤之余，她们不失清醒和勇气。由此，虽然同不少传统女性一样遭遇“多情女子负心汉”的悲剧，但她们以退为进，以独立自主的态度坦然面对，既赢得了尊严，也保留了希望。

幸运的是，在惨遭背叛后，婚姻的大门并未就此对毛彦文和柳溪关闭；不过，她们的婚姻依然悲喜交杂，令人叹惜。1935 年，37 岁的毛彦文与年逾花甲的熊希龄喜结连理，夫妻相差近三十岁的年龄，这在当时着实罕见，而此次堪称大操大办婚礼之超级豪华阵容，亦令几乎整个上海滩为之沸腾。高官、巨贾、名流、明星……各行各业有头有脸的人物亲临现场，可谓是“车盖云集”“群贤毕至”，其中除了贺喜之外，恐怕不能排除有些人其实是抱着一种“猎奇”的心理去关注此事，人们很难不为这对“白发红颜”的结合而惊叹。考虑到熊希龄的显赫身份以及两人社会地位的巨大反差[5]，难免有人感慨毛彦文的“高攀”，于是有论者揣测其心理：“毛彦文决定嫁给熊希龄，利益上有自己的考量，这本来无可厚非。”（桑农 60）如其所言，毛彦文家境平平，身为长女，她不仅自己要独立谋生，还得照顾两个妹妹，又因身逢乱世而难免颠沛流离，其中艰辛可想而知。但毛彦文终究并非攀附权贵之类，否则该会毫不犹豫地欣然应允，但实际上她却因辈分[6]及年龄关系断然拒绝了熊希龄的提亲。当然，毛彦文最后还是答应嫁给熊希龄了，只不过其显赫身价固然令人不容小觑，但除此之外，更难能可贵的是，熊希龄为人正直善良、才华横溢，且对毛彦文情真意切、关爱有加。当时的毛彦文早已过了谈婚论嫁的最佳年龄——其实即便就今天的标准看，大龄、高知的女性面临婚姻困境亦算是颇为常见吧。正是这样，顶着“大龄青年”“高知女性”[7]的双重头衔，毛彦文若想觅得各个方面都让人满意的伴侣谈何容易，明白了这一点，恐怕也就多少可以理解为什么在丈夫猝然离世[8]后毛彦文始终保持独身了吧。更何况，“曾经沧海难为水”，要想找到一位像熊希龄那样对自己百般呵护的伴侣，几乎可以说是可望而不可及了。还值得思考的是，站在熊希龄的角度看，毛彦文有哪些优点让他念念不忘乃至穷追不舍呢？在给毛彦文的信中，熊希龄这样描述自己眼中的爱人：“不好虚荣”“不尚形式”“坦白直实”“不好世俗娱乐”“立志创立事业”“骨肉孝友”“挚爱儿童”（178）。由此可见，固然是“老夫少妻”式的组合，在熊希龄的心目中，毛彦文绝不仅仅是一个只供赏玩的“花瓶”，而确乎一个理想的助手、同事，毛彦文在丈夫去世之后的所作所为，尤其是在香山慈幼院[9]建设方面的努力及成果，也完全证实了这一点。换言之，固然也曾因“夫贵”而“妻荣”，毛彦文终究不同于传统女性之一味仰仗于丈夫的荫庇，而向世人彰显出自我的独立性和价值。

与毛彦文的婚姻相比，柳溪与谢湘的结合显得更为被动。在当时特定的形势下，经由“组织”的干预，“结婚”俨然成为一桩政治任务，令柳溪猝不及防且不容推托。正是这样，在仅仅只有一面之缘、彼此完全不了解的情况下，柳溪不得不火速收拾行李，赶去与谢湘结婚。此时，她忐忑不安地把自己与王昭君相比：“前去和番远嫁的王昭君，也不过是我这样祸福未卜、前途迷茫的一种心态吧？”（118）谢湘比柳溪年长 11 岁，是军区的大干部，就此而言，似乎同毛彦文与熊希龄的结合一样，以世俗的眼光看，柳溪嫁给谢湘可算是拥有靠山、后顾无忧了。

然而，无论毛彦文还是柳溪，事实上都未能长久地享受婚姻的安宁与幸福。对于毛彦文而言，丈夫熊希龄的突然去世让她猝不及防、悲痛欲绝。至于柳溪，则在婚后认真反思上次与陈毓森的婚变，意识到自己当时过分专注于工作，缺乏女性的温柔，这次应该有所改正——若换作陈毓森，又有多少人会因为他的忘我工作而责备他对妻子不够温柔体贴呢？柳溪虽然接受过高等教育[10]，但显然并未从根本上摆脱男尊女卑的传统思想观念，用激进的女权主义者的话来说，此即女性群体的“自我憎恨和自我厌弃”，其根源则在于“对女性卑下观点的反复宣扬，无论这种宣扬是多么含蓄，最后，女性对此也信以为真”（米利特 65—66）。正是在这种传统观念的耳濡目染之下，柳溪难以免俗地想要迁就丈夫，千方百计地讨丈夫欢心：“我像别的妇女专心照顾自己的丈夫那样，每天照顾他的吃喝……我不愿意有一丁点儿事情悖拗着他，更不能流露出些许不愉快的情绪。"（122）然而，柳溪要做丈夫背后的"小女人"的想法，终究被残酷的现实击得粉碎。因为家庭成分是地主，柳溪在"土改"运动中沦为被整治的对象，贫民出身的谢湘为了免受牵连，不顾女儿刚刚满月，坚决要跟妻子离婚。此次的离婚危机虽然因为后来土地改革政策调整、柳溪转危为安而化解，但谢湘不顾妻子死活、只求自己平安的心理可谓暴露无遗。面对丈夫的胆怯和自私，柳溪不得不警醒："这次的婚变事件，严酷的事实，打破了我要做一个'贤妻良母'的想法，我的灵魂中有了一种醒悟，那就是唤醒了我早年的那种意识，要做一个独立的女人，要做一棵树，而不做一根藤缠在丈夫身上，享受'夫荣妻贵'的荣华。"（146）明白了这一点，柳溪开始有意识地疏远丈夫，直到小儿子出世，夫妻关系才真正有所缓和。然而好景不长，后来柳溪又受政治风波的冲击，被打成右派，善于明哲保身的谢湘毫不留情地抛弃妻子，他打着"假离婚"的幌子诱使妻子同意离婚，使得柳溪在蒙冤受难之际又遭遇"被离异"的窘境，孩子也被谢湘带走，为此，柳溪大病两个月，为自己的人财两空、一无所有而悲叹不已。但柳溪终究没有被婚姻的不幸击垮，她清醒地意识到自己"现在的关键是先把身体养好，然后还是要发奋图强，……独立地迈向人生"（206）。一个是贴心伴侣的猝然离世，一个是无情丈夫的恶意抛弃，毛彦文和柳溪的婚姻在时代风云以及种种个人因素的作用之下很快变得支离破碎，她们为此惊慌失措、痛不欲生，但终究没有一味沉浸于自己的悲哀当中，而是振作起精神，勇敢地迎接一个个接踵而至的更加严峻的困难，以自己的实际行动书写出现代女性独立自强的新篇章。

由此可见，毛彦文和柳溪在婚姻上都历经坎坷，其中"幸"抑或"不幸"很难划分、厘定，但值得一提的是，在遭遇婚姻挫折时，她们没有像传统女性那样一味地隐忍、退让，而是不随波逐流，亦不委曲求全，有情有义、有理性有胆识，由此，她们终究未拘囿于婚姻的围城，而变被动为主动，彰显出一份现代知识女性特有的自信与成熟。究其"主动"的根源，则不能不提她们安身立命之本——事业。凭借着才华与努力，毛彦文和柳溪积极投身于事业当中，由此既有效改善了自己的客观处境，也在心理上收获了一份难能可贵的幸福与满足。

毋庸讳言，按照男权文化传统，女性其实是没有什么事业可言的，甚至不少历史上赫赫有名的智者在这一点上也不能免俗，对女性表现出无可掩饰的偏见，比如亚里士多德声称："男人是主动的，他很活跃，在政治、商业和文化中有创造性。男性塑造社会和世界。在另一方面，女人是被动的。她天性就是待在家中的。她是等待着活跃的男性原则塑造的物质。"卢梭断言："女人依靠男人的感觉而活，依靠男人对她们的奖赏而活，依靠男人对她们的吸引力、对她们的美德所设定的价值而活。女人一生的教育都应该依照和男人的相对关系而计划，女人要取悦于男人，要贡献给男人，要赢得男人的爱和尊重，要哺育男人，要照顾男人，要安慰、劝慰男人，并要使男人的生活甜蜜且愉悦。"叔本华提出："女人从本性上来说意味着服从，对于这一点，我们可以把它看作这样一个事实，即每一位处于完全独立的非自然位置上的女人都要直接依附于某个男人，使自己接受他的统治和支配。这是因为她需要一位丈夫和主人。"（李银河 8—9）智者尚且如此，其他人更不必说了。按照这样的逻辑，女性与事业显然便没有什么关系了，女性也因此长期以来处于被歧视、受压迫的地位。毛彦文和柳溪便是如此，因为没生儿子[11]，毛彦文的母亲饱受婆家的虐待，毛彦文姐妹自然也常遭欺侮；柳溪则因为出生时母亲难产而死，再加上是个女孩，从小便被视为"丧门星"，挨饿受打几乎成了家常便饭。不幸之中万幸的是，由于时代风气的变化，加上种种机缘巧合以及她们自己的刻苦努力，毛彦文和柳溪得以冲破旧家庭的牢笼，接受正规的学校教育，并取得优异的学习成绩，"知识改变命运"　　应当承认，这为她们以后的事业准备了必要的条件。

相比较毛彦文，柳溪在事业上的开拓显得更为艰难，也更具传奇色彩。革命战争年代，她是机智勇敢的女战士，曾经在沦陷区从事困难重重、危机四伏的地下工作，打入敌人内部、印刷抗日传单、建立地下交通站……柳溪不知疲倦地努力工作，也取得了令人惊叹的成果。然而尽管如此，她却在后来一系列的政治运动中蒙冤受难，接二连三地遭遇迫害，由此，她无法正常地工作，不得不下工厂、去农村、蹲牛棚，看大门……甚至连自由都被剥夺，从身体到精神都饱受摧残。即便在这种暗无天日的情况下，柳溪也没有放弃学习和工作的热情。比如在刚刚离开牛棚，又被下放农村期间，她省吃俭用，购买《水稻》《小麦》《玉米》等农业科技类书籍，一边用心阅读，一边结合劳作予以实践总结，从而逐渐掌握了一些农业科学知识。正因为这样，她敏锐地注意到农民们播种的麦种已经退化，建议改种适合当地土质的新麦种，农民们采纳了这一建议，结果第二年收获了大面积的丰收。后来，柳溪又积极钻研杂交多穗高粱育种、红薯温床育秧等的科学方法，帮助农民增种高产作物，补充粮食的不足。这样，柳溪以自己广博的学识以及认真、踏实的工作态度博得了农民们的信任，朴实、善良的农民一开始曾经因为柳溪的“右派”身份而对她的到来抱怨不已，后来则由衷地为柳溪的落户感到庆幸，乃至自觉地保护她，比如找借口阻止她去参加批斗会，以“免受那撕肝裂肺的奇耻大辱”（342）。正所谓“知识就是力量”，这句话在柳溪身上得到了充分的验证，她想方设法地把知识与工作实践结合起来，以卓有成效的工作结果显示出自己存在的意义，最终也获得了人们的理解和尊重。同毛彦文一样，柳溪出于形势所迫，从事过五花八门的工作，尤其对文学创作情有独钟。早在上中学时，她便在当时的《河北日报》发表小说《失意者》，成为保定城学生群中的“明星”人物。此后，柳溪始终对文学兴趣不减，但由于种种原因，写小说只能成为她的“副业”，甚至为了避免引发怀疑和迫害，只能偷偷摸摸地进行，她不无苦涩地自我解嘲：“我不得不把这光明正大的工作，巧妙地转变成‘地下作战’。”（259）尽管如此，写作对柳溪而言绝非可有可无的消遣，用她的话说：“我把写作当成了我自立自强的事业，更应该多干多写。”（209）在被批挨整的苦难日子里，写作更可谓精神支柱，给柳溪带来巨大的、无法估量的心理安慰。西方现代哲学的肇始者叔本华主张人生即痛苦，因为人有着永远也无法满足的欲求，而艺术则为人们提供了一种从痛苦中暂时获得解脱的途径，为此，叔本华把艺术比作“人生的花朵”“生命中一时的安慰”（叔本华 367—368）。叔本华或许太过悲观，但柳溪的经历却为叔本华的理论提供了一个很好的注脚，因为她的痛苦确乎深重而漫长，文学创作亦确乎成为她暂时摆脱现实苦难的有效途径。不仅如此，事实证明，柳溪在文学创作方面的确颇有天赋且成绩斐然。[12]

至于毛彦文，她虽然性格相对沉静、平和，却绝对不是无所事事的“依人小鸟”。因此，即便是嫁给熊希龄这座“大靠山”，她也自觉以协助、辅佐丈夫为己任，尤其时时注意学习处理与香山慈幼院有关的各项事务，因而备受丈夫赏识。熊希龄在新婚喜宴之上，曾应宾客要求，报告自己与毛彦文的恋爱经过，坦言：“毛女士曾留学美国，学识、经验俱丰富，尤其挚爱儿童，可协助吾办香山慈幼院。……毛女士以理想、职业相同乃允婚。”（63）限于当时的情形，熊希龄的此种说法难免给人以“冠冕堂皇”的印象，但以后的事实表明，此说法其实并非虚妄。熊希龄去世之后，毛彦文接任香山慈幼院院长一职，她不负众望，在兵荒马乱的年代，不仅尽力维持北平慈幼院，还陆续开办了桂林分院、柳州小学分院、芷江香山女中分院等，由此，熊希龄生前所热衷的慈善事业并未由于他的溘然长逝而告终，反倒奇迹般地发展壮大起来。这中间固然不能否认毛彦文须仰仗丈夫遗留下来的各方面资源，但同样不能否认的，当然还包括毛彦文自己的卓越才能以及致力于慈善事业、教育事业的高尚情怀。不仅如此，基于开办香山慈幼院所引发的积极的社会反响，毛彦文先后当选北平市参议员和“国民大会”代表。后来，毛彦文离开大陆赴台，因为走得太匆忙，几乎算是两手空空地来到台湾，迫于生计，她不得不远赴美国，先后做过编辑、大学研究人员、图书管理员等工作，离美返台后则以教书为主要职业，直至年过古稀才正式离职退休。[13]纵观毛彦文动荡漂泊的一生，无论在大陆、香港，还是在美国以及我国台湾地区，她始终保持着旺盛的工作热情，在诸多行业尤其是在教育领域用功至深、令人钦佩。

如前所述，男权文化传统不主张女性开创自己的事业，认为女性天生不具备这样的能力。与此相关，女性受教育的权利被忽视乃至剥夺，于是，“女子无才便是德”之类的说教一时之间广为流传。而教育的缺失无疑会导致传统女性在事业上的捉襟见肘、难有成就，从而客观上也助长了女子对男子的依附性。正如波伏娃不无遗憾地写道：“西方一般男人的梦想，是女人自由地忍受他的主宰，她不经过争论不会接受他的想法，但向他的理智让步，明智地抗拒他，最后让他说服。……他心里所要求的是，这场斗争对他是一场游戏，而女人将自己的命运投进去；这是作为解放者或征服者的男人的真正胜利：因为女人自由地承认这是自己的命运。”（波伏娃 256）当然，这种男尊女卑的偏见其实不止于西方。毛彦文和柳溪也曾饱受性别歧视之苦，幸运的是，她们终究没有受制于家庭的狭小空间——固然此类结果并非完全出于她们的主观意愿，有时也是客观条件使然——但她们无疑不属于传统的贤妻良母，而以事业为依托，在逆境中奋力坚持，不仅实现了自力更生，而且积极地回报他人、回报社会。因此，她们谈不上真正意义上的女权主义者，但却以自己的行动为女性的自我塑造提供了生动、有力的个案。

“写作自传需要强烈的自我意识和自传冲动”（杨正润 325），毋庸置疑，《往事》与《我的人生苦旅》都蕴含着作者深挚的情感和表达自我的热切要求，但总体上看，两部自传的叙事风格差异明显。大体言之，前者冷静，后者热烈。这一点在两本书的标题上亦体现出来：“往事”不过是一种客观陈述，没有透露出什么感情色彩；“我的人生苦旅”则有一定的主观抒情意味，尤其一个“苦”字更明显可见作者的感慨。与此同时，两部自传的“冷”“热”之分亦非绝对，毛彦文在冷静追述中也有热烈的情绪流动，柳溪在激动描绘之余亦不乏冷静的剖析和反思。

在《往事·自序》中，毛彦文谦虚地表示：“我是一个平凡的人，所写的都是平凡的事，虽其中有几件突出的记载，乃事过境迁，也成为平凡的了。”（2）她怀疑自己经历的往事是否值得留下、写出来给谁看、谁又会关心，最后在好友胡适的鼓励下，才终于决定动手撰写这本自传。其实难怪毛彦文不够积极，中国人一向不热衷于写自传，究其原因，“中国主流意识形态形成了一种不利于自传发展的文化环境，中国封建专制对个性的压制从本质上说是极大地限制了自传的存在空间，而且中华民族传统的价值取向和思维方式也不利于自传的发展”（杨正润 325）。由此，直至耄耋之年⑭，毛彦文才终于起笔写作自传，而且起初也未曾打算将之公开出版，不过“仅赠少数亲友作为纪念”（2）。这样一种较为平和的创作心态决定了《往事》的叙事风格以冷静为主，毛彦文更戏称其为“流水账”，谓之“谈不上格局，也没有文采”

(2)——这是毛彦文的谦虚，实际上当然不至于此。在回顾往事时，毛彦文以看似平淡无奇的笔调追忆自己的生平经历，但因为其本人有着极其丰富的人生阅历——有些甚至堪称富于传奇色彩，加之毛彦文外“冷”内“热”的性格特点，使得《往事》的叙事并不给人以枯燥乏味之感，故而平淡只是表面的。在冷静、超然之余，《往事》当中的激情叙事亦偶尔闪现，比如同情母亲因为没生下男孩而在婆家受尽欺辱：“这真是欲加之罪，何患无辞，祖母这种近似疯狂的无理取闹，不知给母亲带来多少痛苦和虐待。”(6)痛斥高高在上的官僚：“人性何在?”⑮(106)震惊于日本战后恢复之迅速、重建之惊人，感慨：“这是一个了不起的民族，仍是我们的强邻，我们中国人争气觉悟，努力奋斗，迎头赶上，与之并驾齐驱，否则屈辱的历史仍将重演。”(134)如此等等直抒胸臆，作者内心的激荡显而易见。

如果说毛彦文的写作心态相对较为平和，柳溪则不然，因为蒙冤长达二十余年，她很难平静地面对往事；此外，身为作家，柳溪也似乎比其他人更多了几分感性。比如和陈毓森发生婚变后，柳溪迫于形势不得不紧急离开那个曾经无比温暖的小屋，不由得百感交集：“那曾经使我感到幸福、温暖胜过宫殿的茅屋，这时对我那么冷酷无情，我像冲出牢笼和樊篱般地离开了这里，永远地离开了。”(92)在肃反运动中无端被拘禁，这让一向忠诚于革命事业的柳溪悲叹不已：“革命，怎么这么难哪！……不仅受敌人的盯梢、追捕、监禁，还要受自己组织的怀疑、审查、批斗，真是不可想象，跟我当年那么热切地追求革命，诚恳地玩命工作，那么单纯与幼稚的傻乎乎的干劲相比，差距是多么大!”(179)当暂时获得自由、被释放回家时，柳溪又欣喜若狂：“啊！天空是多么蔚蓝，太阳是多么光艳！我的心情也突然晴朗了。自由是多么可贵!”(193)……诸如此类饱蘸情感的语句在柳溪的自传中时常可见。总之，因为无辜受难，柳溪的自叙有着浓厚的控诉及辩护的色彩。有国外学者曾经指出：“中国文人写自传，归根到底都是为了强调自己的正确。”(川合康三 206)就柳溪的自传而言，应当是确乎如此。与此同时，正所谓“爱之深、恨之切”，对于曾经帮助过自己的人，柳溪也毫不掩饰地表达了感激、赞颂之情。

此外，身为小说家，柳溪很自然地将小说笔法带入自传写作中，于是，细腻生动的场面描写、细节描写、心理描写等在《我的人生苦旅》当中可谓常见，读来着实引人入胜。比如开篇的“出生丧母”一节，气氛的紧张——不知何故全城戒严，即将临盆的大龄产妇因此无法去医院；接生婆的野蛮——用整个身子去挤压产妇肚子，甚至准备用秤钩“先把婴儿的头骨砸穿勾住，然后把婴儿大卸八块地勾将出来”（2）；母亲的痛苦——“疼得嗷嗷直叫”“几次昏厥过去”（1）；父亲的慌乱——吓得六神无主，“随便什么人都能指挥他”（2）；“我”的无助——被扔在桌子底下三天无人问津；如此等等。撇开历史实录的残酷不论，这部分描写生动传神，惊心动魄，与小说并无二致；又因为此部分系全书开篇第一节，上述小说笔法客观上也起到了激发阅读兴趣的作用。又比如“文化大革命”时柳溪被下放到农村喂猪，她工作尽心尽责，除喂仔猪外，还喂过一只专供繁殖后代用的母猪，为此特意在它发情时赶它去和三里之外的一只种猪交配，“以后这聪明的母猪自己走三里地，于夜间自己找那头种猪去偷情、去做爱，比《西厢记》中跳墙的张生还勇敢”（339）。这样生动活泼的描写极富生活气息，也透露出柳溪苦中作乐的乐观精神。其实同《我的人生苦旅》一样，《往事》当中也不乏大悲大喜之处，但往往点到即止，并无太多的渲染或者修饰。比如在成功解除包办婚约后，毛彦文最终返回家中，父母则很快重新接纳了这个曾经那么“忤逆”的女儿，对此，毛彦文感慨：“父母跟以前一样的爱护我，关切我，证明骨肉之爱，永不变质。”（34）新婚燕尔，毛彦文与熊希龄夫唱妇随，她难掩内心的喜悦：“我深切体会到秉[16]是我的理想丈夫，同时也是知己，彼对我亦夫亦友的深情，令我陶醉，令我庆幸。”（77）得知熊芷[17]去世的消息，毛彦文痛悼：“熊芷是我国女界不可多得的人才，她的逝世是教育界及妇女界的大损失。”（159）此外，还值得注意的是，《往事》虽以冷静叙述为主，但在行文过程中夹杂着一定量的信件、书画、诗词、照片等，这些材料在表情达意方面无疑起到了推波助澜乃至画龙点睛的作用。至于其中几篇悼念性的文字，如《悼君毅》《抗战胜利祭告先夫秉三文》《五妹同文》《三妹辅文》等，采用直接向对方倾诉的口吻，更是写得情真意切、感人至深。

总之，毛彦文和柳溪一生经历坎坷、阅历丰富，身为知识女性，她们利用手中的笔书写自己的喜怒哀乐、悲欢离合，无论冷静抑或热烈，均富于可读性和史料价值。

有论者云："女性自传记录了女性意识的发展，是研究女性运动史的重要资料，也在推进着女性解放运动。"（杨正润 344）《往事》与《我的人生苦旅》两部自传便在以小人物的独特视角去反映大时代的离乱沧桑的同时，客观上写出了传主毛彦文和柳溪隐忍与反抗兼具的特点，是一代独立自强的知识女性的成长历史，可谓现代女性自我塑造之真实而生动的范例。

注释【Notes】

① 毛彦文：《往事》。天津：百花文艺出版社，2007 年。本文所引该自传中的话均出于此，以下仅在引文后标示页码，不再另注。

② 柳溪：《我的人生苦旅》。武汉：长江文艺出版社，2000 年。本文所引该自传中的话均出于此，以下仅在引文后标示页码，不再另注。

③ 毛彦文生于 1898 年，卒于 1999 年；柳溪生于 1924 年，卒于 2014 年。

④ 指吴宓的前妻陈心一女士。

⑤ 熊希龄曾经担任北洋政府国务总理、财政总长等职，既是显赫的政治家，也是著名的实业家、社会活动家、慈善家；毛彦文则出身平民，与熊希龄相识之初不过是一个普通教师。

⑥ 毛彦文与熊希龄的一个内侄女朱曦系同学，且私交甚笃，朱曦也是最早在毛彦文面前为熊希龄提亲的人，而此前毛彦文一直比照朱曦，以"老伯"称呼熊希龄。

⑦ 毛彦文系南京金陵女子大学高才生，后赴美深造，在密歇根大学主修中等教育行政，辅修社会学，获得硕士学位，如此高学历，在当时女性中实属少见。

⑧ 熊希龄于 1937 年在香港去世，适逢抗战全面爆发，北平、上海、南京等相继沦陷，熊希龄关心国事，因心情沉重诱发中风而撒手尘寰，此时距其与毛彦文大婚尚不足三年。

⑨ 香山慈幼院系熊希龄创办的一家慈善性质的学校。

⑩ 柳溪曾经就读于北平师范大学历史系。

⑪ 毛彦文的母亲曾经诞下一男孩，但该子于五岁时夭折。

⑫ 比如柳溪创作的通俗小说《燕子李三传奇》《超级女谍金璧辉外传》深受读者大众欢迎，其长篇小说《战争启示录》荣获中宣部"五个一工程"奖。

⑬ 据《往事》记载，1976 年秋季开学前，毛彦文以年事已高和照顾亲人为由，坚决拒绝了校方的盛情邀约，教书生涯就此告终。

⑭ 毛彦文于 1985 年开始撰写自传《往事》。

⑮ 《华北日报》社占用熊宅，导致熊家遭遇大火，损失惨重，毛彦文向当时的宣传部长吴国桢报告灾情，吴不仅不予以救助，反而仅以"五分钟谈话"打发毛彦文，态度极其粗暴无礼。

⑯ 熊希龄字秉三，毛彦文昵称其为"秉"。

⑰ 熊芷系熊希龄之女，曾任台北女子师范的校长，亦曾力促毛彦文与熊希龄的结合。

引用文献【Works Cited】

西蒙娜·德·波伏娃：《第二性 I》，郑克鲁译。上海：上海译文出版社，2011 年。

[Beauvoir, Simone de. *The Second Sex I*. Trans. Zheng Kelu. Shanghai: Shanghai Translation Publishing House, 2011.]

金梅：《论毛彦文之不嫁吴宓》，《文学自由谈》2000 年第 1 期，第 86—92 页。

[Jin Mei. "On Mao Yanwen's Refusal to Marry Wu Mi." *Free Forum of Literature* 1(2000): 86-92.]

川合康三：《中国的自传文学》，蔡毅译。北京：中央编译出版社，1999 年。

[Kawai Kozo. *Chinese Autobiographical Literature*. Trans. Cai Yi. Beijing: Central Compilation & Translation Press, 1999.]

李辉：《"历史备忘书系"总序》，柳溪：《我的人生苦旅》。武汉：长江文艺出版社，2000 年，第 1—2 页。

[Li Hui. Preface to *Series of Historical Memoranda*. *My Miserable Life*. By Liu Xi. Wuhan: Changjiang Literature and Art Press, 2000: 1-2]

李银河：《女性主义》。济南：山东人民出版社，2005 年。

[Li Yinhe. *Feminism*. Jinan: Shandong People's Publishing House, 2005.]

柳溪：《我的人生苦旅》。武汉：长江文艺出版社，2000 年。

[Liu Xi. *My Miserable Life*. Wuhan: Changjiang Literature and Art Press, 2000.]

毛彦文：《往事》。天津：百花文艺出版社，2007 年。

[Mao Yanwen. *The Past*. Tianjin: Baihua Literature and Art Publishing House, 2007.]

凯特·米利特：《性政治》，宋文伟译。南京：江苏人民出版社，2000 年。

[Millet, Kate. *Sexual Politics*. Trans. Song Wenwei. Nanjing: Jiangsu People's Publishing House, 2000.]

桑农：《花开花落：历史边缘的知识女性》。桂林：广西师范大学出版社，2010 年。

[Sang Nong. *Flowers Blossom and Fade: The Intellectual Women on the Edge of History*. Guilin: Guangxi Normal University Press, 2010.]

叔本华：《作为意志和表象的世界》，石冲白译。北京：商务印书馆，2009 年。

[Schopenhauer, Authur. *The World as Will and Representation*. Trans. Shi Chongbai. Beijing: The Commercial Press, 2009.]

杨正润：《现代传记学》。南京：南京大学出版社，2009 年。

[Yang Zhengrun. *A Modern Poetics of Biography*. Nanjing: Nanjing University Press, 2009.]

余斌：《吴宓先生的昆明岁月（下）：总是失败的婚恋与他的学术写作滑坡》，《新文学史料》2008 年第 4 期，第 55—66 页。

[Yu Bin. "Mr. Wu Mi's Life in Kunming(II): His Forever Failed Love and the Retrogression of His Academic Writing." *Historical Materials of New Literature* 4(2008): 55-66.]

象征身份的剥离与重塑

——阿克罗伊德笔下的王尔德

吴铁群

内容提要：彼得·阿克罗伊德创作传记注重在一定现实基础上的小说化创造，《一个唯美主义者的遗言——奥斯卡·王尔德别传》中，他用王尔德拟日记的手法，主观性地重构了王尔德追求象征身份的一生。传记中由姓名符号确立的民族、家庭身份和由理想填充中获得的艺术名人身份构成了王尔德的社会和内在身份，但生活的变故使他的多重身份被层层剥离于他的社会存在与心理真实。而传记中的王尔德用叙事言说的方式重建了自己坍塌的多重身份，并将自己重塑为伟大的唯美主义艺术家和时代先行者的象征身份。

关键词：阿克罗伊德　王尔德　象征身份　《一个唯美主义者的遗言——奥斯卡·王尔德别传》

作者简介：吴铁群，南京大学文学院比较文学与世界文学专业博士研究生，主要研究方向为外国文学和西方文论。

Title: Stripping and Remodeling the Symbolic Identity: The Image of Oscar Wilde in Peter Ackroyd's Literary Narrative

Abstract: Peter Ackroyd's biography shares something of novel writing on the basis of life reality. In *The Last Testament of Oscar Wilde*, Ackroyd subjectively reconstructs Oscar Wilde's life in pursuit of his symbolic identity in the form of Wilde's pseudo diary. The national and family identities acquired from the name symbol and the artistic celebrity status obtained from the ideal filling constitute the social and internal identity of Oscar Wilde. However, the change of life has caused his multiple identities to be stripped from his social existence and psychological reality. Ackroyd's Oscar

Wilde in the biography by way of the biographer's peculiar narrative rebuilds Wilde's collapsed multiple identities and reconstructs him as a symbolic identity of the great aesthetician artist and forerunner of the times.

Keywords: Peter Ackroyd, Oscar Wilde, Symbolic Identity, *The Last Testament of Oscar Wilde*

Wu Yiqun is a doctoral candidate at Nanjing University. Her research concerns foreign literature and western literary theories. E-mail: 15242871@qq.com.

彼得·阿克罗伊德是英国当代著名的后现代主义作家，他的创作理念是，小说是提供娱乐的，“我要做的就是给人们一点快乐”（Ackroyd 47），他认为传记作品也是如此，“传记作家没有任何理由去教育和指导读者。传记作家的工作是提供娱乐，就像小说家一样”（Ackroyd 47）。阿克罗伊德认为传记作品是传记作家的小说家化创作，是对历史人物主体性的文学建构，传记写作的目的不是提供真相而是表现人物独有的内在结构，传记写作的原则就是传记要像小说一样具有趣味性和可读性。在他的观念里，传记与小说没有区别，“我不认为它们是传记，我只觉得它们是另一些小说。传记中你可以做所有的事情就像小说里一样，而不只是单调的叙述”（Ackroyd 46），传记中很多的事情和情感都是传记作家杜撰出来的，而“他们不得不如此。你必须找到你独有的有限方式将事情串联起来，创造一个人物也许和任何真实的人从没有任何关系”（Ackroyd 47）。

获 1984 年毛姆奖的《一个唯美主义者的遗言——奥斯卡·王尔德别传》中的王尔德即阿克罗伊德以历史上王尔德的真实经历为基础创造的一个小说化的人物。王尔德是 19 世纪著名的戏剧家、小说家、唯美主义文学的代表人物，他的艺术成就和传奇人生一直吸引人们对他进行不断研究和解读。在对他个人生活的研究中，他从一个著名的艺术家沦为阶下囚的经历和在面对如此巨变时他的反应和感受是人们最为关注的部分，也由此产生了很多解读他人生的传记、戏剧和影视作品。而阿克罗伊德的传记匠心独运地以王尔德自己拟日记的形式，用小说化的手法重述了王尔德一生。传记用以假乱真的王尔德式的语言，打破传统传记线性时间的限制，“将王尔德的引语与对王尔德口吻的模仿相结合，创造出一个极度合理的小说化的虚构日记体传记作品”（Finney 244），让王尔德的内在本质和性格特点在假设性的王尔德自我叙述中逐渐展现，用主观性的诠释重塑了王尔德的形象。“这部小说正是要挑战我们对真实的认识。阿克罗伊德糅合了正史和文学中的王尔德形象。”（晓风）在王尔德拟日记记述中，阿克罗伊德用层层的身份叠加建构传记中的王尔德的社会身份和自我认知，并让他自省性地叙述多重身份被剥离于自身的经历，最后让他在主观化的叙事中重塑了自己的社会身份和内在秩序。传记用拟日记的方式小说化地记述了阿克罗伊德设定下的独一无二的王尔德象征身份的确立、剥离与重塑，与普通的编年体人物生平考证式传记作品具有明显区别，非常具有文学研究价值。

一、象征身份的确立

王尔德在《王尔德狱中记》中写道“人是象征”（77），“我自己是处于我的时代的艺术和文化的象征联系中的人（74）”，他认为人是象征，是某种象征秩序的表征。王尔德本人对于人的象征归属观念被阿克罗伊德在传记中延续，传记人物王尔德的一生被阿克罗伊德小说化地重塑为一个追求象征身份的过程。阿克罗伊德是一位后现代主义作家，他的思想深受20世纪后现代思潮中语言学维度的影响，相信语言符号对人类的决定性作用。而法国后结构主义理论家拉康对于象征的研究极能代表后现代思想。拉康认为象征界是人类存在的现实世界，象征秩序是人类信奉的文明和必须遵守的规则，人们必须遵守象征的法则并得到象征界的认同才能获得自己的存在属性。象征界是由语词所结构的，象征界中的一切都由语言和象征过程主宰，而语言是符号结构，“一旦出现了象征符，那么一切事物就都会按照那些象征符和象征界的法则而被规定或结构，包括无意识以及人类主体性”（霍默 60），所以语言符号的先行存在和主体符号意义的确立即人存在的依托。而建立主体的符号意义则要求人们在符号系统中为自己争取到一个合理的位置，并将这一符号背后的意义缝合到自己身上，用符号内涵书写自己的外在身份和内在本质，最终完成在象征界自己合法身份的注册。而这被象征界认可的身份即象征身份，即王尔德本人所说的人的象征归属，也是阿克罗伊德塑造他笔下的王尔德的一个逻辑思路。

阿克罗伊德为自己笔下的王尔德确立的第一重象征身份是他姓名符号和其代表的民族和家庭身份。传记中的王尔德在日记中热情洋溢地描述名字对自己的重要意义，“我对自己的大名是很在乎的，每次写奥斯卡·芬格尔·欧弗莱赫蒂·威尔斯·王尔德，我的心里都洋溢着莫大的喜悦。这个名字里寄托了爱尔兰的所有传说，这名字似乎能给我力量和现实”（4）。而这样的语言正如王尔德本人对自己姓名的看重，“她（母亲）和父亲把一个在我们国家的发展史上都是高贵的、受人尊敬的名字给了我”（52）。人是象征，姓名作为一种象征符号使人与世界建立了第一份联系，对任何人来说，“从他出生之时开始，即使那时只是以他的姓名的形式，他已经加入了话语的广泛活动之中去了”（拉康 426）。人在出生时就获得了被他人命名的名字，姓名的确立是人在象征界的初次登记，代表人拥有了自己的符号指代和符号背后表征的社会关系。而命名是个人被迫对一个符号的认同，主体的人外化为一个姓名指称，并且因为这一符号在各种时间和空间被反复询唤，使这一外在符号最终转化为主体的自动重复，内化成为主体的内在秩序。阿克罗伊德对名字的重点提及即让传记中的王尔德在接受自己姓名的过程中实现象征身份的确立。

奥斯卡·芬格尔·欧弗莱赫蒂·威尔斯·王尔德的姓名首先为王尔德带来了与他人相连的原因，在现实生活和传记再现中都是如此。王尔德的姓氏来自父亲的家族，王尔德是他父亲威廉爵士的孩子，在他出生之前就因血缘而被接纳入家族之中，确定了他在家庭中的亲缘关系。威廉爵士是当时英国著名的医生，是维多利亚女王的御医，获得过北极星勋章，王尔德对姓名的自豪部分就来源于父亲姓氏代表的社会地位。王尔德家族是爱尔兰民族，爱尔兰战士和行吟诗人欧西恩的儿子名叫奥斯卡，欧西恩的父亲芬格尔也是爱尔兰的英雄人物，王尔德的父母用爱尔兰英雄的名字为他命名，寄托了对他人生的美好希望。因为这原初的命名，王尔德在出生前就被赋予了家庭和民族身份，后来他结婚又获得了丈夫和父亲的身份，延续了家族的姓氏，更加稳固了源自家庭的身份。

命名也表征了家人对王尔德未来的期望，他是爱尔兰王尔德家族的奥斯卡，是该成为成功人士的人。传记中的王尔德由于被重复询唤姓名，于是这姓名符号表达的意义自然被他内化为自我理想；又因为对由语言符号创造的文学的喜爱，更将文学文本中关于成功的内涵认定为自己的人生追求，“我从心底涌出对成功的强大而甜蜜的渴望。看到书上的大人物，我一概把自己比作他们”（41）。传记中的王尔德在对命名的内化和符号结构的接受中，确定了成为社会名人的人生理想。他强烈地“渴望成名，但不知如何成名”（52），直到他发现了自己艺术的天分，“我怀有天才的脱俗，通过自我探索，能够发掘新的诗歌题材和新的艺术形式”（65）。于是，他怀揣着成为杰出艺术家的梦想来到伦敦，“我是来征服的”（65）。阿克罗伊德用艺术的想象讲述了王尔德开启艺术生涯的深层原因，用细致的心理描写展现了他定义中的王尔德对名利的憧憬，并根据王尔德真实的家庭背景将姓名对他身份确立的重要性用逼真的王尔德式的语言凸显出来。

唯美主义杰出作家是阿克罗伊德为传记中的王尔德确立的第二重象征身份。传记中的王尔德在日记中感慨地回忆当年的自己为了成名而做出的努力和获得的成绩。那时的他创作优美的唯美主义作品，努力宣讲唯美主义的原则，身体力行唯美主义的教义，成为英国独树一帜的艺术家，影响力更遍布世界各国。他用艺术的创造得到了社会和大众的认可，成为声名显赫的人物，成为绝对的唯美主义者，“我创造了一个新世界，在这个世界里唯美主义的种种行迹成为可能”（75）。唯美主义的秩序更内化成为他的心理结构，知行合一地表现在他的艺术和私人生活中，他本人就成为唯美主义理想在现实中的具象显现，“我是一个惊世骇俗的形象，我坚决不和现在这个世纪牵连在一起”（75），唯美主义艺术家就此成为传记中的王尔德深信不疑的内在本质。阿克罗伊德用形象化的语言塑造了一个无比自信、春风得意的王尔德，用艺术的天赋和特立独行的性格将传记中王尔德的名字在象征界注册为独一无二的存在，他不再是只具有民族和家庭身份的王尔德，而是拥有了唯美主义艺术家身份的王尔德，他的姓名即唯美主义的表征和成功与声望的象征，“我成了上流社会的象征性人物，成为英国名流们力求创造的艺术行列中的中坚人物”（137）。自此，传记中的王尔德为自己的姓名赢得了社会象征身份的确立，阿克罗伊德也完成了对自己笔下的王尔德形象的第一步建立。

二、象征身份的剥离

传记中的王尔德在日记中继续讲述他成名后的经历。那个时期的他，在艺术上，每部剧作都获得了成功，成为英国戏剧界独领风骚的人物；在个人生活上，发觉了自己真实的感情取向，并遇到了一生的挚爱，而他也因此招致灭顶之灾。昆斯伯里侯爵是他的爱人道格拉斯的父亲，因为对道格拉斯与王尔德间感情的憎恶而不断侮辱他们，这使王尔德将其以诽谤罪告上法庭。然而，在对昆斯伯里侯爵审讯中，王尔德的私生活却被添油加醋地暴露在公众面前，结果被告无罪释放，作为原告的他却因有伤风化罪入狱。姓名意义加上后来填充的社会名望是阿克罗伊德为传记中王尔德最初确立的象征身份，是他核心的内在结构。而当这两项基底都不再成立，当姓名和姓名代表的社会地位都失去，他的象征身份也就此失落，剥离于他的自体生命了。剥离是人们在象征界中合法地位的丧失，是在社会和群体中基本认可的失去，是自我原有符号化身份在象征现实中的脱落。由于身份的剥离，人们相信并内化为自身特质的一切外在结构都不再指称主体的特质，人与世界失去了关系，与原有的主体性也失去了关联，人的存在濒临毁灭。

阿克罗伊德虚构了一个身世真相，将传记中王尔德的第一层家族身份剥离于他的象征属性。传记中的王尔德在日记中悲痛地讲述了在他被保释回家后母亲告知他的真相，“在那个宿命的晚上，母亲告诉我，我的生父是个爱尔兰诗人和爱国者，我并不是威廉爵士的亲生儿子，我是私生子”（49）。拉康认为父亲是一个隐喻，父亲之名是一种法，是维系社会秩序的基本之法，其功能就类似语言的结构，是象征界通过父亲的名义宣讲的律令，而父亲代表的象征法则就是子女必须接受的社会身份和自我定位。王尔德从小就生活在威廉爵士父亲之名的教导下，也在家族姓氏中认可自己的血缘身份和生存意义，可他坚信的这一切就在他遭逢人生重大危机时雪上加霜地瓦解。原来，他的生命从起源处就是个错误，他的家庭身份从来只是误认，他引以为傲的姓名根本就不属于他，根本就不能指称他的家族身份和内在结构。传记中的王尔德就此失去了原初的名字，丧失了家族的身份，“我确信我也一样应被归为被遗弃者的行列”（48）。但其实有关王尔德的所有资料中都没有威廉爵士不是他生父的记述，阿克罗伊德这一虚构之笔充分表现了他传记创作小说化的主张，“用叙事逻辑挑战固定历史的观点，将想象重造的历史小说优先于实证史实的独裁”（Murray 85），用姓名符号不再能表征王尔德的身份的虚假身世揭示将传记人物王尔德的第一层家族身份彻底剥离，用小说般的情节否定了他的血脉起源，为王尔德的悲剧命运更增加了绝望的色彩，更用艺术的想象印证了符号秩序对人存在的重要性。

阿克罗伊德为王尔德制造的第二层象征身份剥离是他开始被审判后与世人关系的转变。万众瞩目的唯美主义艺术家本是传记中的王尔德为自己打造的社会身份，成就和声望就是他在象征界中的属性。而当他不被大众接受的感情取向和言行被公示于众，他所有正面的声名都消失殆尽，他再也不是受人崇拜的才子，不是众人眼中成功的代名词，而变成了违背法律和道德的人，成了他回顾性叙述中自己所说“都市文明种种疾病的一个象征”（68）。传记中的王尔德悲痛地回忆身边人在他入狱后的表现：债主将他的家洗劫一空，妻子和孩子被迫搬离住所，母亲不堪打击离世，朋友对他避如蛇蝎，曾经崇拜他的人们对他无情驱逐，他的儿子改换了姓氏，妻子死后的墓碑不见他的姓名。于是，儿子、丈夫、父亲、朋友、名人的符号身份就这样一一剥离于他的象征属性。而因遭逢此重创，他作为艺术家的信心和创造力也被摧毁了，“艺术家所需的自信已经离我远去，我无法创作出我本应创作出的作品”（209）。而世人对他的认可来自艺术的成就，当他失去艺术品格与能力，他也就失去了象征界的地位，“作为艺术家的我已经死了”（248）。阿克罗伊德借王尔德自己之口想象性地还原了一个天才艺术家对自己艺术生命终结的悲怆，并由此将王尔德身上的一切象征符号全部剥离于他的生命存在。传记中的王尔德自省性地回忆过往，悲哀地认识到，“丑闻的全部历史将伴随着我的名字，我永远无法摆脱”（217），“我的真名实姓已经死了”（4）。阿克罗伊德根据王尔德的真实经历细腻再现了王尔德所有社会身份被剥离于自身的绝望，让他用自己的语言讲述自己的经历和感受，“阿克罗伊德有时比王尔德自己还要更具王尔德风格”（Lewis 40），比单纯讲述客观事实的传记作品更具心理真实感。

阿克罗伊德为传记中的王尔德营造的最根本的第三层象征身份剥离是他内心秩序的倾覆。在王尔德入狱后，他先天被授予和后天获得的象征符号都剥离于他的自身存在，他过去获得的社会地位和自我认同都被彻底否定，他的生存空间只剩下囚室的方寸之地，他基本的衣食住行都被他人管控，他作为一个人基本的被尊重和有所归属的需要完全丧失。这种对身体的禁锢和被人类共同体驱逐的经历是严重的创伤事件，而创伤事件的打击会粉碎人所有的生活常态和内心秩序，使主体不再能在象征界中指认自己的位置，无法再从自我内心结构中找到自身存在的符号意义。传记中的王尔德因为强烈的创伤感受颠覆了所有的自我认知和自我认同，心理系统完全被击溃，内心象征身份被彻底剥离于主体存在。“在暴烈的创伤性侵扰抹去了所有实质性内容之后，留在人的主体性中的，便只有主体性的纯粹形式”（齐泽克 114），阿克罗伊德设定的王尔德在入狱之初即成为一个没有内容和实质的单纯客体，彻底失去了所有，“我的个性已经从我身上剥离了”（230），“灾难花了我的眼，夺了我的思想，把我变得像个初离母体的婴儿”（144），“我看到我镜子中的自己，是奇怪的白色影子”（115）。真实的王尔德遭遇的创伤事件在传记中被阿克罗伊德以王尔德切身心理体验的方式细致呈现，进行自述的王尔德用极具个人情感化的创伤叙事回忆他内在身份的层层剥离，很具有艺术震撼力和情绪感染力，展现了这部实验性传记作品的独特魅力。

三、象征身份的重塑

王尔德本人在《狱中记》中说过，在经过了一心求死的牢狱生活初期阶段后，他决心要活下去。根据这一真实情况，阿克罗伊德塑造的王尔德也是坚强的，或者说阿克罗伊德相信人类是坚强的，相信人的心理因素中永远有求生意志和自救本能维护自己的存在。所以，传记中的王尔德在日记中写道"我想活着"（262）。人的世界是象征的世界，象征化的存在是人们唯一能获得的真实，在象征界获得合法身份才能保证人们的存在。所以，即使人们被剥离了从前的象征身份，也必须重建新的象征关系以重塑自己与世界的关联。而人们的言说就是重入象征的手段，是象征界对人类的天赋馈赠。人们是通过言语来进行言说，人们通过言语互相言说和聆听从而建立起各自的存在秩序和相互间的象征关系。"主体的历史是由发送给别人的言语构成的"（Lacan 214），人们利用具有创建性的言语，"重新组织过去的偶然事件，赋予它们必将出现的必然性意义"（Lacan 213），站在时间的此刻叙述过去，用后知之明的理解重构事件的意义，用诉说与叙事为自己重塑象征属性。阿克罗伊德也让王尔德用他最熟悉的言说来重塑自己的象征身份。

阿克罗伊德笔下的王尔德的生命本能在入狱一段时间后开始恢复，求生意志使他在极度的精神困境中开始用言说填充内心的空洞，用新的符号秩序为自己建造存在的意义，"我开始和自己说话。这些谈话的机智让我自己都不禁发笑。我和上方一动不动盯着我看的蜘蛛说话"（231）。阿克罗伊德用艺术的想象细致地构建王尔德在狱中自我解救的过程，让传记中的王尔德用与自己对话、与假想对象对话的言说抵御因丧失所有象征关系而造成的恐惧，并将言说的自我拯救延续到他出狱之后，让他撰写日记回顾一生，于是才有了名义上王尔德的日记实则传记的这部作品。传记中的王尔德清醒地了解自己在进行自我拯救，在用叙事的言说为自己建构新的生存意义，"我在回溯"（266），"我不能中断叙述的思路，我必须为过去注入意义，而只有现在。我心中才盈满这些意义"（118）。而他如此的认知即阿克罗伊德对于语言符号对人巨大影响力的相信，是阿克罗伊德对语言言说重塑符号身份的相信。所以，传记中的王尔德必须用叙事为自己过往的生活做出合理解释，用符号秩序的重新建构延续自己的存在，用言说重塑自己的象征身份。

阿克罗伊德为王尔德重塑的第一层象征身份由通过言说获得的二次命名产生。真实的王尔德出狱后化名为"塞巴斯廷·美墨斯"，寄居在小旅馆里。

阿克罗伊德用想象性的描述探究王尔德化为此名的原因，为自己笔下的王尔德重建与世界的初步关联，“我感觉奥斯卡·王尔德的名字好像是一个巨大的虚空，一不留神就会跌下去，把自己迷失”（5）。所以他只能改换别的姓名。美墨斯是集流浪汉、倒霉鬼、邪恶者为一身的可怕人物，来源于王尔德母亲的舅舅杜撰的爱尔兰传说。传记中的王尔德叙述自己曾经同众人一样厌弃美墨斯，而当他经历过人生的起落后，他意识到人们对美墨斯的厌恶不是因为他犯了什么罪责，而是因为他行踪不定，冷眼旁观世间一切，“正由于他看透了世界，才不为世人所容”（28）。所以，传记中的王尔德认为美墨斯的故事正如他自己的艺术创作和人生经历，他的作品是俯看世事的冷嘲热讽，感情生活是惊世骇俗的不合常规，而且爱尔兰民族是饱受流离之苦的流浪民族，就像美墨斯的居无定所，也如他不羁的灵魂游荡世间没有皈依，所以美墨斯其名更能指称他自己的本质属性，“对我来说流浪是一生一世的传奇，爱尔兰民族是在苦难中讨生活的，但就在苦难当中，站起了一个伟大的诗人和演说家的民族”（11）。阿克罗伊德让传记中的王尔德通过言说为自己二次命名，用爱尔兰的传说，用母亲家族编纂的故事重新确立了自己爱尔兰民族身份和母系家族的血缘身份，用新的符号结构重新表征了自己的象征归属。

阿克罗伊德笔下王尔德的第二层象征身份重塑由他用悔悟的态度重塑与他人的象征关系中产生。《狱中记》中，王尔德讲述在审判官对他进行痛斥时，他感觉：“如果这一切都是我自己说出来的，那该是多么辉煌啊！一个人最高尚的时刻就是他跪在尘土中，敲打着自己的胸膛说出自己生活中的一切罪恶的时候。”（115）依据这样的描述，阿克罗伊德让传记中的王尔德写下几乎一样的句子，用逼真的王尔德语言打造传记中王尔德的形象，“一个人的高峰时刻是他在尘土中忏悔一生所犯的罪的时候。现在我要讲述我的罪了”（157）。真实的王尔德在之后的文字中并没有做出反省性的叙述，而是将自己的遭遇归因于道格拉斯的错误。而传记中的他在日记中重述自己的一生，自省性地回望过去，勇敢剖析自我并努力重塑自我身份，“这里，阿克罗伊德是招募王尔德来为他自己对王尔德的拯救作证”（Finney 244），理性和清醒的王尔德是阿克罗伊德小说化的创造，是他笔下独特的王尔德。

阿克罗伊德用艺术的想象细致描写他定义下的王尔德劫后重生的心理活动，“经历过世事轮回，时光逆转，我必须换个眼光来看待过去”（5），原来“凡我经行之处，皆有毁灭之人，凡是我有所接触的人都遭受了我的创伤，我实在是生活在他人的眼泪和痛苦之中”（23）。传记中的王尔德忏悔自己与妻子的婚姻是建立在他的软弱和谎言之上。当年他发现了自己对希腊式爱情的渴望，为了不让自己脱离正轨而与妻子结婚，想用婚姻的象征关系将自己稳定在常规之内，但他最终还是背叛了婚姻而由欲望控制了言行，为妻子和孩子带去了种种伤害。妻子在他出狱前去世，并放弃了王尔德的姓氏；他的母亲在他被审判之初就备受打击，不久后就郁郁而终。面对过去的自己带给他人的伤害，传记里的王尔德无限悔恨，饱受良心的谴责，“我最大的灾难是对享乐的热爱”（144），“我的内在诅咒超过了我的世纪给我的诅咒”（24）。阿克罗伊德用对他人的愧疚的心情重建起传记中王尔德与亲人间被剥离的象征关系，儿子、丈夫、父亲的多重身份在他的内心中被自省性的言说重塑起来。

阿克罗伊德用传记中王尔德对象征现实的反省性认知重塑他的第三层象征身份。“我被迫用一种新的方式看待事实。这个世界所依据的基本原则似乎和我的想象有天壤之别”（215），“我以前并没有真正的认识世界”（233），“我现在意识到了我的力量——以及我个性的力量——原来取决于我在社会上的地位，这种地位没有了，个性就一钱不值”（23）。传记中的王尔德认识到他获得的一切热爱都来自艺术名人的地位，而当他成功人士的声名不在，追捧他的人也不复存在。他了解到自己从前太热衷成功和成名，但其实名人的位置是世界上早已存在的象征事实，个人不可能占有它，只可能将其用某种方式缝合于自己的外在属性，名人的身份根本不能构成人的本质，所以他之前将成功人士的身份纳入自己的心理结构是根本的误认。“我太春风得意。我当时把世界想象成我的世界；我觉得自己无所不能。我被自己的成功束缚了”（143），“我生活的意义全在于别人的脑子里，并不存在于我自己的生活中”（3）。阿克罗伊德塑造的书写日记的王尔德是极具思想力的形象，他在经历过人生起伏后深刻认识到是他对自我属性的误认造成了他对现实的错误感知，世界不是他以为的样子，人们也不是热爱他本人，让人们推崇的是那个功成名就的符号地位，而他从来只是占据了名人的位置，活在人们对成功的狂热中。“别人的生活蜂拥而来，围住了我，推挤着我”（11），“我的生活是空虚的，我的成功是欺骗性的”（146）。在《狱中记》和王尔德出狱后的书信中，我们并没有看到对象征现实得出如此深刻理解的王尔德，这个自省和清醒的主体是阿克罗伊德为传记中的王尔德在他自己假想性的叙事言说中塑造的又一层新的内在象征身份。

最后，阿克罗伊德让传记人物王尔德总结性地重塑自己的象征身份。传记中的王尔德在重建了对世界和自我的认知后，开始为自己确立新的象征身份。“要是我爱艺术多一点，爱名望和欲望少一点，我应该有更大建树。我的个性败坏了我的艺术：这乃是我一生中不可宽恕之罪。”（103）从前的他被外在的名利所塑造，如今他看透名利的虚妄，要用自己的内在力量重塑自己的身份与价值，“我可以自行决定新生活的本质”（241）。传记中的王尔德在记述中首先确认自己唯美主义的艺术成就。他认为自己的作品涵盖多个文学体裁，将喜剧带回了英国舞台，用英语开创了象征戏剧，创造了散文诗，将文学批评创立为独立于文学实践的学问，开创了唯美主义的新风格，为艺术界奉献了杰出的作品和观念。他强调自己虽然作为杰出人士的名望不在了，但他艺术的思想和作品却是伟大而永久的，“我的艺术生涯圆满了，再想添点什么都是画蛇添足。我从韵文至散文，再到戏剧。我一生颇不平凡”（55），“我是这个时代最伟大的艺术家，我对此毫不怀疑”（256）。

传记中的王尔德更将自己确认为超越时代思维的思想家。“我的悲剧也是这个时代最大的悲剧”（256），因为“我本可以成为时代的声音，因为我宣扬的全是我这个时代不知道的东西——也就是每个人都应力求完美”（267）。他总结说美是自己的终极理想，虽然因为太过急切而偏离了美的本质，但对于美的信仰从来都是世界的本真，“我只看到美。没有美，世界上会一无所有”（278）。但他追求的美在世人眼里却是丑闻，于是他站在后知之明的位置理性分析：“我们的时代落后又可怕”（270），只以局限的思维命名它不能了解的事物，所有它不能接受的生活方式和生命存在即被认定是病态和邪恶，而他是拥有与众不同的、革故鼎新的思想的一个，于是就成为被守旧的时代驱逐的一个，而如果在具有开阔思维的时代，他不会是被排除的一个，是时代的狭隘错误判定了他。"我既是自己又是他人，既属于自己的时代也属于他人的时代"（271），他认为自己即便被定义为时代的丑闻，也是"伟大的丑闻"（278），因为他实质上是被狭隘界定但思想超越局限的新时代开拓者。阿克罗伊德塑造的王尔德由此在自己的迷失和时代的捆缚加诸于身的苦难中找到了超越悲伤和屈辱的自我认同，"我发现了延续生命的内在力量，从卑微中站起来，勇敢地面对世界"（23）。但其实根据王尔德本人生命最后一段时间写给友人的信件，我们看到的是一个濒临死亡和疯狂的人，完全看不到他尝试重塑自我的努力。所以，传记中这个通过一系列回溯性的自我言说和语言符号的叙事重组，将自己的象征身份重塑为伟大唯美主义艺术家和超越时代思想家的传记中的王尔德，即阿克罗伊德小说化塑造的阿克罗伊德式的独特王尔德。

四、结　论

阿克罗伊德根据王尔德本人有据可考的经历和文字，模仿他的语言以王尔德拟日记形式创作了这部实验性的传记，让王尔德作为一个文本人物为自己发声，用主观性的视角重述了他的一生。阿克罗伊德延续王尔德本人对人的象征归属的理解，让传记中的王尔德回溯性地记录了自己在符号命名和名人位置获取中建立的民族、家庭和社会身份在命运辗转中被一层层剥离于他的社会存在与心理真实，而后又让他用自省性的叙事言说重塑了自己多重的象征身份。阿克罗伊德以小说化的手法将王尔德作为一个文本人物加以塑造，"在历史的革新和文学的发明之间画了一条界线"（Moran 357），传记中，王尔德最后为自己确立的伟大艺术家和时代先行者的象征身份即阿克罗伊德对他笔下的王尔德的理想诠释。

引用文献【Works Cited】

Ackroyd, Peter. "Interview by Patrick McGrath." *Bomb* 26 (1988): 44-47.

彼得·阿克罗伊德：《一个唯美主义者的遗言——奥斯卡·王尔德别传》，方柏林译。南京：译林出版社，2014 年。
[Ackroyd, Peter. *The Last Testament of Oscar Wilde*. Trans. Fang Bolin. Nanjing: Yilin Press, 2014.]

Finney, Brian. "Peter Ackroyd, Postmodernist Play and Chatterton." *Twentieth Century Literature* 38.2(1992):240–246.

Lacan, Jacques. *Écrits: A Selection*, Trans. Alan Sheridan. London: Tavistock, 1997.

拉康：《拉康选集》，褚孝泉译。上海：上海三联书店，2001 年。
[Lacan, Jacques. *Écrits: A Selection*, Trans. Chu Xiaoquan.Shanghai: Shanghai SDX Joint Publishing Co, 2001.]

Lewis, Roger. Rev. of *The Last Testament of Oscar Wilde*, by Perter Ackroyd. *The American Spectator* 17.3(1984):39–41.

Moran, Joe. "'Simple Words': Peter Ackroyd's *Autobiography of Oscar Wilde*." *Biography* 22.3(1999):356–369.

Murray, Alex. *Recalling London-Literature and History in the Work of Peter Ackroyd and Iain Sinclair*. London: Continuum, 2007.

奥斯卡·王尔德：《王尔德狱中记》，孙宜学译。北京：中国人民大学出版社，2004 年。
[Wilde, Oscar. *De Profundis*. Trans. Xun Yixue. Beijing: China Renmin University Press, 2004.]

晓风：《召唤王尔德的幽灵》，《中华读书报》2014 年 11 月 19 日，第 011 版。
[Xiao Feng. "Summoning the Ghost of Oscar Wild." *China Reading Gazette*, 19 Nov. 2014:11.]

斯拉沃热·齐泽克：《事件》，王师译。上海：上海文艺出版社，2016 年。
[Žižek, Slavoj. *Event*. Trans. Wang Shi. Shanghai: Shanghai Literature and Art Publishing House, 2016.]

发轫期传记：亲友眼中的艾米莉·狄金森

卢 婕

内容提要：艾米莉·狄金森作为享誉世界的女诗人，她的创作发展、生平经历和心灵历程吸引了大量的狄金森研究学者和普通读者的兴趣。早期的狄金森传记作家以亲友为主，他们共同塑造出一个神秘的、传奇的、天才的女诗人形象。尽管这些作品还存在许多虚构成分和人为矫饰、夸张、扭曲、疏离和变形，但是早期传记与狄金森作品之间形成的双向互构、相互推进的文学传播途径为推动狄金森在美国的文学地位的迅速上升起到了不容忽视的作用。

关键词：艾米莉·狄金森 传记 经典化

作者简介：卢婕，四川大学文学与新闻学院博士研究生，成都信息工程大学外国语学院副教授。主要从事比较文学与世界文学研究，近期发表了《关于比较文学研究的反思》（《湖南师范大学社会科学学报》，2017 年第 4 期）、《译介·比较·阐发：艾米莉·狄金森中国化三路径》（《复旦外国语言与文学论丛》，2017 春季刊）等。

Title: Emily Dickinson in the Eyes of Her Relatives and Friends: The Early Biographies

Abstract: Emily Dickinson is a world-renowned poetess and thus her writing career, life experience and mental evolvement have drawn interest from many specialists and common readers. Dickinson's early biographers used to be her relatives or friends, who co-shaped an image of mysterious, legendary and ingenious poetess. Despite the fictional elements and some artificial pretension, exaggeration, distortion, alienation and deformation, these early biographies did play an indispensable role through the establishment of mutual-forming and propelling way of literature dissemination in the rapid elevation of Dickinson's literary status in America.

Keywords: Emily Dickinson, biography, canonization

Lu Jie is Associate Professor at Chengdu University of Information Technology and a PhD candidate of Comparative Literature and World Literature in College of Literature and Journalism at Sichuan University. Her research interests include comparative literature and translation studies. Her publications include "Reconsiderations on Comparative Literature Study" in *Journal of Social Science of Human Normal University* 4(2017) and "Translation/Comparison/Illustration: Three ways for Sinolization of Emily Dickinson" in *Fudan Forum on Foreign Languages and Literature* spring, (2017). E-mail: 81740948@qq.com.

从1924年到20世纪50年代末是艾米莉·狄金森传记的发轫期。发轫期的狄金森传记有很大一部分是由其亲友撰写的。其中，玛莎·狄金森·比安奇（Martha Dickinson Bianchi）是狄金森的侄女；米莉森特·托德·宾厄姆（Millicent Todd Bingham）是狄金森生前好友梅布尔·卢米斯·托德的女儿；马积高·詹金斯（Macgregor Jenkins）是狄金森的邻居。最初的狄金森传记几乎都是狄金森的亲友根据手头的资料和心中的回忆而整理的怀念性文字。这些材料成为后来的非亲友作家撰写传记的重要资料依据和发挥无数浪漫想象的出发点。发轫期由亲友撰写的传记主要偏重于渲染诗人的神秘隐居与隐秘的爱情故事，具有浓郁的传奇色彩。安娜·玛丽·威尔斯（Anna Mary Wells）认为狄金森的生平之所以成为当时传记作家感兴趣的对象主要有两个原因：（1）狄金森诗歌的传播与接受年代正是文学界对作者私人生活好奇的年代；（2）对于广大读者而言，狄金森的生活本身就是一个谜，传记作家可以利用读者的好奇满足名和利的双向需求（Wells 455—458）。她的评论可谓一针见血地道出了当时狄金森传记作品迅速发展的重要原因。

一、玛莎·狄金森·比安奇撰写的传记

狄金森的侄女玛莎·狄金森·比安奇作为狄金森哥哥奥斯丁和嫂子苏珊

唯一的女儿，成长于阿默斯特大街。她的住处仅与狄金森的房间相隔一道树篱。狄金森去世那年她年方 19 岁，虽然有可能她并不是狄金森所最青睐的三个侄子女辈的孩子。但是她的弟弟吉尔伯特（Gilbert）早夭，而哥哥内德（Ned）又是个大男人。因此，回忆过往与姨母狄金森的点点滴滴这样细腻的“小事”只得由她独自完成。1924 年，比安奇出版的《狄金森生平与书信》（*The Life and Letters of Emily Dickinson*）是世界上第一部狄金森传记作品。它的面世标志着狄金森传记和传记研究这艘大船从狄金森的老家阿默斯特镇起航。

在《狄金森生平与书信》中，作者一方面否定诗人具有天赋异禀，另一方面极力渲染诗人的神秘主义气息。尽管她宣称她的传记要揭开面纱，让凡间的曙光照进害羞的诗人的现实生活，然而她并未以狄金森侄女的身份尽可能地搜集事实资料与访谈故友，而是认为狄金森自己为她的传记提供了唯一线索，这唯一的线索就是诗人生前的书信。但是，众所周知，由于诗人临终前曾嘱托亲友烧毁她的书信，因此仅有部分珍贵书信侥幸地得以保留至今。比安奇就凭借着这些残留的书信以及她自己偶尔从诗人口中听来的只言片语勾画和想象出诗人生前与外部世界为数不多的脆弱联系。在比安奇的这本传记里，狄金森的少女时期与常人无异，她是个聪敏、对自然和音乐有本能的热爱、天真烂漫、不明世故、幸福快乐的姑娘，怎么看也算不上是“奇才”（prodigy）。比安奇承认狄金森并不是人们想象中的那样生来就是一名令人难解的隐士，少女时期的狄金森并不反感社交活动，比如，她很乐于参加大学毕业典礼以及一年一度的家畜博览会等当时流行的社交和娱乐活动。但是随父亲去华盛顿后在恋爱中的挫折以及父亲的去世导致她逐渐断绝了与外界的交往，仅仅与少数亲友保持着密切的书信往来。毫无疑问，玛莎把艾米莉的神秘隐居仅仅归结为恋爱的挫折与父亲的离世是过于简单和肤浅的。但是，比安奇把狄金森的诗句与其独特的生活经历联系起来相互阐发的做法得到了日后许多狄金森传记作家的认可和继承。比如，从狄金森的诗句“家就是上帝的定义”（Home is the definition of God）发展开来，比安奇解释狄金森鲜少出门远游是因为她有着中世纪僧侣的灵魂和清教徒血统的肉身，因此，她的诗歌总让人觉得有一种宗教插画中的巨大省略和惊人简洁，在那里地狱可以被描绘在方寸之间，天堂也可以被一枚硬币覆盖。比安奇对于狄金森对宗教的态度的解释也非常独特。她举出一些狄金森书信中掺杂的《圣经》典故来证明狄金森并不是抗拒皈依上帝，而是以自己独特的方式热爱上帝。总之，比安奇的传记一方面将少女时代的狄金森描写成一位寻常的邻家姑娘，另一方面又大力渲染她在隐居之后的神秘脱俗。通过不同时期的强烈反差来凸显狄金森作品高超的艺术性与思想性。简言之，她以刻画小说人物的技巧塑造出一个与19世纪日常生活中的美国女性既非常接近又截然不同的艺术形象。通过这种对日常女性共有特质的靠近和疏离，比安奇成功地为自己赢得了足够的读者，也为她的姨母争取到了更多的拥趸。

对于比安奇对狄金森隐居后的生活的描写，评论界褒贬不一。埃塞尔·帕东（Ethel Parton）指出比安奇传记中刻画的狄金森具有双重隐秘的特点：一是拒绝发表，二是独居避世。因此，就算是她的书信得以公开，或者她的旧友足以证明之前的误解，随着时间的推移，她在文学与个人的双重隐秘身份仍然会导致人们关注的重点从她性格中更显著、更重要的特点上偏离开来。人们容易形成一个错误印象：她是一个病态、神经质、自闭的人（Parton 701）。然而，尽管埃塞尔的批评言之有理，我们却不得不承认，在狄金森作品经典化的初期，被陌生化和神秘化的狄金森形象恰好是使她的诗歌被大众熟悉和了解的最便捷、最有效的途径。正因为比安奇对这“陌生”与“熟悉”二者之间神秘的张力的巧妙利用，她的传记成功地吸引了当时不少的批评家对狄金森诗歌的关注。斯蒂芬·文森特·贝尼特（Stephen Vincent Benet）在1924年狄金森的书信传记出版之际，在《一月书评》（*Book of the Month*）中评价道：“对于那些对美国诗歌或者事实上对世界最优秀的诗歌感兴趣的读者来说，《狄金森生平与书信》应该是一本必读之书……在这里，你可以了解一位杰出人物灵魂的内在历史，即便在我们的时代，这样的灵魂都难得一遇。”（Benet 732—735）斯蒂芬的话明显地印证了比安奇的传记对早期狄金森诗歌成为美国熟悉的通俗文学作品的推动作用。事实上，比安奇的传记在狄金森离世后40年出版，彼时正是英美两国都对其诗、其人产生新一轮的兴趣之际。她在传记中刻画的狄金森形象可以说也许是美国书信中最迷人的女性形象。对于像狄金森这样一位沉默的天才，比安奇以其后裔的身份完成了一项非常必要并且异常艰难的使命。

当比安奇在58岁之际出版《狄金森生平与书信》之后，美国评论界出现了两大阵营的交锋：一大阵营以埃塞尔·帕东、斯蒂芬·文森特·贝内特、甘梅利尔·布拉德福特（Gamaliel Bradford）和凯瑟琳·贝茨（Katharine Bates）为主将，他们非常喜爱这本传记，也满足于简单地告知狄金森是一个从"小精灵鬼"成长而来的"神秘女诗人"这一事实。另一阵营则由赫伯特·戈尔曼（Herbert Gorman）、罗尔夫·汉弗莱（Rolfe Humphries）、吉纳维夫·泰格特（Genevieve Taggard）、爱德华·萨皮尔（Edward Sapir）、乔治·弗里斯比·惠彻（Gorge Frisbie Whicher）和牛顿·阿尔文（Newton Arvin）等人挂帅。他们不满足，更不喜欢他们在传记中读到的内容。他们认为在1924年，离开狄金森的诗歌而去"想象"出一本关于诗人的传记是非常不切实际的。在1924年，一本传记与它传记之外的东西脱节是无法被人们容忍的。毕竟，对于不仅仅满足于以阅读逃避现实生活的普通读者而言，不依靠诗歌分析，仅仅依靠叙述是不足以自立的。批评阵营中的重要人物不满于毕安奇对狄金森过于简单化的叙述，更不满足于比安奇撰写的传记对狄金森诗歌分析的缺失，他们中的不少人身体力行，为了弥补比安奇传记中的这一缺憾而亲身投入狄金森的生平和诗歌研究中，成为日后狄金森传记作家中的佼佼者。

在介绍狄金森作品的编辑与出版时，笔者曾指出，由于各种版本的狄金森诗集的问世，读者对这位神秘诗人的兴趣也日益增长。在这样的读者需求刺激之下，早期的狄金森亲友首先采取的是以书信代替传记的做法来满足读者的好奇，期望狄金森的书信可以为读者打开"窥见作者灵魂之窗口"（Earle 5）。但是，事实证明，仅仅凭借狄金森的书信并不能反映狄金森的生平经历，也满足不了读者进一步了解狄金森生活细节的愿望。因此，比安奇在出版了书信传记的八年之后，终于推出了一本真正意义上的狄金森传记——《与艾米莉·狄金森面对面》（*Emily Dickinson Face to Face*）。

与前一本书信传记相比，1932年比安奇出版的《与艾米莉·狄金森面对面》加入了更多狄金森未出版的书信内容和家庭生活的介绍，闪耀着狄金森与普通读者相通的情感与人性光辉，这淡化了前一本传记刻意为狄金森营造的神秘形象带给读者的疏离感，为读者开辟出一条较容易接近狄金森的幽曲小径。这本传记打破了之前狄金森传记只能在阅读作品的基础上发挥想象去构建狄金森生平的惯例，为读者提供了一些新鲜而可靠的素材。这本传记的出版背景是狄金森去世半个世纪之后，一些与狄金森毫无关系的圈外人（比安奇称之为“rank outsiders”）肆无忌惮地出版书籍或发表文章来对她的姨母大加评说。比安奇作为生活优越的贵族妇女，加之已经步入暮年，本想对此保持沉默，然而这些圈外人的作品却有很多失实之处，直到她决定出版新传记之时也没有一本能满足她的期待的作品面世。因此，作为“权威人士”，她觉得自己有必要，也有义务出版一本“正统”的传记以正视听。读者从她的新传记的开场白中可以体会到这种强烈的责任感和义务感：“狄金森家族成员三代同堂，住在阿默斯特镇树篱隔挡着的两栋房子里。我们称之为‘老屋’（The Mansion）和‘新屋’（The Other House）。作为狄金森唯一的侄女——哥哥奥斯丁与‘苏珊姐姐’的女儿，现在来独自回忆一些陈年往事的真相。”（Bianchi 1）然而，较之对前一本传记的反响，读者对这本传记的反响却不那么热烈。

1933 年，一位署名“R.H.”的评论人在《新英格兰季刊》（*The New England Quarterly*）上发表书评。他首先对于比安奇新书中收录了一些狄金森未发表的书信和对狄金森家庭背景的介绍表示感谢。他认为这是持有狄金森手稿和书信的两大家族之间长期竞争达到白热化的结果，尽管对此公众甚少提及，但是大家却都心知肚明。他预言比安奇这本传记的出版必然刺激其竞争对手托德一家曝光更多的新资料。因此，《与艾米莉·狄金森面对面》的出版可谓是一把双刃剑：一方面，它提供给我们更全面了解狄金森的机会；另一方面，两大家族的激烈竞争和众说纷纭导致的乱象与迷雾会使读者根本不可能“面对面”地注视狄金森。读者能真正注视她的方法可能只有通过投身在她的诗歌作品中细品慢读，因此他期待能有更多的狄金森的手稿能被发掘，而不是各说各话的传记的出版。在文章结尾处，他呼吁：“只有当狄金森的每张手稿都被印刷出来供大家公正地进行学术分析和编辑，在过去这些年里不同的分歧与争议才能得到最终解决。”（R.H. 417）同年 3 月，莫里斯·U.斯卡普斯（Morris U.Schappes）在《美国文学》（*American Literature*）上发表相关评论。他认为读者不断被提醒作者是狄金森的侄女这个事实，但是 175 页篇幅的作品却并没有为我们提供多少之前读者不知道的新鲜材料。斯卡普斯相当尖刻地讽刺道：“由于不愿意一些圈外作家因为在她的书中被提及而获得永垂不朽的机会，比安奇只有偶尔在脚注中纡尊降贵地反驳一下那些非家族成员传记作者在书中提及的一两件事……不过，尽管如此，吉纳维夫·泰格特（Genevieve Taggard）、哈维·艾伦（Hervey Allen）、约瑟芬·波利特（Josephine Pollitt）和托德夫人等人还是在不同程度上受到了打击。”（Schappes 82—85）从上文可以看出，斯卡普斯对比安奇的作品极尽讥讽的主要原因是要为“圈外”传记作家打抱不平。他认为这些作家都没有得到比安奇足够的尊重，甚至是遭到了侮辱。其中，泰格特受比安奇攻击最多，她所持的“乔治有可能是狄金森的情人”的观点原本就没得到学界的一致承认，现在更是受到比安奇的痛批。比如，根据该传记第 24 页的脚注，比安奇指出，迪肯·卢克·斯威彻尔（Deacon Luke Sweetser）过去常常通过麦琪（Maggie）这个中间人把古尔德（Gould）的信送给狄金森。仅仅凭此就下定论说“乔治”是狄金森的情人，而斯威彻尔在他俩之间传递书信、穿针引线这件事毫无疑问是不合适的。在《与艾米莉·狄金森面对面》这本传记中，比安奇坚持了她以前的看法。她认为狄金森的爱人是牧师沃兹沃思（Wadsworth）。事实上，除了对泰格特的传记关于狄金森的感情生活这一重要问题提出异议之外，比安奇的新传记对其他人的错误批评没有那么严重。她仅在第 5 页的脚注中指出托德夫人在再版的书信集中使用的照片真实性存疑；在第 61 页的脚注中修正了艾伦在 1931 年 11 月 7 日《太阳报》（*The Sun*）的一则关于狄金森葬礼上抬灵柩的人是大学学生的评论；在第 61 页的脚注中修正了波利特在其传记第 307 页提及的关于诗人遗体存放地点的谬误，比安奇指出诗人遗体停放在图书馆而不是会客室。

在斯卡普斯眼中，从比安奇的新传记中，学者只能了解一些为数不多的逸闻趣事，而普通读者还不得不忍受比安奇令人倒胃口的以深情和亲密为特点的行文风格。斯卡普斯还指出："对狄金森自己的书信、便条和诗歌的热情关注还是有所回报的。尽管这并不能增加我们目前对她的认知，但比起其他传记作家而言，这本传记更乐于承认狄金森与嫂子苏珊之间长久的亲密感情。"（Schappes 82—85）这一评论貌似客观而中肯，但细细读来，读者不难体会斯卡普斯委婉地暗示比安奇的特殊身份反倒有导致事实真相扭曲的可能：她可能刻意夸大了狄金森与她的母亲苏珊之间的友谊。直到 1970 年这本传记再版之际，仍有人质疑《与艾米莉·狄金森面对面》的价值。斯科特·唐纳森（Scott Donaldson）在 1970 年发表书评时质疑把 1932 年狄金森侄女搜集的那些未出版的书信、笔记和回忆录再版有什么价值呢？那些未出版的书信和笔记现在当然已经不再是"未出版"的了。而那些比安奇的回忆虽然偶尔有使人领悟狄金森诗歌的作用，但也并不总是值得信赖的（Donaldson 161—163）。但是不能否认的是，这本传记最令人信服之处首先在于它不仅以狄金森亲属的身份，更是以一个孩子的视角观察狄金森的日常生活。其次，比安奇以脚注和附录的形式更正了一些当时的匿名作家对狄金森的错误认识。尤其是谣传在狄金森 20 岁时曾与阿默斯特一位叫乔治（George）的学生有暧昧私密的书信往来，而关于迪肯·卢克·斯威彻尔在他俩之间传递书信、穿针引线这个说法，比安奇感到极为愤慨，她专门用两处尾注对此事做了说明。这些极为隐秘的个人事件当然是圈外的其他传记作者难以得知的，只有比安奇以其特殊身份可以恰当地纠正谬误。比安奇的《与艾米莉·狄金森面对面》的价值主要在于为我们解读狄金森的诗歌提供文献参考。不过，总的来说，1970 年当比安奇的《与艾米莉·狄金森面对面》再版之际，经历了近 40 年的大浪淘沙，她的传记在数量众多、黎献纷杂、泥沙俱下的狄金森传记中尽管没有获得批评界的一致好评，但其作为探寻狄金森这一丰富文学宝藏不可或缺的钥匙的地位已经得到公认。

总的来说，比安奇的两本传记没有逃脱探寻狄金森隐秘的爱人和渲染其隐士生活的俗套。乔纳森·摩尔斯（Jonathan Morse）甚至认为比安奇一边抚摸着姨妈狄金森留下的唯一一张照片，一边试图将她与记忆中的理想美女形象协调一致。这样做的结果就是，她写出了一部“小说”（fiction），而不是传记（Morse 259—272）。阿尔弗雷德·哈贝格（Alfred Habegger）在其2001年出版的狄金森传记《我的战争都埋在书里：艾米莉·狄金森传》（*My Wars Are Laid Away in Books：The Life of Emily Dickinson*）中也有一段文字指责比安奇的狄金森传记中提供的一些逸闻趣事并不可靠。他认为：“1924年，诗人不太诚实的侄女玛莎·狄金森·比安奇讲述了一个传奇故事。”（哈贝格 161）从以上评价可知，比安奇的传记中虚构与失实的情况是多么严重和普遍。作为狄金森的侄女的特殊身份使得她的传记有以下几点特点：（1）笔调轻松，感情真挚，以孩童的眼光观察狄金森的生活为原本单调的狄金森隐居生活增添了一些不为人知的趣味性；（2）在“熟悉”与“陌生”中寻找平衡，既试图通过传记让读者多了解狄金森的日常一面，使狄金森更“接地气”，又适度地渲染她的卓然独立以保持其神秘的吸引力；（3）由于过分强调她作为狄金森亲属的特殊身份，同时贬低或批评其他传记作者的成果和真实性，她为自己的传记招致了一些好打抱不平的人士的批评和不满，他们要么以其人之道还治其人之身，怀疑她的特殊身份会导致她的传记对狄金森的生活有所隐瞒或失真，要么贬低她作传的文笔，认为她的叙述惺惺作态、矫揉造作，远远不如其传记中收录的狄金森的书信和诗歌本身具有研究价值。安娜·玛丽·威尔斯认为比安奇的《狄金森生平与书信》显然不足以满足大众的好奇心。吉纳维夫·泰格特、约瑟芬·波利特也反驳她的传记有失真之处（Wells 455—458）。不过，总的来说，比安奇撰写的两部传记引发了美国社会大量的关于狄金森的讨论，无论她的传记得失多寡，对于狄金森在美国文学地位的上升是有百利而无一害的。借着比安奇无意或有意制造的“话题效应”，更多的美国读者开始关注到狄金森这样一个已故的可以作为流行的文学话题谈资的诗人。

二、米莉森特·托德·宾厄姆撰写的传记

米莉森特·托德·宾厄姆（Millicent Todd Bingham）是梅布尔·卢米斯·托德（Mabel Loomis Todd）的女儿。她母亲是狄金森诗集第一辑的编

辑者、狄金森哥哥的情人和狄金森生前友人，具有多重身份。宾厄姆从母亲那里得到了当年狄金森妹妹拉维尼亚交由其母亲保管的狄金森的部分诗稿和书信。这些有利条件为她撰写狄金森传记提供了有利的身份支撑和材料支撑。

除了拉维尼亚交给托德夫人的诗稿和书信之外，狄金森的哥哥奥斯丁也曾将掺杂了狄金森过去写给马萨诸塞州洛德法官的部分书信草稿和信函残张装在一个包裹中委托宾厄姆的母亲梅布尔保管。宾厄姆从母亲手里得到这些独占性的手稿，从中进行筛查和挑选，找出了她认为可能是狄金森写给洛德法官的书信，在此基础上进行加工创造，为狄金森谱写出一部颇具浪漫色彩的黄昏恋曲。

1954 年，她出版的传记《艾米莉·狄金森：启示录》(*Emily Dickinson*：*A Revelation*）主要以狄金森的书信为证据，证明狄金森爱情故事的男主角是狄金森父亲的朋友兼同事洛德法官（Judge Otis Lord)。洛德法官比狄金森年长 18 岁，与狄金森的父亲年纪相仿。他与狄金森的父亲是马萨诸塞法院和政界的同僚兼朋友。宾厄姆通过狄金森的书信草稿为原始资料，为读者呈现出两人以鸿雁传情的方式而维持的真挚爱情。传记中狄金森开始这段感情时已经年逾五十，她与洛德法官的激情洋溢的书信一直持续到洛德法官生命中的最后两年（1882—1884 年)。不过至于这段感情开始于何时，宾厄姆也不得而知。但是她断言从狄金森的书信内容可以推测这是一段早已存在的感情。她甚至为读者留下开放的空间去判断这段感情是开始于 1874 年狄金森的父亲去世之前还是之后，或者甚至是开始于 1877 年洛德法官的夫人去世之前还是之后。至于书中提出洛德法官是不是导致狄金森在 19 世纪 60 年代发生精神危机的原因这个问题也相当令人浮想联翩。不得不说，宾厄姆将狄金森浪漫的爱情故事中的“男主角”指向洛德法官的确在很大程度上提高了狄金森的知名度。在 18 世纪美国，当女性身份还被局限于父权体系下的附庸之际，人们对于女性诗人作品本身的兴趣或许还远不如对她们的浪漫故事的兴趣。传记中关于女性诗人与有名望的男性的交往这类浪漫插曲虽然从一方面而言使得作品流于庸俗，但从另一方面来看，它又的确令“狄金森”这个位于新英格兰小镇的默默无闻的“家庭妇女”为更多的美国读者所耳闻。这种情况在中国也是如此。中国女诗人李冶、薛涛、鱼玄机被称为“唐代三大才女”，她们都留下了许多优秀的诗歌作品。然而，在文学横向（跨地域）和纵向（跨时间）传播时，不少读者都是通过传记作品初识她们，然后才进一步去阅读和钻研她们的作品，探索她们的思想精神。在数量众多的唐代女性诗人中，许多目前不为人知的女性诗人曾经创作出优秀的作品，然而她们却在文学经典化历程中被大浪淘沙。而李冶、薛涛、鱼玄机三位女诗人能够从中脱颖而出成为中国女性古代诗人经典化历程中的成功案例，首先要归功于她们作品本身的魅力，但也不得不提她们与同时代的男性名人的情感故事和文学友谊。李冶与陆羽和释皎然、薛涛与元稹和韦皋、鱼玄机与温庭筠，这些女诗人与当时的名流雅士的书信和唱和无疑对于其诗歌的流传和诗名的彰显起到了推动作用。

宾厄姆撰写的传记出版之后不久，沃尔特·麦金托什·美林（Walter McIntosh Merrill）于1955年在《新英格兰季刊》上发表书评认为，宾厄姆提出的洛德法官是狄金森的爱人的说法很好地解释了狄金森选择独居的原因。而且，从狄金森总是更欣赏比自己年长很多的男性来看，洛德法官也符合条件。因此，宾厄姆提出的洛德法官是狄金森的爱人这一说法看上去是一个经得起推敲的猜测。但是仅从狄金森一向更青睐在心智上远比自己成熟的男性就断言狄金森的爱人可能就是洛德法官，则显然缺乏原因和结果之间的必然联系。在沃尔特·麦金托什·美林眼中，这本传记更重要的价值在于其中新公开的书信为读者提供了一睹狄金森充满魔力的意象、迷人的诗歌节奏以及非凡的表达个人内心激情的能力的机会。但是，对于宾厄姆传记以“启示录”为名，而且在讲述中从始至终故弄玄虚这两点，沃尔特·麦金托什·美林做了猛烈的批评：“从标题往后读，一个接一个的悬念让读者急切地希望能从中了解什么轰动性的爆料。因此等读到传记倒数第二部分，宾厄姆得意扬扬地公开狄金森五花八门、林林总总的既没有标注日期，也没有寄出的那些未被出版的信件，并且这些信件中也没有几封是关于狄金森的爱人洛德法官时，读者感觉这简直就是赤裸裸的欺骗。”（Merrill 283）美林认为无论是从传记作家而言，还是对读者而言，狄金森的感情生活虽然是她的传记中不可或缺的一部分，但却也没有必要过于较真。读者对于作家对狄金森的爱情故事的想象和发挥是持比较宽容的态度的。然而，关于狄金森的具有史料价值的文献部分，读者的态度就严肃得多。这从另一方面证明，狄金森的作品正逐渐从"通俗读物"悄然向着"严肃读物"转向。美林对宾厄姆的严厉批评正体现了当时意欲以狄金森为严肃的学术研究对象的群体对于所谓的狄金森研究的"圈内人"的不满。

但是，与美林的观点相反，同年杰伊·利达（Jay Leyda）在《美国文学》上发表的书评却高度评价了宾厄姆所撰写的传记中公开的狄金森书信的价值。杰伊·利达说："这些新出版的书信非常了不起……也许对于批评家而言，拒绝接受这本书和它的观点要比改变他们对狄金森之前的偏见更为容易。"（Leyda 436—437）从中可见宾厄姆撰写的传记具有多大的颠覆性。这些书信改变了之前狄金森在公众心中的固有形象。通过基于书信的研究和阐发，狄金森不再是一个郁郁寡欢的"阿默斯特修女"，宾厄姆的传记在传统的刻板平面的狄金森形象中注入感情、思想和灵魂而使她立体鲜活起来。抛开学术研究者对更确切和丰富的研究资料的需求不说，单从宾厄姆传记本身对狄金森形象的塑造，以及对推广狄金森作品所起到的效应而言，这本传记仍不失为狄金森传记中的佳品。

三、马积高·詹金斯撰写的传记

在狄金森诞生100年之际，马积高·詹金斯出版了《艾米莉·狄金森：朋友与邻居》（*Emily Dickinson*：*Friend and Neighbor*）一书。用弗雷德里克·卡朋特（Frederic I. Carpenter）的话来讲："詹金斯写的是一本令人愉快的回忆录，根本不是一本传记。"（Carpenter 753—757）詹金斯的传记与其他作者撰写的传记最大的区别在于，他的作品实际上应该是19世纪的产物而不是20世纪的产物。早在1891年，他就完成了一篇名为"一个孩子对艾米莉·狄金森的回忆"（A Child's Recollections of Emily Dickinson）的文章。《艾米莉·狄金森：朋友与邻居》其实是在这篇文章的基础之上扩展和延伸而来的。值得一提的是，他非常反对以心理分析的方法去解剖他所认识的“艾米莉小姐”。他在传记中反复强调狄金森是一个充满活力的人，远非那些追随奥地利精神病医生弗洛伊德的精神分析学者所臆想的难以与人共处的“神经症”患者。他传记中的狄金森形象与其他人所刻画的“古怪的隐士”形象大不相同。詹金斯回忆道：“我记忆中的她身材清瘦、灵敏、优雅而且总是充满活力……留着漂亮的赤褐色头发，眼睛闪着亮光。”（Jenkins 2）在詹金斯笔下，狄金森是一位亲切的长者和玩伴：她和他们一起玩游戏，在困难时期她坚强地保护他们，她无视麦琪的权威，在食品储藏室搞偷袭给孩子们足够的曲奇和甜甜圈，从她的窗口把用篮子装着的姜饼分享给他和伙伴们享用……传记中记载着一连串充满温情和乐趣的小事件。总体而言，詹金斯笔下的狄金森不是外界想象的不食人间烟火的样子，相反，她非常真实，是个活生生的朋友和“战友”。孩子们觉得和她在一起比和任何其他长辈在一起都自在。这本传记的绝大部分内容都是由詹金斯的回忆再现和编织而成的。他唯一用到的文献是一些很久以前“艾米莉小姐”和“这个孩子”（作者本人）玩游戏时随意涂写在废旧纸片上的便条。回忆内容过多而文献资料相对不足导致这本传记在结构上显得比较零散。但是，从另一方面而言，随笔的形式和回忆的内容又使这本传记在可读性和趣味性上占据了一定优势，尤其是一些逸闻趣事对于读者，尤其是低龄读者而言相当具有吸引力。

在詹金斯的传记中，狄金森最后的遗言是对嫂子苏珊说的。她说：“我的答案是绝对的可以。”（My answer is an unmitigated *Yes*）从这句遗言来看，詹金斯认为狄金森是一个不善于拒绝的人。她接受这个世界和她自身，不管身处其间是多么复杂和矛盾。她总是那样快乐和坦然，既不后悔遗憾，也没有痛苦哀愁。詹金斯撰写的传记对于我们清楚了解狄金森性格中最重要的特点是很有帮助的。在他的传记出版之前，其他作家对艾米莉·狄金森性格的刻画导致美国文学批评界为狄金森贴上了一个看似不太贴切的标签——“女版瓦尔特·惠特曼”（the feminine Walt Whitman）。人们倾向于用弗洛伊德关于“压抑和抵抗”的理论来解释狄金森诗歌创作的动因。他们认为狄金森强烈的表达自我的本能的欲望不被社会风俗、习惯和道德所容，因此，欲望与规范就产生激烈的斗争，最后狄金森秘密地创作出数量惊人的诗歌——这恰好就是欲望反抗规范的结果。因此，尽管狄金森与同时期的美国诗人惠特曼二人诗风截然不同，但是，从这种强烈的自我表达的激情来看，狄金森从一定程度而言是类似于惠特曼的。但是，在詹金斯眼中，狄金森性格中“顺从”天命的成分要大于“抗争”或“抵抗”的因素，认识到狄金森的亲善和乐观，而没有被其他作者误导，把狄金森看作“斗天、斗地、斗自己”的精神疾病患者。

总体而言，当时的读者普遍认为阅读詹金斯的这本传记就像在一大堆无关紧要的浮渣中搜索真正宝贵的金矿石一样。不过，如果有幸拾到了金矿石，那么之前耗费的时间与精力倒也没有白费。因此，尽管这本传记内容比较零散，思绪比较漂浮，但还是值得读者一览。

四、结　语

狄金森传记几乎是紧随狄金森作品集出版而诞生的。但是由于资料不足，加之狄金森本身的自我封闭和其亲友的有意塑造与隐瞒，早期狄金森传记带有很浓厚的“小说”般的虚构成分。狄金森一度被塑造成一位与世隔绝的、谜一般的、被多个爱情故事缠绕的传奇女诗人。相较于她的诗歌成就，传记作家更感兴趣的是把她刻画成一位两耳不闻窗外事，患有陌生环境恐惧症，因而尽管有各种浪漫爱情但却终身不敢步入婚姻殿堂的老姑娘。简言之，早期的狄金森传记倾向于以“神化”和“陌生化”的方式把狄金森当作小说中的人物形象来塑造以满足读者的猎奇心理。总的来说，早期由其亲友撰写的传记为扩大狄金森在美国的知名度以及奠定狄金森研究的基础做出了较大贡献。他们撰写的传记有大量的虚构成分和人为矫饰、夸张、扭曲、疏离和变形，为狄金森隐晦的诗歌意义蒙上了一层灰色的面纱，但是，在狄金森还没有成为专业领域的学术研究对象之前，这些狄金森传记在当时都为读者解读谜一般的狄金森诗歌提供了不同的参考和启发。更重要的是，他们共同塑造的一个神秘和超然的狄金森形象极大地满足了在狄金森经典化初期通俗读者对于一个天才女性诗人的想象。狄金森传记与狄金森诗歌和书信作品之间形成的双向互构、相互推进的文学传播途径和文学经典化模式值得我国在推动“中华文化走出去”时加以借鉴。狄金森的传记研究向我们展示了传记在文学研究中的巨大价值：以传记打造作者形象，以传记激发读者兴趣，以传记阐释文学作品，以传记介绍历史文化，以传记提升文学品格，以传记助推经典的形成。

引用文献【Works Cited】

Benet, Stephen Vincent. “The Book of the Month.” *The Bookman* (1924): 732–735.

Bianchi, Martha Dickinson. *Emily Dickinson Face to Face: Unpublished Letters with Notes and Reminiscences*. Boston and New York: The Houghton Mifflin Company, 1932.

Carpenter, Frederic I. “Emily Dickinson: Friend and Neighbor.” *The New England Quarterly* 3.4 (1930): 753–757.

Donaldson, Scott. Rev. of *Emily Dickinson Face to Face*, by Martha Dickinson Bianchi. *The New England Quarterly* 44.1 (1971): 161–163.

Earle, Rebecca. *Epistolary Selves: Letter and Letter-writers*. Aldershot: Ashgate, 1999.

阿尔弗雷德·哈贝格：《我的战争呈现在书里：艾米莉·狄金森传》，王柏华、曾铁峰、胡秋冉译。北京：北京大学出版社，2013年。

[Habegger, Alfred. *My Wars Are Laid Away in Books: The Life of Emily Dickinson*. Trans. Wang Baihua, Zeng Yifeng and Hu Qiuran. Beijing: Beijing University Press, 2013.]

Jenkins, MacGregor. *Quotes: From Emily Dickinson: Friend and Neighbor*, Boston: Little, Brown, and Company, 1930.

Leyda, Jay. Rev. of *Emily Dickinson—A Revelation* by Millicent Todd Bingham. *American Literature* 27.3 (1955): 436–437.

Merrill, Mc Intosh, and M.T.Bingham. Rev. of *Emily Dickinson: A Revelation* by Millicent Todd Bingham. *New England Quarterly* 28.2 (1931): 283–284.

Morse, Jonathan. “Memory, Desire, and the Need for Biography: The Case of Emily Dickinson.” *The Georgia Review* 35.2 (1981): 259–272.

Parton, Ethel. “Emily Dickinson.” *The Outlook* 23 April 1924: 701.

R.H. “Emily Dickinson Face to Face by Martha Dickinson Bianchi.” *The New England Quarterly* 6.2 (1933): 417.

Schappes, Morris U. “Face to Face: Unpublished Letters with Notes and Reminiscences by Emily Dickinson, Martha Dickinson Bianchi and Alfred Leete Hampson.” *American Literature* 5.1 (1933): 82–85.

Wells, Anna Mary. Rev. of *Emily Dickinson: The Human Background of Her Poetry*, by Josephine Pollitt; *The Life and Mind of Emily Dickinson*, by Genevieve Taggard; *Emily Dickinson: Friend and Neighbor*, by Macgregor Jenkins; *Emily Dickinson: A Bibliography*, by Alfred Leete Hampson. *American Literature* 12.4 (1932): 455–458.

小说作为一种精神自传

——契诃夫和他的《带小狗的女人》

高　永

内容提要：安东·契诃夫的短篇小说《带小狗的女人》书写了一对男女陷入"黑暗的秘密之恋"的故事，但这个故事却绝不是道德批判的文本。契诃夫借助这样一个婚外情故事，写出了现代人不得不戴着面具活着的生存境况，小说主人公陷入了一场出于自己内心深层需要的自欺之中。事实上，小说主人公纠结的情感正是契诃夫对自己爱情观的戏仿，从这个意义上说，《带小狗的女人》是一部带有精神自传性的作品，其中蕴含着契诃夫的内在精神强力。

关键词：安东·契诃夫　《带小狗的女人》　精神自传

作者简介：高永，文学博士，河北大学文学院副教授。主要从事中外文学比较研究、西方文学与文论研究，近期发表了《哈罗德·布鲁姆的"美国宗教"研究》（《宗教与美国社会》，第13辑）、《哈罗德·布鲁姆的撒缪尔·约翰逊批评》（《北方工业大学学报》，2017年第3期）等。

Title: An Autobiography of the Author's Inner World: Chekhov and *The Lady with the Dog*

Abstract: Anton Chekhov's *The Lady with the Dog* tells a story in which a man and a woman get involved in a "dark secret love", but this story is not a text of moral criticism. Chekhov insinuates the living conditions of modern people in masks. The protagonists are caught in self-deception. We might say that the "dark secret love" of the protagonists parodied Chekhov's concepts of love. In this sense, *The Lady with the Dog* contains the inner spiritual strength of Chekhov and becomes the autobiography of author's inner world.

Keywords: Anton Chekhov, *The Lady with the Dog*, autobiography of the inner world

Gao Yong is Associate Professor of Literature at Hebei University, China. His research concerns comparative literature and western literature and literary theory studies. He is the author of "Harold Bloom's Samuel Johnson Criticism" (*Journal of North China University of Technology*, 3 2017) and "Harold Bloom's Study of American Religion" (*Religion and American Society*, volume 13), etc. E-mail: bajinhanye@163.com.

一个女人，孤身一人，牵着一只小狗，一天几次出现在人们的视野中。这样的女人给我们的通常印象是：生活富足，衣食无忧，但也孤独、寂寞。契诃夫写于1899年秋季的短篇小说《带小狗的女人》，将这样一个年轻女子带到了男主人公德米特利·德米特利奇·古罗夫的身边。其时，他从莫斯科来雅尔塔已经两个星期，"对这个地方已经熟悉，也开始对新人发生兴趣了"（322）①。

故事开始时，对于情场老手古罗夫来说，安娜——这个带小狗的女人——只是他多个猎艳对象中的一个。于是，一系列惯常的勾引手段被古罗夫用到单纯少妇安娜身上，一切顺理成章地发生了：安娜成了古罗夫的情人。其间的试探、暧昧、勾引的过程被契诃夫用简洁、平淡的文字交代得一清二楚，包括安娜无论如何也说不清楚她的丈夫在什么地方工作，这连她自己都觉得好笑。我们很容易就知道了：她不爱她的丈夫——那个她口中的"奴才"，正如古罗夫也不爱他的妻子——那个自称"有思想""读过很多书""在信上不写'ъ'这个硬音符号，不叫她的丈夫德米特利而叫吉米特利"（322）的女人，在他眼中则"智力有限，胸襟狭隘，缺少风雅"（322—323）——一样。

在两人正式成为情人前的那个傍晚，在防堤坡码头上，在等待轮船开来的人群中，安娜丢失了她的长柄眼镜。纳博科夫认为这一句简单的交代——"后来在人群中把带柄眼镜也失落了"——被契诃夫说得漫不经心，而且"对故事没有任何直接影响——只是偶然提了提，但不知怎么的，它恰好符合小说早就暗示出来的那种不能自已的、使人凄恻的情调"（262）。以一个作家的敏感，纳博科夫洞见了这句简单的交代所具有的暗示情调的作用，如果联系安娜在等待轮船到来的人群中的表现，那么我们就会发现，眼镜丢失这个细节所具有的暗示意味似乎还要丰富得多。她在人群中寻找着谁？为什么在转过身来对着古罗夫时"她的眼睛亮了"（326）？这是否意味着如果从那轮船上下来的人群中有她要找的人（小说中已经交代过，她丈夫可能会来），她的眼睛会一直暗淡下去呢？在这样的情境下，眼镜的丢失是否暗示着她暂时要抛弃那个她要寻找的对象呢？她很快投入了古罗夫的怀抱，成了他的情人，这也许印证了我们的猜测。在人群中，她前言不搭后语，明显心绪烦乱地说了许多话，这样的表现是因为紧张于可能的面对吗？这既可能是与其丈夫的面对，也可能是与古罗夫的"面对"。当终于证实那轮船上没有她刚才寻找的人后，她安静了下来，表面安静地等待着与古罗夫的"面对"。

如果故事到此为止，或者按照所谓"现实主义"的逻辑发展下去，无论他们在分离之后是继续约会还是永不再见，这个故事最多只是一个惯常的婚外情故事，《带小狗的女人》也最多成为"现实主义"小说长廊中的普通一篇而已。事实上恰恰相反，《带小狗的女人》被普遍认为是契诃夫最好的小说之一。契诃夫的巨大创造力在这里得到充分体现，他将大量笔墨泼洒在描写两人分开后的精神煎熬上。正如屠尔科夫所指出的那样，古罗夫和安娜之间相互关系的起点很平常，但在以后"两个主人公，特别是古罗夫，发生了惊人的变化"（374）。故事发展的逻辑在这里发生了"陡转"。从一种"格调崇高"的相识到最后堕入一种"生活俗套"，也许不失其生活批判的意义，更合乎道德评判的需要，但这却绝非契诃夫的洞见。契诃夫通过这个"陡转"暗示，他的《带小狗的女人》在根本上是反道德批评的，因为他并没打算把故事局限在狭隘的道德小说范畴。

作为情场老手的克罗夫觉得，回到莫斯科后，过一段时间就可以把这段风流艳遇抛诸脑后，"安娜·谢尔盖耶芙娜在他的记忆里就会被一层雾盖没，只有偶尔像别人那样来到他的梦中，现出她那动人的笑容罢了"（332）。但事情并不如他所料，他发现自己终日思念着她，饱受相思之苦，安娜在他的记忆中，不但没有被一层雾盖没，反而越来越清晰了。"他久久地在书房里来回走着，回想着，微微地笑，然后回忆变成幻想，在想象中，过去的事就跟将来会发生的事混淆起来了……”（332）原本习惯并沉浸在莫斯科冬季生活的古罗夫，突然觉得周围的人那样令人厌恶，自己的工作和生活变得那样没有意义。这一切都证明安娜于古罗夫具有一种特别的意义，虽然我们难免怀疑他对安娜的感情到底是不是真正的爱情。但有一点是肯定的，古罗夫开始怀疑，甚至是厌恶自己原来那种浑浑噩噩、半死不活的生活。

古罗夫像是着了魔，借口出差，跑去安娜居住的斯城，并在剧院中与安娜见了面。突然见到古罗夫的安娜惊慌失措，几乎昏厥过去。她对古罗夫的爱是无可怀疑的：“她带着恐惧、哀求、热爱瞧着他，凝视着他，要把他的相貌更牢固地留在她的记忆里。”（337）但她请古罗夫快些离开，并赌咒会到莫斯科去与他相会。自此以后，他们每过两三个月就会在莫斯科相会一次。至此，他们真的陷入了最复杂、最困难的境地——枉顾现实的羁绊，陷入没有结果的私情之网。连古罗夫这位老牌的花花公子、情场老手，也不得不承认，他以前经历过那么多女人，但他一次都没有爱过，他与这些女人的关系无论被说成什么都可以，但绝不能说是爱情，“直到现在，他的头发开始白了，他才生平第一次认真地、真正地爱上一个女人”（340）。哈罗德·布鲁姆套用威廉·布莱克《病玫瑰》中的伟大诗句——“黑暗的秘密之爱”——来概括安娜对他们之间爱情的抱怨：“她哭，是因为激动，因为凄苦地体验到他们的生活落到多么悲惨的地步；他们只能偷偷地见面，瞒住外人，像窃贼一样！难道他们的生活不是毁掉了吗？”（339）这何尝不是古罗夫体会到的呢？虽然他似乎更享受这种“黑暗的秘密之爱”。但也正是在这里，契诃夫作为一个作家的伟大表现到了极致，他将一个婚外情的故事终于引向了对人之存在的关注，他这样描写古罗夫去幽会时的心理活动：

> 他一边说，一边心里暗想：现在他正在去赴幽会，这件事一个人都不知道，大概永远也不会有人知道。他有两种生活：一种是公开的，凡是要知道这种生活的人都看得见，都知道，充满了传统的真实和传统的欺骗，跟他的熟人和朋友的生活完全一样；另一种生活则在暗地里进行。

由于环境的一种奇特的，也许是偶然的巧合，凡是他认为重大的、有趣的、必不可少的事情，凡是他真诚地去做而没有欺骗自己的事情，凡是构成他生活核心的事情，统统是瞒着别人，暗地里进行的；而凡是他弄虚作假，他用以伪装自己、以遮盖真相的外衣……却统统是公开的。(338)

推己及人，古罗夫不再相信他看到的事情，总是揣测每一个人都在秘密的掩盖下，“就像在夜幕的遮盖下一样，过着他的真正的、最有趣的生活。每个人的私生活都包藏在秘密里，也许，多多少少因为这个缘故，有文化的人才那么恓恓惶惶地主张个人的秘密应当受到尊重吧”(338)。

谁又能否认，这不正是我们所有人的生活写照呢？高尔基在读到这篇小说后写信给契诃夫说：“你杀死了现实主义。”已有论者就此指出了契诃夫这篇小说具有一种超越时空的力量：“这是否意味着高尔基已经看出了它的更高可以与未来的读者产生共鸣的可能性？重读契诃夫的这篇写于19世纪最后一年的小说，我们会发现，生活在20、21世纪的人，肯定会比19世纪末的读者，更能体会到这个小说的男女主人公不得不戴上面具过着双重生活的痛苦。”(童道明)

后期的契诃夫是一个书写日常生活悲剧的伟大剧作家，这在他的这篇小说作品中也得到了体现。我们无法确定古罗夫是否真的陷入爱情之中了，但我们却可以确定安娜真的爱上了古罗夫，无论他是不是值得她去爱。这场爱情必然会是一个悲剧，因为“出走”——逃离没有希望的婚姻——是不可能的，至少契诃夫暗示我们安娜和古罗夫也确实都没有“出走”的意图。无意出走意味着身陷一个日常性（或陈腐）的惨况之中，实实在在地沉浸于“黑暗的秘密之爱”中，这份爱带给他们的欢乐也只能与悲伤相伴，这不就是最平凡的生活吗？对此，契诃夫既不歌颂，也不试图去歪曲，只是如实地呈现出来。正是在这一意义上布鲁姆说：“契诃夫最伟大的力量是在我们阅读时给予我们这样一个印象，也即这里终于揭示了人类存在中陈腐的惨况与悲剧性的欢乐之永久混合的真理。”(27)

但笼罩着这场“黑暗的秘密之爱”的迷雾并没有散去，我们不禁要问，他们之间的爱情，特别是安娜对古罗夫的爱是如何发生的？古罗夫从与安娜的秘恋中得到了什么？他真的如他宣称的那样身陷爱情无法自拔了吗？

当古罗夫对镜看到自己苍老的白发时，我们更加怀疑安娜对克罗夫的爱是如何发生的。孤单、寂寞与沉闷占据了这个女人的生活，成了她日常生活的主旋律。她向自己的丈夫撒谎说自己病了，于是来到雅尔塔，她在寻找什么？她在成为古罗夫的情人后的倾诉道出了她的心思：

> 我嫁给他的时候才二十岁，好奇心煎熬着我，我巴望过好一点的日子，我对自己说：“一定有另外一种不同的生活。”我一心想生活得好！我要生活，生活。……好奇心燃烧着我，……这您是不会了解的，可是，我当着上帝起誓，我已经管不住自己了，我起了变化，什么东西也没约束我了，我就对我的丈夫说我病了，我就到这儿来了。……到了这儿，我老是走来走去，像是着了魔，发了疯。(328)

潜在的心思——渴望改变压抑的生活现状，找寻一次生命自由释放的机会——在这近于呼告又近于自责的表白中被淋漓尽致地体现出来。其实这又何尝不是古罗夫的心思呢？古罗夫不断与不同的女人发生的风流韵事，不正是他排解孤单、寂寞与沉闷的方式和手段吗？他冒险与不同的女人偷情不同样也是因为“他渴望生活”，以致因偷情引出的麻烦在面临新的艳遇时，都不再是复杂的大问题，也不再令人难以忍受：“一切都显得十分简单而引人入胜了。”(323) 这让我们想起卡夫卡给爱情下的那个定义——爱情是偶然在场。原来爱情的发生有时就是那样简单——两个追求真实生活的人在一个容易发生风流韵事的地方相遇了，特别是对于只有在爱情中才真正活着的安娜而言，与古罗夫的相遇，是偶然也是必然。

布鲁姆说：“读者可以相信安娜的眼泪，但不会相信古罗夫边搔头边说：‘到底怎么办？到底怎么办？到底怎么办？’”(27) 确实，相对于深陷爱情无法自拔，以致只能求助于眼泪的安娜来说，古罗夫看待这场婚外情的立场则要“客观”得多，他似乎一直站在一个审视者的角度思考着二者之间的关系。但我们也无法否认，这场婚外情带给古罗夫的情感震动，远非其他任何一次风流韵事可比，他甚至从中体会到一种幸福：在雅尔塔的黎时时分，与安娜坐在一起，面对周围神话般的环境，他甚至感到了世界的美好，一种得救感油然而生，“我们会永恒地得救，人间的生活会不断地运行，一切会不断趋于完善”(329)。在斯城的剧院里，当古罗夫看到安娜时，他的表现绝非一个惯于艳遇的情场老手应该有的：“古罗夫一眼瞧见她，他的心就缩紧了，他这才清楚地体会到如今对他来说，全世界再也没有一个比她更亲近、更宝贵、更重要的人了。……占据了他的全部生命，成为他的悲伤、他的欢乐，他目前所指望的唯一幸福。”(335) 在莫斯科宾馆的房间里，当他看见镜子里那个苍老的自己时，他手扶着安娜温柔、颤抖的肩膀，突然怜悯起安娜的生命，这其中不无自责之意——这个温暖、美丽的生命“大概已经临近开始凋谢、枯萎的地步，像他的生命一样了”(339)。

人生的无奈——有能力爱时不能爱或没机会爱，深陷爱时才发现生命已韶华不在。一种屠格涅夫式的悲凉感让古罗夫痛苦不堪。但人在本质上需要爱情。爱情对于每个人都是一样的，无论他是不是真的拥有爱情，无论他是不是有爱的能力，他都需要，就是这样，与他是不是风月老手无关，也与其社会地位、婚姻状况无关，这是一种几近本能的需要。人需要爱情，这种激烈的情感发自内心，在这种激烈的情感中，人得以证明作为个体的自我的存在——正如古罗夫在与安娜的关系中感受到的那样。但爱情毕竟不是人生的全部，于是我们常常失去爱情，常常没有能力去爱，结果，当爱情不在时，我们有意无意地编织着身陷爱情的谎言，或者步入“黑暗的秘密之恋”中，最后连自己都认为这就是真的爱情，正如古罗夫不断暗示自己已身陷爱情之中无法自拔一样。而此时，我们拥有的还是纯粹的爱情吗？安娜不知道，古罗夫不知道，契诃夫心里可能有答案，但他不告诉我们。这不正是对现代人的精神困境的最好注解吗？

在现代社会的重压下，那与自我紧密相连的爱情，哪怕真的在我们身上发生了，也是值得怀疑的，因为现代生活褪尽了神话的可能性，而纯粹的爱情不就是一个典型的神话吗？从这个意义上说，古罗夫与安娜之间的感情是不是爱情已不再重要。萨特曾经对“说谎”与“自欺”进行了区分，在他看来，说谎意味着对现实的超越，说谎者完全了解他所掩盖的真相，他在自身中肯定真情，但在说话时又否定它，并且为了自己否认这一否定。自欺则不同，它虽有着与说谎相同的结构，但它在本质上是真诚的，是一种脆弱的相信，其目的是“使自身逃避其所是”（84）。古罗夫宣称自己生平第一次认真地、真正地爱上了一个女人，他没有说谎，安娜更没有说谎。但谁又能肯定他们不是陷入了一种自欺的境地呢，一种出于内心深层需要的自欺？无论这种自欺指向什么，至少证明了他们都在试图逃离以往的生活，通过这场“黑暗的秘密之爱”，古罗夫与安娜都更加深刻地认识到了自己原有生活的荒谬，他们试图摆脱那些日常的庸俗生活。可以说，安娜与古罗夫的痛苦“爱情”，“纯洁了安娜·谢尔盖耶芙娜和古罗夫的心灵，使他们高于庸俗生活”（屠尔科夫 375）。

当安娜对古罗夫说，他们的爱情是“黑暗的秘密之恋”时，我们对这样的爱——有妇之夫与有夫之妇的越轨偷情——无法做出任何道德的评判。与契诃夫的《带小狗的女人》颇类似的作品是维谢利特斯卡娅（笔名 B. 米库利奇）的中篇小说《米莫奇卡的温泉疗养院》。这两篇小说描写的环境和情景非常相近：《米莫奇卡的温泉疗养院》中主人公之间的艳史“正好就是契诃夫笔下的古罗夫起初所幻想的那种艳史”（屠尔科夫 369）。维谢利特斯卡娅的这篇小说，无疑是道德批评的绝佳对象，也正是在这个意义上，得到了列夫·托尔斯泰和苏沃林的热情赞许。虽然托尔斯泰是契诃夫爱戴的作家，而苏沃林是他的好友，但契诃夫还是对《米莫奇卡的温泉疗养院》提出了自己的看法，认为这是一篇辞藻浮华、矫揉造作的作品。而他写作《带小狗的女人》，则是要按照自己的观点来评价生活，从自己的伦理观出发思考爱情问题。在这里，我们看到的是契诃夫对独创性的坚守，哪怕这样会使自己陷入与同时代的伟人发生争论的困窘中，也在所不惜。

纳博科夫说，契诃夫从来不想为人们提供一种社会的、道德的训诫，但这并不意味着他的小说“比那些凭借一系列着色傀儡来炫耀其社会见解的诸如高尔基那样的许多其他作家”（259）的作品更少批判意味，只是他的天才让他“在不经意之间就揭露了那充满饥饿、前途茫茫、遭受奴役、满腔愤怒的农民的俄罗斯最黑暗的现实”（259）。如此，在这篇小说中，契诃夫没有给我们提供任何对人物进行道德评判的可能。如果联系契诃夫的人生经历，特别是他的情感经历，我们一定能更深刻地理解契诃夫之所以用这样一种超然的态度书写这对男女之间的情感故事的动因。

1898 年，契诃夫在艺术剧院排演他的《海鸥》时，认识了自己未来的妻子奥尔加·克尼佩尔。很明显，契诃夫很快坠入了爱河。在经历了与莉季娅·米齐诺娃（莉卡）和莉季娅·亚沃斯卡娅等人的感情波折后，契诃夫遇上了这个他真正爱上的女人。《海鸥》演出获得巨大成功，这一定程度上也促进了契诃夫与克尼佩尔之间的感情。但他们分居两地，只能靠鸿雁传书，以解相思之苦。克尼佩尔深爱契诃夫，希望与他结婚，长相厮守。但是，一如他与所有女性的关系一样，面对爱情，契诃夫似乎永远保持一种若即若离的姿态。契诃夫需要爱情，他认为在生命中，爱情是不可或缺的，但爱情并非生活的全部，将爱情等同于生活，爱情也会失去美感，变得丑陋。契诃夫情愿饱受相思之苦的煎熬，也不愿让爱情成为束缚他的枷锁。从契诃夫对古罗夫与安娜“爱情”的书写中，从契诃夫对待婚姻与爱情的态度中不难发现，契诃夫珍视自由，厌弃束缚，哪怕是给予人自我认知机会的爱情也不能成为束缚人之自由的枷锁。从这个意义上说，布鲁姆的看法不无道理——他认为相比于契诃夫在《海鸥》中的特里戈林身上戏仿自己，“古罗夫是一个变形得更厉害的自我戏仿”（27）。

确实，也许契诃夫用这样一篇小说对自己的爱情观进行了自嘲，只是这种自嘲太过曲折了。他将自己对爱情既向往又恐惧的心理透过变形镜投影到了这篇小说中。早在 1895 年，当一位记者极力劝契诃夫结束独身生活时，契诃夫在回信中写道：“好吧，如果你希望这样，我就结婚。不过我的条件是：一切必须照旧，即她必须住在莫斯科，而我住在乡下，我将经常到她那里去。那种天天如此、朝夕如此的幸福我可受不了……我答应做一个出色的丈夫，不过得给我这样一个妻子，她要像月亮一样，并不是每天都升上我的天空……”（转引自赵佩瑜 101）他更享受那种两地分居、互不干扰，而又能得到爱情滋润的生活。当安娜为这种“黑暗的秘密之爱”折磨时，“古罗夫似乎陶醉于这种秘密生活，他觉得这种生活揭示了他真实的自我”（布鲁姆 27）。这何尝不是克尼佩尔与契诃夫的写照呢?

由此，我们不难发现，契诃夫需要爱情，也赞美爱情，因为在他看来，人在爱情中可以发现自我，正如在他在小说中书写的古罗夫与安娜那样。契诃夫在有关小说《三年》的构思札记中说：“可能，我们在热恋中所体验的东西乃是一种正常状况。爱情可以向人指出，他应该是什么样的人。”（转引自屠尔科夫 375）显然这是契诃夫那一时期关心的问题，这一问题虽然没有被写进《三年》中，却在《带小狗的女人》中被呈现了出来。从这个意义上说，与其说《带小狗的女人》是在讨论爱情问题，不如说是作家试图借这个“黑暗的秘密之恋”的故事，探讨找寻自我、发现自我的问题。

将自己的个体生命体验融入小说创作中，成为小说的灵魂，是所有伟大作品必备的品质。如果说伟大的作品都只有一个主人公的话，那这个主人公一定是作者本人。从这个意义上说，其实任何一部伟大作品在某种意义上就是作者的精神自传。在《带小狗的女人》中，作家契诃夫的内在精神，是文本中隐在的一个重要形象，他坚守独创性、勇于对抗庸俗生活、努力发现自我、珍视自由。这个形象，不是契诃夫，也是契诃夫，同时还是我们每个人该有的状态。从这个意义上说，契诃夫在小说创作中实现了自己的写作理想——既要写出“生活的本来面目”，也要写出“生活应当是什么样子”（契诃夫 216）。

传记式的批评固然显得幼稚而笨拙，但作家的内在精神与文本中人物精神的契合，却似乎永远是文学具有个性化特色的源泉。如果将作家的内在精神视作文本的外在之物，并试图将其置于雷内·韦勒克与奥斯汀·沃伦所定义的“文学的外部”研究[②]的范畴内，那是刻板的学究的专利。凭着这种内在的精神强力，文本得以具有普遍性——每当我们看到这个词时，都不由自主地会想起另一个词——“个人性”。

注释【Notes】

① 本文所引契诃夫小说原文，皆出自契诃夫小说《带小狗的女人》（汝龙译），见《契诃夫小说全集》第10卷（北京：人民文学出版社，2016年），文中只注明引文页码。
② 雷内·韦勒克和奥斯汀·沃伦在他们合著的《文学理论》一书中，区分了“文学的内部”研究和“文学的外部”研究两类，并将传记式的研究方法作为“文学外部研究”的典型方法，对之提出了质疑。

引用文献【Works Cited】

哈罗德·布鲁姆:《如何读,为什么读》,黄灿然译。南京:译林出版社,2011年。

[Bloom, Harold. *How to Read and Why*. Trans. Huang Canran. Nanjing: Yilin Press, 2011.]

契诃夫:《契诃夫论文学》，汝龙译。北京：人民文学出版社，1958年。

[Chekhov, Anton. *Chekhov on Literature*. Trans. Ru Long. Beijing: People's Literature Publishing House, 1958.]

——:《契诃夫小说全集》（10），汝龙译。北京：人民文学出版社，2016年。

[——. *Complete Works of Anton Chekhov*. Vol. 10. Trans. Ru Long. Beijing: People's Literature Publishing House, 2016.]

弗·纳博科夫：《论契诃夫》，薛鸿时译。《世界文学》1（1982）:256—268。

[Nabokov, V. "On Chekhov." Trans. Xue Hongshi. *World Literature* 1(1982):256-268.]

萨特：《存在与虚无》，徐宣良译。北京：生活·读书·新知三联书店，1987年。

[Sartre, Jean-Paul. *Being and Nothingness*. Trans. Xu Xuanliang. Beijing: SDX Joint Publishing Co., 1987.]

童道明：《伟大的俄罗斯戏剧家契诃夫》，《人民政协报》2010年11月22日，第C03版。

[Tong Daoming. "Chekhov: The Great Russian Dramatist." *CPPCC News*. 22 Nov. 2010: C03.]

安·屠尔科夫：《安·巴·契诃夫和他的时代》，朱逸森译。北京：中国社会科学出版社，1984年。

[Turkhov, A. *Anton Chekhov and His Time*. Trans. Zhu Yisen. Beijing: China Social Science Press, 1984.]

赵佩瑜编著：《契诃夫》。沈阳：辽海出版社，1998年。

[Zhao Peiyu, ed. *Chekhov*. Shenyang: Liaohai Publishing House, 1998.]

独特的战争叙事

——评宋谭秀红的战时回忆录

沈　忱

内容提要：宋谭秀红在回忆录中记录了她一路从南京到香港，再到广东，最后落脚重庆的战时逃难经历。回忆录着眼于个人及社会生活，通过生活实录反映战争之残酷。回忆录中，作者表现了对民族主义的疏离，从人性悲悯的视角关注战争。除此之外，基于作者海外华人和女性的边缘身份，她将故土寻根和对家庭生活的渴望融入了战争反思，具有独特价值。

关键词：战争回忆录　宋谭秀红　战争反思　夏威夷华人

作者简介：沈忱，上海交通大学人文学院比较文学与文化理论方向博士研究生，研究兴趣为传记研究。

Title: The War Narrative in Irma Tam Soong's Refugee Memoir

Abstract: Irma Tam Soong records her story as a refugee fleeing from Nanjing, via Hong Kong and Guang Dong, to Chong Qing. Soong's memoir exposes war's cruelty by writing about her personal and social life. From the perspective of humanity, other than nationalism, the author makes a profound reflection on war. The author also explores her identity as a Chinese American and a woman through writing her tale of survival, making her war reflections insightful.

Keywords: war memoir, Irma Tam Soong, war reflections, Chinese in Hawaii

Shen Chen is a PhD candidate in School of Humanities at Shanghai Jiao Tong University. Her research concerns life writing studies. E-mail: shenchen90@sjtu.edu.cn.

宋谭秀红（Irma Tam Soong）是夏威夷华人的一个杰出代表，她是夏威夷华人历史研究中心的创建者，也是华人历史研究者，她对孙中山和兴中会的研究在相关领域影响深远。她的《美国华侨在中国战时的经历》（*Chinese-American Refugee，A World War II Memoir*）出版于 1984 年，是一部写抗战时期生活的回忆录。这部回忆录为第二次世界大战时期中国的这段历史提供了独特视角的见证，作者的海外华人身份和女性身份也使得回忆录对战争的反思蕴含了更为丰富的内涵。

一

宋谭秀红 1936 年重回中国，1945 年离开，正好经历了从 1937 年第二次世界大战在中国战场开始到结束的历史跨度。作者在中国的这九年，为了躲避战火，从南京逃到香港，香港沦陷后又逃到广东，最后辗转到重庆。回忆录既记录了惨绝人寰的日军暴行，也有暂时安宁的避难生活，还有艰辛的逃亡旅程，给我们展现了丰富而生动的战时生活图景。

现今出版的战争回忆录多以战地纪实为主要内容，比如有代表性的《陈诚回忆录》《陈布雷回忆录》《长沙、常德、衡阳血战亲历记》《我的 1945：抗战胜利回忆录》等，其主要内容是抗战将领回忆自己的峥嵘岁月，展现中国军人在正面战场、敌后战场浴血奋战之情形，再现各大战役的细节，分析战争之得失。这些回忆录有着极高的历史价值和军事价值。但战争不局限于战场，它对整个国家的社会生活都产生了影响。近年一些记录战时社会生活的回忆录相继出版，反映了战争回忆录写作的新趋势，比如记录上海沦陷期间的市民生活的《抗战时代生活史》、记录抗战爆发初期从南京南下逃难故事的《小难民自述》等。这些回忆录反映了普通民众在战争中的艰难处境，从另一个角度反映了战争的残酷。

宋谭秀红的回忆录同样是一部由普通人视角写作的战争蒙难记，个人生活是回忆录的主要内容。回忆录的主体部分详细描写了三个生活片段：一是 1941 年香港被日军占领后的生活；二是作者从香港逃出，在丈夫的祖籍地广东花县的生活；三是作者辗转逃亡到重庆，和丈夫重聚的故事。作者写到香港遇难、广东避难等经历，既记录了个人生活，也展现了战时香港、广东等地的社会情况。回忆录的主体部分是曲折而艰辛的逃难故事，为了离开被日本占领、举目无亲的香港，作者独自带着孩子，加入了亲戚的逃难队伍。一路上路途遥远，环境恶劣，体力透支，食不果腹，席草而眠，精神和身体都处在崩溃边缘。在花县老家，宋谭秀红和孩子暂时度过了一段平静的生活。不过为了和丈夫团聚，她得继续往内地逃。经水路到桂林，又坐火车到贵阳，和丈夫团聚后又一路坐车抵达重庆。作者写这段经历时，一方面记录了逃难过程的艰辛，另一方面也不忘观察所到之处的社会生活情形，记录了途经之处在战时的民生情况。比如，作者写到广东农村的生活。花县暂时没有受到战火的侵袭，人们一如往常过着日出而作日落而息的农家生活，在这里能够暂时摆脱生命危险。不过这里物资极度缺乏，每日只能吃青菜和粗粮，过年时才能吃到一点猪肉。作者也关注到路途中遇到的各种不同人的生活状态，比如她在花县遇到的农妇，不得不每天背着孩子早出晚归，在地里做农活时还要把孩子背在背上，十分操劳。然而即便在这里，战争的阴影也存在着。男丁都被征入战场，村里只留下了老弱病小。作者注意到村口有一块地上立满了墓碑，是女眷为他们在战场牺牲的男性家属所立的。作者的回忆录是一部生活实录，她没有写到战场的刀光剑影，却用这种日常生活透露出的非正常状态来表现战争之残酷，反思战争对整个民族和社会的影响。

除此之外，作者经历了香港沦陷，这段个人史的记录是一份珍贵的历史见证。1941 年 12 月 8 日日本轰炸夏威夷的珍珠港，同一天香港九龙也被轰炸了，英国不得不无条件投降，香港被日本占领。由于作者的孩子刚刚出生，为了家庭团聚，她选择放弃回美，留在香港面对战争。她和家人躲到朋友家里，胆战心惊地等待日本军队的进入。日军进驻后，为了保护自己，他们只得躲到密室里，很少出来活动。日军一步一步地控制着整个香港，他们不得不偷偷转换躲藏地点。作者目睹了日军攻占香港时所实施的各种管制政策，通过详细的个人生活描写来反映在异族侵略的压抑中人的生存状态。比如，作者非常清晰地回忆起等待日军进来的心理活动，“在黑暗中我们听着雨滴落在街上的声音。它们重重地敲打着地面。这雨滴好重，我对自己说。哒哒哒哒。是行军的脚步声？但这是谁的脚呢？日本人的？他们不可能！不会这么快！英国人？不！不，上帝！他们要去哪儿？”（Soong 7）这种细腻的心理描写让读者感受到战争给人们带来的极度恐惧，以切身感受表达对战争的谴责。作者还写到被占之后香港满城皆兵、家宅门户紧闭、城市中满目疮痍的情形，由于粮食物资紧缺，路边到处都是因饥荒饿死的人，一队队的难民结伴逃回内陆家乡。关于第二次世界大战时期香港地区的回忆录并不多，作者记录了香港被占之后自己和朋友们的避难生活，以及香港沦陷后的民生状况，展现了日本占领香港时香港人的生存状态，弥补了空白。

作者还写到了日军的暴行。比如，她写到日军刚刚入驻香港时，还比较收敛，有一两个日本人白天来家里也并没有抢夺财物。不过没两天便暴露了非人的本性，不仅强占民宅，还抢夺妇女实施暴行。从这个方面看，作者作为战争受难者和见证者，她所见证的日军所为也是一份直接而有力的历史证词。

二

正如很多大屠杀回忆录研究者所认为的，虽然回忆录是一种非常个人化的写作形式，但很多这类回忆录都表达了强烈的道德意识和公共意识，出现了非个人化倾向。[①]研究者们普遍认为，这些回忆录的作者由于受到意识形态的束缚，不得不把被主流文化不能认可的内容剔除。当然我们不能责备这样的回忆录违背了自传写作的原则，格里莫尔认为，“受创者在写作回忆录的时候常常受到法律、道德、文化等外在条件的制约，这导致他们在进行自我表达时，有时候不得不选择部分沉默，而选择那些能引起普遍认同的内容表达”（Gilmore 128）。这种迎合主流文化的写作立场是国内的很多抗战书写所持有的，作者多是站在民族主义和英雄主义的角度，歌颂抗战所体现的民族精神，呼吁国民奋勇抗敌。比如前几年被重温的抗战回忆录《小难民自述》，作者写到逃难途中遇到了很多没有团结意识只顾自我保全的人，认为这是国人的劣根性，缺乏民族意识。这种回忆录的写作立场便是迎合了主流意识形态重集体而轻个人的道德标准。

现在也有学者对这种写作视角进行反思。肖向东曾论述了只关注政治性的战争写作的局限性：

> 战争文学如果一味地表现战争或单纯地阐释政治，而在主题深度的开掘上舍弃对“战争中的人”的审美关照，尤其是强调战争的政治主题并以“政治性”审美规范制约战争文学的写作等强制性做法，既易于造成对复杂的“战争人性”的遮蔽，影响战争文学在“能指”向度上的深刻掘进，又难以实现“战争美学”的目的，即在战争情境下从个体、他人、群体、民族、国家、人类的视野，透视战争个体的生命体验及其命运遭际，刻画战争与人的关系纽结，显示战争的本相与实质，反思战争的荒谬，进而达到控诉战争罪恶、呼吁和平、警示来者的文学预想。（肖向东 197）

宋谭秀红的回忆录正是体现了对民族主义的疏离。从回忆录的题目就可看出，作者将抗日战争放在第二次世界大战中来看，她所记录的中国不是“抗战时期”的中国，而是“战时”的中国。作者对战争的反思是站在一个世界的立场，取消了“抗日”这种政治性的审美，从人类悲悯的角度来关注战争带来的灾难。

作者在回忆战争和逃难经历时，十分关注战争中个人的生存状态。比如，写到香港被占领时的情形，作者那时经常看到人死在路上无人收尸。“路上经常躺着一个老头或老太，他们本该在福佑下寿终正寝。一旦他们的尸体被收走，另一个垂垂欲死的人会过来躺在空出的位置上。”（Soong 23）活着的人也无法有尊严地活着，路过日军关卡时，他们被迫像动物一样从栅栏里钻过。每每叙述至此，作者便格外激动，严苛的生存条件和紧张的物资还尚能克服，而战争环境中苟且的生命状态让她感到十分痛苦。在写重庆生活时，她回忆到一个片段：一个面容枯黄的妈妈在门前照顾一个本该上学的孩子。作者由此感叹："我非常反对战争，它是不正常的，它让成千上万的人变得更加贫穷、受忽略，他们完全不知道更好的生活是什么样。"（Soong 73）战争使人们不得不生活在一个异常的状态下，这种异化状态是不可修复的，即便赶走侵略者获得解放也无法扭转。

作者的美国成长背景还使得她格外注重个人隐私，而在战乱中个人的独立和尊严总是受到破坏。她不止一次提到在逃难中通过日军关卡，每次她都祈祷守关的日本人是个文明人，但结果都令她很恼火，因为他们会拿走她行李中一些值钱的东西。特别是从香港进入内陆时，每个人都要经过传染病检查，她认为这是"借着科学的名义，某一种族为了显示它的威权，让无助的受难者承受非现代方式的羞辱"（Soong 28）。

战争不仅造成生灵涂炭、家国沦丧，其泯灭人性、违背道德的罪恶是更为深重的。在非正常的环境中暴露出的荒谬人性和畸变人格是对人类文明和人道的挑衅，这才是战争带给人类最可怕的创伤。作者能够站在民族主义之外，从人道主义的普世性视野反思战争是深刻而难得的。

三

宋谭秀红对民族主义的疏离与她独特的个人身份也不无关系。首先，作者在民族身份上和本土中国人有所不同。和一般受难者不同，宋谭秀红作为归国华裔，在战时的受难经历除了让她肉体上忍受流亡之苦，精神上也有失根漂泊感。这种海外作者所独有的离散情结使得回忆录对战争的反思拥有独特的角度。作者的逃难过程，也是一次对故国进行生活体验、文化认知的过程，自身对家园的渴望和对和平的希冀融合在一起，形成一种独特的战争写作视角。

宋谭秀红夫妇是海外归国的华裔。第二次世界大战前，在海外的中国人就不断受到歧视和排斥。从 20 世纪 30 年代的报刊文章中可以看到，他们认为弱小的祖国不能保护他们在海外免受不公，所以他们想通过自己的力量建设一个富强现代的中国。夏威夷的中国人也是如此，他们在《新中国报》上发表了很多文章，思考如何改变中国贫穷积弱的现状，试图利用自己的西学背景为中国出力。他们中有的人作为孙中山和康有为的支持者走上革命的道路，有的人向中国捐资助学修路，还有一些人选择回到中国。从夏威夷回中国的人只是夏威夷华人的一小部分，但包括了很多高学历、有专业技能的人才。至于他们的回国原因，有一部分是为了建设新中国，还有一部分是在美国无法取得更高的社会地位。因此，1930 年到第二次世界大战期间，夏威夷兴起了一股回国浪潮。不过第二次世界大战后，中国不稳定的政治经济环境让他们望而却步，又回到了美国。宋谭秀红夫妇就是属于这样一小批夏威夷华人。他们选择回到中国，一方面是想寻根并且帮助建设现代的中国，另一方面也是受美国的历史环境所迫，尤其是当时美国遇到经济危机，本来就受歧视的华人更难找到工作。1939 年，宋谭秀红夫妇曾有机会回到檀香山，但是因为当时美国经济崩溃，他们根本没办法在美国找到工作，只好回到了中国。

由于文化背景的差异，虽然回到中国，作者却时时感到身份的差异，体会到被边缘化的苦恼。宋谭秀红在回忆录中多次表达了这种身份意识。在广东花县，她来到丈夫祖籍所在地，看到祠堂里祖先的牌位也心生感动，特别是因为血脉的关系，让她得以在战乱中有亲人可以依靠。战争环境加速了她中国化的转变。为了不被日本人发现真实身份，她在穿着打扮上向中国妇女靠拢。在广东的农村，她了解了很多客家习俗，也遵守规矩。她学中国妇女洗衣服，也会用中国的偏方来治病。这是作者为了在逃难中生存不得不在生活方式上做出的转变，但她还是没有办法抛除美国文化背景，在精神上仍是飘零的状态。比如，在广东，她极力想和客家孩子们交朋友，但他们很怕她，不敢跟她说话。她也无法像其他女性一样操持家务。这让她感觉格格不入，被边缘化了。作者曾表示："此刻，我很感激。我站在了亚洲的土地，我祖先的土地，在家里，虽然不是实际的家，我和周围的人都有一样的皮肤、眼睛和头发，但是我走路、说话和衣着看起来又是夏威夷—美国式的。"（Soong 3）在去重庆的火车上，她遇到了两个讲英语的白人，虽然她跟他们讲流利的英语，但他们却对她很冷漠。她很郁闷，觉得自己和那两个白人其实是一类人，也是有着美国国籍、以英语为母语的人。到了重庆，她终于和美国人坐在一起，但她发现自己在他们中间也显得格格不入，无论是衣着打扮还是生活理念，作者都不再是美国式的了。战争加速了宋谭秀红生活方式的中国化，但在精神上，她意识到自己处在两种文化之间的尴尬境地。

除此之外，作者的女性身份也让她的战争叙事处在远离主流文化的立场。作者在书的扉页上引用了自己1939年写作的一首诗：

> 女人，你坐在门外/他还没有从战场回家/他还没有走远/敌人比以前更靠近/女人们在等候，坐在家门外/女人，她坐在门外/他还没有从战场回家/他走远了/敌人打到了北城墙/女人们在门前哭泣/女人，她坐在门外/他还没有从战场回家/他永远离开了/谁的眼泪掉下来，掉下来/一个女人坐在门外。(Soong vi)

这首诗既是她自己的心理写照，也代表了很多被孤立在公共生活边缘的女性心声。作者写到很多跟她有着同样命运的女性，比如她的难友马贵贞，给她孩子做过保姆的王妈、阿九，广东农村的客家妇女们。战争造成了她们的家庭破裂，就她自己而言，也多次提到战争中和丈夫聚少离多的苦恼。

宋谭秀红是在双方父母的建议下，为了和丈夫团聚才离开夏威夷来到中国的。然而由于战地记者工作的特殊性，夫妻婚后有一大半时间都不能见面，而且丈夫总是穿梭在战场前线，随时都有生命危险。作者在回忆录中常常表达自己每天对丈夫安全的担忧，每次听到丈夫要离开便陷入恐慌。她多次提到自己是为了追随丈夫才来到中国，但丈夫的工作让他们的婚姻生活聚少离多让她非常痛苦。在她的叙事视野里除了战争所带来的恐惧阴影，支离破碎的家庭生活和独自面对危险的情形也常常让她陷入孤独无助。她没有多少参与公共生活的欲望，到了重庆后，她为了生存，应聘了美军驻中国军队的一个秘书职位，本也可以在战争年代发挥作用，但对宋谭秀红本人来说，她选择留在中国经受战争是为了和丈夫团聚，建立安稳的家庭，这种信念支撑着她度过战时的危难。当工作和家庭事务产生冲突时，她毫不犹豫选择了离职。

和渴望安定平安的家庭生活的太太不同，丈夫宋德和（Norman Soong）

则是公共生活的积极参与者。宋德和是第二次世界大战期间著名的战地记者。他写的通讯报道刊登在西方主流杂志上，将日本在中国所行的暴行公之于世，他在战场上的传奇经历也令他成为一个英雄般的人物。他选择留在中国是因为某种天赋使命感："如果我在战争一开始就离开中国，我的孩子会怎么想我？"（Soong x）香港被日本袭击后，他立刻选择深入前线。他于1942年发表过一篇《香港脱险记》（Flight from Hong Kong），写自己深入港九亲眼目睹的日军暴行，以及作为日军通缉的抗日人士，是如何乔装打扮混在难民中从香港逃脱的。宋德和的战地报道让国际人士了解了中国的抗战和日军暴行，为中国争取了国际同情。他在战场上九死一生，也是某种程度上的民族英雄。

当然，有很多灾难回忆录的描写对象都是宋德和式的人物，有强烈的意识形态和政治理想，企图在普遍的道德框架中构建自己的身份。这样的形象已经成为一种幸存者形象的符号。[②]而宋谭秀红的回忆录则表现了对主流话语的疏离，这和她的性别身份不无关系。当宋德和式的男性角色在政治给定的道德谱系和现实中构建自己的身份时，人们觉得这才是蒙难者应有的形象。而像宋谭秀红这样没有受到战争的直接戕害，只是战争所波及的弱者，甚至在和平时期就处在社会边缘的人，往往被主流话语所遗忘，

黄心村曾经指出："在文学批评中，家庭性被当作一套反话语，也就是说，作为一种话语表达，家庭性具有瓦解主导意识形态或男性统治范畴的潜能。正如诸多理论家所言，家庭性的表达是一个边缘群体的话语宣言。"（黄心村 44）作者为了家庭完整选择面对战争，并一路逃难，会为了家庭放弃在美国军队的工作，这在战时主流意识形态中是会遭到批判的。但家庭完整是宋谭秀红这类边缘女性所追求的生活理想。战争对社会、国家等公共空间造成破坏，代表个人空间的家庭也由此破裂。宋谭秀红对渴望重建家庭的书写，表达了边缘群体的生活状态，挑战了主流意识形态，是对个人生命价值的关照。这种边缘话语对我们反思历史有着重要的意义。

宋谭秀红处在民族和家庭的双重边缘状态，对故土的寻根和对家庭生活的渴望交织构成了她回忆录独特的话语体系。在战争中，被边缘化的人大多并不会选择出来发声，以致他们的经历也就逐渐被遗忘。但是历史中既有宋

德和式的英雄，也有宋谭秀红式的平凡弱者。宋谭秀红在回忆录中表达了自己作为平凡个体的心声，也写到了很多像她一样平凡众生，虽然没有表现出任何使命感，但也让我们看到了历史的另一面。我们不能说这样的话语是自私或狭隘的，相反，脱离意识形态的局限、关怀人性的写作同样是弥足珍贵的。这是通过另一种话语来反映战争的残酷和对个体生命造成的心灵创伤。

注释【Notes】

① 比较有代表性的论述包括：Cathy Caruth. *Unclaimed Experience*：*Trauma*，*Narrative*，*and History*；Leigh Gilmore. *The Limits of Autobiography*；Lawrence Langer. *Admitting the Holocaust*。这几位学者均探讨了大屠杀回忆录中作者的道德意识和公共意识。

② 关于这种幸存者形象的阐述见 Marianne Hirsch. "Surviving Images：Holocaust Photographs and the Work of Postmemory"。作者认为幸存者在叙说自己的劫难经历时，往往会迎合公共道德的要求。

引用文献【Works Cited】

Caruth，Cathy. *Unclaimed Experience*：*Trauma*，*Narrative*，*and History*. Baltimore：Johns Hopkins UP，1996.

Gilmore，Leigh. "Limit-Cases：Trauma，Self-Representation，and the Jurisdictions of Identity." *Biography* 24.1(2001)：128–139.

——. *The Limits of Autobiography*. Ithaca：Cornell UP，2001.

Hirsch，Marianne. "Surviving Images：Holocaust Photographs and the Work of Postmemory." *Yale Journal of Criticism* 14：1(2001)：5–37.

黄心村：《乱世书写——张爱玲与沦陷时期上海文学及通俗文化》，胡静译。上海：上海三联书店，2010 年。

[Huang Necole. *Women*，*War*，*Domesticity*：*Shanghai Literature and Popular Culture of the 1940s*. Trans. Hu Jing. Shanghai：Shanghai SDX Joint Publishing Company，2010.]

Langer，Lawrence. *Admitting the Holocaust*. New York：Oxford UP，1994.

Soong，Irma Tam. *Chinese American Refugee*，*A World War II Memoir*. Honolulu：Hawaii Chinese History Center Press，1984.

肖向东：《论中国当代战争文学——基于"战争文化"与"人学"视角的观察》，《江海学刊》2013 年第 6 期，第 195—202 页。

[Xiao Xiangdong. "A Theoretical Study on Chinese Modern War Literature—from the View of War Culture and Humanity." *Jianghai Academic Journal* 6(2013)：195–202.]

自传中的死亡书写与自我确立

——评朱利安·巴恩斯《无可畏惧》

黄莉莉

内容提要：朱利安·巴恩斯的《无可畏惧》是一部交融着死亡书写与自我确立的自传作品。作品表面看来很像一部散文随笔，但其中呈现出异常鲜明的自我讲述冲动，文本不仅涉及作者的家庭背景和成长经历，更重要的是，它表现出完整的自我确立过程，又因作者对死亡的敏感，这一过程与死亡书写紧密融合，从而形成这一独具特色的自传文本。

关键词：自传　死亡意识　死亡书写　自我确立

作者简介：黄莉莉，南京大学博士研究生，阜阳师范学院讲师，研究方向为英国当代文学和西方文论

Title: Death-Writing and Self-Confirmation in Autobiography: Julian Barnes' s *Nothing to Be Frightened of*

Abstract: Julian Barnes's *Nothing to Be Frightened of* is an autobiographical work that combines death-writing and self-establishment. The work looks like a collection of prose essays apparently; however there is indeed an unusual and obvious impulse of self-telling in the text which not only involves the author's family background and growing-up experience, but more importantly, shows a complete process of self-establishment. Meanwhile the text is closely related to the writing of death owing to the author's sensitivity to death and therefore this unique autobiographical text can be formed.

Keywords: autobiography, death consciousness, death-writing, self-establishment

Huang Lili is a doctoral candidate at Nanjing University and a lecturer at Fuyang Normal College. Her research centers on contemporary British literature and contemporary western literary theories. E-mail：kklily113@163.com.

朱利安·巴恩斯（Julian Barnes，1946— ），英国当代最具先锋性的写作者之一，其自传《无可畏惧》出版于2008年，彼时作者年过六十，多次获布克奖提名。巴恩斯的父母早在20世纪90年代离世，但他却始终不能释怀，自我讲述的根源往往来自身份焦虑和精神困境，看似一生顺遂的朱利安·巴恩斯彼时也陷入精神困境。首先，父母之死在其心中盘旋不去，引发身份危机。早年巴恩斯曾以想象父母死去的方式进入写作，而当父母真正离世，预想中的释然却并不能轻易到来，通过写作铸就的隔离之墙却被打破，在废墟中反思和父母的关系并重新找到写作的意义成为巴恩斯亟待解决的精神困境。其次，父母之死具象化了其长期以来的死亡幻象。巴恩斯从少年时期开始，就被“死亡恐惧”所困扰，他承认自己“一直打算创作一部以‘让我们来直接谈谈死亡吧’为开篇的作品”（Barnes 100），“无可畏惧”这一书名表面是作者劝解自己要直面死亡，隐含之意却是点出“死亡”最令人可怕之处——“虚空”（nothing）（此意来自巴恩斯所引用法国作家儒勒·列那尔（Jules Renard）之言：“那个更真、更精确、更充满意义的词儿就是‘虚空’。”（Barnes 100）。于是《无可畏惧》就成为这样一部交融着死亡书写与自我确立的自传。巴恩斯似乎有要打破“自传契约”的意图，譬如在作品中直接说：“这不是我的‘自传’，也不是对父母往事的追忆。”（Barnes 34）这来自他一贯的先锋作家特质：“我恨一部传记的开头是：‘他的曾祖父出生于……’然后接着是童年趣事之类的，我知道这些挺重要，可我就是不耐烦写这个。”（Guignery 63）同时他也刻意打破线性叙事传统，文本因此具有极明显的散文随笔风格，但是作品中表达出的自我讲述冲动异常鲜明，不仅涉及作者的家庭背景和成长经历，更重要的是，它表现出完整的自我确立的意图，又因作者的敏锐性和独特性，这一过程被他自己心中盘旋不去的死亡意识所缠绕，从而形成这一独具特色的自传文本。

一、自传中的死亡书写

巴恩斯的死亡书写肇始于小说，处女作《伦敦郊区》即被安吉拉·卡特称为“拥有成熟的死亡观”（Guignery and Roberts 162），随着年纪渐长，他对此主题关注更甚，在《无可畏惧》这部自传中，他终于能得偿所愿地直接书写自我和死亡的关系。这种书写从各个层面展开，并与作者的家庭背景和成长经历交融在一起，读者可以感受到作者备受死亡意识折磨的成长历程。

首先，将死亡恐惧作为一种身心感受去描写。巴恩斯坦言自己是一个“极其怕死”的人，面对死亡，他首先感到的是一种弥漫身心的恐惧。这种恐惧起始于对“必死性”（mortality）的认知，巴恩斯对此做了充分描述：“就像在一个陌生的旅馆，那儿有一个闹钟，被前一位客人定了时，于是，在一个邪恶的时间点，你突然从睡梦中被抛出，落入一片黑暗，残酷地意识到置身于一个被临时租借的世界。”（Barnes 23）他认为“死亡觉醒”这种说法已不能表达出那种“特定的漫天遍地的恐慌”，只能借用法国批评家查理·德波（Charles du Bos）所言之“死神的闹钟”来形容。这种来势凶猛的死亡恐惧开始于13岁，在此后的岁月，它几乎每个夜间都会突然来袭：“从皮肤上的针刺痛感，到大脑一片空白的恐慌，从陌生旅馆的粗鲁闹钟声，到弥漫城市的刺耳警报声。”（Barnes 65）直至写作自传之时，巴恩斯也未能视之如常，它依然新鲜而强烈：“就在几天以前的一个夜里，它又突然来临，突然被刺入意识，清醒，孤独，决然孤独，拳头捶在枕头上，嘴里喊着：‘不！不！不！’止不住地嚎哭，可怕的时刻，完全被淹没。”（Barnes 126）对于这种反应，作者表示感到“羞耻”却无法自控，因为那是一种“强烈的精神上的痛楚”。

除此之外，作者还产生各种死亡幻觉和死亡想象，早在少年时代，他就有过灵魂离开身体的体验，成年之后他更是经常想象自己的死亡——最好的可能性与最坏的可能性。最好的死亡的想象是被医生确认绝症，“有一段足够长的时间，有着足够的清醒，可以让我写成那最后一本书——那本我所有关于死亡的想法的书”（Barnes 100）。因此这本自传的写作几乎是巴恩斯对其心目中理想死亡过程的预演，然而他清楚地知道："不，事情不会是这样的，所以最好还是先把书写出来。"（Barnes 101）最坏的死亡想象则极为可怕："我最坏的想象中往往包含着禁闭、水以及一段明知必死无疑却必须忍受的时间。"（Barnes 100）轮船失事溺水，飞机失事溺水，被抢匪捆绑着塞进车厢扔进水里，被鳄鱼拖走扔进洞里……最糟糕的可能性在于："我们倾向于想象我们死得顺畅而清醒，知道一切是怎么回事……但是假如疼痛和恐惧依旧，又加上了混乱呢？你不知道自己是谁，身在何处，是死是活。"（Barnes 101）就这样，巴恩斯在想象中无限接近和体验死亡，对他而言，死亡的可怕之处不仅在于肉体的痛苦，更是自我意识的消失，因此在混沌中死去是最为悲惨的，而最好的死亡过程必须是清醒的，而且是最大程度的清醒，能够对死亡本身有着明确的意识和自主思考——在对死亡的书写中走向死亡。

除了耽于死亡想象，巴恩斯还不自觉地去咀嚼现实中的死亡。在访谈中，他明确地说这本书的写作起点就是父母的死亡，而自传出版之时，距父母去世已有十余年时间。在此期间他并未让父母之死沉寂于内心，而是反复回忆和体味，这在自传中深有体现，譬如开篇不久就写到母亲的葬礼，读之宛如昨日，细节之处更是写到母亲死后侧卧的身姿、微斜的嘴角、整齐的发丝、"我"印在她脸颊的一吻、葬礼的音乐、历历在目的遗物，等等。巴恩斯和母亲的关系并不融洽："在她死时，我和她的关系已经恶化并继续恶化着。"（Guignery and Roberts 166）在自传中，他并未美化其形象，但却直面她的死亡带给他的情感和思想冲击。总之，巴恩斯对于死亡有着独特的敏感，他充分体验死亡给他带来的各种身心感受，在想象中，在现实中，在自己，在他人，这些感受成为他个人精神生活中不可忽视的一部分，也是他在自传中反复去诉说和强调的。

其次，将死亡作为理性认知对象去思考。强烈而持久的死亡恐惧促使作者不断对其进行思考，而最初的思考只能借助阅读展开。少年时期的巴恩斯在现实中无法找到引导者——无宗教传统的家庭、无从交流的父母和兄长、思想尚未开化的同龄人，他只能从书和艺术中寻找答案。在自传里，他这样宣称："这本书里有大量的作家，一些是作曲家，大部分都已死去，大部分都是法国人……这些艺术家——这些死去的艺术家——是我日常的伴侣，也是我的先辈，他们是我真正的血脉来源。”（Barnes 38）这些“先辈”对死亡有着同样的敏感，他们的见解安抚了少年的恐慌并引导他走向更理智的死亡观。大量的引述使作品几乎成为读书随笔，但是这些引述和巴恩斯的家庭背景并列，作为其成长的另一条重要线索——精神的家园的血统共同构成了自传的主体。譬如耽于思考死亡的法国作家蒙田，是最早“尝试用一种现代的、成熟的、非宗教性的态度接受这不可避免的结局”的作家，具有“恬淡的书卷气，可抚慰人心”（Barnes 42）的气质，在他身上，巴恩斯找到了最可接受的面对死亡的姿态——“现代的”“非宗教的”“书卷气的”，而他那些精神上的“亲人”们，几乎无一例外地拥有此种相同的气质和相似的死亡观。

用理性对抗死亡这一过程中最大的挑战是如何无条件接受“必死性”。在这个问题上，巴恩斯遇到的最大诱惑是宗教（基督教），基督教所允诺的“不死”与“重生”对于极度怕死的人来说是一个大诱饵：“为何不能有重生？如果可以，我想要完全不同的生活，体验另一种失望和悔恨。那是完全值得期待的。如果有来生。”（Barnes 63）如果接受，就一劳永逸地在精神上勾销了“必死性”，但是对于巴恩斯而言，接受“上帝”这件事本身隐含着极大的矛盾性，他对此反复进行思考：首先，信仰在信众和哲学家（譬如笛卡尔和维特根斯坦）那里都有可能沦为赌博般的功利行为，而这是背离信仰的真谛的；其次，信仰上帝的根本又在于对尘世的弃绝，这是与其热爱生活的本性相悖的——“我从未真正地否定生命，一本小说，一个朋友，一场足球赛事，都可以重新激活我的生趣”（Barnes 61）；第三，即使放任自己对“不死”和“重生”的想象，接受上帝的存在，“我也意识到我所怀念的那个神可能看起来会更像一个无关宗教的自我沉溺的私人概念的神”（Barnes 114）。由此可见，巴恩斯在自传中展现出一个用理性竭力对抗死亡恐惧，并拒绝用宗教带来解脱的自我形象。

而这种对自我形象的期待，与在文化血脉上“我的祖先”确是一致的——在否认或者说拒绝了宗教的方式后，只能采取一种“现代的”“非宗教的”“书卷气的”方式去面对死亡：在蒙田那里，是“因为我们不能战胜死亡，所以最好的办法就是将其铭记心间，时刻不忘咀嚼品尝死亡之味”（Barnes 42）；在福楼拜那里，是“要注视脚下深渊，保持冷静”（Barnes 24）；在儒勒·列那尔那里，是要对死亡的本质时时保持清醒的认知，时刻面对可怕的“虚空”；对于肖斯塔科维奇来说，是“我们不能让死亡恐惧在不期之间爬上来，我们必须让恐惧变成熟面孔，一个方法就是书写他”（Barnes 26）。这些态度的共通之处，其一是保持对死亡的敏感性。人不怕死往往并非出于勇气，而是思维的怠惰或对生命的麻木，所以巴恩斯说：“除非你知道而且感觉到良辰美景有其时，美酒会酸掉，玫瑰也会枯萎烂成一滩臭水——不然那些愉悦和乐趣就没有了语境，而只是通向坟墓的漫漫长路。”（Barnes 126）其二是要对死亡进行表达，也即儒勒·列那尔所言“只有面对死亡，我们才能变得书卷气”（Barnes 26）。巴恩斯反复谈论19世纪福楼拜、屠格涅夫、左拉等人定期在“马格尼聚餐”（Magny Dinner）中讨论死亡以及20世纪20年代芬兰音乐家西贝柳斯参加的“柠檬桌子”（Lemon Table）死亡主题聚会，参与者都是无宗教信仰的文化人，他们用讲述、书写或艺术创作让死亡成为可以触摸之物。这也成为巴恩斯从前人那里继承而来的一种对抗死亡的有效方式。

第三，探讨死亡与写作之间的关系。对于巴恩斯而言，如果说死亡最可怕之处在于“虚空”，写作就是一条可以直抵“虚空”的蹊径。“虚空”首先表现为“自我”的消失。就动机而言，写作可以对抗“虚空”，将“自我”延续至有限生命之外，巴恩斯在自传中想象某人对他这样说：“你编织故事，以让你的名字，让你个性的某些难以定义之处，能够在你死后继续存在，这种期望给你带来某种安慰。”（Barnes 66）他无法否认自己存在这种潜在动机的可能性，虽然他也意识到这种想法的有限性：“所有的作家最后都会被忘记，整个人类最后也会消亡。”（Barnes 66）然而即便如此，写作依然是对抗人类有限性的有效方式之一，但是它同时导致一种无可解脱的循环。死亡恐惧根本上来源于自我意识——清醒意识到自我的存在，因而难以割舍，而用写作（同样来源于自我意识）对抗死亡带来了一种悖谬的结果：“不管作家的美学宗旨如何——自传写作还是作者隐退，为了完成作品，‘自我’一定会得到强化和定义。"（Barnes 88）被强化的"自我"更加难以接受"弱化"和"消亡"。因此，写作并不能抚平或击退死亡恐惧，它只是逐渐建构起一个更加明确的恐惧死亡的"自我"——更清楚地意识到必死性，意识到"虚空"的必然降临，意识到恐惧本身。写作由是确立了一种基本的生命方式——向死而生/写（这其中，写作是主动性的选择，死亡恐惧更是主动性的选择）——而这就是巴恩斯这类所谓"极度怕死"的写作者的真实面目。他在自传中设想过一个交易，假若有一种新发明的设备，可以特定消除大脑中的死亡恐惧，但同时也会消除写作的欲望，他如此回应想象中的这种诱惑："我肯定会考虑一下的……但是我希望我最好还是拒绝。"（Barnes 66）

而让死亡成为写作对象，就是时刻体验"虚空"和"边界"的存在，体验福楼拜所谓的"注视脚下深渊，保持冷静"的感受。首先，关于死亡恐惧，巴恩斯认可肖斯塔科维奇的看法："这是一种最强烈的情感，也可能是人类最深沉的情感。"（Barnes 26）死亡恐惧虽然带来痛苦，却也带来对生命本身的珍视，但它并不是一种策略性的选择："我不能说直面死亡，让我变得更聪明、更严肃或什么别的。我只能说，如果不经常性地意识到死亡，可能也不能很好地品味生命。就像在柠檬汁里加一勺盐，更够味。但是我真的认为我那些不去想死亡的朋友们的生活就缺滋少味了吗？不。"（Barnes 65）它只是使得生命体验变得更真实、更复杂，而这对于一个写作者而言是无比珍贵的，虽然并不是绝对必要。其次，"注视脚下深渊，保持冷静"也是一种最有利于写作的姿态。在福楼拜的原意中"冷静"并不是作家们的真相，而是大众对他们的想象和期待，但是它同时赋予作家一种自我身份感。在这种身份幻觉中，艺术家或写作者一面是貌似冷静地驻足崖边，一面内心波澜汹涌不可自抑，他将自己推到真相的边缘，看似勇敢实则恐惧万分地伸出自己的触角，这种看似错位或矛盾的状态实际却暗合艺术创作最核心的秘密。于是，那些"时刻咀嚼品尝死亡之味"的人，实际上是在采撷艺术之珍果，这就是巴恩斯在自传中通过反复讲述而表达出的——"写作就像是与死神共舞，虽然危险甚至痛苦，却也令人迷醉，不可自拔"（Barber 47），艺术创作的迷醉反而填补了死亡恐惧带来的痛苦。

二、死亡书写中的自我确立

正像书名所体现的，这是一本直接以“死亡”为主题的书——满足了作者一直以来的写作愿望，但同时，它也是一部侧重于自我精神成长的自传，在其中，可以看到一位写作者思考死亡这一终极问题时的精神探索和挣扎，也可以看到一个写作者的“自我”如何挣脱死亡的威胁和束缚而逐渐得以确立的过程。

首先，作者剖析了其面对父母之死时的自我意识，从而更明确其在精神上的独立性。作品以父母之死带来的复杂感受为开篇，其后逐步呈现家庭中的矛盾关系。巴恩斯 1946 年出生于英国中东部莱斯特的一个教师之家，后迁至伦敦郊区，其父母均是法语教师，巴恩斯和哥哥先后进入牛津大学，其兄长乔纳森·巴恩斯后成为日内瓦大学的哲学教授。父母在文化上保守刻板：“在我的童年时代，宗教、政治和性这三个话题在家里是从来不被允许出现的。”（Barnes 5）子女被寄予中产阶级家庭的普遍期望：“我们理所当然成绩好，上大学，工作，结婚，生孩子。”（Barnes 158）其性格严谨而冷漠：“他们最鲜明的性格特征——这可不是时代特色——是完全，几乎完全，缺乏感情，在任何时候，都缺乏公开的情感表达。”（Barnes 158）因此家庭缺乏文化氛围和情感交流，兄弟二人在成年以后都选择逃离：“我的哥哥自从上了大学后就再也没有回过家。”（Guignery and Roberts 105）后来乔纳森的住所在法国，银行账户在英国，工作在瑞士，成为“一个生活在‘无处之地’（nowhere）的人。”（Barnes 155）而巴恩斯自己的逃离则是隐藏在写作生涯中的：“我刚开始写作的时候，给自己定了一个原则，一个心理上的前提——我应该写得好像我父母已经死去了一样。”（Barnes 66）

在艺术道路的选择上，巴恩斯受到家庭更多的排斥，大学毕业后，他曾尝试过教师和编辑工作，甚至一度考取了律师资格证，他的作家之路“开始得犹疑又艰难”（March 60）。他厌恶布尔乔亚式的仅仅将艺术作为装饰物的观念，小说处女作《伦敦郊区》出版之初，巴恩斯还很在意父母的反应：“我担心他们会认为我在否定童年，虽然我并没有，但是它就是在制造这样的误解。”（Holland 16）结果父亲委婉地挑出其语法错误，母亲则明确地说受不了那些“污言秽语的轰炸”：“我可能会给我的朋友们看看封面，内容就算了。”（Barnes 161）母亲从小就认为巴恩斯“过于爱幻想”，她谈起巴恩斯兄弟：“我的一个儿子（指乔纳森·巴恩斯）写的书我想读却读不懂，而另一个儿子（指朱利安·巴恩斯）写的书我读得懂，却不想读。”（Barnes 161）这使巴恩斯意识到自己陷入了一种困境：“在大部分写作者那里，某种层面上，都有着一种退化的取悦父母的渴望。你可能忽视他们，冒犯他们，甚至刻意写出让他们憎恨的书，但是某一部分的自我依然在经历不能取悦他们的痛苦。”（Barnes 161）他甚至在一部以父母为原型的短篇小说《水果笼子》里刻意地“夸大了母亲的疯狂和罪过”——一个小说写作者对自己母亲的报复，虽然他一再提醒自己“不要利用和滥用他们作为题材，也别想着去冒犯他们和讨好他们。”（Barnes 162）

这些矛盾使巴恩斯和父母在精神上非常疏离，死亡一度拉近了他们之间的关系。巴恩斯详细描述父亲弥留之际嘶哑着说再见的情形、他蜷曲的指甲和他那种在精神上完全被“耗尽”后而自甘“放弃”的状态，他也详细描述了一向强势而自信的母亲中风之后的懊恼以及随后到来的那种既清醒又糊涂的痛苦状态，他对父母努力“死于性格之中”（die in character）表达敬意。然而巴恩斯体验到的并非仅仅是丧亲之痛——而是“死亡”本身，在母亲死后，他并没有为尊者诲般展开温情的回忆，而是更加清醒地对其做不乏苛刻的评价：“四十六年的生命，都是这样，母亲在那里，唠唠叨叨，组织话题，大惊小怪，掌控局面。”（Barnes 164）对于父亲，他也一度为其面对生死的麻木态度而感到困惑：“为什么，你不仅仅表现得缺乏勇气，还缺乏人类最基本的好奇心？”（Barnes 153）巴恩斯质疑其父母的生命存在极大的缺陷：“如果我的父母变得更有感情，更坦诚，更感性，他们是否就能死得更好一些？”（Barnes 221）由此可见，巴恩斯既没有逃避父母死亡所带来的复杂感受，同时也仍然坚持面对那条难以跨越的鸿沟，他追求一种和父母全然不同的更富精神价值的生活，虽然其结果并不可预料：“或许，一个人越想逃离自己的父母，他们最后死的姿态就会越相似。”（Barnes 222）但这一坚持的态度正是巴恩斯在《无可畏惧》这部自传中所要坚定展现出来的。

其次，即使对死亡怀着强烈的恐惧，作者依然在上帝与艺术之间做了坚定的选择，进一步明确其小说写作者身份。虽然在进入牛津大学后，巴恩斯曾坚定地宣称自己是“一个快乐的无神论者”，但是这种“快乐”有其代价，尤其因为巴恩斯对于死亡有着特别的敏感，而这带来了他对宗教复杂的观感：“如果我为从上帝老人家那里解脱的自由而快乐，就要为其后果而受苦。没有上帝，没有天堂，没有来生；那样，死亡，不管看起来多么遥远，它在议事日程上的次序就不同了。”（Barnes 18）随着年龄渐长，他的宗教立场变得更难以清晰界定：“我在二十岁时称自己是无神论者，到了五十和六十岁，我称自己为不可知论者。原因不是我懂得更多了，而是我更加知道自己懂得太少了。我们怎么能这么确信我们都知道了呢?”（Barnes 22）这既是对母亲强势控制的反思，直至去世前一年，她还试图施加影响，看到巴恩斯在电视节目中谈论宗教便致电指责：“到底是怎么回事？你就像你父亲一样……”（Barnes 7）更是来自长期对终极问题的思考，他反复阅读前人对“上帝”和“死亡”问题的探讨，同时在作品中通过人物进行表达，譬如在其小说《凝视太阳》中，主人公格里高尔曾经罗列十几条关于是否信仰上帝的后果的可能性。这种不可知论倾向，不代表他像自己笔下的柯南道尔爵士那般走向神秘主义和回魂术，而是试图超越二元论对更广大的不可知领域表达敬畏的一种方式，也是巴恩斯对于宗教情怀和宗教审美之中合理性的一种认同，即《无可畏惧》的开篇所表达的“我不相信上帝，但是我想念他”（Barnes 1）。

巴恩斯成名后曾多次公开谈论自己的死亡恐惧，而收到很多宗教信众的皈依劝解，对此，巴恩斯往往不无遗憾地表示拒绝。在《无可畏惧》中他花了大量篇幅来谈论此问题，首先，在经验层面他无法接受一个人格化上帝的存在，其次，在理性层面，他更倾向于用思考和写作直面恐惧，并在其中发现这种恐惧本身对于生命的价值。与此同时，他清醒地意识到人类的经验和理性都有着自身的限度，而对这种限度之外的可能性抱持敬畏之心，因此他不愿意像母亲一样轻易地宣称无神论是唯一的真相。不信教，同时也不决然否定——巴恩斯通过讲述家庭和自我的宗教经验，确立起这样一种个性化的不可知论态度，而这也是他精神世界的基础。同时他也认识到，在他成长的时代，宗教早已被大众所抛弃："我觉得我的家庭连续几代人对宗教的态度典型地反映了宗教在英国的现状。"（Guignery and Roberts 166）但是他拒绝随波逐流，不经思考、毫无留恋就轻易地放弃信仰，信仰与不信仰都必须是经过个体独立思考之后的慎重选择。巴恩斯曾引用某学者对维特根斯坦的评论："他不是一个信教的人，但是在他身上，某种意义上存在着宗教的可能性。"（Barnes 22）这句话其实也可以用于巴恩斯自身。

20岁的巴恩斯在宣称自己是无神论者的同时，也称自己是"唯美主义者"，他引用泰奥菲尔·戈蒂耶（Théophile Gautier）的诗句"上帝死了，但诗歌复活了一切"，以表达对艺术的绝对推崇。但是，巴恩斯并不是真正意义上的"唯美主义者"，他认为艺术之美可能并非仅仅来源于其形式，譬如在面对宗教艺术时的质疑："我们可以把宗教从宗教艺术中抹去吗？仅仅从色彩、结构、声响去欣赏他们，把那些内在的意义仅仅看作童年记忆一样遥远的东西？或者这是个无意义的问题，因为我们并没有选择？"（Barnes 54）也因此，巴恩斯对宗教态度矛盾："怀念上帝，对我而言，最为关切的，是在面对宗教艺术时，我怀念那种潜在的动机和信念。对于不信者而言，始终有一个悬而未决的假想——假如一切是真的，那将会怎样。想象在大教堂听莫扎特的《安魂曲》……会不会增加一些不一样的热情？"（Barnes 54）宗教与艺术的结合，即在形式美中赋予了更宏大的意义，巴恩斯认为这为艺术带来了更多的可能性。他所怀念的，是充满了意义和严肃性的曾经的世界，他引用菲利普·拉金的诗句："有些人永远会感到震惊/他内在的饥渴会更厉害"，表达出自己也存在一种"内在的饥渴"——一种感受到意义缺失后面对艺术、面对世界的空虚感。

吊诡的是，在《无可畏惧》中，一向被冠以"后现代主义者"的巴恩斯，不断表达着自己对于意义和宏大叙事的渴望，然而，这与其说是一种矛盾，不如说是某些所谓的"后现代主义者"们更真实的写照。巴恩斯以为，即使除去宗教光环，《圣经》依然"是一部最好的、伟大的小说"（Barnes 57），而“小说”对于巴恩斯而言，又是真和美的载体：“它要讲述一个美丽的精致的巧妙的谎言，而其中包裹着坚实的、闪闪发光的真相。”（Observer 15）因此宗教与艺术存在某种相通之处，欣赏艺术的先决条件是在心理上要悬置所有的“不相信”：“它们只是纸上的文字、舞台上的演员和帆布上的颜料，这些人物从不存在、不可能存在，或者只是存在过的复制品，一个短暂的幻影而已。但是当我们欣赏时，我们相信：爱玛活过，爱玛死去。哈姆雷特杀死了雷阿提斯等等。”（Barnes 78）巴恩斯认为，这种对“不相信的”悬置就离信仰行为不远了，他因此而得出结论：“宗教就是小说写作者最初的最伟大的创作。”（Barnes 78）小说写作就是意义建构的过程，而身为小说家的巴恩斯也由此将自我的文化身份推向了更难以言说的境地——在后现代主义的表象下暗中折返一种A.S.拜雅特所言的“复杂的怀旧之境”（Byatt 34）。

第三，在对死亡的阅读和书写中，作者进一步明确自己在文化上的血脉渊源。巴恩斯是典型的书斋型作家，他将大量的时间用于阅读和写作，并在其中建构自己的精神世界。在《无可畏惧》中，巴恩斯不断引用其“没有血缘的亲人们”对于死亡、上帝、生命、艺术之美等问题的观点，以建立与他们之间的精神连接，为自己确立了文化上的血脉渊源，他也对自己的这种所为有着清醒而坚定的意识：“这种血统也许不是那么直接，也许没有什么证据，但是不管怎样，我就是愿意这么宣称。”（Barnes 38）这些“亲人们”身上最初吸引巴恩斯的是他们的死亡观，而之后，让他甘愿追随的是一种更为根本的东西——一种在文化裂缝中竭力保持自我精神独立的写作者姿态。譬如福楼拜和列那尔——巴恩斯着墨最多的两位——都是在19世纪50年代的法国社会庸俗的文化氛围中从典型的小资产阶级家庭中破茧而出的写作者，他们都坚定地抨击彼时虚伪的宗教道德并决然放弃信仰，他们在艺术和审美上都超前而精确地触碰到下一个世纪，同时他们又深深扎根在自己的时空里去观察和描写——这些是他们卓越艺术的根本，也是他们直面自我生死的力量之源。他们是最早一批不约而同地以“向死而生/写”为生活准则的那些人，他们不再像前人或同时代庸人那样活在上帝天然的庇护之下，他们也没有像20世纪的先锋派们那样断然去打碎和消解一切。在他们那里，巴恩斯似乎找到了精神归属和自我定位。

儒勒·列那尔似乎是在精神上与巴恩斯最为亲近的人，巴恩斯自传中也展现了列那尔的生平，这位百年前的作家的历史，似乎成为巴恩斯生活经历和精神世界的另一个模版，在彼此的相互映射中，巴恩斯进一步确立了自我的存在方式。列那尔长达二十多年坚持写作，成就了一部长达千页的巨著《日记》，其文字呈现出罕见的真诚和对人性的深刻洞察，即使在讲述自己悲惨的童年际遇时，他依然拒绝以自怜之心回顾过去，反而批判了浪漫化的雨果式孩童形象："孩子不过是一种小小的、有必要存在的小动物，他身上的人性并不比猫更多。"（Barnes 47）他热爱大自然，却摒弃感伤主义，只是精确地去描绘。对于人性，他采取同样的对策——保持距离、观察、写出来，自然是辛辣讽刺的，他笔下的事物往往浸透了自己特异的审美。纪德这样抱怨列那尔的作品："那不是一条河，是一个酿酒厂。"（Barnes 48）但巴恩斯尤为欣赏特种特异性，他意识到这种特异性来源于一种绝对独立的精神——列那尔行事特立独行，公开质疑上帝的存在，在小说盛行的年代写散文，所以萨特说他其实处在"所有更为现代性的尝试的源头上"（Barnes 48），这也是巴恩斯自己一直向往并追求的艺术理想。

在列那尔那里，他尤其感受到一种由真诚言说自我而带来的力量。列那尔关于上帝的不敬言论、列那尔对于面对父母和兄弟死亡的复杂感受、列那尔对自己的死亡的看法，都让巴恩斯极为着迷，他看到列那尔的家庭"就像我的家庭的更极端和更戏剧化的版本"："母亲的喋喋不休和偏执，父亲的安静无聊……列那尔对母亲不能忍受，我也是，和她在一起，会感觉整个精神、整个生命、所有的时光都被吸走了，永远不能解脱……列那尔的父亲对他的处女作不置一词，我的父母处心积虑地表达了对我的处女作的否定。"（Barnes 159）列那尔深刻批判自己的家庭："对布尔乔亚们来说，最可怕的东西就是布尔乔亚们自己。"（Barnes 160）对无力面对自我而庸碌生活的亲人们表达痛恨，而这一点，这正是巴恩斯对自己的家庭最大的诟病。巴恩斯由此而获得自我书写的启示，这种书写的基础是在精神上保持独特性，对死亡保持敏锐的觉知，对生活保持批判态度，而这种书写带来的力量即便不能抹去死亡和死亡恐惧，也成就了一种独具力量和魅力的存在方式。

三、结　语

《无可畏惧》是这样一部奇特的自传，它看来散逸不羁地“充满了书籍、轶事和观念”（Groes 104），却完整地勾勒出一个写作者的世界——他直面自我生命中最敏感和脆弱之处，感受、思考并书写那挥之不去又深入骨髓的死亡恐惧，同时他竭力超脱出现实环境和父母的影响，致力于找到真正可抚慰自我的“无血缘的亲人”。在这一过程中，他逐渐完成自我确立——一个保持精神独立并用写作为自我存在赋予意义的小说写作者，对于一向被冠以“后现代”的朱利安·巴恩斯而言，这好像是一种并不那么“后现代”的形象，但却似乎又暗中通向所有他那些独具先锋性的作品的更根本之处。巴恩斯曾在《福楼拜的鹦鹉》中用“网”来形容传记，可捕物的线索是它的一个维度，遍布的“洞眼”是它的另一个维度，也可以说，在这部给自己写的传记中，一个作家的真实自我既纠结于这些丝线上，也游走于这些洞眼之间。

引用文献【Works Cited】

Barber, L. "Julian Barnes Dances around Death". *Telegraph*. 5 March, 2008:47.

Barnes, Julian. *Nothing to Be Frightened of*. London: Vintage Book, 2009.

——. "Interview by Vanessa Guignery." *Sources*. 8(Spring, 2000):59-72.

Byatt, A.S. "People in Paper House." *The Contemporary English Novel*. Ed. Malcolm Bradbury. London: Edward Arnodl, 1979: 6-36.

Groes, Sebastian, and Peter Childs. *Julian Barnes*. London: Continuum Books, 2011.

Guignery, Vanessa, and Ryan Roberts. *Conversations with Julian Barnes*. Jackson: University Press of Mississippi, 2009.

Holland, Caroline. "Escape from Metroland." *Islington Gazette*. 31 July, 1981:16.

Kota, Rahul. *Life and Word of Julian Barnes*. London: LBP, 2012.

March, Michae. "Into the Lion's Mouth: A Conversation with Julian Barnes." *The New Presence*, 1997:56-62.

Observer. "He's Turned Towards Python." *Guardian* 30. Aug. 1998. Web. 13 Jun.2018. (https://www.theguardian.com/books/1998/aug/30/fiction.julianbarnes.)

为她们立传：生命书写视域中的《我是女兵，也是女人》

朱 研

内容提要：诺贝尔奖得主阿列克西耶维奇以其口述实录见证和保存了苏联和后苏联时代许多普通女性的生命故事。在其女性生命书写中，女性的个体经历不仅折射出以往被男性声音遮蔽的时代和民族的历史，也作为一种生命本体显示出其独立的价值。《我是女兵，也是女人》这部作者以女性生命之声成就的文献文学处女作就充分体现出对女性主体的探寻。复调风格将女兵们流动的主体性刻画得淋漓尽致，集体叙述为她们构建和巩固社群，书写女性自己的历史提供了有力的平台，对女性战争体验的捕捉则产生超越性的审美价值，呈现出女性生命的夺目辉光。

关键词：阿列克西耶维奇　女性生命书写　《我是女兵，也是女人》

作者简介：朱研，湖南大学文学院讲师，主要从事比较文学与当代外国文学研究。近期发表了《阿列克西耶维奇的创伤书写：以〈来自切尔诺贝利的声音〉为中心》（《当代外国文学》，2016 年第 2 期）等。

Title: Writing Lives for Women: A Case Study of S.A. Alexievich's *War's Unwomanly Face*

Abstract: In the form of oral history, the Nobel laureate S.A. Alexievich witnessed and preserved the life stories of many Soviet and post-Soviet females. In her women's life writings, the personal experience of females not only reflects the history of the nation that was obscured by male voices, but also shows their independent values as individual lives. *War's Unwomanly Face* which is explicitly devoted to women in wartime fully reflects the self-exploration of the female subject. As the writer's first documentary work, the polyphonic style, the narration of group lives, and the aesthetic characteristics of such prose make unique contribution on women's life writing.

Keywords: S.A. Alexievich, Women's Life Writing, *War's Unwomanly Face*

Zhu Yan is Lecturer in College of Chinese Language and Literature at Hunan University, China. Her research interests are comparative literature and world Literature. She is the author of "S. A. Alexievich's Trauma Writing: *Voices from Chernobyl*: A Case Study", in *Contemporary Foreign Literature*, 2(2016). E-mail: Zhuyan1104@126.com.

在 2001 年出版的《生命书写百科全书：自传和他传的形式》一书中，英国学者玛格丽塔·乔利曾经指出，"life writing"（生命书写）这一在 18 世纪就出现的术语，自 20 世纪 80 年代以来在学术领域得到了更广泛的接受，它包含书写自己和他人生平的作品，具有跨文类的开放性与包容性。视觉艺术、图传、口述史、证词等用来描写和记录"真实的人"的文类都应纳入"生命书写"的范围（Jolly ix）。如其所说，自 20 世纪 80 年代始，聚焦真实人生与人性的生命书写日渐繁荣，不仅吸引了大量读者，也成为文学批评、文化研究、女性研究、后殖民研究、心理学、人类学等西方学术领域探讨的热点。特别是在后结构主义理论崛起的背景下，如何对那些被权力主宰的宏大叙事有系统地边缘化的妇女、底层、不同族裔、性向、能力的弱势群体进行全新的书写成为一项严峻的课题，而口述史、民族志、博客、电子邮件等非传统传记的生命书写文类则成为作家与学界开拓与关注的新领域。

依据后现代论述，女性也并不是一种生物或自然的独立个体，而是由权力和知识所塑造的，是从她们的文化处境中生成的，她们的生命故事也同样不可为一种霸权主导或主流意识所产生的宏大叙述统摄，而是具有多重性、复数性、演进性的。女性口述作为女性生命书写的一种重要形式，通过重现以往被忽视的女性的声音和视角，以及她们在历史上的主观能动性，来揭示形成社会性别的历史过程，其目的就是要去捕捉女性经验的社会建构意义，及其所蕴含的主体性。

2015 年的诺贝尔文学奖得主阿列克西耶维奇就是一位擅长以基于口述实

录的“文献文学”书写苏联与后苏联时代普通女性生命故事，构建其心灵与情感编年史的作家。正如作家自己所说，她的写作要为这些淹没在宏大历史叙事中的女性“建造一座感情的圣殿”（阿列克谢耶维奇 413）。她们有的在卫国战争中惊恐地度过童年，有的为抗击侵略者勇敢地投身战场，有的被无助地卷入阿富汗战争，有的在切尔诺贝利核灾难中经历爱与死亡，还有的在告别了苏联的新时代后依然彷徨、迷惘。在阿列克西耶维奇的女性生命书写中，女性的个体经验和经历不仅折射出以往被男性声音遮蔽的时代和民族的历史，也作为一种生命本体显示出其独立的价值。

《我是女兵，也是女人》这部完全以女性生命之声成就的作品就充分体现出对女性主体的探寻。在这部作品中，作者以其典型的复调风格将女兵们流动的主体性刻画得淋漓尽致，集体口述则为她们构建和巩固社群，在群体中重新发现自我，进而凝聚、转化群体的力量，书写女性自己的历史提供了有力的平台，对女性战争体验的捕捉更产生超越性的审美价值，呈现出女性生命的夺目辉光。

一、复调风格与女性流动的主体性

经过五百多次的采访，数百盒录音带的记录，在阿列克西耶维奇最终创作出的这部巨著中，女兵们由她们的口述树立起同样可以承担参战义务、争取公民权利的女性主体形象。她们可以胜任军事领域的几乎所有岗位，从记录文书、传递讯息、医疗抢救、洗衣做饭、修鞋理发、饲养马匹，到输送物资、修理汽车、架桥修路以至狙击、轰炸、飞行、爆破、埋雷扫雷、冲锋肉搏……只有通过言说，通过讲述自己的生命故事，进行一系列经济、社会及政治话语的竞逐，女性才能和其他弱势群体一样，建立自己的主体地位，阿列克西耶维奇用她的作品充分证明了这一点。

“多声音的写作——当代痛苦与勇气的纪念碑”（Treijs）是诺贝尔奖评委会对阿列克西耶维奇的高度评价，而这种复调风格，在《我是女兵，也是女人》这部作品中不仅表现为口述者们众声齐发，每一个口述者个体的言说也都表现出两面或多面，她们从语言到思想再到感情的复调性都在自己的讲述中被阿列克西耶维奇捕捉下来。

如前所述，后结构主义女性主义者亦怀疑女性身份的稳固性，持续性。相反，她们认为女性自我是多变的、流动的。她们的身份可以有私人领域的特征，也可以有公共领域的特征，社会生活的各个领域原本不能分割，而每个领域都能为女性提供不同的身份内涵与主体地位，正如凯茜·弗格森对“流动的主体性”之阐释：“被权柄（这种权力本身就是变动的）所左右，但又不在权力系统之内。‘流动的主体性’是理性的，人们正是在不断变化的遭遇和关系中，既经历变动，又不受羁绊，形成了这种‘流动的主体性’。”（Ferguson 154）阿列克西耶维奇笔下这些苏联卫国战争女兵的口述恰恰展现了女性那些往往被排斥的身份，揭示出作为“流动”的能动者（agent）的女性主体。

从美女到大兵，从女儿、未婚妻、母亲、妻子到遗孀、老姑娘、被抱怨“身上只有毡靴和绑腿布味儿”的弃妇、叛徒老婆，从学生到军人再到会计师、教师、工人、农民，从战斗英雄的光荣称号到隐姓埋名不愿意承认的残废老兵身份，从战场上备受怜惜的女兵小妹到战后被侮辱咒骂为“战场老婆”“前线婊子”……她们的身份在战前、战时和战后迅速变化，在复杂的境遇中，女性主体的构建也成为一个流动的进程。同情、仁爱常常被作为女性天生的特征本质化，而实际上通过这些真实鲜活的口述我们可以发现，女性主体性的形成“这一过程是模糊的：凌乱和多元混杂的，不稳定与持续并存……”（Ferguson 154）

虽然女兵们在战争中的英勇常常不亚于男性，但是阿里克西耶维奇显然意识到，将能够做到与男性相同视为优秀，必然会模糊女性作为主体的差异性。女性因其生育后代的本能和经历产生的关怀、同情及重视生命的特征以及对美与爱的追求，往往与她们在战场上的勇猛无畏、坚毅克制混杂交融。

在阿列克西耶维奇笔下，同样的一个女兵，可以击毙 75 名敌军却为断粮时杀死一匹小马号啕大哭；可以挺身而出带领男兵们发起冲锋，却无法接受战场上枪毙退缩男孩的可怕场景；可以凭精准的枪法让敌军雌雄莫辨，却为不舍一条红围巾牺牲性命；可以穿着肥大笨重的男兵衣履去前线，却在片刻的休息时间仍要绣绣手绢，织织花边；因为看到德军坦克碾压儿童而发疯，却在发现背上烧焦的伤员是德国兵时仍不能抛弃；渴望参加战斗，却不能抛弃孩子，拖儿带女仍坚持完成任务；心疼骨肉，却要为偷运药品通过哨卡故意伤害孩子，转移视线……

这种"自我"的不稳定性，也往往通过女兵们记忆的零散、破碎，讲述的矛盾、分裂表现出来。卫生指导员奥尔佳在看到辛苦抢救的伤员因两名逃兵的抛弃被敌人残忍杀害后，愤怒不已。在对逃兵进行处决时，只有三个人走出队列，奥尔佳也站了出来。在回忆这段经历时，她却不知如何面对当时的行为："我不知道如果是现在的话，我会不会原谅他们？不好说……我从来都不说假话。要是再有一次，我就会哭起来，不能接受了……"（160）

阿列克西耶维奇也曾多次有过口述记录被讲述者删得面目全非的经历。面对更多听众，她们会主动隐去那些生动、有人情味却被视为妇人家的鸡毛蒜皮的细节，表述得像报纸上表彰英雄功勋的官样文章，像权力所期待塑造的榜样那样教育年轻人。正如作家深刻体会到的："在同一个人身上存在着两种真实：一种是被强行隐藏于地下的个人真实，还有一种是充满时代精神的整体真实，散发着报纸的气味……结果我发现的是一种坚固的内心自我保护意识和自我审查，而且还不断地修正。"（101）女兵们的言说往往徘徊于屈从与抗拒权力秩序之间，就像凯特·米莉特所深刻揭示的那样，"在我们的社会秩序中，基本上未被人们检验过甚至常常被否认的（然而已经制度化的）是男人按天生的权力统治女人。一种最巧妙的'内部殖民'在这种体制中得以实现，而且它往往比任何的种族隔离更加坚固，比阶级的壁垒更加严酷，更加普遍，当然也更为持久"（米莉特 33），在这种坚固持久的"内部殖民"中，女性自己的声音被无意识地隐藏起来。

然而，在压抑与妥协中，她们的口述也表达出对性别身份不平等与对战争残杀的强烈质疑。当战后突然发现人们并不是像崇敬男兵一样看待女兵，而是投以异样的目光时，困惑不已，"他们不和我们分享胜利，这对我们是一种屈辱……我们不理解"（126），当硝烟远去，男人们仍给孩子带来玩具枪械时，无法平静，“人类的生命，是非常珍贵的造物……是伟大的恩赐！而人类自己并不是这一造物的主人”（399）。无论是无意识的屈从还是勇敢的思考，阿列克西耶维奇都忠实地记录下来，而正是她的理解、保存与书写，使得女性的能动力在真实的生活点滴间显露出来，成为对建制权力的顽强抵御。通过对个人经验的叙述，即使那些习惯于自我审查、修正的女兵都成为自己生命故事的“创造者”。

二、集体叙述与女性社群的构建

个体的自我认同绝不是仅仅局限于捍卫属于自己的私人领域，而是在有明确的自我意识的同时，积极地与自我之外的他者建立起一定的关系，最终实现一种双向的自我认同。自我叙述本身就是建基于他者的认同，“我”和“他者”在口述中完全是两个不能分割的组成部分。因而，口述史正如科斯莱特、鲁丽和森玛菲尔德所指出的那样，呈现出“主体间性”的交遇（Cosslett, Lury and Summerfield）。阿列克西耶维奇运用口述进行的女性生命书写就成为女兵们跨越阻隔、构建社群、聚集交流的一个平台。

因为总是提醒自己要捍卫沉默的女兵自己的历史、话语和情感，提醒自己用爱去理解，作家自己也成为社群的一员，“你也是我们中的一员，你也是前线的姑娘了”（79）。在每一次采访结束后，阿列克西耶维奇往往又能得到一长串地址和号码，或者一些聚会的时间地点。战后在工作、婚嫁、生育等方面的困境在女兵们讲述、聆听、分享的过程中重新显现出来。原本她们担心，“如果讲出来，谁还会给我工作？谁还会娶我？于是我们都像鱼儿一样沉默，谁都不愿承认自己在前线打过仗”（125）。可是，在与作家的交流中，在与群体的关系中，每一个讲述的女兵都不再是单独、孤立的主体，她们惺惺相惜，互相理解支撑，在社群中重新发现自己，为自己走过的岁月下定义。与之相对的是，在作品的采访正文中几乎没有男性的口述记录，只有正文前的作者手记中零星出现了几位男兵的谈话。例如上文曾提及的男狙击手对作者的诘问：“战争就是男子汉大丈夫的事。你可以写的男人打仗的事难道还少吗?”(83)一方面，让我们透过其视角正视主导社会的男性观念；另一方面，个体的男性声音淹没在浩瀚的女性话语中，丧失权威，更反衬出女性社群构建的必要和重要。

阿列克西耶维奇在回顾自己积累和筛选资料的方法时，曾提到两点：一是通过参加老兵群体的聚会来解决无法完成四面八方海量采访的问题；二是分门别类，尽量记录不同军事岗位上妇女的事迹。她的采访与记录一方面巩固了许多既有群体的联系，另一方面又因为按不同岗位的分类采访使得许多在同一岗位上有相似经历的女兵形成新的群体。在最后创作的过程中，作者进一步打破岗位的界限。所以在成书后，我们可以看到既有集中记录狙击手的章节、聚合大量医护人员口述的章节，也有将洗衣兵、炊事兵、汽车修理工、邮递员等不同岗位的女兵口述集结而成的章节“我们没有打过枪”。正如舍尔纳所指出的，在讲述、聆听和分享的过程中，访谈者和受访的妇女“惺惺相惜”，交流“女性主义”的见地，并通过大众记忆的共同塑造，使口述历史成为一个结聚横跨时空和地域的女性社群意识的平台（Gluck 5)。这些不同岗位的女兵，即使从未谋面，这部作品的出版也会成为她们沟通社群意识的平台。在口述者与口述者之间，口述者与作家之间的“主体间性”交遇中，女性们彼此看见，既有相似的对战争苦难和胜利喜悦的回忆，也有曾经与当下各自的不同处境、不同生活空间；既有各种因性别身份而带来的同样困境，也有每个人的不同解脱方法，因为互相见证而鲜活动人。历史不再仅仅关乎过去，而成为今日与未来的一种建造和再造。

俄罗斯学者伊伦娜兹·德拉沃斯洛娃在回顾当代俄罗斯女权运动时曾经指出，在1979年创办的女性杂志《俄罗斯妇女》和《玛利亚》的撰稿者被迫移居，杂志在20世纪80年代很快停刊之后，接下来为期十年的一个阶段并没有群众性的女权运动出现。在官方的言论中，妇女的社会地位被置于“业已解决的妇女问题”以及“妇女多种角色之间的紧张关系”的一般框架内进行讨论（Zdravomyslova 35)。也就是说，在80年代的俄罗斯历史文化语境中，女性社群几乎无法立足，处境异常艰难。这部作品1983年创作完成后，书稿搁置两年不能出版，作者也被审查官批评以原始自然主义歪曲光荣历史，诋毁卫国战争，而这些在当时还是非常可怕的指控（引自 Alexievich）。但也正因如此，阿列克西耶维奇为女性集体发声，帮助构建女性社群的写作更显示出其特别的意义。

值得注意的是，这是阿列克西耶维奇首次在作品中使用集体口述实录文体。正如苏珊·兰瑟在《虚构的权威：女性作家和叙述声音》一书中所指出的那样，集体型叙述往往是边缘群体或受压制群体的叙述现象，很少在统治阶级男性作家的写作中出现，“在其叙述过程中某个具有一定规模的群体被赋予叙事权威；这种叙事通过多方位、交互赋权的叙述声音，也通过某个获得群体明显授权的个人的声音在文本中以文字的形式固定下来”（兰瑟 23）阿列克西耶维奇正是运用集体型叙述声音，以群体中的个人轮流发言的“轮言”形式，使得女兵们因为过去而凝聚，形成以其话语主体为形式的女性政体的权威，从而在当下与未来互相扶助。当一个社群能集体地生产一定的共同回忆时，它就可以在整体社会找到自己的位置，并因此而结聚成转化的力量（Thompson 7）。1985 年，《我是女兵，也是女人》在明斯克与莫斯科出版后，连续多年不断重印，迄今已售出 200 万册，正如作家自己所说，“只有我们习惯于同心协力一起生活，这才会有所帮助。正所谓‘物以类聚，人以群分’。面对这个世界，我们有共同的快乐和泪水。我们既能承受苦难，又能讲述苦难，正是苦难，成为我们沉重而动荡生活之证明”（408）。女兵们的声音汇集在一起，已然结聚成不容忽视的巨声。

三、审美体验与女性生命的辉光

苏珊·朗格说：“真正能够使我们直接感受到人类生命的方式便是艺术方式”（朗格 66）阿列克西耶维奇笔下的女兵口述之所以五色斑斓，别具光华，正是因为其鲜活动人的生命体验最终上升为一种审美体验，而这一方面是由于其强烈的情感性，另一方面则在于其深刻的超越性。

“在光学上有‘采光性’的概念，说的是镜头采集捕获图像能力的强弱。女人的战争记忆就是按照自身情感张力和痛苦，而呈现的最强采光性能……

女人的战争，是伴随气味、伴随色彩、伴随微观生活世界的战争……”（415）女兵们的生命体验无论豪迈还是哀伤，由于满浸着情感，充溢着具体而微的光影、声色、气味，都生动真实，震人心魄。黎明晨风中扬起的战马鬃毛，冰雪大地上耸立的神奇云杉，小灌木樱桃宁静无涯的蓝色，牺牲战友鲜血与衬衣的红白撞击，狗儿的哭泣，牛羊的尖叫，雪地中无奈逝去的生命与鲜血的强烈腥味，前线上呱呱坠地的婴儿与粉匣的诱人香气……女兵们的叙述往往按照情感体验的逻辑衍生，不按时间、事理的逻辑展开，虽然很少有确切的纪年，而常以“那是一个春天”“就这样又过了两三年”“两三个月过去了”等虚化的时间表述带过，但是那些浓烈的、激动的、感伤的情感都在场景的还原中凝固了，正如加斯东·巴什拉在其《空间的诗学》中所说的那样，“在空间的无数蜂巢中储藏了浓缩的时间。……只有借助空间，只有在空间的范围内，我们才能找到时间持续的漂亮化石，通过长时间的停留使之变得具体化”（Bachelard 8—9）。女兵们的回忆将战场空间中各种细节的体验都重新激活，而这些体验恰恰是生命之宝藏，因为“生命就是在体验中所表现的东西……是我们所要返归的本源”（伽达默尔 85）

虽然往往有人质疑阿列克西耶维奇记录的是像随处散落的砖瓦一样没有经过艺术提炼的粗糙生活，但是正如作者回应所说，摘取这些原汁原味的谈话恰恰是因为它们“显露出无法抹去的人生悲剧。人生的混乱和激情，人生的卓越和不可理喻……”（413）。阿列克西耶维奇的书写并不过滤抽泣和痛哭，她呈现给读者的正是那些最有热度的、蕴含着本真、深藏着爱欲的现实生命体验，“在战争中最能看透和开启一个人的内心，还有就是在恋爱中，能穿透皮下表层，触及心灵的最深处。在死神面前，任何思想都是苍白的，死神开启了深不可测的永恒，任何人都没有充分准备面对这种永恒”（417）。

爱情是战争中唯一的个人隐私。无论是执意将牺牲的丈夫带回几千公里外的家乡安葬，还是没有婚礼不被认可，仍然坚持独自生养战场上爱人的孩子，选取女兵们这些不为人知的故事，不仅打破了对战争的宏大叙事，形成了独特的私语式叙述风格，更显示出艺术对个体存在的强烈关注，表达了作者对生命尊严的期许与对道德意义的深度思考。

而死亡则是对生命价值的反观性言说，对死亡的书写是对人灵魂世界的终极探索。阿列克西耶维奇抓住女性对死亡细致入微的感悟和无限哀婉的体察，将死亡以直观、感性、具体的形态呈现出来。当黄色的阴影从发根蔓延到脸庞、衣襟，弥留伤员脸上带着大大的惊异停止呼吸，当倒在草地上的战友望向天空，对着人字形飞过的仙鹤发出不舍的叹息……作者记录的与其说是肉体的消失，不如说是对如何向“生”的诘问。

爱与死的心灵震颤，体现出人内在生命的强烈搏动，并且上升为超越性的审美体验。“横飞滚烫的弹片奈她如何，因为她心中燃着一团火。当我们抬起担架上的女孩，朋友，定要记住那淡淡的秀脸。”（98）保家卫国的英雄情怀与红消香断的无限怜惜融注在这用心浇灌的前线诗篇里：“您知道吗？在战场上经常会出现多么美丽的早晨？就在战斗打响之前……看到那个早晨你马上就会想到这有可能是你人生的最后一个早晨。大地是如此美丽，空气是如此清新……朝阳是如此可爱……”（245）对生命的珍重、对自然的礼赞、对和平的渴望流露在这用爱描绘的战隙图景中。唯有理解爱，才能深刻把握生命自在而又博大的无限意义——其不停息的执着欲念与难以言表的崇高与伟岸；唯有面对死，才能充分展示生命脆弱而又强韧的丰富内涵——其不可解的无奈无常与不能动摇的庄严与尊贵。

阿列克西耶维奇引了一段普希金在《现代人》杂志上曾为抵抗拿破仑战争的少女骑兵娜杰日达·杜洛娃的日记片段书写按语：“究竟是什么原因，促使一个年轻少女，上流贵族的大家闺秀，离开温暖的家庭，女扮男装出现在战场上，去承担连男人们都畏惧的艰难责任呢？（对手是谁？不可一世的拿破仑大军！）……”（20）面对同样的问题，阿列克西耶维奇虽然没有直接给出答案，但是她笔下爱与死亡的生命体验展现出女兵们对个体生命的领悟、对国家民族命运的担当，折射着女性生命的夺目辉光。

四、结　语

“我们已经习惯于把妇女当作母亲、当作未婚妻，然后是美丽的太太……

战争就是男子汉大丈夫的事。”正如阿列克西耶维奇在第二次世界大战后的采访中遇到的一位男狙击手所说（83），男性话语构建出来的女性形象往往柔弱胆怯，被局限于闺阁、家庭的私人领域，排斥在战争等公共政治领域之外，只能处于从属于男性、被男性保护的弱势地位，而这种刻板印象已经深入历史，不易动摇。虽然在第二次世界大战中，有逾 100 万名 15—30 岁的苏联女兵参战，但是关于战争的一切，都是男人在书写，从观念、感受到语言都是男式的，沉默、失语的女性在历史中完全丧失了其主体地位。阿列克西耶维奇在其创作笔记中不禁诘问：“在绝对男性的世界中，女性站稳并捍卫了自己的地位后，却为什么不能捍卫自己的历史，不能捍卫自己的话语和情感?”（406）为她们立传，正是承载着作家这样的使命，《我是女兵，也是女人》将沉默无语的女性带到了历史的前台，典型的复调风格将女性流动的主体性化作复杂多声的生命合唱呈现在读者眼前，集体叙述则为女性们构建社群、结聚群体转化的力量、共同塑造新的女性主体形象发挥了不容忽视的作用，对女性生命体验的审美观照更使得历史长河中被掩蔽的女性生命重绽辉光。

阿列克西耶维奇对女性生命的关注在她后来的作品中仍得到延续，《最后的证人》中恐惧无助的战时女童，《锌皮娃娃兵》中痛苦矛盾的遗属母亲，《来自切尔诺贝利的声音》中伤心欲绝的消防员妻子都给读者留下了难以磨灭的印象。作家的思考不仅深入战争，她还从女性的视角审视和平时代的巨大变迁，在 2013 年出版的《二手时间》中，女性口述者的比例甚至占到全部受访者的近 2/3，从转折期一个个普通女性的人生故事反观历史夹缝中生命的渺小与迷惘，更是别具深意。

正如在《生命书写文集——从文类到实践》（*Essays on Life-Writing: From Genre to Critical Practice*）一书中马琳·卡达所说，生命书写常因其“妇女生活重构”而带有性别立场（Verduyn 29）。作为阿列克西耶维奇首次运用口述实录完成的作品，同为女性的作家投入了更多的个人情感，这部作品中不仅几乎每篇都有作者手记，而且其篇幅有的已接近正文的女兵口述，影响了其声音的独立性，相较后来的作品，还不够成熟。然而，从根本上看，自《我是女兵，也是女人》始，阿列克西耶维奇的创作就既存有性别立场，又超越性别立场，直指生命根基，叩问人性本质，表现出非凡的创作抱负："要去书写生与死的真相，而不仅仅是战争的真实。要提出陀思妥耶夫斯基式的问题：在一个人的身上，到底有多少个人？又如何在本质上保护这个人？"（411）

致谢【Acknowledgement】

本文为"21世纪外国文学的现实观照与生命书写"专题研讨会参会论文，感谢霍士富教授的点评！同时，本文也受益于《现代传记研究》匿名评审人提出的修改意见，作者谨致谢忱！

This paper was presented at the 2017 conference "The Realistic Reflection and Life Writing of Foreign Literature in the 21st Century". The author wishes to thank Professor Huo Shifu for his comments and would also like to thank the anonymous referees of *Modern Life Writing Studies* for their comments and suggestions.

引用文献【Works Cited】

Alexievich, S.A. "The Chronicler of the Utopian Land." Svetlana Alexievich: Voices from Big Utopia. N.y. 〈http://www.alexievich.info/biogr_EN.html〉. Web. 21 July 2017.

阿列克谢耶维奇：《我是女兵，也是女人》，吕宁思译。北京：九州出版社，2015年。

[Alexievich, S.A. *War's Unwomanly Face*. Trans. Lv Ningsi. Beijing: Jiu Zhou Press, 2015.]

Bachelard, Gaston. *The Poetics of Space*. Trans. Maria Jolas. Boston: Beacon Press, 1994.

Cosslett, Tess, Celia Lury and Summerfield Penny, eds. *Feminism and Autobiography: Texts, Theories, Methods*. London: Routledge, 2000.

Ferguson, Kathy. *The Man Question: Visions of Subjectivity in Feminist Theory*, Ithaca: Cornell University Press, 1992.

Gluck, Sherna. "What's So Special about Women? Women's Oral History." *Frontiers: A Journal of Women Studies*, 2, (1977): pp.3-17.

伽达默尔：《真理与方法》，洪汉鼎译。上海：上海译文出版社，1999年。

[Gadamer, Hans-Georg. *Truth and Method*, Trans. Hong Handing. Shanghai: Shanghai Translation Publishing House, 1999.]

Jolly, Margaretta. ed. *Encyclopedia of Life Writing: Autobiographical and Biographical Forms*, London: Fitzroy Dearborn Publishers, 2001.

苏珊·朗格：《艺术问题》，滕守尧等译。北京：中国社会科学出版社，1983年。

[Langer, Susanne. *Problems of Art*. Trans. Teng Shouyao. Beijing: China Social Sciences Press, 1983.]

苏珊·S. 兰瑟：《虚构的权威：女性作家与叙述声音》，黄必康译。北京：北京大学出版社。

[Lancer, Susan Sniader. *Fictions of Authority*. Trans. Huang Bikang. Beijing: Beijing University Press, 2002.]

凯特·米莉特：《性政治》，宋文伟译。南京：江苏人民出版社，2000 年。
[Millett, Kate. *Sexual Politics*. Trans. Su Wenwei. Nanjing: Jiang Su People's Press, 2000.]

Thompson, Paul. *The Voice of the Past: Oral History*. Oxford: Oxford University Press, 1978.

Treijs, Erica. "Nobelpriset i litteratur till Svetlana Aleksijevitj." *Svenska Dagbladet* 2015. Web.8 October, 2015. 〈https://www.svd.se/aleksijevitj-vi-ar-inne-i-radslans-tid/om/nobelpriset-i-litteratur-2015.〉

Verduyn, Christl. "Between the Lines: Marian Engel's Cashiers and Notebooks." *Essays on Life Writing: From Genre to Critical Practice*. Ed. Kadar, Marlene. Toronto: University of Toronto Press, 1992. 28–41.

Zdravomyslova, Elena. "Overview of the Feminist Movement in Modern Russia." *Diogenes*, 49. (2002):35–39.

《特殊教育和我：朴永馨口述史》：个人史与特殊教育史的交织与重合

孙　会

内容提要：《特殊教育和我：朴永馨口述史》是当代中国特殊教育领域的第一部口述史。作为当代中国特殊教育的亲历者、见证者、研究者和倡导者，口述者朴永馨教授有意彰显个人生命经历与特殊教育发展历程之间存在的不可分割性。因此，将个人史融入特殊教育史之中，让二者相互交织和重合，成为这部口述史的重要特色，这也使其具有很强的行业史料价值。同时，这部口述史也暗含了口述者的一种期待和呼吁，希望更多的人来关注这一特殊教育领域和残疾人群体，改变其边缘化的处境。

关键词：朴永馨　口述史　特殊教育　残疾人

作者简介：孙会，文学硕士，南京特殊教育师范学院助理研究员，《现代特殊教育》（高等教育研究）编辑，主要从事特殊教育管理和残疾人传记研究。

Title: *Special Education and I: The Oral History of Piao Yongxin*: Interweaving and Coincidence of Personal History and Special Educational History

Abstract: *Special Education and I: The Oral History of Piao Yongxin* is the first oral history in the field of special education in contemporary China. As a witness, researcher and advocate of special education in contemporary China, Professor Piao Yongxin, the narrator, intends to reveal the inalienability of personal life experience and the development of special education. Therefore, integrating personal history into the history of special education as an integral part becomes the salient feature of this oral history.

It also has strong historical value for the industry. At the same time, this oral history also implies the narrator's expectation of and appeal to the general public for more attention to the special education and the disabled, endeavoring to change their marginalized situation.

Keywords: Piao Yongxin, oral history, special education, the disabled

Sun Hui is Assistant Researcher at Nanjing Normal University for Special Education and Editor of the *Journal of Modern Special Education* (Higher Education). She specializes in special education management and biography of the disabled. E-mail: sunhuiyi226@sohu.com.

特殊教育作为国民教育的重要组成部分，是一个国家和社会文明程度的重要标志，也是其总体教育发展水平的体现。在中国，特殊教育起步较晚，大众对其了解和关注程度并不高。随着社会文明的进步、残疾人事业的发展，这个特殊群体越来越受到社会的关注，特殊教育也愈加受到重视，但仍然处于较为边缘的地位。新近出版的《特殊教育和我：朴永馨口述史》，是北京师范大学特殊教育专业朴永馨教授以个人成长经历为主要线索，通过采访者的访谈、记录和文字加工，最终形成的一部口述史。朴永馨是中华人民共和国成立后第一代从事特殊教育的工作者，被誉为此专业“第一人”。他是当代中国特殊教育的亲历者、见证者、研究者和倡导者，至今仍然活跃于特殊教育领域，其口述史的重点都与此密切相关。从这个意义上说，作为特殊教育领域的第一部口述史，他的个人生命史在很大程度上也是特殊教育史的折射，其人生起落对应的恰是后者的曲折发展历程。因此，将个人的成长经历与特殊教育发展史交织与融合在一起，是这部口述史最重要的特色。

一

在中国特殊教育发展史上，朴永馨有着重要的地位。作为国家“一五”计划时期最早派到苏联学习特殊教育的两名留学人员之一，他的求学经历也可以看作新中国特殊教育的发端，他后来的人生际遇都与此密切相关。因此，这部口述史在以时间顺序追溯口述者不同人生阶段的同时，又以特殊教育领域重要事件的发生发展作为主题和线索，在个人与历史的互相映衬中，较为清晰地展现了朴永馨个人的经历、学术思想的形成与特殊教育发展历程之间的互动关系。

不难发现，除了简洁带过的“少年时代”的零星记忆，朴永馨人生经历追溯的重点始终与特殊教育息息相关。这也就不难理解，他回忆的主体是从“留苏岁月”开始的，因为这是他人生的重要转折点：1955 年，他高中毕业，经考试、推荐和政治选拔被派遣到苏联留学，由国家分配决定学习特殊教育专业。可见，他进入这一领域带有非常大的偶然性。与当时众多的留学人员一样，朴永馨本着“祖国的需要就是我们的需要，祖国需要什么我们就学什么”（21）的精神，开始真正结缘特殊教育。在 1949 年前，特殊教育与民众教育馆、博物馆、图书馆、体育场、电影院、补习学校等归为一类，总称为社会教育。那时的特殊学校多为教会举办和私立，属于社会救济慈善事业。1949 年后，当时的政务院在《关于改革学制的规定》中规定：“各地人民政府应设立聋哑盲等特种学校，对生理上有缺陷的儿童、青年和成人施以教育。”（刘英杰 771）这一规定将特殊教育正式纳入国民教育体系，使其性质发生了根本改变，开启了新的发展之路。朴永馨就是在这一历史背景下被派遣到苏联留学，在特殊教育发生的始端，他是带着一种“祖国的需要”和现实使命去学习的。怀着要报效祖国的信念，朴永馨回顾了自己在苏联五年的留学岁月：攻克语言难关，“先后在国立莫斯科列宁师范学院、国立列宁格勒赫尔岑师范学院和苏联教育科学院矫正教育研究所学习”，并且“系统学习了智力落后教育专业、聋哑教育专业、盲教育专业和言语矫正专业”（34），结识了一批特教领域的专家……这些也为他后来能在这一领域大有作为奠定了坚实的基础。

学成归国后，朴永馨主动提出到基层北京市第二聋哑学校工作，从特殊教育最基础的实践开始。事实上，他的选择也反映了当时特殊的历史环境和特殊教育现状。当时国内的特殊教育刚起步，高等教育中尚未开设这一专业，这方面的师资培养也未开展，与此相关的研究也未建立，很多因素使他所学的很难在高校和研究所派上用场。在基层特殊学校工作阶段，他又赶上了各种社会政治运动，尤其是“文化大革命”期间，特殊学校的教学和科研基本停止，朴永馨也被下放到农村。也正因此，“基层耕耘”一章回顾的内容很少，那段岁月想有作为也很难。不过，这段经历也让他对当时残疾人的生存和受教育状况以及各地特殊教育的情况有了更深入和直观的了解。同时，他展现的这段“难有作为”的人生经历，也让人们了解到在很长一段时间，中国的特殊教育几乎处于停滞不前的状态。

“文化大革命”结束后，各行业都在恢复中，朴永馨在近20年的基层特殊学校经历中也有了自己的认识和思考。他意识到中国的特殊教育必须要在高等教育中有一席之地，作为当年特派留学特殊教育专业的人才，他有责任在高等教育中开辟特殊教育的阵地。随着特殊教育事业的发展，传统的短期集中式培训和分散的“师傅带徒弟”方式已不能满足对专业师资数量和质量的需求，专业人才的缺失开始凸显。当时国内特殊学校的教师几乎没有人受过专门的特殊教育师范训练，因而，师资培养迫在眉睫。1979年，朴永馨调入北京师范大学工作，成立特殊教育研究室，开始筹建这一专业。同时，他协助教育部筹建南京特殊教育师范学校，扶持各地中等师范学校开设特殊教育专业，制定中等特殊教育师范学校教学计划、编写教材、培训师资等。在这部口述史中，他把这一段时期称为“风雨创业路”。

一个专业从无到有，需要师资、教学、科研、社会活动、对外交流等方面的准备，在当时特殊教育专业人才稀缺的状态下，每一步的建设都异常艰辛。1986年，我国大陆高等院校的第一个特殊教育专业在北师大诞生。而随着国家对特殊教育的重视，从20世纪80年代中期开始，国家教育部门统一规划安排，有计划地在全国六个大区的部属师范大学建立特殊教育专业，进一步培养高层次的人才。在这样的历史背景下，朴永馨和所在的北师大特殊教育专业得以迅速成长。人才培养、国内外的学术交流、创办特殊教育杂志、编写《特殊教育辞典》等，这些不仅开创了北师大特殊教育专业在国内外的学术地位和影响力，同时也奠定了朴永馨个人在国内外特殊教育领域的学术影响力，他个人的学术思想也是在这一时期产生并形成。1996年，朴永馨在北师大退休，但回忆却并未止步于此。因为，这一时期中国的特殊教育进入了快速发展期。无论是国家层面还是社会群体，各方面对特殊教育和残疾人事业都愈加重视和关注。国家法律法规、教育行政部门有关特殊教育的政策规章等方面都逐步建立和完善；民办的特殊学校和机构、群众性的科研组织也开始逐渐建立。朴永馨尽管离开一线的岗位，但依旧活跃在特殊教育的各个领域，凭借其声誉和影响力，助推着中国特殊教育的发展。可见，改革开放之后的这几十年是朴永馨个人专长得到充分发挥的人生阶段，也是这部口述史叙述最详细的部分。

二

朴永馨口述回忆其近50年的职业生涯，主线虽是“小我”的个体命运，却也让人清晰地看到了中国特殊教育发展的历史脉络，以及个人成长经历中折射出的社会变迁和历史复杂性。从中，读者不仅可以触摸到半个世纪以来中国特殊教育的发展历程，也可以领略到那一代成长起来的特殊教育者所置身的时代氛围和独特的生命体验。尽管朴永馨不断强调自己只是“一个普通的特殊教育老师，不敢与那些著名学者相比，也没有什么特殊的经历和事迹”(1)，但正如编写组在“后记”中所指出的：

> 先生是新中国特殊教育发展的亲历者和见证人，在我国大陆高等特殊教育事业从无到有再到蓬勃发展的进程中，起着开创和引领作用，其影响遍及中国及海外。他创办了北京师范大学特殊教育专业（1986年），即我国高校第一个特殊教育专业，建立了我国大陆第一个特殊教育研究室（1980年）和第一个特殊教育研究中心（1988年），创办了国内第一本特殊教育杂志《特殊教育研究》，培养了新中国第一批特殊教育本科生和研究生。(273)

因此，将其誉为“新中国特教事业第一人”也并不为过。当然，“第一”的称号背后还意味着，朴永馨作为一名特殊教育的研究者、探索者和实践者，他率先尝试将其学习的理论用于实践，并从实践中进一步修正原有的认识，从而在这一领域做出许多独到的探索。正如肖非所指出的，朴永馨的贡献主要体现在他“对特殊教育对象的科学阐释、对中国特殊教育发展的理论思考、对中国特殊教育学科建设的探索”“他形成了以‘特殊儿童既有共性也有特性’为代表的特殊儿童观和以‘特殊教育既有共性又有特性’为代表的特殊教育观，以及由此提出的残疾儿童的三因素补偿论……”（肖非 3）与此同时，他还注重中外特殊教育观念和教学方式比较，总结其中的规律性成分，并结合现实，积极探索中国特色的特殊教育模式。在他看来，发展特殊教育不仅要考虑经济条件，对残疾人正确的认识和态度也至关重要。基于这样的认识，朴永馨提出了自己的特殊教育模式：在举办特殊学校的同时可在普通学校开设特殊班；支持随班就读工作；强调特殊学校作用的多元化。

不过，从朴永馨自己的追忆来看，他后来的研究和实践都是与尝试构建中国特色的特殊教育学和学科体系密不可分的。他主编的新中国第一本特殊教育学教材《特殊教育概论》和国家“八五”计划重点图书《特殊教育学》，体现了他对构建中国特殊教育学的基本框架和学科群等的总体设想和展望。同时，他在师资培养中也一直渗透着特殊教育学科建设的思想，例如，他助力南京特殊教育师范学校的筹建、受国家教委委托牵头研制中等特殊教育师范学校课程方案等。不过，对其教育生涯而言，最具突破性的还在于，在朴永馨的努力下，1986 年开始，北京师范大学特殊教育专业率先招生。自此，特殊教育高级人才的培养获得了制度化的保证，高等师范特殊教育课程体系也开始建立，丰富了特殊教育学科体系。

然而，值得进一步追问和思考的是，朴永馨之所以取得如此重要的一些成绩和如此多的“第一”称号，固然离不开其个人的执着奋斗、敢于克服各种困难的吃苦精神以及强烈的社会、学术责任感，但从另一种意义上来说，他一枝独秀的突出成绩，恰恰反衬出特殊教育长期的边缘性和“荒芜性”。从朴永馨自述的经历看，他因国家派遣留学分配而偶然与特殊教育结缘，学成归国，也因当时特殊的政治环境而选择到基层特殊学校工作，这些偶然性的背后也折射出当时残疾人群体和特殊教育的艰难处境。改革开放后，他顺应时势开始在北师大发展特殊教育专业，从“一个人的研究室”开始到特殊教育专业首次招生，特殊教育一直处于边缘化发展的境地："第一届特殊教育专业总共招收了15个学生，其中仅有几个学生是通过第一志愿考进特殊教育专业来的，对特殊教育专业有一定了解，大多数是通过第二、第三志愿进来的或服从分配的，对特殊教育一无所知。目前，每年特殊教育专业的招生恐怕还有这样的情况。"（109）这一现象不仅体现了社会大众对特殊教育的普遍化陌生，也反映出多数年轻人对从事这一职业的抵触心理。

三

不容否认，随着社会经济物质文化水平的日益提升，人权意识的增强，残疾人群接受的教育不仅得到了恢复，还有了很大发展。国家为保障残疾人的权益，陆续制定了法律法规，出台相关措施，设立专门机构，实施了很多改善残疾人状况和发展特殊教育的计划和行动……在朴永馨的口述中，他想强调的也正是由于国家层面的政策支持，特殊教育学科才有了这样空前的发展：残疾人受教育安置形式从单一到多种，特殊教育对象在扩大，全方位、多层次的残疾人教育体系在完善，特殊教育逐渐融合为社会系统工程的一部分。人们对残疾人的认识从宿命、无用到接受和尊重其差异性，对待残疾人的态度从歧视、同情到平等、融合，人们开始认识到特殊教育的发展有利于人类更好地认识自己。

然而，朴永馨的口述史中凸显的，恐怕并非仅是其个人成就和中国特殊教育取得的巨大成绩，更有一种深深的忧虑。作为最大的发展中国家，中国残疾人群庞大，这决定了中国的特殊教育也是世界上规模最大的。因此，朴永馨在口述中，有意无意也希望人们看到当下中国特殊教育所面临的诸多问题和挑战。比如：全社会对特殊教育的认识还不够深入和全面，相关的法律法规还有待健全和丰富；各地区和各级各类的特殊教育发展很不均衡；特殊儿童的就学率明显低于普通儿童，其融合教育还面临着诸多困境，毕业生的就业困难重重；特殊教育的研究和学科建设仍然相当薄弱等等。其实，人们也不难发现，在社会生活中，残疾人这个群体也依然处于弱势状态，与健全人之间的隔膜仍然很深。社会对残疾人的歧视现象依然大量存在，使他们很难真正受到公平对待，也难以真的融入健全人的生活中。

教育公平是社会公平的重要体现，在当下的中国，这依然是一个亟待解决的难题，而推进残疾人享受教育公平更是任重而道远。因此，保障残疾人接受公平的教育不仅仅是特殊教育工作者的责任，更是整个社会的责任。这也意味着，中国残疾人的特殊教育要想真正贯彻对人权的保障和尊重，让“平等、参与和共享”的理念在残疾人身上真正得以实现，离不开全社会共同的参与和努力。朴永馨一直强调自己的人生经历是与特殊教育不可分割的，讲自己其实就是讲述特殊教育的发展历程。正如朴永馨自己所说：“先有特殊教育，然后历史的机遇让特殊教育选择了我、培养了我……”（1）所以，在口述中，他始终有意将特殊教育摆在首位，把个体性的“我”放在次要的位置。这本身也可以看作他作为一名特殊教育工作者的呼吁，呼吁更多的人关心特殊教育和残疾人群体，呼吁更多人投入到其中来，彻底改变其边缘地位。

台湾学者王明珂认为：“有两种流行的口述历史。一则是主流历史所界定的当代重要人物之口述历史，另一则是主流史忽略的社会边缘人群。”（37）然而，朴永馨的口述史却介于这两种之间。从特殊教育史的角度讲，他代表着主流，但无论是特殊教育者还是残疾人群体都还处于社会的边缘。那么，这部口述史的意义就具有了双重的价值：一方面它让人们“更深入了解主流史的细部枝节，进一步肯定主流史的典范性”；另一方面“让社会大众知道社会边缘人的声音”（王明珂 37）。的确，朴永馨通过他人生史的回顾，让人们看到特殊教育这几十年来的发展所取得的一些成就。但是他更希望人们从其个人史的回溯反思中，关注这个还没有得到社会大众和主流教育重视的领域和群体，从而为其争取更多的权利和发展空间，也唤起人们对于残疾人更多的关怀和帮助。当然，如果从成熟的口述历史角度来考量，这部口述史的粗糙和单薄之处也是显而易见的。这固然和采访者对口述史的理解、驾驭和设计等有关，毕竟他们作为特殊教育专业的研究生，对口述历史的理论和实务缺少深入的领悟，对特殊教育研究也把握不足，很难有效引导受访者讲述出更为丰富的历史内容。而作为口述者，由于过度希望以自己的个人史来展现特殊教育史，有意将“小我”隐身于“大我”之后，反而造成了“小我”展现不够充分，“大我”也有时流于表面和空泛。究其主因可能还在于，特殊教育历史本身就过于单薄，“单薄”在一定意义上反而彰显出这一领域长期以来的艰难处境。

引用文献【Works Cited】

朴永馨口述：《特殊教育和我：朴永馨口述史》，江小英等整理。北京：北京师范大学出版社，2017 年。

[Piao Yongxin. *Special Education and I*: *An Oral History by Piao Yongxin*. Ed. Jiang Xiaoying. Beijing: Beijing Normal University Press, 2017.]

刘英杰主编：《中国教育大事典 1949—1990》。杭州：浙江教育出版社，1992 年。

[Liu Yingjie, ed. *The Annals of Chinese Education 1949-1990*. Hangzhou: Zhejiang Education Press, 1992.]

肖非：《本土化的特殊教育研究——朴永馨教授学术思想探微》，《国家教育行政学院学报》2007 年第 5 期。

[Xiao Fei. "The Localized Special Education Research: A Probe into the Academic Thoughts of Professor Piao Yongxin." *Journal of National Academy of Education Administration* 5(2007).]

王明珂：《口述历史的事实与社会现实》，《台湾口述历史的理论实物与案例》，许雪姬主编。台北：台湾口述历史学会，2014 年。

[Wang Mingke. "The Fact and Social Reality of Oral History." *The Theoretical Objects and Cases of Oral History in Taiwan*. Ed. Xu Xueji. Taipei: Taiwan Oral History Society, 2004.]

刘孝标《世说新语注》征引僧人别传述微

——兼论僧人别传在中世僧传文献中的学术地位

阳　清

内容提要：刘孝标《世说》注征引僧人别传多种，涉及支道林、佛图澄、尸黎密、释道安等四位高僧行迹。这些僧人别传产生于《高僧传》之前，有些甚至早于《高逸沙门传》和《世说》，并与六朝僧传形成纵向关联，昭示出某种文化背景和文学习尚，有助于僧人类传和综合性传记的文本建构，客观呈现出了史学和文学的双重价值。考察《世说》刘注征引僧人别传，探讨六朝僧人别传的存录情况，梳理唐宋之际的僧人别传文献，同时分析诸种僧传形态及其力量对比，可见僧人别传往往因其数量最多、贡献最大，从而在中世僧传文献中享有至关重要的学术地位。

关键词：《世说》注　僧人别传　中世佛教文学

作者简介：阳清，文学博士，云南师范大学文学院中国古代文学与文献研究中心教授。主要从事汉魏六朝文学与文献研究，近期发表了《孙绰〈名德沙门题目〉考述》（《文学遗产》，2017 年第 6 期）等。

Title: Liu Xiaobiao's Borrowing Monk Biographies for His *Annotations to A New Account of the Tales of the World*: Monk Biographies in Buddhist Literature from China's Six Dynasties to the Tang Dynasty

Abstract: Liu Xiaobiao employs a variety of monk biographies in his *Annotations to A New Account of the Tales of the World*, including life stories of four monks, such as Zhi Daolin, Fo Tucheng, Shi Limi, Shi Daoan. These biographies were written earlier than *Memoirs of Eminent Monks* and some of them were even earlier than *Lives of Eminent and Holy*

Monks and *A New Account of the Tales of the World*. These lives were historically related to monk biographies in the Six Dynasties, manifested certain cultural background and literary trends, contributed to the textual construction of collective biographies and comprehensive biographies, and featured the dual values historically and literarily. By examining the monk biographies quoted in Liu Xiaobiao's *Annotations to A New Account of the Tales of the World*, exploring the record of monk biographies in the Six Dynasties, carding monk biographies in the Tang and Song Dynasties, and analyzing various forms and significance of monk biographies, it is apparent that monk biographies enjoy indispensable academic standing in monk biographical literature in that period for their great number and greatest contribution.

Keywords: *Annotations to a New Account of the Tales of the World*, monk biography, Buddhist Literature from the Six Dynasty to the Tang Dynasty

Dr. Yang Qing is Professor of Chinese literature in the Research Center for Chinese Ancient Literature and Documentation, College of Literature at Yunnan Normal University, China. His research focuses on Chinese literature and document studies from the Han Dynasty to the Six Dynasties in Chinese history. He is the author of "Probing Sun Chuo's *Eminent Shramanas*" (*Literary Heritage*, (6) 2017). E-mail: chdyq2006@126.com.

众所周知,《世说新语》刘孝标注文具有非常重要的文献学价值。高似孙《纬略》指出:"梁刘孝标注此书,引援详确,有不言之妙。如引汉魏吴诸史,及子传地理之书,皆不必言。只如晋氏一朝史,及晋诸公列传、谱录、文章,皆出于正史之外。纪载特详,闻见未接,实为注书之法。"(133)胡应麟《读〈三国志〉裴注》亦认为:"裴世期之注《三国志》,刘孝标之注《世说》,傍引博据,宏洽淹通,而考究精严,辨驳明审,信两君之深于史学也。迄今三国六代小说逸事,往往覆赖二注以存。"(736)譬如,《世说》记载僧人姓名可考者行迹达七十余处,涉及支道林、于法开、佛图澄、法虔、竺法深、慧远、康僧渊、尸黎密、竺法汰、释道安、道曜、康法畅、僧意、僧伽提婆、法冈道人、支愍度、道壹道人等十七位高僧。基于魏晋玄学的时代背景,《世说》"客观展示了名士与高僧的广泛交游,由此塑造出了一批生动可感的僧人形象"(阳清:《〈高僧传〉对于〈世说新语〉的捃拾与展开》48)。而针对上述相关内容,《世说》刘注一方面征引品题僧人之作亦即孙绰《名德沙门题目》及《赞》,另一方面征引僧人类传著作亦即《高逸沙门传》,同时还引及当时突出的僧人传记诸如《支遁别传》《高坐别传》《安法师传》等,“其纠正义庆之纰缪,尤为精核。所引诸书,今已佚其十之九,惟赖是注以传”(永瑢等 1182),故为后世考证家珍重。对此,朱东润明确指出:“《世说新语注》还有一件可以注意的,就是沙门的传叙,在这个时期已经狠发达”“可看见传叙文学在当时的发展和沙门的受人注目”(《中国传叙文学之变迁》 47)。关于《世说》刘注征引《名德沙门题目》与《高逸沙门传》,笔者另有专文探讨。兹考察刘注征引僧人别传,兼论同类著作在中世僧传文献中的重要地位。

一、《世说》刘注征引僧人别传文本

以余嘉锡《世说新语笺疏》为考察对象,可见《世说》刘注征引僧人别传文本实有十三处,涉及支道林、佛图澄、尸黎密、释道安等四位高僧行迹。朱东润在《八代传叙文学述论》第八章中虽已如数指明,但并未对文本作详细梳理。今依类编列并摘录如下:

(1)《支法师传》:“法师研十地,则知顿悟于七住;寻庄周,则辩圣人之逍遥。当时名胜,咸味其音旨。”(余嘉锡 264)

(2)《支遁别传》曰:“遁任心独往,风期高亮。”(余嘉锡 557)

(3)《支遁别传》曰:“遁神心警悟,清识玄远,尝至京师,王仲祖称其造微之功,不异王弼。”(余嘉锡 563)

(4)《支遁传》曰:“遁神悟机发,风期所得,自然超迈也。”(余嘉锡 633)

(5)《支遁传》曰:“遁太和元年终于剡之石城山,因葬焉。”(余嘉锡 757)

(6)《支遁传》曰:“遁每标举会宗,而不留心象喻,解释章句,或有所漏,文字之徒,多以为疑。谢安石闻而善之曰:‘此九方皋之相马也,略其玄黄,而取其俊逸。’”(余嘉锡 990)

(7)《支遁传》曰:“法虔,道林同学也。俊朗有理义,遁甚重之。”(余嘉锡 755)

(8)《高坐别传》曰:“和尚胡名尸黎密,西域人。传云国王子,以国让弟,遂为沙门。永嘉中,始到此土,止于大市中。和尚天姿高朗,风韵遒迈。丞相王公一见奇之,以为吾之徒也。周仆射领选,抚其背而叹曰:'若选得此贤,令人无恨。'俄而周侯遇害,和尚对其灵坐,作胡祝数千言,音声高畅,既而挥涕收泪,其哀乐废兴皆此类。性高简,不学晋语。诸公与之言,皆因传译。然神领意得,顿在言前。"(余嘉锡 119)

(9)《高坐传》曰:"庾亮、周顗、桓彝一代名士,一见和尚,披衿致契。曾为和尚作目,久之未得。有云:'尸利密可称卓朗。'于是桓始咨嗟,以为标之极似。宣武尝云:'少见和尚,称其精神渊箸,当年出伦。'其为名士所叹如此。"(余嘉锡 532)

(10)《高坐传》曰:"王公曾诣和上,和上解带偃伏,悟言神解。见尚书令卞望之,便敛衿饰容。时叹皆得其所。"(余嘉锡 907)

(11)《安法师传》曰:"竺法汰者,体器弘简,道情冥到,法师友而善焉。"(余嘉锡 280)

(12)《安和上传》曰:"释道安者,常山薄柳人,本姓卫,年十二作沙门。神性聪敏而貌至陋,佛图澄甚重之。值石氏乱,于陆浑山木食修学,为慕容俊所逼,乃住襄阳。以佛法东流,经籍错谬,更为条章,标序篇目,为之注解。自支道林等皆宗其理。无疾卒。"(余嘉锡 441)

(13)《澄别传》曰:"道人佛图澄,不知何许人,出于燉煌,好佛道,出家为沙门。永嘉中,至洛阳,值京师有难,潜遁草泽间。石勒雄异好杀害,因勒大将军郭默略见勒。以麻油涂掌,占见吉凶。数百里外听浮图铃声,逆知祸福。勒甚敬信之。虎即位,亦师澄,号大和尚。自知终日。开棺无尸,唯袈裟法服在焉。"(余嘉锡 126)

除此之外,刘氏《世说·文学》注征引张野《远法师铭》云:

> 沙门释惠远,雁门楼烦人。本姓贾氏,世为冠族。年十二,随舅令狐氏游学许、洛。年二十一,欲南渡,就范宣子学,道阻不通,遇释道安以为师。抽簪落发,研求法藏。释昙翼每资以灯烛之费。诵鉴淹远,高悟冥赜。安常叹曰:"道流东国,其在远乎?"襄阳既没,振锡南游,结宇灵岳。自年六十,不复出山。名被流沙,彼国僧众,皆称汉地有大乘沙门。每至然香礼

> 拜，辄东向致敬。年八十三而终。（余嘉锡 284—285）

此则虽不是僧人别传，应为墓志，但可视同当时较为突出的僧人传记。

检读上述文本，《世说》刘注征引《支遁别传》即《支法师传》《支遁传》，《高坐别传》即《高坐传》，《道安别传》亦即《安法师传》《安和上传》。如此种种，可见刘孝标引注僧人别传在文献称名方面并不严谨。如果说，《世说》记载高僧言行较多，同时囊括汉地高僧和西域大德，其中以支道林事迹最为详备，相关内容多达六十处，那么考察上述文本，亦可见《世说》刘注征引支道林别传内容亦属最多，其次则为尸黎密、释道安、佛图澄，可谓基本上符合刘义庆原著所记僧人行迹的比例。要之，《世说》刘注让僧人别传这种文献类型在六朝之际得以客观展示出来，借此证明了中古传记文学与佛教同步盛行的时代印合。

二、《世说》刘注征引僧人别传透析

考察《世说》刘注征引僧人别传，借此得见刘孝标的训诂学体例及其学术成就，前人相关阐述较多，此不待言。值得重视的是，这些僧人别传的撰者与写作时代，这些僧人传记与《名德沙门题目》《高逸沙门传》《高僧传》的时代关联，这些别传出现的文化背景与文学习尚问题，以及它们的史学价值和文本功能等，都是值得我们进一步探讨的重要话题。

先看《世说》刘注征引僧人别传的撰者和写作时代。关于《支遁别传》，余嘉锡认为："《支遁传》不知谁撰，盖必作于《语林》成书之后，故采取其语，今《高僧传》亦仍而不改。"（991）余氏所谓《支遁传》采用裴启《语林》之语，直接关涉前文第六条。据《世说·轻诋》："裴郎又云：'谢安目支道林，如九方皋之相马，略其玄黄，取其俊逸。'"刘注又引《续晋阳秋》曰："晋隆和中，河东裴启撰汉、魏以来迄于今时，言语应对之可称者，谓之《语林》。"（余嘉锡 990—991）那么《支遁别传》应撰于 363 年之后。又据前文第五条，支遁卒于太和元年，那么《支遁别传》理应撰于 366 年之后。又据前文第二条，《支遁别传》云"遁任心独往，风期高亮"，而考察竺法济《高逸沙门传》佚文，其中有支遁"少而任心独往，风期高亮，家世奉法"之语,则《高逸沙门传》曾经捃拾《支遁别传》。考察竺法济其人,得见该僧在"司马曜(373—397年)执政期间,曾经活动于今浙江嵊州一带",应于其师"竺法潜卒(374年)后主持剡东仰山,由此名垂江左"(阳清:《竺法济〈高逸沙门传〉索隐》163—164),其著作《高逸沙门传》应撰于4世纪末。又,《高僧传》卷四《晋剡沃洲山支遁》云林公亡后,"郄超(336—377年)为之序传,袁宏为之铭赞,周昙宝为之作诔"(释慧皎 163),则《支遁别传》应撰于366年至377年之间,远早于《世说》。

道安别传撰者不可考。据《出三藏记集》卷十五《道安法师传》,安"以伪建元二十一年二月八日,斋毕无疾而卒。葬五级寺中"(释僧祐 564)。据《高僧传》卷五《晋长安五级寺释道安》,"是岁晋太元十年也,年七十二"(释慧皎 183),则道安别传理应撰于385年之后《世说》刘注之前。《佛图澄别传》《尸黎密别传》撰者亦不可考。据《高僧传》卷九《晋邺中竺佛图澄》,佛图澄卒于"晋穆帝永和四年(348年)"(释慧皎 356),据《出三藏记集》卷十三《尸梨蜜传》,高坐"年八十余,咸康(335—342年)中卒"(释僧祐 522),《高僧传》卷一《晋建康建初寺帛尸梨蜜》亦同。那么这两种别传分别撰于348年、342年之后,《世说》刘注之前,远早于《高僧传》。至于《远法师铭》,其撰者张野曾入庐山依慧远(334—416年),后卒于义熙十四年(418年),则该文撰写于416年至418年之间,同样远早于《高僧传》。

再看《世说》刘注征引僧人别传与《名德沙门题目》《高逸沙门传》《高僧传》的逻辑关联。前述支遁别传内容为竺法济《高逸沙门传》所吸收,即可见二书的某些内容实际上前后相承。抑又,据前文第十一条,有《安法师传》云竺法汰"体器弘简,道情冥到",而孙绰《名德沙门题目》曰:"法汰高亮开达。"(余嘉锡 570)《名德沙门赞》赏评法汰:"凄风拂林,明泉映壑。爽爽法汰,校德无怍。事外潇洒,神内恢廓。实从前起,名随后跃。"(严可均 1810)又据前文第十二条,有《安和上传》云道安"神性聪敏而貌至陋,佛图澄甚重之","以佛法东流,经籍错谬,更为条章,标序篇目,为之注解。自支道林等皆宗其理",而孙绰《名德沙门论目》曰:"释道安博物多才,通经名理。"(严可均 1811)《名德沙门赞》赏评道安:"物有广赡,人固多宰,渊渊释安,专能兼倍,飞声汧陇,驰名淮海。形虽草化,犹若常在。"(严可均 1809)据此不难发现,孙绰对法汰和道安的品评与道安别传所载颇为契合。因孙绰生于晋愍帝建兴二年(314 年),卒于简文帝咸安元年(371 年),则道安别传明显撰写于孙氏《名德沙门题目》及《名德沙门赞》之后,并且有可能参考了孙绰的相关品评。至于慧皎《高僧传》吸收支道林等四种僧人别传,则属显而易见。前述余嘉锡即谓《高僧传》对《支遁传》"仍而不改",余氏又云:"《高僧传》一《帛尸梨蜜传》与《注》所引《高坐别传》略同。"(119)事实上,倘若我们对照《世说》刘注征引僧人别传前文十三条与《高僧传》中的相关僧人本传,其实不难发现《高僧传》一方面直接或间接捃拾前代僧人别传,另一方面或整合,或改编,或增补文本,从而实现了历史价值、宗教价值以及文学价值的多元同构。至于《高僧传》对《名德沙门题目》及《名德沙门赞》《高逸沙门传》乃至《世说》及其刘注等文献的吸收和利用,同样大致遵循着这一创作规律。

再看这些别传产生的文化背景与文学习尚问题。别传亦即正史和家谱以外的单篇个人传记,大体上属于散传,《隋志》归之于史部杂传类。从很大程度上说,《世说》刘注征引僧人别传的大量出现,其实暗合这个时代所谓史部杂传类著述的创作风尚。人物传记撰写潮流,原本与史学传统、价值判断、考绩制度等存在着某种必然的关联。据《隋书·经籍志》杂传小序,历代"公卿诸侯,至于群士,善恶之迹,毕集史职",众庶乃至"穷居侧陋之士,言行必达,皆有史传","善恶之事,靡不毕集"(魏征等 981)。两汉以来的正史创作之风由此彬彬称盛,人物品评活动抑又推波助澜,六朝杂传可谓直接受其影响。正是基于上述缘由,作为"史官之末事"的杂传于斯为盛,"其内容和主题极为驳杂:既有一家之传,亦有一地先贤、耆旧之传,既有高士、名士、隐逸之传,又有列士、列女、忠臣、良吏、高僧、神仙、孝子、幼童之传,还有感应、灵验、冤魂、鬼神之故事"(阳清:《先唐志怪叙事研究》7),杂传叙事甚至与小说叙事构成杂糅态势,其中的别传与类传、综合性传记前后关联乃至并行不悖,最终融汇成了六朝人物叙事的时代洪流。《世说》刘注征引僧人别传一方面具有这个时代散传和类传的基本特征,亦即表现为"作者率尔而作,不在正史,离史独立,其传主形象反较真实。它对传记作为一种文学样式独立地发展起了促进作用"(陈兰村 7),另一方面无疑促进了僧人类传乃至综合性僧传的文本建构。自两晋伊始,佛教僧传大致经历了从单传亦即别传到类传、通传的自然发展。详究其演变轨迹，诚如汤用彤先生所言，“一方面沿东汉以来品题人物的著作”，“第二方面则出现了当时突出的僧人传记”，“其后始有人据一类一地之僧人相关的材料为书”，“再后则因佛法僧三方面的著述已多”，“此后《高僧传》之名渐通用矣”（释慧皎 557）。如前所述，从孙绰《名德沙门题目》及《名德沙门赞》，至《世说》刘注征引僧人别传，再至竺法济《高逸沙门传》，最后至慧皎《高僧传》，不仅大体上反映了六朝佛教僧传系列著述的发展历程，而且客观彰显出了这个时代的文化背景和文学习尚。

最后看《世说》刘注征引僧人别传的史学价值和文本功能。受司马迁“实录”创作观念的影响，从裴松之到刘勰，六朝批评家大多强调史传文学的真实性，借此成为这个时代的理论共性。从实际情况看，《世说》及其刘注的史学价值是显而易见的，现存《晋书》对于《世说》的捃拾即可见一斑。《史通·杂说》指出：“宋临川王义庆著《世说新语》，上叙两汉、三国及晋中朝、江左事”，“而皇家撰《晋史》，多取此书”（刘知几 450）。《四库提要》亦认为，《晋书》“所载者大抵宏奖风流，以资谈柄。取刘义庆《世说新语》与刘孝标所注一一互勘，几于全部收入”（永瑢等 405）。早在初唐官修《晋书》之际，可供依据的晋史旧作有所谓“十八家晋史”（晁公武 182）之说，房玄龄等学者竟然舍“史”而求“小说”，非但不抛弃《世说》及刘注，反而大加利用，这只能说明其所载事迹大多真实可靠。至于《世说》及其刘注征引僧人品评著作、僧人别传、僧人类传等，均被后来的《高僧传》加以捃拾和展开，同样证明了二书的史学价值不菲。更为确切地讲，前述《世说》刘注征引僧人别传与其前后相关僧传文献的时代关联，事实上已经印证了这类文献的史学价值。不仅如此，从文本功能看，这些僧人别传除了承载着史学内涵以外，还因为与佛教人物和佛教文化交流直接关联，由此对于拓展中世佛教史的具体研究颇有裨益；又因其品评人物独具匠心而又充满文采，写人记事生动鲜活而又严谨有序，并且直接影响着随后的佛教僧人类传以及综合性僧传，由此具有不可忽视的叙事文学价值。要之，作为史部杂传类著述的组成部分，《世说》刘注征引僧人别传对同时代前后相关传记文学的创作有着重要的作用和明显的影响。

三、六朝至宋代僧人别传存录情况考察

值得指出的是,《世说》刘注征引支道林、尸黎密、释道安、佛图澄等四种单独的人物传记,作为一种文献类型而言颇具代表性,但其实并非六朝僧人别传的全部。考察历代公私目录,可见六朝僧人别传作品另有多种,由此充分证实了这种文献类型的时代普遍性。

较为典型的例证是,《隋志》史部杂传类著录有康泓撰《道人善道开传》一卷。姚振宗指出:"案《法苑珠林》二十七引《冥祥记》云:'赵沙门单或作善,字道开,不知何许人也。《别传》云燉煌人,姓孟。'是善为其名,或传讹以为姓,遂改为单耳。"(5367)则南齐王琰或许得见善道开别传。今检读《法苑珠林》,得见《冥祥记》存录单道开别传曰:

> 燉煌人,本姓孟。少出家,欲穷栖岩谷,故先断谷食。初进面,三年后服练松脂。三十年后,唯时吞小石子。石子下,辄复断酒脯杂果。体畏风寒,唯噉椒姜。气力微弱,而肤色润泽,行步如飞。山神数试,未曾倾动。仙人恒来,意亦不耐,每啮蒜以却之。端坐静念,昼夜不眠。久住抱罕,石虎建武二年(336年),自西平迎来至邺下。不乘舟车,日行七百余里。过南安度一童子为沙弥,年十三四,行亦及开。既至,居于昭德佛图,服缕粗弊,背脞恒袒。于屋内作棚阁,高八九尺,上织菅为帐,禅于其中。绝谷七载,常御杂药,药有松脂茯苓之气,善能治目疾。常周行墟野,救疗百姓。王公远近,赠遗累积,皆受而施散,一毫无余。石虎之末,逆知其乱,乃与弟子南之许昌。升平三年(359年),来至建业,复适番禺,住罗浮山。阴卧林薄,邈然自怡。以其年七月卒。遗言露尸林里,弟子从之。陈郡袁彦伯兴宁元年为南海太守,与弟颖叔登游此岳,致敬其骸,烧香作礼。(释道世843—844)

《高僧传》卷九《晋罗浮山单道开》明显吸收了《单道开别传》,并在借鉴其他相关

文献的情况下展开文本内容，遂云该僧“以石虎建武十二年(346 年)从西平来，一日行七百里，至南安”，“至石虎太宁元年(349 年)，开与弟子南度许昌”，“至晋昇平三年(359 年)来之建业，俄而至南海，后入罗浮山”，“春秋百余岁，卒于山舍”，又云“有康泓者，昔在北间，闻开弟子叙开昔在山中，每有神仙去来，迺遥心敬挹。及后从役南海，亲与相见，侧席钻仰，禀闻备至，迺为之传赞曰：‘萧哉若人，飘然绝尘。外轨小乘，内畅空身。玄象辉曜，高步是臻。飡茹芝英，流浪严津’”(释慧皎 361—362)。《晋书》卷九十五《艺术》亦有单道开本传。清代《晋书》补志诸作，譬如丁国钧、文廷式、秦荣光、黄逢元等同名著作《补晋书艺文志》以及吴士鑑《补晋书经籍志》均著录该种别传。

抑又，《隋志》史部杂传类还著录有《梁故草堂法师传》一卷，不题撰名。姚振宗指出：

> 案旧、新《唐志》有陶弘景《草堂法师传》一卷，又有萧回理《草堂法师传》一卷。而《文选·北山移文》注引梁简文帝《草堂传》云：“汝南周颙，以蜀草堂寺林壑可怀，乃于钟岭雷次宗学馆(案起于宋元嘉中)立寺，因名草堂，亦号‘山茨’。”章氏《考证》皆引之，盖以此三家皆近似之也。考《南史》颙本传：“益州刺史萧惠开携颙入蜀，为府参军。”又云：“颙长于佛理，于钟山西立隐舍，休沐则归之。”是钟山草堂寺起于颙，然颙无草堂法师之号，又卒于齐永明中，不当云梁故。考《艺文类聚》七十六有王筠撰《国师草堂法师智者约法师碑》。《梁书·孝义传》云：“江紑第三叔禄与草堂寺智者法师善。”盖即其人也。(5369)

《新唐书艺文志注》著录陶弘景《草堂法师传》亦云：“谨按《艺文类聚》有王筠撰《国师草堂法师智者约法师碑》，当即其人。《隋志》传记类亦有《梁故草堂法师传》一卷，不著撰人，恐即此二传之一也。”(佚名 213)则《隋志》著录之《梁故草堂法师传》与旧、新《唐志》著录之陶弘景《草堂法师传》、萧回理《草堂法师传》，有可能同为南梁草堂寺高僧智者约法师别传，清代王仁俊《补梁书艺文志》在著录前述三种《草堂法师传》的同时，甚至著录有《文选·北山移文》注引“文帝《中堂法师传》一卷”(204)。种种证据表明,在《高僧传》同时代或者稍后,南朝僧人别传作品的撰写依然方兴未艾。

事实上,除了《隋志》著录《道人善道开传》《梁故草堂法师传》,《高僧传》抑又涉及六朝僧人别传多种。该书卷一《汉洛阳安清》引及安世高《别传》云:

> 晋太康末,有安侯道人来至桑垣,出经竟,封一函于寺云:“后四年可开之。”吴末行至扬州,使人货一箱物,以买一奴,名福善,云“是我善知识”,仍将奴适豫章,度郏亭庙神为立寺竟。福善以刀刺安侯胁,于是而终。桑垣人乃发其所封函,财理自成字云:“尊吾道者,居士陈慧;传禅经者,比丘僧会。”是日正四年也。(释慧皎 7)

卷四《晋燉煌竺法乘》云法乘卒后,“高士季颙为之赞传”(释慧皎 155),该卷《晋剡山于法兰》又引及于氏《别传》云“兰亦感枯泉漱水,事与竺法护同”(释慧皎 166);卷五《晋于潜青山竺法旷》云法旷卒后,“散骑常侍顾恺之为作赞传”(释慧皎 206);卷十二《宋庐山招隐寺释僧瑜》云:

> 其后旬有四日,瑜房中生双梧桐,根枝丰茂,巨细相如,贯壤直耸,遂成连树理,识者以为娑罗宝树。剋炳泥洹,瑜之庶几,故现斯证,因号为双桐沙门。吴郡张辩为平南长史,亲睹其事,具为传赞。赞曰:“悠悠玄机,茫茫至道。出生入死,孰为妙宝?(其一)自昔药王,殊化绝伦。往闻其说,今睹斯人(其二)。英英沙门,慧定心固。凝神紫气,表迹双树(其三)。其德可乐,其操可贵。文之作矣,式飘髣髴(其四)。”(释慧皎 452)

与此相关,前述清代《晋书》补志诸作五种大多著录这些晋代僧人别传。抑又,新、旧《唐志》均著录有北齐《稠禅师传》一卷,《太平广记》卷九十一曾转引《纪闻》《朝野佥载》以详录该僧事迹。诸如此类,可证六朝僧人别传别行于世者应为数不少。《世说》刘注征引僧人别传,其实不过是其中的部分作品。尽管这样,缘于其作为单篇个人传记而未成专题著作流传,六朝僧人别传大多数成为类似隐性的存在,并不为世人注目。而事实上,因其史学价值和文学价值兼具,六朝僧人别传又是非常值得我们关注的传世文献。

六朝之后,僧人别传在隋唐宋三代同样不乏其多。这里,李正奋《隋代艺文志》即著录有释灌顶撰《天台智者大师别传》二卷,其《隋代艺文志辑证》另著录有释智顗撰《南岳思禅师传》、释灌顶撰《杭州真观法师别传》以及释彦琮撰《达磨笈多传》四卷、《那连提黎耶舍传》等。欧阳修《新唐书·艺文志》另著录有《高僧嬾残传》一卷、辛崇《僧伽行状》一卷、《法琳别传》二卷、李吉甫《一行传》一卷等。脱脱《宋史·艺文志》著录有元觉《一宿觉传》一卷、辛崇《僧伽行状》一卷、彦琮《释法琳别传》三卷、朱士挺《伏虎行状》一卷、陈嘉谟《僧自严行状》一卷等,黄虞稷、倪灿《宋史艺文志补》著录有《湘山寂照禅师事状》十二卷。焦竑《国史·经籍志》还著录有《大慈恩寺三藏法师传》十卷。上述僧人别传著述大多不存于今世。而考察诸种大藏经,可见《永乐北藏》《乾隆大藏经》均收录有隋灌顶撰《天台智者大师别传》一卷、唐惠立撰彦悰笺《大慈恩寺三藏法师传》十卷。《卍续藏经》收录有唐彦悰撰《唐护法沙门法琳别传》三卷、唐李华撰《善无畏三藏行状并碑铭》一卷、唐赵迁撰《不空三藏行状》一卷、《惠果和尚行状》一卷以及由日本佐伯定胤、中野达慧共编的《玄奘三藏师资传丛书》二卷。除上述僧人别传外,《大正藏》还收录有新罗崔致远撰《唐大荐福寺故寺主翻经大德法藏和尚传》一卷、《惠远外传》一卷等。这些别传终因文献结集而留存至今。至于敦煌宝藏和唐宋总集中收录、佛教类书中摘录、佛教经录中著录以及相关史书中涉及的中世僧人别传文献,同样值得我们重视。与六朝同类文献相比,这些僧人别传在总体上价值更高,有的甚至成为传记文学经典。

四、僧人别传之于中世僧传文献

东晋以来,"传叙文学跟着佛教思想而发展,在传叙底主题方面,尤多关于佛教徒的叙述"(朱东润:《八代传叙文学述论》272),僧人别传正是其中较为常见的形态。通过考察《世说》刘注征引僧人别传,探讨六朝僧人别传的存录情况,梳理唐宋之际的僧人别传文献,有助于我们深入理解僧人别传类著述在中世僧传文献中的地位。撇开诸佛、菩萨以及印度圣贤未至汉地者的相关传记不谈,中世佛教僧传文献可分为品评、单传亦即别传、类传以及综合性传记等四种形态,并且涵括历代僧人行记著作,不失为我国佛教史研究的文本基础。僧人品评类著作譬如孙绰《名德沙门题目》罕见并且早佚,后来的大多数评赞往往依附于其他传记形态。六朝类传著作譬如竺法济《高逸沙门传》绝少抑且亡佚,唐代则以义净《大唐西域求法高僧传》最著声名。综合性僧传存世完帙者,六朝有慧皎《高僧传》,唐有道宣《续高僧传》,宋有赞宁《宋高僧传》,如此最成体系。僧人行记通常以别传形式另行于世。在诸种传记形态中,僧人别传往往因其数量最多、贡献最大,从而在中世僧传文献中享有至关重要的学术地位。

首先,中世僧人别传的数量无疑最多,僧人类传和综合性僧传的数量则非常有限。前述相关的文献梳理已客观证明了这种结论。值得一提的是,晋唐佛教行记其实是僧人别传的某种变体。自佛教传入中国以来,汉地僧侣前往佛国求经巡礼者不乏其人,行记类文献应运而生。佛教行记乃僧人自撰或者他撰以记录其佛国经历的旅行笔记,后亦被僧人类传和综合性僧传加以吸收和利用。据笔者考察,六朝行记诸如支僧载《外国事》、释法显《佛国记》、竺法维《佛国记》、释智猛《游行外国传》、昙无竭《外国传》、释法盛《历国传》、释昙景《外国传》以及记载慧生等人西行求法的《慧生行传》《宋云家记》《道荣传》等著作十种,都曾先后别行于世,唐宋佛教行记诸如玄奘《大唐西域记》、常愍《历游天竺记》、义净《西方记》、慧超《往五天竺国传》、圆照《悟空入竺记》以及范成大《继业西域行程》、无名氏《西天路竟》等著作七种,亦曾先后别行于世,其中以法显《佛国记》和玄奘《大唐西域记》最著声名。晋唐大多数佛教行记虽亡佚不存,其学术价值却不容忽视。要之,僧人别传的数量优势,事实上已决定其在中世僧传文献中的特殊意义。

其次,鸟瞰中世僧传文献,僧人别传的学术贡献无疑最大。一方面,僧人别传在人物品评著作的基础上产生新变,同时又吸收传统史传手法,以全面展示某一高僧的行迹和生命历程,从而为类传和综合性传记提供了重要的素材。换句话说,僧人别传是类传和综合性传记的文本基础,往往有助于僧人类传和综合性僧传的形成,特别是经典性综合型僧传产生过程中必不可少的关键环节。

前述《世说》刘注征引僧人别传有助于《高逸沙门传》和《高僧传》的文本建构，以及《高僧传》文本先后涉及安世高、竺法乘、于法兰、竺法旷、释僧瑜等僧人别传，正是充分证明了这种事实。此不赘述。另一方面，僧人别传在很大程度上是特立独行的，即便是在被类传和综合性传记捃拾和吸收之后，依然可以别行于世，并且产生比较重要的学术价值和人文影响。《隋志》著录《道人善道开传》如此，历代史志、补志、经录著录的《佛国记》以及其他不少僧人别传更是如此。更为重要的是，在僧人类传和综合性僧传产生的同时或者前后，某些高僧的别传不仅成为长篇巨著，而且事实上与类传和综合性传记分庭抗礼，彰显出了巨大的学术张力。以僧人行记《佛国记》为例，其学术影响并不亚于《高僧传》。同理，《大唐西域记》亦不亚于《大唐西域求法高僧传》和《续高僧传》。《大慈恩寺三藏法师传》更是与《大唐西域记》堪称双璧。如果说《大唐西域记》以“地”为主，作为方志的文体特征显而易见，不失为研究中亚和南亚诸国历史、地理、宗教、文化以及中西交通的珍贵资料，那么《大慈恩寺三藏法师传》则是以“人”为主，其中记述现世灵验尤多，追记佛教传说略少，旅行者的形象和情感得以淋漓尽致地展现出来，“此书在古今所有名人谱传中，价值应推第一”（梁启超 412）。作为僧人别传，《大唐西域记》与《大慈恩寺三藏法师传》俱为我国古籍中传记文学和游记文学的名著，其学术价值应在同时代僧人类传和综合性僧传之上。

综上，以《世说》刘注征引僧人别传为线索，通过全面梳理中世僧人别传，我们不难看出这种僧传形态在同时代僧传文献中的显赫位置。从很大程度上讲，《世说》及其刘注征引僧人别传不仅昭示出某种文化背景和创作习尚，而且集体表现出了种种史学价值和文学功能，为六朝僧传著作的发展和繁荣做出了不凡的功绩。更为宏观地说，僧人别传同样是古代僧传文献中不可或缺的关键文本，它不惟让佛教传记文学和游记文学在晋唐时代处于巅峰，更是为后人研究中世佛教史和佛教文化交流史提供了种种可能，由此做出了不可磨灭的贡献。

致谢【Acknowledgment】

本文为国家社科基金项目“中国中世佛教僧传文学研究”（12XZW013）、教育部人文社科项目“衣冠南渡与东晋文学发生研究”（14YJC751028）成果，得到全国哲学社会科学规划办公室、国家教育部的经费资助，受益于《现代传记研究》匿名评审人提出的修改意见，作者谨致谢忱！

My acknowledgement and gratitude go to the research projects "Ancient Chinese Buddhist Biographies" sponsored by China National Social Science Fund(IC：12XZW013) and "The Nobles' Moving South and the Emergence of the Literature of the Eastern Jin Dynasty" by China Ministry of Education(14YJC751028). And I am grateful to the editor of *Modern Life Writing Studies* and anonymous reviewers for their suggestions and comments.

引用文献【Works Cited】

佚名：《新唐书艺文志注》。北京：清华大学出版社，2012年。

[Anonymous. *The Annotated New History of the Tang Dynasty*. Beijing：Tsinghua University Press，2012.]

晁公武：《郡斋读书志》，孙猛校证。上海：上海古籍出版社，2011年。

[Chao Gongwu. *Jun Zhai Reading Catalogue*. Pro-Cor. Sun Meng. Shanghai：Shanghai Classics Publishing House，2011.]

陈兰村：《中国传记文学发展史》（绪论）。北京：语文出版社，1999年。

[Chen Lancun. *The History of Chinese Biography*(*Introduction*). Beijing：Language and Literature Press，1999.]

高似孙：《纬略》。北京：商务印书馆，1939年。

[Gao Sisun. *Lost Notes*. Beijing：The Commercial Press，1939.]

胡应麟：《少室山房集》，江湛然辑。台北：商务印书馆，1986年。

[Hu Yinglin. *Shaoshi Shanfang Corpus*. Compiled by Jiang Zhanran. Taipei：The Commercial Press，1986.]

梁启超：附录：《支那内学院精校本〈玄奘传〉书后——关于玄奘年谱之研究》，《佛学研究十八篇》。上海：上海古籍出版社，2001年，第412—434页。

[Liang Qichao. "Appendix：Postscript to *Xuanzang*：*The Biography*，a Fine Edition by China Buddhist College-Examining Xuanzang's Chronicle." *Eighteen Essays on Buddhism*. Shanghai：Shanghai Classics Publishing House，2001. 412-34.]

刘义庆《世说新语》，余嘉锡笺疏。北京：中华书局，2007年。

[Liu Yiqing. *A New Account of the Tales of the World*. Notes by Yu Jiaxi. Beijing：Zhong Hua Book Company，2007.]

刘知几：《史通》，浦起龙通释。上海：上海古籍出版社，2009年。

[Liu Zhiji. *All About Historiography*(*Shi Tong*). Exp. Pu Qilong. Shanghai：Shanghai Classics Publishing House，2009.]

释道世：《法苑珠林》，周叔迦、苏晋仁校注。北京：中华书局，2003年。

[Shi Daoshi. *The Omnipresent Buddism*(*Fa Yuan Zhu Lin*). Pro. and notes by Zhou Shujia and Su Jinren. Beijing：Zhonghua Book Company，2003.]

释慧皎：《高僧传》，汤用彤校注。北京：中华书局，1992年。

[Shi Huijiao. *Eminent Monks*. Pro. and notes by Tang Yongtong. Beijing：Zhonghua Book Company，1992.]

释僧祐：《出三藏记集》，苏晋仁、苏炼子点校。北京：中华书局，1995 年。
[Shi Sengyou. *The Encyclopedia of Buddism*(*Chu San Zang Ji Ji*). Che. Su Jinren, Su Lianzi. Beijing: Zhonghua Book Company, 1995.]
王仁俊：《补梁书艺文志》。北京：清华大学出版社，2012 年。
[Wang Renjun. *The Catalogue of the Liang Dynasty*: *A Supplementary History*. Beijing: Tsinghua University Press, 2012.]
魏征等：《隋书》。北京：中华书局，1973 年。
[Wei Zheng, et al. *History of the Sui Dynasty*. Beijing: Zhonghua Book Company, 1973.]
严可均：《全晋文》。北京：中华书局，1958 年。
[Yan Kejun. *All Prose of the Jin Dynasty*. Beijing: Zhonghua Book Company, 1958.]
阳清：《〈高僧传〉对于〈世说新语〉的捃拾与展开》，《理论月刊》1（2016）：47—51。
[Yang Qing. "Eminent Monks: Its Exploitation of the Writing Crafts from *A New Account of the Tales of the World*." *Theory Monthly* 1(2016):47-51.]
——：《先唐志怪叙事研究》。北京：人民出版社，2015 年。
[——. *A Study of Mystery Narratives Before the Tang Dynasty*. Beijing: People's Publishing House, 2015.]
——：《竺法济〈高逸沙门传〉索隐》，《文献》1（2016）：162—168。
[——. "Examining the Unexpected Texts of Zhu Faji's *Elegant Shramanas*." *Document* 1 (2016):162-168.]
姚振宗：《隋书经籍志考证》，《二十五史补编》。北京：中华书局，1955 年。
[Yao Zhenzong. "A Textual Research on the History of the Sui Dynasty." *The Supplements to Histories of Twenty-Five Dynasties*. Beijing: Zhonghua Book Company, 1955.]
永瑢等：《四库全书总目》。北京：中华书局，1965 年。
[Yong Rong, et al. *The General Catalogue to the Complete Library in Four Sections*. Beijing: Zhonghua Book Company, 1965.]
朱东润：《八代传叙文学述论》。上海：复旦大学出版社，2015 年。
[Zhu Dongrun. *A Treatise on Biographical Literature in the Eight Dynasties*. Shanghai: Fudan University Press, 2015.]
——《中国传叙文学之变迁》。上海：复旦大学出版社，2015 年。
[——. *The Development of Chinese Biographical Literature*. Shanghai: Fudan University Press, 2015.]

清末民初（1903—1919）商务印书馆汉译传记出版研究

胡　燕

内容提要：商务印书馆自1903年至1919年出版二十三部译传，包括《传记丛书》四部、《少年丛书》中西方人物译传十四部及其他译传五部。《传记丛书》确立新的英雄典范如拿破仑、纳尔逊以及一些冒险家等，以培养具有尚武勇、尚冒险、尚进取等品质的新国民，但由于仓促上马，一版而绝。《少年丛书》模仿梁启超新体评传，采取节译、改写的翻译策略，添加绪言及“批评”，于传主之事迹、品行等可学与不可学之处一语道破，努力构建既禀赋传统美德、又融入西方智识的兼容中西的新型国民范型，成功实现了域外思想文化资源与本土思想传统的对接、融合，故一版再版，堪称近代译传出版奇迹。其他译传包括两部日本维新志士译传、第一部留学生自传、第一部当代哲学家评传，后两部译传的出版彰显了其在译传出版方面的敏锐性与开拓性，具有引时代风气之先的意义。

关键词：商务印书馆　汉译传记　出版　新民

作者简介：胡燕，文学博士，西华师范大学文学院副教授，硕士生导师。主要从事古代散文、近代翻译传记研究，近期发表了《晚清翻译传记出版与政治典范建构》（《中国出版》，2017年第16期）等。

Title: The Publishing of Translated Biography in Chinese by The Commercial Press(1903–1919): An Examination

Abstract: The Commercial Press published twenty-three translated biographies from 1903 to 1919, including four volumes of *Biography Series*

and fourteen biographies of western subjects in *Books for Youth* and the other five biographies. *Biography Series* set the examples of new heroes such as Napoleon, Nelson and adventurers to cultivate the new citizens who embodied boldness, the spirit of adventure and ambitions. Because of insufficient preparation, however, they were not republished any more. *Books for Youth* imitated Liang Qichao's New Biography in adding exordium and criticism, adopting the strategy of abridged translating and rewriting, revealing the biographical subject's exemplary and unexemplary deeds, establishing a new model for fostering new nationals featuring both the traditional virtue of endowment and western intellectual, and realizing the integration of foreign ideology and Chinese cultural traditions successfully. So they were reprinted many times, which is nothing less than a miracle in the modern publication of translated biography. The other translated biographies included two biographies of Japanese reformers, the first autobiography of student studying abroad and the first critical biography of a modern philosopher. The latter two publications manifest his insight and pioneering vision and make great sense in leading the trend.

Keywords: The Commercial Press, Chinese translated biography, publication, innovating nationals

Dr. Hu Yan is Associate Professor of Classic Chinese Literature at China West Normal University. Her research interests are classic Chinese prose and modern translated biography studies. She is the author of "The Publication of Biography Translations in Late Qing Dynasty (1886-1911) and the Construction of Political Models" in *Journal of China Publishing* 16(2017). E-mail: huyanplzh@163.com.

商务印书馆是近代出版汉译传记数量最多、影响最大的民营出版机构。商务印书馆自1903年至1919年出版二十三部译传，包括《传记丛书》四种（1903年）、《少年丛书》中西方人物译传十四种（1908—1919年）①、其他译传五种。单就世俗人物译传而言，仅同时期的广学会②所出译传与其数量相当，远超其他出版机构。其所出译传的传主类型丰富，包括近代欧美政治家、军事家、探险家，日本维新志士，古代欧洲哲学家，当代欧洲学者等。其中，《少年丛书》被民国教育部审定为“学生校外必读”书籍，多次再版，如《大彼得》自1909年12月初版，至1916年4月已出第九版，短短七年时间再版八次，这样的再版速度无论在当时，还是当今均是令人惊讶的。北京团结出版社在2015年再版文白对照本《少年丛书》，表明其在当下仍有阅读之价值。冯玉祥曾言："(《少年丛书》) 每本总有许多地方可以使我们看到中外伟人奋斗的史迹，可以鼓励我们向他们学习，可以扩大我们的心胸，坚定我们的意念。实在是一部良好的丛书。"（冯玉祥 177）商务印书馆所出译传，既有《少年丛书》一版再版的出版奇迹，亦有《传记丛书》一版而绝的出版教训，实值得关注。

一、《传记丛书》

《传记丛书》乃是商务印书馆于1903年出版的一集四编西方人物传记丛书。第一编《克莱武传》，麦可利著，由商务印书馆编译所转译自日文，"克莱武传……今就日本中尾氏重译"[③]。第二编《拿破仑传》，矢岛元四郎著，范枕石译。第三编《纳尔逊传》，据版权页及《绪言》，该传似由中村佐美译，何震彝编。但据笔者考证，《纳尔逊传》基本照录内田成道与冈千仞所译的《纳耳逊传：军人必读》（罗业叟梯即 Robert Southey 著，1888年），仅删掉了序、引言、正文每一节后的"译者曰"，修改了少量的字词，如将"可令伍德"改为"司令伍德"之类。第四编《辟地名人传》，爱德华著，王汝宇译。

商务印书馆翻译出版该丛书的目的在于：其一，确立新的英雄典范以新民。该丛书颂美两类英雄，第一类乃是以武力建功立业之"绝世之英雄"（杨瑜统 2），或以商战殖民印度如克莱武，或以陆战横扫欧洲如拿破仑，或以海战称雄海上如纳尔逊；第二类乃是以一己之力开疆拓土的冒险家，即《辟地名人传》中所言之二十多位欧美冒险家，他们"抗志航海，不避艰险，搜觅新地。风气既开，兴起者众。国家坐享其利，而殖民之地乃愈推愈广矣。……读之可以增人进取之气。"（王云五 35）商务印书馆对军事家及冒险家的颂扬展现出其作为有文化担当意识的出版者着意通过英雄传记以培养具有尚武勇、尚冒险、尚进取等品质的新国民的美好愿望，正如《拿破仑传》的提要所言："拿破仑名震环球，世人无不欲知其生平。……有崇拜英雄之念者，曷取而三复之。"（王云五 35）其二，以印度之覆辙以警世。时人常以中国比印度，而以克莱武等为代表的东印度公司逐渐蚕食印度的前车之鉴引发了国人兔死狐悲之感慨以及强烈的生死存亡之忧患意识。“悲哉！怅怀中国，世事茫茫，印度第二，殷鉴不远。”（麦可利 1）“印度衰颓之状，是书所记颇详，足以警我中国。”（商务印书馆 1）

该丛书是商务印书馆编译所成立起来为顺应时代风潮力推的第一套传记丛书，展示了其作为有出版理想、欲“提撕国民”的出版机构所应有的社会担当与忧患意识，但可能是准备不足、仓促上马，故该丛书的源文本、传主选择、文风、体例等颇为驳杂，故在当时影响不大，一版而绝。原因大致如下：其一，据笔者统计，各类出版机构 1902 年仅出版二十四部译传，而 1903 年共出版了八十部单行本译传，呈井喷式增长。读者面对着纷至沓来的各类译传目不暇接，而商务印书馆编译所在翻译、出版西方传记之时，缺乏对市场的详细调查，导致同一传主的译本在 1903 年重复出版。如关于拿破仑的传记，仅 1903 年就有益新译社、通社、东来译局、文明书局及商务印书馆共出版五部不同源文本及译者的传记。商务印书馆躬奉盛会，一方面可见出其对社会热点的敏感以及追随新思潮的胆气，但也导致其所出译传湮没不闻。其二，其所出译传读者定位不准确，如日人翻译《纳尔逊传》的目的在于为海军军人作战做参考，故音译大量外国地名、人名、军舰名，重在阐明现代海战的战术、战略等军事知识。商务印书馆在出版之时，不加甄别，一仍其旧，对大量的外来词如“磅”之类以及对普通读者而言异常陌生的军事术语等未加以本土化的阐释。这样的直译增加了阅读障碍，影响了阅读的流畅度，故其传播效果大打折扣，亦在所难免。这亦是早期传记翻译出版甚而是早期西文翻译出版的通病，其时尚未找到西方思想资源与本土传统文化情境相契合的最佳途径。

二、《少年丛书》中的十四部西方人物译传

《少年丛书》，又名《中外伟人的传略》，是商务印书馆从 1908 年至 1919 年分六批陆续出版的中外历史名人传记丛书，是 20 世纪中国第一部历史人物

类普通教学辅导丛书。该丛书包括30部人物传记，其中外国历史人物14种，中国历史人物16种。该传记丛书总括东西历史名人的构架及别名明显受到梁启超《中西伟人传》（广智书局，1903年）的影响。《中西伟人传》收录中国伟人张骞、班超，外国伟人噶苏士、马志尼、加里波的、加富尔、罗兰夫人。《中西伟人传》将中西豪杰英雄并列以构建晚清国民效法、学习之政治典范④，乃是其以文学实践“新民说”的具体呈现。所谓“新民云者，非欲吾民尽弃其旧以从人也。新之义有二：一曰淬厉其所本有而新之；二曰采补其所本无而新之。”（梁启超 550）《少年丛书》即秉承这一理念，既淬砺革新本国既有之豪杰以适应新时代，又博采各国特别是欧美之英雄以补国民之缺失，目的在于打造新国民，使其具备完美人格和现代国民素质。“少年丛书”之命名得之于林万里，林万里曾于1903年上半年留学日本，可能接触过其时正风靡日本的五卷本《少年传记丛书》（东京：名友社，1897年），故借鉴之。

据崔文东（崔文东）及笔者的考证（胡燕 326—352），《少年丛书》中的十四部外国人物传记，名为编辑，但除每书开篇之绪论与章节后的“批评”外，其余部分多节译、改写自日文传记。其中《毕斯麦》《哥仑布》《华盛顿》《纳尔逊》《大彼得》《加里波的》《格兰斯顿》《克林威尔》等八部译自日本博文馆出版的《世界历史谭》中的同名传记，《达尔文》译自英文，其余传记的源文本不可考。林万里自1908年至1911年译写了六部传记，即《毕斯麦》《哥仑布》《华盛顿》《纳尔逊》《大彼得》《加里波的》；孙毓修自1917年至1918年5月译写了三部传记，即《格兰斯顿》《富兰克林》《德谟士》；钱智修自1918年5月至1919年译写了五部传记，即《林肯》《克林威尔》《苏格拉底》《达尔文》《拿坡仑》。就传主的身份而言，包括三类：近世欧美政治家、军事家，古代欧洲的雄辩家与哲学家，近世欧洲学者。林万里作为该丛书第一任编者，提出了十三条编辑大纲，明确了《少年丛书》的潜在读者、传记结构、传记语言、与学堂课本之关系、传主选录标准、编辑目的等，继任者亦萧规曹随。

《少年丛书》是“专供青年男女及学校生徒之观览”之“中学国文读本”“中等历史读本”“中等伦理书”（林万里：《〈少年丛书〉编辑之旨趣》 2—

3)，故兼有教科书之功能。有鉴于此，该丛书针对青少年这一特殊读者群在三个方面进行了有效的探索：其一，针对青少年的接受能力与兴趣点，传记的写作“以富于趣味，而引人入胜为主，事实并不杜撰”（林万里：《〈少年丛书〉编辑之旨趣》 3），文字“力求浅明，而又不流于俚俗”（林万里：《〈少年丛书〉编辑之旨趣》 1），令仅有初步知识积累的少年能够阅读。这就首先解决了如何吸引少年阅读的问题。其二，传记既然是叙述一生的经历，少年时代自然是传记写作的题中应有之义。但《少年丛书》既然专门为少年而作，故特别着墨于人物的少年儿童时代，对其辛勤学习、不畏困难处大书特书。如“人但称哥仑布善读书，并不以操业贱而笑之”（林万里：《哥仑布》 4）；加里波的少年时“专究天文、地理、算术诸学，欲为航海业”（林万里：《加里波的》 4）；特别是华盛顿自幼好学，尤好军事游戏，“其性情颇激烈，然极善于自制，生平守规则、慎言行，绝不肯为不道德之事”（林万里：《华盛顿》 7）。译传着意于介绍传主的求学方式，以引导、启迪正处求学阶段少年的求学态度，如在论述哥伦布之所以能最终发现新大陆，就在于“当举世顽迷咸不知地球为何物之时代，而哥伦布独能不为附和，自辟见解”，故“吾辈读书，既不可不信古人，而又不可不疑古人”（林万里：《哥仑布》 17）。以英雄之真实事迹宣扬既“求新”，又“好古”之修业态度，对少年之感染、激励可想而知。其三，所谓金无足赤，人无完人。英雄豪杰并非均是道德完人，其身上亦有诸多缺点、错误，“英雄则多不矜细行者，若果悉存英雄之全面目，则读者流弊所及必有画虎类狗之讥”（林万里：《〈少年丛书〉编辑之旨趣》 3），但因少年缺乏相应的判断力，故译者或改写原文，“只取可法之处，存其一面，其他之一面不足为训者，概从删削”（林万里：《〈少年丛书〉编辑之旨趣》 3），或添加评论，引导读者“批判性”地看待传主，“观毕斯麦之少年，殆无一事可取。为学生时，不守礼法。当兵时，故违命令。此皆彼之极坏处，读者不可不知”（林万里：《毕斯麦》 8）。改写或评论的目的在于避免传主形象与圣贤豪杰的标准发生冲突，以致难以自圆其说。当英雄的某些非原则性缺点、错误对少年有借鉴意义时，译者努力掘发其正面意义，如哥仑布因择友不当，引起数次风波甚而失败，“故吾人读哥仑布传，只可学其冒险，学其忍耐，至于哥仑布此种过失，不可不引之为鉴也”（林万里：《哥仑布》 46—47）。

译传在保留传统章回体的框架的同时，又模仿梁启超的“新体评传”开篇绪论、正文夹叙夹议、末篇结论的结构范式，积极呼应近代评传热潮。故译传开篇绪论多以某一关键词如“名誉心”“冒险”等提纲挈领，正文在叙述其人、其事、其言之后再加格言式的“批评”（评语），“间有应须注意之处，则于每章之下特加批评一段，使读者易资启发。此系参用历史家论赞之体及小说家批评之体”（林万里：《〈少年丛书〉编辑之旨趣》 4—5）。用批评点明传主言行、事迹的意义具有画龙点睛之励志效果，更易为青年读者接受，从中获得某种启发。传记对传主言论、行事一一点评，品评得失与否，多以史带论，而非以论带史，如纳尔逊在进攻西班牙某港失利负伤之后，译者从道德角度批评曰：“右手全断，仆地而复起立，起立而复仆地。一身染血，犹扶上甲板观战，何其勇也。见兵士落水，忍痛指挥小艇救助，自以左手攀绳而立，何其仁也。不悲断臂，不悲失败而以此后不能为国家尽力而悲，何其忠也。忠勇而且仁爱，大军人之资格，固应如是。”（林万里：《纳尔逊》 26）在概括传主的事迹之后，立足于传统儒家立场揭橥人物之精神气质，彰显了中国传统文化与西方现代明的对话，富有说服力与感染力。至于应该让传主自己说话，还是由作者揭破题旨，历来有不同的看法。译者采取先叙后论、夹叙夹议的方式，既是模仿、回应梁启超新体评传如《李鸿章》的结构及表述方式，更是出于对其时青年学生阅读及理解水平的担忧，故意越俎代庖。

其编译出版之目的有二：一是令青少年有模仿学习之榜样，“本书所选辑之人物皆道德完备之圣贤及爱国之英雄、救世之豪杰。与夫勤苦励志、卒成事业之大发明家、大实业家、大军人、大硕士，而要其人多半忠臣、孝子、烈士、义父与国家及世界有关系者。吾国青年男女学生若能取为模范，实足以养成国民之资格”（林万里：《〈少年丛书〉编辑之旨趣》 2）。二是努力构建一种既禀赋传统美德，又融入西方智识的兼容中西的新型国民范型，旨在融合传统伦理与西方品格，顺应提倡修身教育的潮流，故“吾国青年男女学生若能取为模范，实足以养成国民之资格，故本书又可作为中等伦理书读”

（林万里：《〈少年丛书〉编辑之旨趣》 2—3）。译者以教科书特别是伦理学书定位译传，借译传发挥此时方兴未艾的教科书功能，故其笔下的传主大都是大功业之缔造者、道德之化身、求新知之典范，故译者在叙述传主生平、言论之时，一方面着力重新阐释诸如进取冒险、独立、自信力、忍耐、荣誉等构建新国民素质的重要概念以及介绍西学新知如地理学知识等，另一方面出于根深蒂固的文化优越感，又力图凸显传统儒家伦理如忠孝等传统道德。“本书编辑之旨在保存国粹，改良风俗。凡国民固有之美性务须发挥之，凡世界最新之智识务须输入之。”（林万里：《〈少年丛书〉编辑之旨趣》 6—7）故为实践这一目的，译者着意将西方豪杰置于本土情境之中加以阐发与修正，如纳尔逊之所以能成为一代名将，除具名誉心与勇气之外，尚由于忠孝两全，“守其父不却步之训，遂能击退西军。观欧特曼（笔者注：纳尔逊之父）之书，可知老人何等欣慰。纳尔逊真忠臣，纳尔逊真孝子”（林万里：《纳尔逊》 22）。

《少年丛书》各册一版再版，风靡数年，销路大好，发行大都在五六版以上，多的达十来版，直到20世纪40年代末，估计每种书销量不会低于1万册。与一版而绝的《传记丛书》相较，其畅销的原因在于：其一，潜在读者明确且极富针对性。《传记丛书》在翻译出版之初，并无整体的框架设计，故其潜在读者的选择以及版式设计、传主选定、行文风格等皆五花八门；而《传记丛书》中的“翻译之旨趣”开篇就确定了青年及在校生为潜在读者群，并据此采取种种策略以吸引这个最有阅读意愿、最乐于接受新思想的群体。其二，采用节译改写而非全译硬套的翻译策略。《传记丛书》多为全译，音译全部人名、地名，硬译西方谚语、军事术语、度量衡单位等，故极大地影响阅读的流畅感及理解的深度；《少年丛书》多为节译，人名、地名或省略，或以某人、某港、某地代替，意译西方谚语、军事术语等，并将西方公元纪年与中国年号纪年先后列出，便于比较。《少年丛书》的绪言及批评皆由译者添加，目的在于突出主题，对于传主的生平事迹有提纲挈领之概括，于传主之事迹、品行等可学与不可学之处一语道破，试图将西方英雄的言行、事迹及道德加以本土化的解读，以契合构建新型国民之需要，乃是其中西会通观念的生动演绎。其三，篇幅适中、文字浅明。《传记丛书》多为十余万言；而

《少年丛书》均为2万字左右。字数的多寡能极大地影响阅读的成就感与新鲜感，且字数多，则意味着出版成本高，定价自然也就高，《传记丛书》定价多为三角至四角，而《少年丛书》统一定价为一角，价廉亦成为其畅销的重要原因之一。"文字不尚高古，只取浅明。吾国青年男女只须略通文法，便可观览"（林万里：《〈少年丛书〉编辑之旨趣》 1），译传运用浅显的文言文，叙述语言平易简洁，人物语言力求个性生动，富有生活气和趣味性。

三、其他译传

近代商务印书馆在翻译、出版两部译传丛书之外，又翻译、出版了五部单本译传。五部传记中尤为人所注目的译传，大致如下。

其一，日本明治维新志士译传两部，即单传《吉田松阴》与合传《日本近世豪杰小史》。《吉田松阴》（1903年）的源文本乃是德富猪一郎《吉田松阴》（民友社，1893年），译者王钝将原文的二十章缩减为十七章，较为完整地叙述吉田松阴的生平与思想。吉田松阴是日本江户幕府末期著名的启蒙思想家与教育家，师从兰学著名学者佐久间象山，开办松下村塾，培养了高杉晋作、木户孝允、伊藤博文等明治维新早期的领导者，"创尊王覆幕之先声，以成明治维新之基，诚日本近世第一伟人也"⑤。《日本近世豪杰小史》（1903年）由商务印书馆编译所翻译，源文本是西村三郎编辑的《近古慷慨家列传》（春阳堂，1887年），该传包括以佐久间象山、坂本龙马、岩仓具视为代表的明治维新的先觉者、攘夷者等三十余人的传记，翻译出版的目的在于"明治维新以来彼国杰出之材，人人乐为称道。但知其略，未知其详，不无遗憾。本馆因取日本近世之有勋业学问侠义奇行者，搜辑其事实，各列一传，著为是编。读之可灼见其人才之盛"⑥。这意味着以张元济、高凤谦为首的编译所秉承变法求新、立宪改良的理念，试图通过出版日本维新志士的传记以及其他鼓吹立宪的刊物如《帝国丛书》《政学丛书》等，竭力为立宪思潮推波助澜。"以张元济为代表的商务印书馆集体领导对于立宪改良情有独钟，这直接影响到20世纪初期商务印书馆的整个出版倾向——全力支持与赞助立宪思潮。”（史春风 42）以上关于维新志士传记的翻译出版是其时宣传立宪的重要组成部分。

其二，近代第一部留美归国的留学生自传，即《西学东渐记——容纯甫先生自述》（1915 年）。该书作者容闳是第一个留美毕业生，回国后为实现教育救国而备尝艰难挫折，晚年从主张维新变法到最终倾向并支持革命。原书为英文本，英文名为 *My Life in China & America*，于 1909 年由 Henry Holt & Company 出版，记述了其积极寻求中国近代化道路的一生经历。译者徐凤石、恽铁樵将原书仅表示生活经历“我在中国与美国的生活”意译为“西学东渐”，既凸显其“以西方之学术，灌输于中国，使中国日趋于文明富强之境”（容闳 27）之志向，又彰显“藉西方文明之学术以改良东方文明之文化”（容闳 104）即以西学改良中学之良苦用心。“西学东渐”既是对传主一生追求的经典概括，亦言简意赅地揭示出近代以来西方学术思想逐渐影响中国传统思想的事实，故成为研究近代思想、文化的高频词，而译传之影响亦不言自明。

其三，近代第一部当代西方哲学家评传，即《德国大哲学家郁根传》（1917 年）。该书名为钱智修编纂，实为译作。该书的源文本为琼斯·阿贝尔·约翰（Jones Abel John）的《鲁道夫·郁根——一部人生哲学》（*Rudolf Eucken—A Philosophy of Life*，1913），原书九章，全面论述了郁根（现译为欧肯）的著述、人生观、认识论及宗教观。译者将原著前言中的郁根生平及著述概述移入第二章，其余一依原作。该书初于 1916 年分四期连载于《教育杂志》，又于次年纳入《教育丛书》出单行本，后又以“欧根人生哲学述要”之名纳入《柏格逊与欧根》（1923 年）。翻译该书之目的在于“盖郁根所以欲解决宇宙问题者，意固在由此而得鞭策人心之原动力，使其企图高尚生活而证自由与人格之真果也。我国今日人欲横流，民志疲苶，郁根之说或可飧馈精神上之饥渴而为促进人格教育之先声欤”（Jones，Abel John 3）。该传独特之处在于不以其生平行事为叙述重点，而以其理论主张为重点，盖其“学问家而非事业家也”，“以为进读原书之喤引，此亦著学术史之通例”（Jones，Abel John 6—7）。对当代哲学家评传的翻译、出版表明其对哲学界的最新动态有敏锐的洞察力与作为出版机构应有的文化担当。

四、结　论

近代商务印书馆所翻译出版的二十三部传记，其中一半以上的源文本来自日文，表明商务印书馆编译所在有意识地接受明治日本评传的影响，既注重明治维新志士的翻译出版，又通过日文转译欧美近世英雄译传。明治日本评传成为近代译传具有统摄性的影响来源。这可能与编译所创立者张元济曾参与戊戌变法、深受康梁影响有关。其所出译传，除早期有极少数外来译稿如《纳尔逊传》《辟地名人传》之外，其余基本上为编译所职员完成，这保证了译传的翻译质量与水平，更是其如《少年丛书》风靡数载之重要原因。译传的传播效果及范围，主要取决于译者是否善于将西方英雄人物的言行、事迹等加以本土化的再度阐释与修正。《传记丛书》一版而绝，就在于全译硬套以致生吞活剥而缺乏与本土情境的对话；《少年丛书》一版再版，就在于节译改写西方英雄的言行、事迹以契合构建新型国民之需要，成功地实现了域外思想文化资源与本土思想传统的对接、融合。除此之外，编译所又翻译出版了第一部留学生自传、第一部当代哲学家评传，在译传传主选择上的慧眼独具，使得商务印书馆所出译传具有引时代风气之先的先导意义。

致谢【Acknowledgment】

本文为西华师范大学2017年度英才科研基金项目“近代汉译传记的文献整理及研究”（17YC456）阶段性研究成果，得到西华师范大学的经费支持，作者谨致谢忱！

The author is grateful to the Project for the Talented “The study of Modern Chinese Translation Biography”(IC：17YC456) funded by China West Normal University in 2017, which supports the present paper.

注释【Notes】

① 指译传的初版年，若无特别说明，下文所言之出版年均指初版年。

② 广学会是西方传教士在近代中国设立的最大出版机构。广学会从1887年至1919年共出版了四十三部译传，其中有二十部新教人物传记，二十三部世俗人物传记。

③ 引文出自《商务印书馆五月份出版新书》广告，《中外日报》，1903年6月2日。
④ 《新编中西伟人传》（内附意大利建国三杰传）广告："夫振人精神、增人智识，莫过于读人物传记，且以著者之文笔纵横感人尤切。父兄之欲子弟成材者最宜以此等书为读本，使之日渐浸渍，有所模范，有所观感，胜于寻常教科书万万也。"《中外日报》，1903年8月9号。
⑤ 《吉田松阴》广告，《中外日报》，1903年7月25日。
⑥ 《日本近世豪杰小史》广告，《中外日报》，1903年6月21日。

引用文献【Works Cited】

崔文东：《晚清翻译传记研究》。博士学位论文，香港：香港中文大学，2015年。
[Cui Wendong. *A Study of Translated Biographies in Late Qing Dynasty*. PhD dissertation, Hong Kong: The Press of Chinese University of Hong Kong, 2015.]
林万里：《〈少年丛书〉编辑之旨趣》，《少年丛书·哥仑布》，林万里编译。上海：商务印书馆，1914年，第1—7页。
[Lin Wanli. "The Editorial Purport of Books for Youth." *Books for Youth: Christopher Columbus*. Ed. and trans. Lin Wanli. Shanghai: The Commercial Press, 1914. 1-7.]
林万里编译：《少年丛书·加里波的》。上海：商务印书馆，1911年。
[Lin Wanli, Ed. and trans. *Books for Youth: Giuseppe Garibaldi*. Shanghai: The Commercial Press, 1911.]
——：《少年丛书·纳尔逊》。上海：商务印书馆，1909年。
[——. *Books for Youth: Nelson*. Shanghai: The Commercial Press, 1909]
——：《少年丛书·华盛顿》。上海：商务印书馆，1909年。
[——. *Books for Youth: George Washington*. Shanghai: The Commercial Press, 1909.]
——：《少年丛书·毕斯麦》。上海：商务印书馆，1908年。
[——. *Books for Youth: Bismarck*. Shanghai: The Commercial Press, 1908.]
——：《少年丛书·哥仑布》。上海：商务印书馆，1914年。
[——. *Books for Youth: Christopher Columbus*. Shanghai: The Commercial Press, 1914.]
冯玉祥：《我的读书生活》。上海：作家书屋，1947年。
[Feng Yuxiang. *My Reading Life*. Shanghai: Writer House, 1947.]
胡燕：《〈近代汉译西学书目提要〉传记类文献补证》，《励耘学刊》25（2017）：326—352。
[Hu Yan. "The Supplementary Collection and Research of Biographies to *Modern Chinese Translation of Western Books Bibliography*." *Li Yun Journal* 25(2017): 326-352].
Jones, John Abel：《德国大哲学家郁根传》，钱智修译。上海：商务印书馆，1917年。
[Jones, John Abel. *Rudolf Eucken: A Philosophy of Life*. Trans. Qian Zhixiu. Shanghai: The Commercial Press, 1917.]
梁启超：《饮冰室文集点校》（第一辑）。昆明：云南教育出版社，2001年。
[Liang Qichao. *Ice-Drinking Room Collected Works* (the First Series). Kunming: Yunnan Education Publishing House, 2001.]
麦可利：《跋》，《克莱武传》，商务印书馆译。上海：商务印书馆，1903年，第1—2页。
[Malcolm, John: Postscript. *The Life of Robert Lord Clive*. Trans. The Commercial Press.

Shanghai: The Commercial Press, 1903. 1-2.]
容闳:《西学东渐记》,徐凤石、恽铁樵译。上海:商务印书馆,1915年。
[Rong Hong. *My Life in China & America*. Trans. Xu Fengshi and Yun Tieqiao. Shanghai: The Commercial Press, 1915.]
商务印书馆:《凡例》,载麦可利:《克莱武传》,商务印书馆译。上海:商务印书馆,1903年,第1页。
[The Commercial Press, Explanatory Notes. *The Life of Lord Robert Clive* by John Malcolm. Trans. Commercial Press. Shanghai: The Commercial Press, 1903. 1.]
史春风:《商务印书馆与中国近代文化》。北京:北京大学出版社,2006年。
[Shi Chunfeng. *The Commercial Press and the Culture of Modern Chinese History*. Beijing: Peking University Press, 2006.]
王云五:《商务印书馆与新教育年谱》。南昌:江西教育出版社,2008年。
[Wang Yunwu. *The Commercial Press and New Education in China: A Chronicle*. Nanchang: Jiangxi Education Publishing House, 2018.]
杨瑜统:《序》,《克莱武传》,商务印书馆译,上海:商务印书馆,1903年,第1—2页。
[Yang Yutong. Preface. *The Life of Lord Robert Clive*. Trans. The Commercial Press. Shanghai: The Commercial Press, 1903. 1-2.]

为信仰殉道

——托马斯·莫尔之死

蔡青辰

内容提要：托马斯·莫尔的名字为世人所知，不仅因为他的著作《乌托邦》，而且得益于罗伯特·博尔特的著名电影《四季之人》塑造的银幕英雄形象。影片中的莫尔作为英国国王的大法官，为官清正廉洁，却因为反对亨利八世的离婚案，遭受反派克伦威尔的贪污罪的控告。最终他毅然决然地走上断头台。而现实中，托马斯·莫尔的死亡更为曲折，死因更为复杂。这与他本人的性格特征、他对婚姻的看法、他对宗教的态度、他与马丁·路德领导的宗教改革的对抗等，都有密切关系。

关键词：托马斯·莫尔　乌托邦　马丁·路德　亨利八世

作者简介：蔡青辰，浙江大学人文学院中文系博士研究生。主要研究方向为文艺学。

Title: A Martyr to Faith: The Death of Thomas More

Abstract: Thomas More is known all over the world, not only because of his book *Utopia*, but also because of Robert Bolt's well-known film *A Man for all Seasons* in which he was shaped as a hero. In the film, More was Lord Chancellor of Great Britain, honest and upright. He bitterly opposed the case of Henry VIII's divorce. For this he was charged by Cromwell, who played the part of the villain. In order to ingratiate himself with Henry VIII, Cromwell bought off a mean person to claim that More had been guilty of corruption. Ultimately, More chose with a firm determination to walk to the scaffold. In reality, Thomas More's death was more complicated. It was closely related to his own character, his attitude towards marriage and religion along with his antagonism to the famous religious reformation launched by Martin Luther.

Keywords: Thomas More, utopia, Martin Luther, King Henry VIII

Cai Qingchen, a PhD candidate in College of Arts and Humanities at Zhejiang University, is majored in literary theory. E-mail: caiqingchen.cqc@163.com.

作为《乌托邦》一书的作者，托马斯·莫尔之名百世流芳。在政治上，他更是担任了英国大法官的要职。然而令人唏嘘的是，托马斯·莫尔的一生终结在了血腥的断头台上，不得善终。

在罗伯特·博尔特根据托马斯·莫尔生平创作的著名电影《四季之人》（*A Man for all Seasons*）中，莫尔的死因非常戏剧化。莫尔作为清正廉洁的大法官，反对亨利八世的离婚案，反派角色克伦威尔为了讨好亨利八世，收买小人构陷莫尔贪污，最终将莫尔送上断头台，为亨利八世顺利迎娶新王后扫清障碍。主人公为了正义，宁愿牺牲性命而不愿屈服的品格令观众赞佩不已。然而电影中的莫尔与传记中的莫尔并不完全等同。现实中，莫尔不仅与亨利八世关系密切，与前任大法官红衣主教沃尔西也相交甚笃。莫尔一步步与亨利八世反目成仇，最终陷入绝地，其中的缘由比起电影情节更为复杂而跌宕。

一、托马斯·莫尔的性格

博尔特的电影的最后一幕是莫尔登上断头台。这一幕被渲染得如英雄就义一般悲壮。莫尔虽然身着粗布衣，头发凌乱，手脚被沉重的刑具束缚，但眼神却平静而坚毅（Bolt 99）。博尔特的电影大获成功，正因为他所塑造的莫尔是这样一位刚正不阿、为自己的良心而献身的英雄形象。实际上影片为了渲染悲剧氛围，塑造英雄人物而采用艺术手法，着重刻画了莫尔性格中宁折不弯的一面。

然而现实中的莫尔并非只有影片里所表现的刚直不屈的一面。他的个性更为复杂而丰满。作为一个活生生的人，生活中的丈夫、父亲，职场上的国王的臣子，他面临着更多的诱惑，有更多的顾虑，也有更多的选择会动摇他的心神。所以他比影片中的英雄莫尔形象走过了更多的心路历程，经历了更多的踟蹰犹豫。这样的莫尔，与影片中供人敬仰的英雄莫尔殊途同归，反而使得传记所表现的莫尔形象更加鲜活动人。

与博尔特所塑造的形象一样，现实中的莫尔是一位谈吐幽默且博学多知、温文尔雅而据理力争的英国绅士。这与他良好的成长环境关系密切。莫尔出生在伦敦的一个富庶而有教养的家庭。“根据一切情况判断，约翰·莫尔不仅是一个青云直上的人，而且还是一个十分富裕的市民，所以，他在伦敦这块富人生活的街区才能拥有一座漂亮的住宅。”（奥西诺夫斯基 3）优渥的家庭环境给莫尔提供了接受优质教育的条件。因为父亲人事关系之便，莫尔十五岁时便进入当时的坎特伯雷大主教、国王的大法官约翰·莫顿的宅邸中担任侍从，锻炼出了优秀的语言技巧与文艺才能。随后在莫顿的建议下，莫尔进入牛津大学坎特伯雷学院学习文法、修辞和伦理学，又到过法国和意大利游学，研究神学和古希腊罗马文化。回到伦敦以后，他在专门的法律学校里攻读英国国王的法律，并进入林肯大学学习，成长为一名“完美无缺”的律师。

莫尔为人正直、两袖清风的美誉，形成于他全身心投入律师事业的时候。莫尔早早地便在伦敦享有颇高的声望。他结识了当时著名的学者伊拉斯谟。这位荷兰牧师称赞莫尔“无论谁也没有像莫尔那样审理过这么多案件，无论谁也没有比他更为光明磊落地处理这些案件；在大多数情况下，他宁可自己蒙受损失，而降低诉讼人因立案照例应支付的费用”（奥西诺夫斯基 8）。“我从未见过任何人比他更不讲究饮食。一直到他成年，他爱饮的是清水……他衣着朴素，从来不穿绸披紫也不戴金链，除非万不得已，为了应付礼节。”（莫尔：《乌托邦》 126）

莫尔能够赢得美誉，不仅因为他的美德，也得益于他的聪明睿智、八面玲珑。所以他作为一名出色的律师，并晋升为后来的大法官，却能自始至终保持着清正廉洁的作风。“在社会交际中，他彬彬有礼，风度不凡，能使郁郁不欢的人心情舒畅，能使一切棘手的难题显得轻松。”（莫尔：《乌托邦》

127）在博尔特的电影的高潮部分，莫尔离开伦敦塔接受最后的审判，克伦威尔极尽所能、花样百出地制造逻辑陷阱，意图迫使他认罪，但是都被莫尔逐一识破，轻松化解。最后，狗急跳墙的克伦威尔只能栽赃莫尔在担任大法官期间收受贿赂。在此之前，影片曾埋下伏笔——他收下了某位诉讼人的杯子，并把它扔进了湖中，却被狼心狗肺的小人拣去，成为莫尔的把柄，最终致使他被判定有罪。然而在传记中可以发现，莫尔总是能够游刃有余地处理各种贿赂问题。在莫尔的传记中，记录了他两次巧妙应对诉讼者礼物的事情："胜诉者的妻子曾经把一个镀金的杯子当作礼物送给了莫尔。但当斟满酒，为这女士的健康祝福后，莫尔又把它当作新年礼物送还给了这位女士的丈夫。莫尔曾接受过另一位诉讼当事人赠送的杯子，但莫尔用珍贵得多的古董回赠了他。"（肯尼 97）事实上，安王后加冕之后，莫尔确实接到了他在担任大法官期间收受贿赂的控告。控诉者是王后的父亲，根本原因则是莫尔拒绝参加新王后的加冕仪式。这些控告也一样被莫尔轻松处理了。所以博尔特的电影中，莫尔被小人抓住把柄，因诬陷而被定罪的情节，则是看轻了莫尔的智慧机敏。

除却大部分时间的温和冷静，他本人的性格中也有尖锐暴烈的一面。在那时的英国，异教徒问题由来已久。莫尔担任大法官之后，一直致力于用法律手段反对异教徒。他认为异教使得人的思想堕落，诱使人们变得暴力，在处理他们时也毫不手软。莫尔的上司、前任大法官沃尔西在职期间，从未处死过异教徒。然而莫尔接手大法官一职之后，则有六个异教徒被处死，其中三个是他亲自审讯的。同样，在博尔特的电影中，温文尔雅的莫尔唯一一次情绪失控，则是女儿玛格丽特宣布要和后来的丈夫威廉·鲁伯交往的时候。鲁伯因为是马丁·路德的狂热支持者，而遭到了莫尔的强烈反对。二人唇枪舌剑、不欢而散（Bolt 36）。

在与异教徒的交锋中，性格温和的莫尔总是难以保持冷静。在与马丁·路德的纸笔论战之中，莫尔也表现出了不为人知的一面。亨利八世发布《维护七件圣事》一书之后，立刻遭到了路德的回击——他发表了一本充满谩骂、言辞轻蔑的小册子。受到亨利八世的委托，莫尔立刻用笔名写了一篇刻毒的拉丁语文章作为回击。肯尼的传记中引用了一个段落："既然他已写道，他已经有在先的权利用胡说八道来玷污和糟蹋王冠，我们难道没有一个在后的权利用来表示后来批评者的被玷污的舌头最适于舔前者那个雌骡屁股，直到他学会更正确地从前者的前提中推断出后者的结论?”（转引自肯尼 72）这些措辞的粗鲁，对于沉浸在博尔特电影中的观众而言无疑是一次打击。但是材料中表现出的莫尔对异教激烈的反抗和排斥，恰恰是促使他与路德展开长达十数年论战的原因之一。也正是这样的性格才使得莫尔丝毫不动摇不妥协，最终走向断头台。

二、托马斯·莫尔对婚姻的态度

托马斯·莫尔本人对待婚姻的态度是十分严谨的。在《乌托邦》的第二部中，详细地记录了乌托邦人的婚姻制度。在他设想的乌有之乡里，人们对待婚姻的态度严肃不苟到令人感到愚笨可笑的地步。婚姻的一切环节都是由法律规定并保护的。在法律之外，也有道德规范着住民的婚姻行为。“乌托邦的法律对这种罪行施以重罚，因为他们预见到，如对婚前乱搞男女关系不认真禁止，结成夫妇的人将很少，而夫妇同居是一辈子的，并且要忍受伴随这种生活的一切艰辛。”（莫尔：《乌托邦》 87）如果违背了婚姻法律，不仅当事者会受到法律的惩罚，其家族亲属也会受到道德上的指摘。

在《乌托邦》中，世人表达了对乌托邦人严谨的婚姻观的轻蔑。莫尔借助世人的嗤笑，展现现实的英国人对待婚姻的轻浮态度，字里行间表达出对现世人的婚姻观的不满，和对乌有之乡的住民的做法的赞同。“我们非笑这样的风俗，斥为愚蠢。乌托邦人却对所有其他国家的极端愚蠢表示惊异。”（莫尔：《乌托邦》 87）莫尔认为在结婚之前，男女双方应当坦诚相待，彼此了解对方身体的全部。比起美貌，男人应该更加注重女方的品德。莫尔本人十分重视自己子女宗教信仰、古典文学和人文知识的教育。他写给子女的家庭教师威廉·戈内尔的信中提道：“由于女性的博学是一种新事物，是对男性懒惰的一种羞辱，许多人会欣然接受这样一种观点，即学习知识本身是错误的，他们从恶习中思考，将自己的无知视为美德。”（Rogers 103）所以莫尔在

《乌托邦》中批评那些依靠外貌选择妻子的庸俗男人："并非一切男人都很明智，只重视女方的品德。即使明智的男人，在婚姻问题上，也会认为美貌大大地增加了美德。"（莫尔：《乌托邦》 88）

乌托邦人实行一夫一妻制度和婚姻终身制度。一旦结婚之后，便要求他们终生相伴，不离不弃。法律不允许他们抛弃身体罹患疾病的对方，并且在道德上认为这是残酷不仁的。"乌托邦人是唯一实行一妻制的民族，除非发生死亡，不致婚姻关系中断……如果妻子无任何可非议之处，身体不幸罹病，乌托邦人就不允许男子违反她的意志而强行和她分离。"（莫尔：《乌托邦》 88）在乌托邦里，人们不能因为一己之私，抛弃对配偶的责任而离婚。他们通过诸多条件、第三方调查者的介入和复杂的流程保证这一点。而后来莫尔所面对的亨利八世的离婚案，恰恰展现出国王对婚姻轻浮的态度。这正是莫尔和《乌托邦》一书所强烈反对的。

亨利八世的第一任妻子阿拉贡的凯瑟琳原本是亨利的哥哥威尔士的阿瑟亲王的妻子，也就是亨利八世的嫂嫂。亨利八世想要迎娶自己的嫂嫂是教会法律所禁止的，遭到了当时的教皇亚历山大六世的反对。但是在 1503 年，朱利叶斯二世继承了亚历山大六世之位，成为新的教皇。这位新教皇选择特许英国国王的这桩本当不合法的婚姻。于是 1509 年，亨利八世得以同他的王后一同加冕。而 1527 年，在亨利八世与凯瑟琳王后结婚 18 年后，亨利八世提出了离婚。原因之一是凯瑟琳王后多次流产，他们只有玛丽公主唯一一个后嗣。然而研究者普遍认为，亨利八世着急结束他的这段婚姻，最主要原因还是他移情别恋——他与凯瑟琳王后的妹妹安·博林坠入了情网。

莫尔本人对于婚内通奸等有碍婚姻关系的行为十分厌恶。在《乌托邦》中，乌托邦法律对于破坏夫妻关系的人受到的惩罚也做出了详细的规定。"发生通奸行为或脾气坏到不能相处，则是例外。当男方或女方感到自己感情上受到这种伤害，议事会就准许其另行择配。被离异的一方从此终身蒙受耻辱并过孤单的生活。"（莫尔：《乌托邦》 89）夫妻一方若在婚内有通奸行为，不仅另一方有选择离异的权利，通奸者亦不允许结婚，并且终身在耻辱中孤单生活。"破坏夫妻关系的人罚充最苦的奴隶……但如果受害者之一对于不义的对方仍然依依不舍，并不禁止他们的婚姻继续生效……但重犯前罪者判处死刑。"（莫尔：《乌托邦》 89）破坏婚姻的人将受到重罚。如果婚姻的破坏者得到了受害者一方的原谅，并表现出痛悔，则可以得到总督的怜悯而获得自由。但是如果再次发生婚内通奸，甚至要判处死刑。

当亨利八世向莫尔征求关于他与凯瑟琳王后离婚并迎娶安·博林一事的意见时，莫尔虽然没有明确地表达对于这段既不合法也不道德的离婚案的态度，但却将教会牧师对于《圣经》原文的相关评论翻阅给亨利八世看。这些评论显然不会支持国王的离婚案。

此时的红衣主教沃尔西担任着英国的大法官职务。亨利八世不满沃尔西对于离婚案拖延的处理方式，竟然借口教皇尊信罪撤销他的职务并剥夺他的财产，将大法官之位交给了莫尔。亨利八世意图莫尔上任之后尽快通过他新的婚姻。但是他不仅没有看到想要的结果，而且当巴结国王的贵族和主教联合起来向教皇签名请愿，请求通过国王的离婚案时，莫尔选择了拒绝在请愿书上签字。1531 年，莫尔不得不将亨利八世收集来的有利于他离婚案的材料提交给议会。但是在对下议院的讲话中，他却没有表达对离婚案的看法。甚至暗中鼓励那些为凯瑟琳王后辩护的人。此后，莫尔委托诺福克公爵向国王要求解除他的大法官的职务。通观《乌托邦》对于婚姻的态度，莫尔在国王离婚案中的种种作为，恰是他对自己的良心的坚持。

三、托马斯·莫尔对宗教的态度

在《乌托邦》中，岛上的居民还未能听说基督的名字。有一部分居民崇拜日月星辰，而大多数人认为有一个唯一的神，巨大永恒，奥妙无穷，超越人类领悟的能力。尽管乌托邦人信仰不一，但是所有居民都相信，至高的神只有一位——密特拉。"他们称他为父，把万物的起源、生长、发育、演化、老死都归之于他，只有对他，乌托邦人才加以神的尊称。"（莫尔：《乌托邦》 103）尽管他用尽量旁观的视角和客观的口吻论述《乌托邦》中信仰小神的异教徒，但是他又将这些信仰与唯一的神相互对比，称其他信仰为"混乱的盲

目信仰”，将信仰近似基督的神的宗教称为“最合情理的一种信仰”。（莫尔：《乌托邦》 103）

莫尔认为少数异教徒的信仰是错误的，他认为不信仰主神“密特拉”的异教徒应当放弃他们错误的信仰，皈依正确的信仰。“毫无疑问，其他的信仰本来早就应该消失，可是他们的一名成员在考虑改变信仰时，偶然遇到不幸的事，于是出于恐惧的心理不将其解释成出于偶然，说成是来自天谴，仿佛不继续受到某人礼拜的神对于这种不虔诚施以报复。”（莫尔：《乌托邦》 103）他认为这些异教徒已经被正确的大众的宗教信仰收服，只是因为出于不理智的迷信和畏惧，害怕受到谴责、报复，才仿佛是被异教所威胁一样，不敢抛弃错误的宗教信仰。所以在他描绘的《乌托邦》中，即便是那些少数信仰其他神灵的人，也趋向于被大多数人所信仰的宗教吸收。

由于乌托邦人的主流宗教与基督教极其相似，主人公一行人便在乌托邦岛上传教，并得到了乌托邦人的普遍接受。但也受到了一些阻碍。基督教相比于乌托邦岛上的原生宗教，便等同于一个新的宗教与被普通民众广泛信仰接纳的宗教之间的关系。通过他所描述的一个狂热的基督教徒向乌托邦人传教的故事，莫尔对基督教与异教的关系的态度、对新的宗教的传播者的态度可见一斑。基督教在乌托邦的传教过程中，只有一个狂热的教徒受到了处分。这个教徒四处宣扬基督教是至高完美的宗教，谴责蔑视其他一切宗教，声称它们是渎神的，信仰者将永远受到天罚。即使如此，乌托邦人给这个狂热的基督徒所定的罪名却是“煽动事端”，而非“蔑视宗教”。可见，莫尔在《乌托邦》中对待异教的态度是相当温和的。即使他认为这些异教是错误低等的、迷惑性的，他也反对用暴力手段剿灭异教。“一个人也可以向别人宣传自己的教……如果他劝说无功，不应将其他一切的教都恶毒地摧毁，不得使用暴力，不得诉诸谩骂。”（莫尔：《乌托邦》 104）

《乌托邦》认为灵魂是不朽的。虽然乌托邦人有权利选择自己的信仰，但是他们不允许有人相信形随身灭。所以人在现世的作为必将报偿于他们死后。“人死后有过必受罚，有德的必受赏。如果有人有不同看法，乌托邦人甚至认为他不配做人，因为他把自己灵魂的崇高本质降到和兽类的粗鄙躯体一般无二。”（莫尔：《乌托邦》 105）而莫尔给出的理由是，如果人们不相信死后的报应，那么在现世中他就不会忌惮法律，而是为了满足自己的私欲肆意触犯法律。对于这种意义上的异教徒，乌托邦人并不会处罚他。只是会视他为懒惰下流的人，不允许他担任公职。因为乌托邦人认为，他人信仰什么不是由自己能控制的，所以乌托邦人不会强迫相信灵魂消亡的人掩盖他们的观点。“在这个问题上，他们不容许假装说谎。他们最恨假装说谎，认为这和欺骗几乎毫无区别。”（莫尔：《乌托邦》 106）

托马斯·莫尔笔下的《乌托邦》对于异教徒的态度温和而宽容，与后来宗教改革如火如荼地开展之后，他现实中对待异教徒的做法大相径庭。在他任职大法官期间，他一共处死了六名异教徒，但是莫尔认为他对异教徒的审讯中并无任何不当，也没有任何残酷的折磨，对他们的裁决也是公正公平的。托马斯·莫尔在1529年出版的《与异端邪说的对话》中，为他惩罚异教徒的行为进行辩护。“但是，异教徒们是在我们自己中间产生，而且在我们自己中间成长的，所以只能在其滋生之时加以镇压和平服，不能给予一点宽容。因为与他们的任何盟约，基督教世界都不会有收益。”（转引自肯尼 84）

莫尔本人是最虔诚的天主教徒。他在坎特伯雷大主教家中度过童年。24岁便受邀请在圣劳伦斯尤里教堂作关于圣奥古斯丁的《天堂》系列的演讲。他有四年的时光在卡尔特修道院中过着清贫而淳朴的生活，每日在小屋里苦修冥想。结婚之后，莫尔仍在外套里穿着粗毛衬衣作为苦行赎罪，过着修道士般简朴严肃的生活。即使当时的教皇已经丑闻不断，因为强征苛税而背负骂名，因为买卖神职而臭名昭著，但正如同莫尔后来在与新教徒的争论中反复声明的，他认为教廷的占有者的卑劣并不会影响到教廷本身的神圣。

1517年《乌托邦》完成时，莫尔只有37岁左右，那一年的亨利八世还没有移情别恋，爱上凯瑟琳王后的妹妹；马丁·路德刚刚把《关于赎罪券效能的辩论》贴到维滕贝格大教堂的门上；那时的莫尔还没有接替沃尔西成为大法官。也许那时他并不会预料到十年之后，当自己面对着新教的挑战时，会采取怎样的态度对待异教徒，是否能像《乌托邦》中所设想的那样宽容，也不会预料到他将怎样细数路德教的罪恶，并用法律严惩异教徒。

四、托马斯·莫尔与王权和教权之争

在著作《乌托邦》中，托马斯·莫尔引用了《理想国》中的观点，认为学者不应该担任国王的臣子。“柏拉图作了一个很美妙的比较，指出何以哲学家有理由不参与管理国家。”（莫尔：《乌托邦》 42）但是现实中的莫尔无法拒绝来自亨利八世的三番五次的邀请，进入了宫廷。莫尔与亨利八世的关系异常亲密。亨利八世频繁地召见莫尔，以至于他大部分时间都在行宫中陪伴亨利八世。亨利八世崇尚学问，欣赏莫尔的才华。他与莫尔的话题也不曾局限于公共事务，而是从天文学到神学无话不谈。他数次光临莫尔在切尔西的宅邸，与他散步谈天，享用午餐（Ackroyd 131）。

原本莫尔也远离了这件亨利八世的离婚案，将自己的工作重心放在处理日益增长的路德教“异端邪说”上。孰料在担任大法官之后他又被迫接手处理离婚案。在处理离婚案的进程中，莫尔正如国王所首肯的那样凭借自己的良心做出选择。三次事件，三个重要的选择，既将莫尔推向了死亡的铡刀，也将他不肯牺牲良心保全性命的伟大展现给世人。当讨好国王的贵族和主教上书向教皇请愿通过亨利八世的离婚案时，莫尔拒绝在上面签名。1533 年亨利八世没有得到教皇同意，便加冕安为王后时，莫尔拒绝参加安王后的加冕仪式。1534 年，亨利八世通过了一个王位继承权的法案，宣布安王后的子嗣享有继承王位的权力，而凯瑟琳王后的女儿玛丽公主被废黜时，莫尔拒绝对这条法令宣誓。

莫尔作为一个虔诚的天主教徒，他不愿违背自己的良心，看着亨利八世践踏基督教的教义。在他看来，尽管教廷腐败不堪，但是占有者的卑劣不能玷污教廷的神圣。亨利八世作为世俗的君主，也不能任意践踏教廷的尊严。在他被囚于伦敦塔中时，他仍旧创作了数篇祷文表达愿意为坚守天主教的信仰而与现世决裂的信念。“让我踏上通往灵魂的窄路，让我背上十字架跟随基督……让我终止不必要的娱乐，为了基督的胜利，让我对世间的财产、朋友、自由、生命以及一切弃如敝履。”（莫尔：《塔中书》 223）

亨利八世处死莫尔的另一个更加重要的原因，是因为莫尔的这些选择，不仅仅表达的是他对于离婚案的拒绝。事实上此时亨利八世在离婚案中已经表现出试图全盘否认罗马教会的司法权，他想成为英国最高的、唯一的法。莫尔拒绝在国王的继承法案上签字，表达了他不认同亨利八世作为世俗君主，其权力可以凌驾于教皇和教廷之上，世俗的法律凌驾于宗教的法律之上。莫尔此时虽然已经从权力的中心退出，但是在与路德教的论战中，他仍是反对者的代表，维护教廷的中坚者。他的存在依旧是亨利八世的绊脚石，亨利八世必然会除之而后快。

在博尔特的电影中，并没有表现出莫尔与路德的直接对抗。而是通过莫尔同他的女婿的对话，含蓄地展现。现实中莫尔与路德教的论战激烈而持久，从 16 世纪 20 年代到 30 年代，莫尔的全部文艺上的活动都是围绕着欧洲的宗教改革运动展开的。1520 年 10 月，马丁·路德以维登堡大学神学教授的身份，对教皇的权威发起了挑战。是年为了筹建圣彼得大教堂，教会发布公告宣称通过捐款可以获取免罪。路德用拉丁文撰写的《教会的巴比伦俘虏》尖锐地针对此事。他由此向受过高等教育的人提出前所未闻的观点——只承认七件圣事中的两件，猛烈抨击天主教会，要求废除僧侣阶层。这本书引发了教廷的恐慌。罗马教皇先后发布了反对路德的训谕，下令焚烧没收路德的著作。由于路德派早已在剑桥、牛津等高校中获得了有力支持，教皇的这些手段成效甚微。在此事上，亨利八世选择支持教廷，反对路德派。1521 年底，亨利八世向罗马教皇赠送了《维护七件圣事》以极力推崇教皇权威。除了参与编写《维护七件圣事》，从 1521 年到 1526 年，莫尔私下里用笔名与路德进行了多次对峙。对比路德的《致英吉利人书》和莫尔的《答路德》，可以发现他们的文笔的尖锐激烈不相上下。在后来付梓的《与异端邪说对话》中也可窥见他们论战的激烈。

在宗教改革初期，莫尔与路德以及他的支持者的论战，是暗中代表国王，维护教会的权利的。从亨利八世写给德国公爵们的书信可以了解到，他认为路德对圣事的亵渎，目的是推翻基督教君主以及贵族的统治。路德的阴谋是鼓动人们造反，废除僧侣，反对国王，否定法律，推翻国家政权。《维护七件圣事》的成书一事中也可见一斑。这本书是由国王的谋士和学者集体创作的，莫尔仅仅选择了担任校对职务。他曾经提醒国王应当未雨绸缪，在书中稍微触及一下教皇的权威——因为虽然国王和其他基督教君主当下与教皇结盟，但是未来也许会产生分歧甚至引发战争。

然而随着时间的推移，亨利八世从路德教的论战中，看到了一举击溃教会，完全控制司法自治权的机会。他放弃了最初反对路德宗教改革、支持罗马教廷的路线，转而策划一场自上而下的温和改革，兵不血刃地取代罗马教皇，成为英国教廷的至尊。在英国封建社会末期，资本主义萌芽的时期，路德新教顺应了英国社会的政治与经济发展的趋势。亨利八世倾向了路德教的学说，而莫尔从代表国王的利益，逐渐倾向于代表自己的良心和教廷的威严向路德宣战。这也使得他从亨利八世的口笔沦为了他改革之路上的障碍。

莫尔在这场教会与新教的论战之中，并不是输给了学识口才，而是输给了渺小的个人无法溯洄的时代的洪流。亨利八世看准时机利用宗教改革者的论战成果，迫使教会彻底放弃了司法自治权，将之完全控制在国王权力之下。

五、托马斯·莫尔之死的意义

莫尔为了保有自己的良心，一生为守护自己的信仰而战，不惜以身殉道的事迹为人称道。在西方，人们称他为圣托马斯。1886 年，他被罗马天主教会册封为圣徒。随后卡尔·考茨基的著作《莫尔及其〈乌托邦〉》付梓，在这位马克思主义者的帮助下，在托马斯·莫尔的事迹感动了人们三百年之久后，他的著作再次在全球掀起波澜。恩格斯赞誉他为时代之子。1953 年，苏联历史学家沃尔金在《〈乌托邦〉的历史意义》中称赞他为空想社会主义鼻祖和空想社会主义最伟大的代表。无数人从他的著作中获得灵感启发，在他铺垫的基石之上取得了更高的成就。时至今日，他仍享有世人的赞誉。

莫尔坚持的是王权与教权之间的平衡，无法接受一方对另一方的完全压制。作为天主教徒，他更是无法接受教会臣服于世俗政权。在作为臣子之前，他首先是一个天主教徒。他的一生拥有一个令人羡慕不已的开端，年轻时代平步青云登上让很多人望尘莫及的高位。他有无数次机会可以从政治的漩涡中脱身，也有无数次机会可以选择掩藏自己的良心，保全自己的性命。他的处境万万不到进退维谷的绝境。他的建树已经让他成为时代的佼佼者，他的著作中的养分足以在他死后三五百年仍被人们汲汲渴求，他的智慧和才华使他可以毫不困难地全身而退。但是正是这样一个全世界的美好都向他开放的人，云淡风轻地选择了为信仰殉道。他的殉道正如他在《乌托邦》中赞许的死亡——人们讲述他的性格和事迹，对他临死前怡然自得的精神赞不绝口。

引用文献【Works Cited】

Ackroyd, Peter. *The Life of Thomas More*. New York: Anchor Books, 1999.

Bolt, Robert. *A Man for All Seasons*. London: Pearson Education Limited, 1996.

安东尼·肯尼：《托马斯·莫尔》，倪慧良、巫苑之译。北京：中国社会科学院出版社，1992 年。

[Kenny, Anthony. *Thomas More*. Trans. Ni Huiliang and Wu Yuanzhi. Beijing: China Social Sciences Press, 1992.]

托马斯·莫尔：《塔中书》，殷宏译。北京：经济科学出版社，2013 年。

[More, Thomas. *Prison-letters*. Trans. Yin Hong. Beijing: Economic Sciences Press, 2013.]

——：《乌托邦》，戴镏龄译。北京：商务印书馆，1982 年。

[——. *Utopia*. Trans. Dai Liuling. Beijing: The Commercial Press, 1982.]

И.Н.奥西诺夫斯基：《托马斯·莫尔传》，杨家荣、李兴汉译。北京：商务印书馆，1984 年。

[Осиновский, И.Н. Osinowski, H. *Biography of Thomas More*. Trans. Yang Jiarong and Li Xinghan. Beijing: The Commercial Press, 1984.]

Rogers, Elizabeth Frances. *St. Thomas More: Selected Letters*. New Haven, CT: Yale University Press, 1967.

传记电影的时效性

——以《血沃中华》和《可爱的中国》为中心

吴凑春

内容提要：方志敏在中国犹如一个不灭的灵魂，时常在各类文艺作品中复活。20世纪“十七年”时期创作了电影剧本《方志敏》，但由于各种原因一直没有成功拍摄。“文化大革命”后不久的《血沃中华》（1980年）和新世纪的《可爱的中国》（2008）是目前完成且仅有的两部方志敏传记电影。这证明了一个事实：在特定的历史时期，某些人禁止被观看，某些人被允许观看，甚至可以被反复观看。两部方志敏传记影像的彼此差异，尤其是一个着重批判党内斗争历史，一个着重歌颂清贫廉洁精神，说明了传记电影都是制作之时主流政治催生的产物，具有一种时效性特征。

关键词：传记电影　方志敏　《血沃中华》　《可爱的中国》　时效性

作者简介：吴凑春，博士，上饶师范学院副教授，主要从事传记学研究，出版学术专著《当代中国传记片创作现象批评》（2013年）。

Title: The Historicality of Film Biography: Case Studies of *Shedding Blood for China* and *Lovely China*

Abstract: Fang Zhimin, the revolutionary stays lively in a variety of Chinese literary works, as an immortal soul in China. Produced in the period from 1949 to 1966, the screenplay “The Biography of Fang Zhimin” for some reasons failed to be filmed. The only two biopics of Fang Zhimin are *Shedding Blood for China* (1980), shortly after the Cultural Revolution, and *Lovely China* (2008), which proves a fact that during a certain period, some viewers are forbidden, while others are allowed to be watched, even repeatedly. The significant difference between the two biographical movies, one focusing on criticizing the internal rifts within the party, and the other on praising the lofty spirit and integrity, demonstrates that film biography is the product of contemporary mainstream ideology, featuring the historicality on the part of the viewers.

Keywords: film biography, Fang Zhimin, *Shedding Blood for China*, *Lovely China*, historicality

Wu Couchun is Associate Professor at Shangrao Normal University.His research interest is biography study. His recent publication is *A Critique of the Making Of Contemporary Chinese Biopics*(2013). E-mail: wzchun9999@126.com.

传记起源于人类本能的自我纪念，力图写出人的本真，因此，真实也就成了传记的生命。时至今日，现代传记学认为，传记不仅是一种文类，还是一种文化，“主要以文字为媒介、以文本的形式存在，但传记也可以使用其他媒介、在不同的文化形式中出现”（杨正润 57）。传记故事电影即其中新的形式之一，它也应追求真实。但是，传记电影的真实性却很难做到，反而具有鲜明的当代性，甚至具有一种即时性特征，也就是说传记电影实为其制作之时的国家主流意识形态的精神投射。比较同一传主方志敏的两部不同传记电影《血沃中华》和《可爱的中国》即可明了。

一、经久不衰的方志敏题材文艺创作

“敌人只能砍下我们的头颅，决不能动摇我们的信仰！因为我们信仰的主义，乃是宇宙的真理！”（方志敏 141）

来自江西上饶的方志敏的这段名言，写于 1935 年 5 月 25 日。当时，他身陷囹圄，以诗明志，振聋发聩。在中国，方志敏烈士的革命事迹和英勇精神，代代传颂。早在 1937 年 1 月，中共机关报《斗争》就刊出了“纪念民族英雄方志敏专号”。1964 年毛泽东为方志敏题写墓碑名。1984 年《方志敏文集》出版，邓小平为其题写书名。2012 年 6 月人民出版社出版《方志敏全集》。

在国家政治话语层面没有忘记方志敏的同时，文学艺术工作者也多次在文艺创作中对其进行讴歌，将其复活。早在 1956 年，石凌鹤就创作了话剧

《方志敏》。这是当代中国最早出现的革命领袖人物传记话剧。该剧在1959年由江西省话剧团进京演出，参加第一届全国话剧观摩演出会，荣获二等奖。1958年工人出版社出版缪敏以回忆录的形式创作的《方志敏战斗的一生》。进入新时期，方志敏题材的文艺创作更是呈现繁荣景象。1977年江西“弋阳腔剧团”创作弋阳腔戏曲《方志敏》，获得了观众的好评。1982年张品成创作《方志敏传》，次年张知《方志敏将军传》由解放军出版社出版。2005年江西省话剧团创作了大型音乐诗画剧《可爱的中国》。2013年江西省文艺院团创作话剧《生如夏花》歌颂方志敏的精神……

总之，方志敏以其伟大精神，成为当代中国大地上一个不灭的灵魂，时不时在文艺作品中复现；以其为题材的文艺创作经久不衰，成为一道无法忽略的风景。方志敏题材文艺作品除了上面所涉之外，还有其传记电影。方志敏传记电影，即以传记故事片的形式塑造方志敏形象。当代视觉文化研究告诉我们，在当今世界，除了口传和文本之外，意义还得借助于视觉传播。因此，对有关方志敏的传记电影创作的分析还是非常有意义的。

方志敏传记电影，目前有两部：一部是1980年制作的《血沃中华》，另一部是2008年创作的《可爱的中国》。影片相关信息如下。

《血沃中华》：编剧方兰、周翼如、孙勃，导演尹一青，主演魏新，由长春电影制片厂制作。这是第一部方志敏传记电影，第一次在银幕上再现了方志敏的革命英雄形象，是介绍和宣传方志敏精神的一次重要尝试。

《可爱的中国》：编剧钟韧、胡雪杨，导演胡雪杨，任程伟主演，出自上海电影（集团）公司上海电影制片厂。

《血沃中华》讲述传主被捕入狱后直至牺牲的这段时间所发生的故事。该片着重突出传主的英雄气概，着重讲述他被捕在狱中斗争的情况，由此凸显他的坚贞不屈和崇高的革命精神境界。所以，影片虚构了他启发国民党将领武耀宗、感动狱卒张怀志、亲见有身孕妻子被拷打也不投降以及蒋介石劝降失败等情节。《可爱的中国》讲述的故事时间则更长，通过传主第一人称自述艰难的革命历程，以及在狱中的誓死抗争过程。这两部影片均为方志敏传记电影，都浓彩重墨地塑造了传主在被敌人俘虏后，坚持革命气节，最后慷慨就义的伟大形象。二者共同之处有：

首先，都是国家电影工程产品。“文化大革命”结束后不久的1980年，电影制作、生产、放映还是完全的计划经济体制，电影创作必须阐述主流政治意识形态，对革命英雄的塑造还是文艺创作的主旋律。《血沃中华》正是一部讴歌早期共产党人光辉形象的典型作品。《可爱的中国》创作于2008年，由国有大型电影集团上海电影集团联合九江市委制作，自然也要肩负宣传教育使命——该片当时被中宣部、国家电影总局列为庆祝新中国成立60周年重点影片，即证明了这一点。因此，二者都是国家级电影产品。

其次，在创作之时传主都具有入传的合法性。20世纪50年代初《武训传》因为选择了不当的人（武训）进行歌颂，被认为“污蔑了农民革命斗争”“污蔑中国历史”而遭遇大批判运动。从此，传记电影创作的首要问题就是选择谁作为传主，即必须考虑传主入传具有足够的合法性。这成了传记片创作的前提，也是一个敏感的政治问题。如果选错了人物，对创作人员来说无异于引火烧身。在极左年代，因为敏感性，方志敏传记电影难以成功拍摄。据石凌鹤先生晚年回忆，他在1956年和1959年，先后写了名为《方志敏》的话剧和电影剧本，得到了中央领导和文艺界同行们的关注。1960年元旦，在人民大会堂的迎新晚会上，周恩来总理曾当面关照电影的拍摄。因为《方志敏》牵扯到王明路线，电影剧本送中央审查。1961年，在第三次文代会期间，中宣部的某部长却对石先生讲，这个戏牵涉到王明路线的“钦差大臣”曾宏易投降国民党当了叛徒。这样的历史资料，不好公之于众。于是，《方志敏》就未能拍成电影。（邱忠毅 4—5）也就是说，方志敏在当时进入传记片不具有合法性。而在1980年和2008年这两个不同的时间点，方志敏则都具有入传的合法性，创作其传记电影都没有问题，都能顺利完成制作。纵观几十年间方志敏传记电影创作历程，证明了一个现象：在特定的历史时期，某些人被禁止观看，某些人被允许观看，甚至反复被观看。当然，不同的历史点对同一个传主方志敏的倚重点也即传主入传的合法性原因之所在是不完全一样的，后文将要论及。

最后，都要塑造传主的革命英雄形象，为宣教所用。刚刚走过“文化大革命”历史的1980年，需要《血沃中华》类作品为革命先烈正名。因此，此类作品遵循传统的革命文艺模式，塑造革命英雄形象。该片因而也就极其强调传主的浩然正气，始终刻意呈现其绝无贪生怕死之态。至2008年，虽然《可爱的中国》在艺术表现和追求上有所不同，但是，最终的创作旨归是和《血沃中华》一样的，也是国家宣传教育工作的一次实践。所以，该片上映伊始，上海市教育部门就已经为150万中小学生预订了电影票（蔡杰 48）。

二、方志敏传记影像的嬗变分析

虽然《可爱的中国》和《血沃中华》同为方志敏传记影像，但毕竟相隔近30年的时间，在传主叙事视角、传主形象设计、历史真实性的追求、创作旨归等各个方面有着很大的变化和差异，而这些历史嬗变，甚至比二者的相同点还更具有研究价值。

第一，从他传到自传：传主叙事视角的转变。《血沃中华》采用传统的第三人称叙事，由幕后“大影像师”操作，营造了一种真实、客观、权威的叙事风格。这是新中国电影中常见的叙事方式，也是一种更加体现话语霸权味道的叙述。进入20世纪90年代，许多电影尤其是传记电影开始走出这一传统叙事模式，而是尝试采用自传叙事，即由传主讲述自己的人生故事，观众能够听到传主自我叙事的声音。这种叙事视角显示了对传主的尊重，更具亲和力、更人性化。《可爱的中国》即是一例。方志敏传记电影，从他传叙事转向自传叙事视角，是人性化叙事的演进——当然，自传叙事也更有利于表现传主的自我反思意识。

第二，从真理在手到自我反思：传主形象设计的变异。《血沃中华》中的传主，是一个智者，一贯正确。外形上，他一副铮铮铁骨，时刻准备着，始终一副与敌人做斗争的英雄形象。在政治思想上，他代表真理，经常讲正确的大道理。在他的影响下，许多将要误入歧途的人走上了正确的道路。如原先内部不和的共产党人，在传主的正确引导下，最后摒弃前嫌，成为好同志，结成新的集体，手拉手一同走上刑场。这样，一方面显示了共产党人在面对阶级敌人的时候最终是团结的，另一方面更加凸显了传主的光辉形象。再如，国民党将领武耀宗被囚禁期间，灰心丧气，对国家前途非常悲观，整天借酒浇愁，颓废不堪。最后在传主的启发下，他领悟到自己的不足，重新振作起来。另如，影片还突出描写了方志敏感化年轻看守张怀志的过程。后者在传主的影响下，认识到生命的价值，冒着生命危险为传主送出书稿。总之，此时的传主是真理在手、始终正确的正面英雄人物形象，无自我反思意识，只会教导他人，而周围的人都成了塑造传主光辉形象的衬托之物。可以说，该片传主的形象塑造还具有极左时代文艺作品的影子。

进入 2008 年的传主，则不再是 20 世纪 80 年代所塑造的苍白的英雄形象。他不再是始终正确、掌握宇宙中一切真理的智者，而是具有反思意识和反思精神的人的形象。影片用自传叙事形式传递其反思意识。他在所率领的部队遭遇严重伤亡后，经常反思自己的军事指挥失误，在狱中用纸和笔书写下来以供党组织参考。传主的反思意识，还突出表现在他对生命的念念不忘上。影片情节设计他曾经收留过一位小脚齐大妹。这位妹子长大成家后，背着一个多月的小孩参加了一次残酷的战斗。当时，传主是阻止她上前线的，但是没有成功。最后母子二人尸首难寻，在战场上只找到了一只被炸得不成样子的小脚布鞋。对此，传主甚为内疚，在狱中批评自己当初没能阻止她上战场，以致一位年轻的母亲和一个弱小的生命就此消失了。此时的传主，流着眼泪反思自己，没有以往革命英雄的“高大全”形象。他平视众生，珍惜生命，具有鲜明的自我反思意识和自我批评精神。这是《血沃中华》中所没有的。

第三，从无所顾忌到力求真实：历史真实性的追求态度不同。《血沃中华》为了塑造传主的革命英雄形象，在历史真实性的态度上是无所顾忌，虚构并篡改了很多重要情节。如：方志敏在监狱里眼睁睁地看着敌人严刑拷打有身孕的妻子缪敏；缪敏在狱中生下一个男婴；蒋介石和宋美龄专门到南昌劝降，由此观众看到，在一个公园里，蒋介石要方志敏陪他下象棋，宋美龄则在一边做缪敏的工作……

但是，历史的真相是，传主在狱中没有和妻子见面的可能，历史上蒋介石从来没有见过传主。可以说，该片塑造传主革命英雄形象的功利心理过于迫切，以致不顾基本的历史事实，甚至在明知是篡改历史真实的情况下依然故我——理由就是为了塑造英雄形象的需要。但是，事实上艺术效果适得其反。影片甫出，就遭到许多观众的驳斥。有论者指出："《血沃中华》中脱离生活、凭空编造的某些重要情节和人物，表面上增加了情节的曲折性和影片的戏剧性，实际上却削弱了影片的真实性和艺术感染力，也不能使观众受到很好的革命传统的教育。"（石明 25）当年方志敏的堂弟方志纯、方志纯的夫人、戏剧家石凌鹤等人也都提出了质疑（危春勇 54）。十多年后石凌鹤先生谈及此事还非常生气、非常难过。

进入21世纪，观众对历史、对革命英雄有了更多的个人理解，像方志敏传记电影再也不能走《血沃中华》这条路了。相比《血沃中华》，《可爱的中国》创作上更加努力追求真实，尤其是细节的真实。具体表现在：第一，传主说话使用并非标准的普通话，而是带有浓重的南方口音。这与方志敏其人来自江西上饶，显得更协调自然。第二，传主在外形上看并非健康强壮，而是一种病态。有时他是趴在担架上，因为他有严重的痔疮。在狱中他咳嗽不停，窝着身子面对敌人，说话则始终哑着嗓子。第三，革命先驱在绝境之时，也会寻求自杀，如独臂将军刘畴西、红十军团二十一师师长胡仰山、团长乔兴民等。显然，这些设计看似有损正面人物形象，但更符合战争情境中人的真实状态。第四，影片编辑使用了大量纪录片和纪实照片，和主体的虚构叙事相互讲述传主故事。第五，传主平缓的话语表达，传递真情。如在审讯中被问及家人，传主说："我有五个孩子，都很小。我与我妻，爱情不坏。"在狱中谈及齐大妹和孩子牺牲的往事，传主满含眼泪。这些细节都是追求艺术真实的表现。此外，该片作为传记电影，非常注意历史时间的真实，如传主被捕、写作、牺牲等具体时间均以字幕呈现，准确到某年某月某天，努力营造一种历史真实感——这些都是《血沃中华》所没有做到的。总之，比之于《血沃中华》，《可爱的中国》在真实性的追求上更具有严谨态度，至于《血沃中华》中虚构的重大情节则完全没有被沿用。

综上所述，《血沃中华》在当时电影体制下，无须考虑艺术性，无须考虑票房，更多关注英雄形象的塑造和正确的政治思想的传达，因而，影片未能脱离“文化大革命”中的反现实主义、反历史主义的夸张手法，拔高英雄人物的精神境界。正面人物概念化，反面人物则漫画化。至《可爱的中国》创作之时，中国电影迈入产业化阶段，作品的观赏性、艺术性、票房收入等都是必须要考虑的。由此，后者在传主叙事视角、传主形象设计、历史真实性的追求等方面都有很大的不同。

三、对党内斗争历史的批判与对清贫廉洁精神的颂扬

尤其重要的是，《血沃中华》和《可爱的中国》各有一个内在的创作主题：一个指向党内斗争历史，对其进行批判；另一个则指向清贫廉洁精神，报之以热烈的歌颂。这两个不同的创作主题，也是传主在这两个不同时代都具有入传合法性之所在，都吻合了各自时代的主流政治的需要。

对不正常的党内斗争历史进行批判，是《血沃中华》所强调而在《可爱的中国》中是缺席的。在“极左”年代，方志敏等老一辈革命家被诬陷，在世亲属更是受到牵连、迫害。如方志敏的兄弟方志纯被打成“大叛徒”“死不悔改的走资派”。夫人缪敏也受到冲击，在1968年临近春节时被关进“牛棚”（任正 18）。“文化大革命”结束后，党中央开始了拨乱反正工作，对遭受迫害的老一辈革命家进行平反，制作他们的传记电影自有拨乱反正、“将颠倒的历史颠倒过来”的意义，从而间接地批判“极左”历史、尤其是批判刚刚过去的“文化大革命”。因此，《血沃中华》和《从奴隶到将军》《曙光》等电影作品一样，触及党内斗争历史，表现左倾统治路线给革命造成的重大损失。该片有意设计了这个情节：传主被捕入狱，相遇昔日战友娄仁海、游海江等人。但是，这些同在狱中的共产党人内部却很不和睦，因为在苏区曾经有过“肃反扩大化”的历史，一些人如游海江对当时执行“极左”路线的娄仁海非常不满，不太搭理他，而娄仁海也有惭愧之色。在此，作为智者的传主对娄仁海加以劝导：“对于个人没有什么不可以原谅的。但是，残酷打击同志的做法，确实不能再重复了。”对游海江等人传主则劝说：“不要过多追究个人责

任。过去我们党有过不少血的教训啊。”传主的这些台词，对同志相残的历史不要重演的希望以及把党内斗争历史视为血的教训的强调，显然是电影创作者的表白，也是当时整个时代主流话语的心声。

与此不同的是，创作于21世纪的《可爱的中国》则突出传主清贫廉洁奉公的一面，因为其时对党内路线斗争的否定已经没有什么政治意义了。相反，此时的中国现实是，精神标准混乱，道德价值迷失，党的廉洁性、清正之风面临严峻考验。正如导演胡雪杨所说：

> 进入21世纪，表面上我们看到的是家和万事兴，全球一体化。但事实上由于我们对于物质欲望的强烈要求导致我们作为一个普通人对基本道德标准和美学鉴赏标准，都产生了怀疑。我们现在很少听到有人说或拿实际行动去说人的清廉、清贫，人的公正、正义。(胡雪杨、侯庚洋 13)

因此，该片创作不再是强调传主的革命大气，而是其“清贫廉洁奉公”精神，而这则是对应了党风廉政建设这一现实政治课题。

方志敏曾任赣东北省苏维埃政府主席兼财政部长，掌管大权，手握重金，但他严于律己，廉洁奉公，恪守清贫。为了革命理想，他不爱爵位，也不爱金钱，留下了《清贫》这样的言志杰作。他的这精神本应得到后人很好的彰显和传承。但是，在20世纪80年代以前的中国，更强调的是革命意志和精神，在艺术上注重的是张扬崇高的革命理想和对英雄献身精神的渲染。因此，《血沃中华》对传主的清贫廉洁人格是忽略的。

2008年的《可爱的中国》，则侧重世俗生活中的传主如何秉持党的宗旨，清正廉明，不徇私情，由此去塑造党的人民公仆形象，树立当下党员教育的形象标本。由此，观众在影片中看到以下几个情节：(1) 在苏区，妻子缪敏因为从缴获的布匹里扯了几尺给宣传队做戏服，被丈夫策马十五里追赶制止，传主做妻子的思想工作，因为那是公家的，不可挪作他用。(2) 传主被捕的时候，敌人以为捞到大鱼，搜肠刮肚地想从他身上找到金银细软、银元大洋，甚至以拉手榴弹要挟。然而，除了传主一身孱弱的皮包骨外，只有一支笔、一块怀表，令敌人大惑不解。(3) 敌人多次审讯，要求传主交代钱物藏在哪里，最后搜索出来的竟然就是几套旧汗褂裤，还有几双缝上底的线袜。这让敌人大跌眼镜。该片不惜大量篇幅讲述这些细节，就是为了塑造一个舍己为公、清贫廉洁的先进党员形象，告诉大家，那才是每个共产党人应该具备的美德。而这正是影片创作之时主流政治的渴求。

可见，《血沃中华》和《可爱的中国》对传主形象塑造的内在主题并不相同，前者借传主的故事批判党内斗争的左倾路线，后者借塑造传主的清贫廉洁精神以呼应新阶段的党风廉政建设。

四、结　语

"一切历史都是当代史。"克罗齐 1917 年提出的观点，为其后越来越多的史学家接受。因此也可以说，一切传记电影都是与时代的对话，都是制作之时主流政治催生的产物。"文化大革命"后拨乱反正成为时代主题，拍摄方志敏传记电影具有"将颠倒的历史颠倒过来"的作用，因而要批判党内斗争的"极左"政治，同时顺应了当时高扬的革命主旋律。进入新世纪，对党内斗争历史的批判已经失去了现实政治意义，随着党的廉政建设摆在头等重要位置，讴歌方志敏清贫廉洁的传记电影自然呼应了时代诉求。纵观方志敏传记电影可知，传主形象的设计与呈现，其所作所为及其精神表征，与其说是历史还原的尝试，毋宁说是国家主流意识的需要，是现实的一种质的规定性的体现，具有一种时效性特征。其实，这并非中国独有现象。在好莱坞，许多传记电影如《青年林肯》《巴顿将军》等传主形象的塑造，无一不与美国当时主流政治、价值观有着紧密的联系。

英国当代图像与视觉文化研究领域的代表人物伊雷特·罗格尔在《视觉文化研究》中指出，在视觉文化竞技场中，被允许说了些什么才是关键的政治问题。一个方志敏，不同的两部传记电影，所呈现的视听语言就是为各自所处时代代言的内容，而分析这些被允许说出的代言内容以及彼此的差异，也就不是一件枯燥无用的工作了。

致谢【Acknowledgment】

本文为江西省文化艺术科学规划青年项目“上饶题材电影创作现象研究”（YG2017209）研究成果，得到江西省文化厅的资助，作者谨致谢忱。

My acknowledgement and gratitude go to the research project, “The Phenomenon of the Making of Theme Movies in Shangrao”（YG2017209）sponsored by Jiangxi Culture and Art in Scientific Planning.

引用文献【Works Cited】

蔡杰：《国庆献礼大片〈可爱的中国〉》，《大江周刊（焦点）》2009年第10期，第48—49页。

[Cai Jie. “*Lovely China*, the Movie Dedicated to the National Day.” *Dajiang Weekly, Focus* 10(2009):48-49.]

方志敏：《方志敏全集》。北京：人民出版社，2012年。

[Fang Zhimin. *The Complete Works of Fang Zhimin*. Beijing: People's Publishing House, 2012.]

胡雪杨、侯庚洋：《拍一个永恒的方志敏——访电影〈可爱的中国〉导演胡雪杨》，《电影新作》2009年第6期，第13—16页。

[Hu Xueyang and Hou Gengyang. “To Film an Everlasting Fang Zhimin: An Interview with Hu Xueyang, Director of *Lovely China*.” *New Works in Movie* 6(2009):13-16.]

邱忠毅：《石凌鹤谈历史题材的真实性》，《上海戏剧》1992年第6期，第4—5页。

[Qiu Zhongyi. “Shi Linghe's Reflections on the Truthfulness in Works of Historical Themes.” *Shanghai Theatre* 6(1992):4-5.]

任正：《〈可爱的中国〉背后的家庭悲剧》，《法律与生活》1995年第1期，第17—21页。

[Ren Zheng. “The Family Tragedy in *Lovely China*.” *Law and Life* 1(1995):17-21.]

石明：《电影创作要加强历史的真实性》，《电影艺术》1981年第4期，第24—25页。

[Shi Ming. “Enhancing Historical Truthfulness in Film Making.” *The Art of Movie* 4(1981):24-15.]

危春勇：《三十年前银幕首现方志敏——我所知道的电影〈血沃中华〉》，《党史文苑》2010年第8期，第52—55页。

[Wei Chunyong. “The Debut of Fang Zhimin on the Screen Thirty Years Ago—What I Know about the Movie *Shedding Blood for China*.” *The Corpus of the Party's History* 8(2010):52-53.]

杨正润：《现代传记学》。南京：南京大学出版社，2009年。

[Yang Zhengrun. *A Modern Poetics of Biography*. Nanjing: Nanjing University Press, 2009.]

一个故事的诞生

——从传记《爱因斯坦：生活和宇宙》到影视剧《天才》

刘　涛

内容提要：本文将沃尔特·艾萨克森的传记作品《爱因斯坦：生活和宇宙》与其改编而成的影视剧《天才》进行比较研究，发现二者在叙事时序、情节甄选以及对于传记真实问题的态度上都存在明显的差异。这些差异产生于两种文本之间不同的文本目标，传记《爱因斯坦：生活和宇宙》力求真实详尽地记述爱因斯坦的人物事迹，而影视剧《天才》则致力于将爱因斯坦的人生经历改编为具有文学性的人物故事。在传记《爱因斯坦：生活和宇宙》改编为影视剧《天才》的过程中，传记文本实际上成为影视文本改编的素材来源，而影视文本所采取的文学性改编也最终促成了爱因斯坦人物传奇故事的诞生。

关键词：《爱因斯坦：生活和宇宙》　《天才》　传记文本　影视文本

作者简介：刘涛，文学博士，南京师范大学文学院在站博士后、讲师，近期主要从事文学图像关系研究、中国现当代文学研究。

Title: The Birth of a Story: From *Einstein: His Life and Universe* to *Genius*

Abstract: This paper aims to conduct a comparative study of the TV drama *Genius* with its original *Einstein: His Life and Universe* to discover that they have obvious differences in the narrative sequence, the plot selection and the attitude to biographical truth. These differences arise from the different text goals of the two texts, for the biography *Einstein: His Life and Universe* endeavors to faithfully tell about Einstein's deeds in detail, while the TV drama *Genius* is devoted to adapting Einstein's life experience to a literary story and attracting the general public. In this process where the biography *Einstein: His Life and Universe* is adapted into the TV drama *Genius*, the biographical text actually becomes the TV playscript's source for its adaptation, and the literary adaptation of the TV playscript in turn contributes to the emergence of Einstein's legendary story.

Keywords: *Einstein: His Life and Universe*, *Genius*, the biographical text, the TV playscript

Liu Tao is Lecturer and post-doctoral researcher in College of Liberal Arts at Nanjing Normal University. His recent research mainly focuses on relationship between literature and images and modern Chinese literature. E-mail: 274886695@qq.com.

爱因斯坦，这位现代物理学的开创者，几乎已经成为普通人心目中人类最高智慧的化身。2017 年美国国家地理频道制作的《天才》（*Genius*）系列传记影视剧再次将爱因斯坦带入到了大众视野之中，爱因斯坦是这部系列剧第一季的主要人物，该剧共 10 集，讲述了爱因斯坦的科学成就与生平事迹。它改编自沃尔特·艾萨克森的传记作品《爱因斯坦：生活和宇宙》（*Einstein: His Life and Universe*）（以下简称《爱因斯坦》），而正当这部影视剧在全球吸引大约 4 500 万观众而大获成功之时，艾萨克森的原著也趁势再版，再版封面极力强调这部传记作品与影视剧《天才》之间的密切联系。[①]然而，通过对传记文本和影视文本的比较细读，笔者发现影视剧对于传记的改编并非桴鼓相应的，在从文字铅华到声光化电的文本转换过程中，二者之间存在着扑朔迷离的文本关系，而这正是值得我们仔细探讨的问题。

一

沃尔特·艾萨克森撰写的《爱因斯坦：生活和宇宙》在副标题中就已经说明了这部传记的写作视角，作者一方面关注爱因斯坦的个人生活，另一方面注重介绍他的科学成就。这部传记以线性叙事的方式向读者讲述了爱因斯坦非同寻常的人生轨迹与科学探索之路，作者始终将生活和科研作为一以贯之的两大主题，几乎每个章节都是围绕爱因斯坦的生活状态与科学研究进行叙述的。

可是，这一叙事方式在影视剧《天才》中却被完全重构。一方面，影视文本中的叙事时序被重建。传记文本中的顺时线性叙事被改编为倒叙与顺叙的结合，影视文本中的爱因斯坦被分为青年和老年这两大叙事时间，故事以老年爱因斯坦作为叙事的起点，而青年爱因斯坦的经历则是在此基础之上以一种叙事回溯的方式得以呈现。影视剧从第一集开始就以老年爱因斯坦作为主线，其中不断以回忆的形式穿插青年爱因斯坦的故事，而随后的五集内容则完全是以倒叙的方式回溯他在青年时代的生活。接着，故事又跳回到老年爱因斯坦，在余下的四集内容中主要以顺叙手法讲述老年爱因斯坦被迫从纳粹德国移民美国之后的人生经历。从表面来看，似乎以何种时序或者叙事方式来讲述爱因斯坦的生平都只是影视文本创作者个人的喜好问题，对于传记文本时序的改编貌似只是艺术手法的运用方式不同，然而，这种叙事顺序的重建其实暗含了影视文本创作者微妙的意图。仔细分析影视文本叙事重建的时序节点，我们会发现爱因斯坦筹备前往美国之前的这段时间被作为了两条叙事线索的分水岭，而这一时间节点的选择显然不是一种巧合。这是一部面向美国观众的传记影视剧，这又是美国国家地理频道首次涉足这一领域，所以影视创作者对于题材的处理自然要照顾到普通美国观众的接受喜好，而将爱因斯坦移民美国作为全剧叙事的中心节点，可以拉近这个移民国家的观众与爱因斯坦之间的文化距离和身份认同。

另一方面，传记文本中的叙事主题被重置。时序重建仅体现了这部影视剧的第一层意图，而它的第二层意图则是在时序重建的过程中对于传记文本的原有主题进行重置。在传记文本作者看来，爱因斯坦移民美国不过是人生中数次重要转折中的一次，但是在影视文本中这次转折的意义明显被强化，而与之相配合的就是叙事主题的变化。如前所言，传记文本的作者将爱因斯坦的生活经历和科学探索贯穿于整部著作之中，虽然影视文本的创作者并未改变传记文本中的这两大主题，但是伴随着时序的调整，这两大主题却被重置于不同的叙事线索之中。在影视剧中，青年时代的爱因斯坦被塑造为一位才华横溢的科学家，重点突出他是如何获得一项项令人瞩目的科学成就，讲述他的生活经历其实就是在讲述一位天才科学家的诞生。相较之下，当叙事线索进入爱因斯坦的老年时期以后，特别是从纳粹德国移居美国之后，对于爱因斯坦的叙事重心明显偏向他对于现实政治的干预和对于社会公众的影响。根据艾萨克森的说法，“虽然他在去世前再也没能做出什么重要的科学成果，但他所不懈追求的仍然是物理而非政治”（艾萨克森 365），但是，影视剧中的老年爱因斯坦显然对政治更感兴趣，他是一位具有自由主义精神的和平主义者，他与美国联邦调查局局长胡佛的恩怨，对于核能技术运用于武器的抵制态度以及对于黑人平权运动的支持等这些情节共同呈现了爱因斯坦非同寻常的生活经历。传记中一以贯之的两个主题在影视剧中被一分为二，科学探索成为青年爱因斯坦的叙述主题，现实经历则化作了老年爱因斯坦的故事核心。这种主题叙事的故意重置并非对于艺术创作多样性的尝试，而是一种价值观念的巧妙植入。当爱因斯坦移居美国之后，影视文本的叙事主题就从科学探索滑向了现实生活，而影视文本所再现的这段现实经历主要集中于爱因斯坦的价值观念与政治态度，而无论是他的自由主义精神，还是他的和平主义立场都与当下美国社会的价值观念十分契合。影视文本在时序重建基础上的主题重置是在有意将爱因斯坦的形象进行美国式的阐释，此时的爱因斯坦不是犹太人，也不是德国人，而是一位符合美国精神的新移民，他在公共领域中所展现的价值精神能够获得美国观众的认可，从而在保障了这部影视剧的经济收益的同时又能够达到意识形态言说的目的。

二

目前较为著名的爱因斯坦传记往往侧重于以严谨专业的科学视角撰写爱因斯坦的学术生平。例如，亚伯拉罕·派斯的《爱因斯坦传》，由于作者曾与爱因斯坦长期共事，故而十分清楚其学术脉络，这本传记详细梳理了爱因斯坦各个人生阶段所取得的科学成就以及他的研究方向和思维方式的变迁。这部传记虽专业有余，却生动不足，它更像是在以爱因斯坦的视角回顾整个现代物理学的发展史，故而对于缺少专业背景的读者而言十分晦涩。此外，爱因斯坦的另一位同行——菲利普·弗兰克，也创作过一部《爱因斯坦传》，这部传记据说得到了爱因斯坦本人的写作授权，它以爱因斯坦的人生经历为叙事架构，可是由于是传主授权难免存在“为尊者讳”的情况，不能完全真实再现爱因斯坦的个人生活，而且这部传记依旧倾向于展现爱因斯坦的学术生涯，故而仍不是十分通俗。反观艾萨克森的《爱因斯坦》，它是爱因斯坦所有文稿档案于2006年公开出版之后的第一本关于爱因斯坦的传记作品，虽然它不及派斯和弗兰克的爱因斯坦传学术气息浓厚，但是也不至于像传记译者所言“这是一本爱因斯坦的生活传记”（447），可以说它的一部严肃而通俗的传记作品。作者艾萨克森以严谨中立的态度征引了大量的原始文献客观地讲述了爱因斯坦的事业与人生，他往往只是根据现有资料断定情节真伪，基本是以一种事无巨细的态度秉笔直书。然而，就《天才》而言，它对于传记文本的改编明显带有强烈的主观意图，最为直接的表现就是对于传记文本既有情节的选择性改编。这种影视文本对于传记文本的情节甄选实际上是影视文本对于传记文本的价值植入和二次创作的过程，而这一过程又最能直观反映二者之间的差异。

影视剧文本对于传记文本的情节甄选主要体现在对于某些情节的强调或者凸显。这部影视剧最大的“卖点”就是对于爱因斯坦私人生活的披露，爱因斯坦在影视剧中登场的第一个场景就是他与秘书贝蒂·诺依曼在办公室里偷情，并且还试图以一夫一妻制并非人类的天性这样的说辞劝诱贝蒂搬到他家里与他的第二任妻子爱尔莎一起生活，这着实让人诧异。随着故事的逐渐展开，爱因斯坦对初恋玛丽的始乱终弃，对待妻子米列娃的冷酷无情，甚至与苏联女间谍之间的风流韵事都被一一呈现在观众面前。这些对于爱因斯坦私人生活的揭露确实颠覆了大众心中的既有印象，对于名人隐私强烈的窥视欲也成为这部传记影视剧吸引大众眼球的直接原因。传记作者同样认为“爱因斯坦似乎终生都无法摆脱与女性的暧昧关系”（258），他也确实在传记中将这些风流韵事毫不遮掩地如实道来。但是，与影视剧为了满足观众的猎奇心理而大肆渲染这些桃色情节有所不同，爱因斯坦的风流韵事显然不是传记的讲述重点，并且所占篇幅也十分有限。可是，影视文本刻意强调这些私人情节，它以一定的内容虚构和适度的合理想象提升了这些情节的叙事地位与内容比重，就是为了迎合大众的接受趣味。传记作品避讳传主不大光彩的事迹是一种非常普遍的现象，而对于爱因斯坦个人隐私的大胆揭露既能够满足世俗的口味，又能塑造这部影视剧真实客观、直言不讳的叙事假象。不过，需要强调的是，这种媚俗的情节甄选仍暗含了一定的意义言说。在传记中与爱因斯坦关系暧昧的女性人数远不止影视剧中所呈现的，甚至艾萨克森不得不以“伴侣”为题专门单列一节讲述与爱因斯坦有过露水姻缘的女性。[②]显然，即使是同一主题的情节，影视剧也是经过了一番甄选，这些情节要么在全剧中至关重要，例如与米列娃之间持续终生的虐恋；要么能够体现爱因斯坦天马行空的浪漫性格，例如他向贝蒂所表达的对于正常人伦关系的不屑。事实上，影视创作者绝无批评爱因斯坦私生活的意思，而是希望通过爱因斯坦轻浮放浪的情感生活表现他人格中的自由不羁以及对于世俗常规的反叛，而考虑到这部影视剧产生于美国大众文化语境之中，以这种形式展现爱因斯坦抗拒陈规的自由主义精神也确实容易得到当今美国观众的认可。

除了对于情节的强调（或曰凸显），《天才》还对《爱因斯坦》中的一些情节采取了视觉符号技术的“转译”，其中最值得一提的也是全剧最为成功的地方就是影视文本以视觉特效的方式演示了传记文本中复杂难懂的专业理论问题。虽然《爱因斯坦》并非一部纯粹的学术传记，但是爱因斯坦所创立的各种物理学理论又绝对是传记不可或缺的组成部分。可是如艾萨克森所言：“爱因斯坦年少时所取得的成功部分来自他的一种本能，使之能够发现背后的物理实在。他能够直觉地感受到一切运动的相对性的含义、光速的恒定性以及引力质量与惯性质量的等效。由此他可以基于对物理学的感受去构造理论。”（337）这种天才般的本能直觉也使得他的物理学理论晦涩艰深，难以通过文字语言进行准确清晰地描述。即便艾萨克森尽量以详尽而通俗的语言解释爱因斯坦的光电效应、相对论、能量守恒、宇宙常数等专业理论，对于普通读者而言这些理论依旧艰涩乏味。不过，影视文本敏感地寻找到了打开爱因斯坦理论的密匙，艾萨克森对于爱因斯坦的思维方式有一句精辟的总结：

“他一般倾向于以图像的方式进行思考，最为典型的莫过于那些著名的思想实验，比如想象从火车上发出的闪光，或者在下降的升降机中体验引力。”（7）“以图像的方式进行思考”说明爱因斯坦偏重于通过视觉符号去理解和表达客观世界，“视觉的能指可以在几个向度上同时并发，而听觉的能指却只有时间上的一条线；它的要素相继出现，构成一个链条”（索绪尔 106）。视觉符号是一种共时符号，语言符号则是一种历时符号，所以爱因斯坦基于视觉符号思维所创立的各种理论自然难以被完全转化为语言符号加以表述。然而，爱因斯坦的图像思维方式恰恰与影视文本所仰仗的图像视觉艺术相契合。例如，爱因斯坦曾经构想过一个关于火车的“思想实验”来解释时间的相对性。在传记中艾萨克森描述了这个火车实验的内容，但是他的表述显得十分吃力，并且不得不借助图示配合说明。③ 对比影视文本而言，“思想实验”的呈现过程则顺畅得多，影片设计了爱因斯坦为他的朋友贝索讲解火车实验的情节，它直接将复杂的实验内容转化为直观的视觉图像，运用空间蒙太奇技的技巧将贝索（当然还有观众）从现实带入到虚拟的实验情境之中，这样就可以使人身临其境地观看到爱因斯坦的理论演绎。影视剧中对于升降机引力、宇宙常数等其他“思想实验”也都采取了符号“转译”的策略，毕竟，影视作为一种“热媒体”相对于书籍这样的“冷媒体”，在观者体验上具有更高的“可悦性”，这种将不易用语言叙述的理论问题转化为简洁明了的图像话语的过程，其实也是一个影视文本对于原文本中情节的二次创作的过程，其目的当然是适应普通观众的认知能力，从而达到最佳的传播效果。

三

归根究底，影视文本对于传记文本的情节改编就是为了讲述一个有关爱因斯坦的生动有趣的故事，也就是说“故事性”是这部影视剧最为关注的地方，而它导致的一个结果就是在影视文本中不可避免地出现了一些文学性想象甚至偏离事实的情况。不过，这种影视文本在改编之中的对于传记文本的文学想象或者失实之处，我们也应该以一分为二的态度加以看待。

有一些想象或者失实源于两种文本之间的叙事差异。叙事的自然不是文学，而文学的自然则是叙事。艾萨克森的叙事语言并非文学性的，他追求以语言的言说功能客观地讲述爱因斯坦的生平，而影视剧则强调在完整流畅的文学叙事系统之中演绎一个跌宕起伏的爱因斯坦故事。二者是以完全不同的方式构建爱因斯坦的形象，对于叙事功能不同层面的运用是传记《爱因斯坦》与影视剧《天才》之间重要的叙事差异。我们将以爱因斯坦"私生女事件"为例，展现这种叙事差异对于传记真实的影响。爱因斯坦与米列娃在正式结婚之前就已经生下了一个名为"莉色儿"的女婴，但是双方生前对此事都讳莫如深，直到1986年爱因斯坦与米列娃的私人信件被公开之后，这段往事才重见天日。但是，由于年代久远，这位爱因斯坦从未谋面的私生女的命运就产生了两种都有迹可循却又完全矛盾的说法：一种说法认为"莉色儿"在1903年9月死于猩红热；另一种说法认为这位私生女后来被米列娃的密友萨维奇收养。在无法确定真相的情况下，出于对事实的尊重，传记作者选择将两种观点都呈现在读者面前，并且详细引述了佐证这两种观点的原始材料，让读者能够了解到事件的全貌。但是，这种做法在影视文本中就不大可取了，因为虽然视觉符号具有非线性的叙事特征，但是这部传记影视剧的故事内核却是建立在完整流畅的线性叙事基础之上的，而这种存在于一维线性叙事的两难不确定性会打断故事的进程。当然，传记影视片并非不能做到兼顾两种叙事可能，假如这里采用先锋电影中的"间离效果"或者按照传记历史（文献）片的方式对于"私生女事件"进行客观呈现，那么这里的两难问题就迎刃而解了。然而，根据杨正润先生的分类，传记历史（文献）片与传记故事片存在根本的区别，前者"强调历史的真实性"，后者则"把镜头主要集中在一个人物身上，这个人物是真实的，影片就是讲述他的故事，同时也是在讲述一段历史"（杨正润 470）。显然《天才》是一部传统意义上的传记故事片，它的叙事并非全然是从历史真实出发，而是为了讲述一个故事，所以无法借助影视文本的视觉符号优势回避这个两难的叙事境地。在影视文本中虽然创作者出于一种对于真实的补偿，安排了米列娃向好友萨维奇提议收养她和爱因斯坦"私生子"的情节，但是最终它还是不得不以"私生子"的离世作为明确的结局。这虽然与传记中的讲述不一致，但是影片为了讲述故事的流畅，将两难的局面化为一元的存在也是一种迫不得已的叙事妥协。“传记片的历史感实际上代表着一般群众对历史的理解和想象，它不同于传记文本中专家对历史的研究和解读。”（杨正润 475）《天才》对于“私生女事件”的处理方式恰恰反映了普通观众内心所期望的故事结局，既能够为这个私生女找到一个妥帖的归宿，又能够让爱因斯坦的故事继续轻装上阵，不会因为这种不确定性影响传记片所呈现的整体真实性。可以说，由于不同的叙事目标，影视文本对于传记文本的偏离或者想象理应被视为一种客观存在，它并非主观上的刻意失实。

然而，另外一些影视文本中的想象与失实则是由于改编者的主观意图所造成的。一个故事的文本就是一个观念的文本，“当历史学家成功地发现历史事实中隐含的故事时，他们便为历史事实提供了可行的解释”（怀特 163）。同样，当影视文本发现了爱因斯坦事迹中所包含的故事时，他们便会为这个故事中的爱因斯坦形象提供可行的意义。不过，为了让爱因斯坦的形象符合影视文本所阐释的故事意图，影视剧中的许多情节明显是有悖传记文本原意的过度想象和刻意失实。例如，在专利局度过的七年时光是爱因斯坦人生中最具创造性的时期，在这期间他发表了光量子假说，解决了光电效应问题，并且提出了狭义相对论。在《爱因斯坦》中艾萨克森援引爱因斯坦的原话：“我非常喜欢这项办公室里的工作，因为它极为多样，可以做许多思考。”（艾萨克森 57）这句话表明爱因斯坦十分享受在专利局工作的时光。然而，这段时光在《天才》中则被曲解为爱因斯坦人生中最为失意与低落的时期。在爱因斯坦赴职的第一天，影视剧就通过仪式化的隐喻将专利局描绘为暮气沉沉、机械单调的官僚行政机构。爱因斯坦在这里备受压抑，由于经常在上班时间从事研究工作，他与上司的关系也十分紧张。影视文本对于这段人生经历的重现与传记文本（亦与真实情况）存在很大的出入，在传记文本中，爱因斯坦认为“专利局是一个‘让我构想出最美妙思想的世俗隐居之地’，无论在当时还是以后，他都认为在那里工作有助于他的科学，而不是一个负担”（58），并且，“他的上司哈勒尔性情温和、风趣幽默，对一些事情虽然心知肚明，却愿与人为善”(57)。影视文本之所以要走向真实的反面，是因为创作者希望在这里植入“世俗/天才”二元对立的话语结构，专利局成为世俗的象征，爱因斯坦则是一个被世俗牢笼所禁锢的天才。压抑的专利局生涯其实是影视文本刻意虚构的产物，目的就是在爱因斯坦与世俗生活之间构建一种戏剧冲突，进而让故事的情节更加扣人心弦。影视改编者的主观意图是造成此处传记失实的根本原因，而这种出于特定意图人为修改事实的做法显然有悖于传记的真实原则。可是，在《天才》中，这种虚构事实的做法却成为影视改编者增加传记故事性的一种手段，例如青年时期的爱因斯坦经常与两位好友索洛文和哈比希特聚在一起讨论哲学问题，因此他们成立了一个名为“奥林匹亚科学院”的小团体，也正是在这个时期，爱因斯坦阅读到了对他日后影响颇深的大卫·休谟的哲学著作。这个小团体虽然有一些游戏意味，但是对于爱因斯坦而言确实是他人生中一段十分有益的经历，他与索洛文和哈比希特也成为终生不渝的朋友。然而，在影视剧中“奥林匹亚科学院”则完全是另一番景象，它被描绘为一群纨绔子弟纵欲享乐的声色场所，索洛文和哈比希特变为了游手好闲的富家子弟，他们不断引诱爱因斯坦走向堕落，沉沦于声色犬马的浪荡生活之中。最终爱因斯坦出于对家庭和事业的责任心脱离了“奥林匹亚科学院”，断绝了与索洛文和哈比希特的来往。影视剧中对于“奥林匹亚科学院”的故意改写是一种十分媚俗的失实，这种刻意虚构一方面迎合了大众的低级审美趣味，另一方面杜撰的这段迷途知返浪子回头的人物经历又增添了爱因斯坦的传奇色彩。可是，即便这是一部通俗的传记影视剧，如此违背传记伦理的失实改编是不应当被原谅的。

这里的传记文本和影视文本在本质上都是有关爱因斯坦的通俗传记，它们都是旨在让受众更加轻松地了解爱因斯坦的生平事迹。不过，相较于传记文本，影视文本的媒介载体具有大众文化的性质，视觉符号的直观体验比文字符号更加能够吸引普通受众的关注。当然，同时作为一种大众文化传播工具，影视文本的创作也必然会自觉地选择易于大众接受的传播形式。故而，《天才》对原作改编的首要任务就是讲述一个引人入胜的故事，它与传记文本之间的根本区别在于具有文学性的故事传记与叙事传记之间的差异，这也就造成了影视文本不可避免地出现一定程度的失实或文学性想象。正是如此，影视传记改编中所涉及的真实问题远比一般传记写作中的真实问题复杂得多，这就需要以辩证的态度加以区分造成不同失实情况的具体原因。

四

总而言之，从传记《爱因斯坦》到影视剧《天才》的改编过程就是一个从纸质媒介走向大众荧屏的过程。在改编过程中，无论是影视文本对于传记文本叙事时序的重建，或者是对于传记情节的选择性运用与视觉“转译”，抑或是对于传记文本的文学想象与刻意虚构，这些改编策略都指向了一个共同目标，那就是将传记文本改写为一个具有文学性的故事文本。伊格尔顿认为：“我们所说的‘文学性’，一定程度上就是指用怎么说来衡量说什么。”(3) 这其实也道出了《爱因斯坦》与《天才》之间的根本差异，前者强调传记书写的客观事实就是注重“说什么”的问题，后者将文学性改编引入传记之中则是更加关注“怎么说”的问题。反过来讲，二者之间的道路又是殊途同归的，它们都是在尝试以各自的文本形式撰写一部通俗的爱因斯坦传记，只不过传记文本着重于将爱因斯坦的事迹视为一种知识结构，努力以平易的叙事和浅近描写将其通俗化，而影视文本则侧重于以主观叙事态度和戏剧性的情节讲述爱因斯坦富有趣味的人生故事。对于影视剧《天才》而言，传记《爱因斯坦》更像是为其文学性改编提供了基础的传记素材，影视文本则可以被视为对于传记素材的二次创作，这个创作过程其实就是爱因斯坦故事诞生的过程，无论是在故事结构上还是在价值趋向上，它都已经与爱因斯坦传记拉开了距离。当然，传记文本与影视文本之间并不存在绝对的优劣之别，二者之间的差异恰恰反映了当下传记作品在阅读传播过程中所面临的一个共同的困境：如何统一传记的真实性与趣味性，让传记在遵守真实伦理的同时还能够适应普通大众的接受喜好，在把握大众口味的同时又教寓大众的灵魂。可以说，这里考察的传记影视改编问题是当下“读图时代”的普遍现象，对于这一问题的研究是为了让传统意义上的传记作品在视觉文化领域绽放新的光彩。

致谢【Acknowledgment】

本文为中国博士后科学基金第61批面上资助项目"外国来华作家与中国现代文学"(2017M611850)成果,得到中国博士后科学基金会的资助,作者谨致谢忱。

My acknowledgement and gratitude go to the research project "Foreign Writers to China and Chinese Modern Literature" sponsored by the China Postdoctoral Science Foundation.

注释【Notes】

① 沃尔特·艾萨克森所著《爱因斯坦》英文版初版时间为2007年,封面主体是一张爱因斯坦的照片(这张照片可能不是爱因斯坦本人,而只是他的模仿者)。然而,几乎是在《天才》开播的同时,这部传记所属的西蒙与舒斯特出版社(Simon & Schuster, Inc.)以简装本的形式再版了这部作品,并且将封面换为了影视剧《天才》的宣传剧照,直接向读者表明《天才》改编自这部传记作品。

② 这些女性中还包括一位名叫托尼·曼德尔的富有寡妇、社会名流埃塞尔·米沙诺夫斯基、一位名为玛格丽特·勒巴赫的奥地利女性。参见传记第十六章中的《伴侣》一节,第259—260页。

③ 在传记中艾萨克森尽管十分努力地想要借助文字语言说明爱因斯坦火车实验的原理,但是由于语言符号的局限性,他依旧不得不将图示作为说明实验原理的补充手段,具体情况参见传记第90页。

引用文献【Works Cited】

特里·伊格尔顿:《文学阅读指南》,范浩译。郑州:河南大学出版社,2015年。

[Eagleton, Terry. *How to Read Literature*. Trans. Fan Hao. Zhengzhou: Henan University Press, 2015.]

沃尔特·艾萨克森:《爱因斯坦:生活和宇宙》,张卜天译。长沙:湖南科学技术出版社,2009年。

[Isaacson, Walter. *Einstein: His Life and Universe*. Trans. Zhang Butian. Changsha: Hunan Science and Technology Press, 2009.]

费尔迪南·德·索绪尔:《普通语言学教程》,高名凯译。北京:商务印书馆,1999年。

[de Saussure, Ferdinand. *Course in General Linguistics*. Trans. Gao Mingkai. Beijing: The Commercial Press, 1999.]

海登·怀特:《作为文学虚构的历史文本》,《新历史主义与文学批评》,张京媛主编。北京:北京大学出版社,1993年,第160—179页。

[White, Hayden. "The Historical Text as Literary Artifact." *New Historicism and Literary Criticism*. Ed. Zhang Jingyuan. Beijing: Peking University Press, 1993: 160-179.]

杨正润:《现代传记学》。南京:南京大学出版社,2009年。

[Yang Zhengrun. *A Modern Poetics of Biography*. Nanjing: Nanjing University Press, 2009.]

对于撰写作家传记之我见

桑逢康

内容提要：从“反思”历史的角度撰写现代作家传记，是新时期文学创作的重要收获之一。当前传记写作在不同程度上受到历史虚无主义思潮的影响，需要引起注意和防范。提倡用作家独特的艺术风格写作家的传记是对《鲁迅传》的要求与希望。对于单纯的作家，为之写传相对来讲比较容易，最难的是为既是作家又是学者的大师级人物写传，这需要传记作者具备相当丰富的学识，否则就写不好甚至难以下笔。

关键词　反思　风格　鲁迅　胡适　郭沫若

作者简介：桑逢康，中国社会科学院文学研究所研究员，中国作家协会会员。主要从事现代文学研究和传记与小说创作。已出版学术专著、长篇传记和小说20余种，总计400余万字。

Title: My Reflections on the Craft of Literary Biography

Abstract: It has been one of the important achievements since 1978 that lives of modern Chinese writers are composed from the perspective of looking at history critically. However, the current life writing is passively influenced by the tendency of historical nihilism to a greater or lesser extent, which we should guard against. It is suggested that the life of a writer be written in his or her unique artistic style. It is relatively easy to write a biography for a less-known writer, but very difficult for a colossus who is both a writer and a scholar. It is imperative for biographers to build on their rich academic expertise, otherwise it will be difficult or even impossible to work out a good biography.

Keywords: reflections, style, Lu Xun, Hu Shi, Guo Moruo

Sang Fengkang is Professor of Chinese Literature in the Literature Institute at Chinese Academy of Social Sciences, and a member of China Writers Association. Over the years he involved himself mainly in the studies of modern Chinese literature and the writing of biographies and novels. So far he has published more than 20 academic works, biographies and fictions with a total of over 4 millions of words. E-mail: sangfk@126.com.

一

传记是历史的参照物，它具有历史与文学的双重属性。

从理论上来说，人类的历史实质上就是人与事的结合：什么人（从个体、一群人到一个民族），从事了什么活动（基本上又大致分为改造大自然与改造社会两个方面）。任何活动都是由人所从事的，而传记的着眼点就是什么人做了什么事，而且把人作为主体。从这个意义上讲，传记在本质上就是历史，是记述历史的一种重要形式，虽然它不是唯一的形式。有时候“传记”后缀“文学”二字，只是需要将它同一般的史书适当区别，运用一点文学手法罢了，并不是改变传记的历史属性。

要讲好中国故事，传记是最好的形式。因为传记的历史属性决定了它讲的中国故事最真实，最可信；传记的文学属性又使得它远比一般史书、教科书更富于感染力，更容易为广大读者所接受，从而达到“教化”的目的。各种各样的传记汇总起来，洋洋大观，称得上是新时期的《资治通鉴》——传记作家们应当具有这样宏大的气魄与抱负。

党的十一届三中全会以来，由于政策调整，改革开放，社会变化，中国的传记文学呈现出了相当活跃的可喜局面。像“文化大革命”期间及前十七年因为写了一部传记而遭批判甚至于获罪的情况一去不复返了，代之而起的是从事传记写作的人愈来愈多，传记作家们的观念得到了更新，视野不断扩大，叙述的角度也愈来愈多样化。各种传记作品源源不断地、大量地涌现出来，受读者欢迎的程度愈来愈高，成为最受欢迎的图书品种之一。就以为现代作家立传而论，新时期的作者们写的现代作家传记大多基于“反思”的立场，从“反思”历史的角度看待过去的人和事，属于“反思”文学的范畴，同政治上“拨乱反正”正相合拍。与此同时，由传记引发的各种争论以至诉讼也随之增加了，从而更加引起社会各方面的关注，形成了一个又一个热点。进入 21 世纪以后，传记创作的良好发展势头更加显著。

这当然不是说不存在问题与不足。就近年来的传记写作而言，我以为需要特别注意以下几点。

第一，克服和防止历史虚无主义的影响甚至侵蚀。历史虚无主义是近年来频频出现的一种社会思潮，在知识界和部分青年学生中有一定市场。最突出的表现，就是在政治上否定中国共产党领导的革命与建设成就，在思想上否定马克思主义，在道路与制度上否定社会主义。其惯用的手法是对党和国家领导人极力丑化或矮化，而不是历史地、辩证地、有分析地看待过去在前进道路上出现的曲折与错误，正确地吸取教训。他们往往在泼脏水的同时把婴儿也扔掉了，更有甚者某些所谓知识“精英”只是为了扔掉婴儿。而我们所需要的，是坚持真理，修正错误，不忘初心，开拓未来。

历史虚无主义在文学上的表现，就是否定现代革命与进步文学的优良传统，否定左翼文学，否定《在延安文艺座谈会上的讲话》。抑损鲁迅、咒骂郭沫若、贬低茅盾，几乎成为一种时尚，同时却把一些“自由派”甚至汉奸文人捧上了天。这是对现代文学历史的严重歪曲。如果年轻学生只知有周作人而不知周树人，只知有张爱玲而不知茅盾，岂不是笑话？

传记作家不能正确看待历史，就不能正确地选择传主，在“歌颂”与“暴露”的问题上就会迷失方向，进退失据。历史虚无主义思潮对传记创作的危害恰恰就在这里。随着时间的推移，随着社会关注点的变化，随着读者阅读兴趣的更新，“反思”虽未完全过时，但仅仅停留在“反思”阶段是远远不够的，开拓新的角度，扩展新的视野，显得更有必要。一大批现代革命与进步作家和他们的作品，代表着自“五四”新文化运动以来中国先进文化的正确方向，对此应当坚持而不能有任何的动摇与怀疑。从个人欣赏的角度喜欢或不喜欢哪位作家与哪部作品是正常的现象，不足为奇，但怀着政治偏见曲解中国现代文学历史则绝对不能听之任之。在传记领域同样需要唱响主旋律，因为只有这样的现代作家传记才更真实，更全面，因而也更符合历史。

第二，虽然传记具有历史和文学的双重属性，但前者即历史属性是主要的，两者不能本末倒置。传记必须真实，这是无可怀疑的，但在实际操作上，由于材料的限制，由于突出传主形象的需要，传记作家有时又不得不有所虚构。虚构究竟多少才算合适？这个分寸很难把握，不少传记作家为此感到困惑，为此绞尽脑汁。我以为在保证传记真实的前提下，做适当而又适量的虚构还是可以的，但这个口子不能开得太大，否则许多乱七八糟的东西都会侵入到传记作品里面，从而失去了真实性。失去了真实性就失去了可信度，而真实性与可信度的缺失意味着传记的堕落，以致被读者最终抛弃。

第三，成熟的作家都会有自己独特的风格。所谓“风格就是人”，就是指通过作品的独特风格可以显示作者独特的个性，让读者认识作者独特的为人——也就是恩格斯所说的“这一个”。这一个而非那一个，既是对作家的要求，也应该是对传记作家的要求。所以，我主张——或者说我希望——最好能用作家的独特风格去写作家的传记。具体一点说要做到两点：一是传记能表现出传主的独特风格；二是作者能用和传主相同或相近的风格来写他的传记。

比如说：能否尝试用“京味小说”的风格写老舍？用“山药蛋”派的风格写赵树理？用“荷花淀”派的风格写孙梨？大家茅盾非久居大上海的大手笔是写不好的，土老帽儿写不出洋派“新月”诗人徐志摩，正如小家碧玉型的演员演不出一代才女林徽因大家闺秀的神采一样。你写沙汀就得熟悉茶馆、袍哥、“麻辣烫”，连四川都没有去过怎么写得好？巴金有没有自己的风格？各说不一。“有的人写了一辈子小说也没写出风格”，这是老舍挖苦巴金的话；王蒙则按风格而不是根据实际年龄将作家分为“少年”“青年”和“老年”，多年前他在中国社科院文学研究所的一次讲演中，说巴金一生都像是个“青年”[①]，这或许正是巴金的特点与风格，他总是怀着一颗青年人的赤诚之心，在字里行间燃烧着青春的炽热的火焰。这也是巴金的作品尤其是《家》《春》《秋》感动了几代青年人的原因。正是这一特点与风格让巴金成为现代文学史上为数极少的几位语言艺术大师之一，也就是通常说的“鲁（迅）郭（沫若）

茅（盾）巴（金）老（舍）曹（禺）”。

郭沫若“五四”时期火山爆发式的诗作，充分体现了狂飙突进的时代精神，具有鲜明而又强烈的积极浪漫主义风格特征。孱弱萎缩、囿于小我的男人，且不说根本就写不出来，即使让他们朗诵也朗诵不出那种黄钟大吕般的雄浑的诗风。曾经有学者提出鲁迅是“中国最忧郁的灵魂”甚或“苦魂”，从鲁迅忧国忧民的角度来看确有一定的道理，但却未必是对鲁迅及其精神的最本质、最妥帖的概括。鲁迅的灵魂不仅是“最忧郁的”，同时也是最热烈、最真挚的，他就像一个高明的医生用手术刀无情地解剖着中国人的国民性，“哀其不幸，怒其不争”，而在这样做的时候，冷峻而又严肃的面孔下面其实有一颗滚烫的心，犹如“地火在地下运行，奔突”。热得发冷这才是鲁迅。请问：谁能有本事用郭沫若的风格写出郭沫若？谁能有本事用鲁迅的风格写出鲁迅？恐怕谁都没有这种本事，尽管已出或将出的《鲁迅传》《郭沫若传》为数并不少。这也很难怪罪谁，因为风格的形成绝非朝夕之功，需要传记作家们长期努力，提高修养，丰富自己。

二

我有一个困惑：假若一百个作者撰写鲁迅的传记，就会有一百部《鲁迅传》，但世上却只有一个鲁迅，究竟哪一部《鲁迅传》才是真实的鲁迅呢？同样的疑问国外也不少，比如世上只有一个拿破仑，但据说《拿破仑传》已经有三百多种，究竟哪一部《拿破仑传》才是真实的拿破仑呢？

如果这多达一百部甚至三百多部的《鲁迅传》或《拿破仑传》可以共存的话，那么只能理解为它们基本上都大同小异，或者各自从不同角度写出了鲁迅或拿破仑的某一方面或仅仅某一个小小的侧面，但绝不会是全部。

拿破仑不是作家，不是本文所要探讨的对象。我们探讨的是撰写鲁迅等中国作家的传记，需要注意和思考的一些问题。

一部好的传记，既要写得真，又要写得像。

所谓“真”，不仅指材料必须真实、准确、可靠，尤其是传主的主要经历和重要的思想观点不能有任何的虚构，而且其生活的时代背景、社会及人文环境都应当真实可信，从而营造出具有时代特征的历史氛围。特定的时代产生特定的人物，特定的人物代表着特定的时代。今天的作者对昨天的历史往往难以把握，这就要求传记作家具备渊博的历史知识和深厚的人文科学功底。

所谓“像”，是指传记的写作不应满足于材料的堆积与罗列，仅仅对传主一生的经历作编年史叙述是不够的，还应着重刻画出传主的个性特征（包括内心世界、独特的行为方式、语言习惯等等）。传主的形象应当是鲜明的、立体的、活生生的、有血有肉的。为此，就不仅要叙述传主一生做了些什么事，更要写出做这些事情的传主究竟是怎样的一个人，从而说明这样的人只能做这样的事，做这样事情的必定是这样的人。在保证真实性的前提下，调动一切艺术手段，对于刻画传主的形象是很有必要的。

写得失真，无疑是传记的最大诟病；写谁不像谁，只能被看作作者欠缺功力。

就以鲁迅为例来说。作为一个读者，我希望看到以下三种鲁迅的传记。

第一种，史料翔实的鲁迅传。生平事迹、创作历程、思想变化、人际交往等等，叙述既详尽又准确，类似于年谱却又不像年谱那样仅仅罗列事实，而是有重点，有层次，并且运用比较生动的文学语言。这样的传记通常称为文学传记，以中国现当代作家为传主的文学传记数量相当多，北京十月文艺出版社的《中国现代作家传记丛书》就属于这一类。由中国作协主持、正陆续出版的中国一百多位历史文化名人传记丛书，也应该属于这一类。

第二种，论述精辟的鲁迅评传。观点正确，有独到的见解，既不随波逐流，又不因时而异。鲁迅是现代中国最伟大的作家之一，但在他生前及逝世以后，一直到现如今，誉之者甚众，毁之者也不少。毛泽东曾经高度评价鲁迅“不但是伟大的文学家，而且是伟大的思想家和伟大的革命家”（毛泽东：《新民主主义论》 658），但有些人并不赞成甚至极力反对，而且这种现象近些年有愈演愈烈之势，不仅大陆的某些学者持有异议，前不久台湾出版了《民国文化与文学研究文丛》，其中一册书名就叫《鲁迅：东方的文化恶魔》。看来如何正确评价鲁迅，仍然是文学界乃至整个思想文化界绕不开的重大而又严肃的话题。

第三种，描写鲁迅的传记小说。选取鲁迅一生中最生动、最典型、最富个性特征、最能突出人物性格，本身又带有某些故事性的事例（包括情节和细节），把鲁迅的形象活生生地再现于读者面前。换句话说，就是以刻画鲁迅人物形象为主的《鲁迅传》。之所以称其为“传记小说”而非通常意义上的小说，是因为主要的情节还是必须要依据事实的，只不过采用了一些小说的技巧。

“传记小说”这种形式的始作俑者可能是法国作家莫洛亚。胡适在1928年就说过：“近几年中，西方出了一种新式的传记文学，其法用传记改作小说体，删除繁重的史料，单挑出最精彩的片断，其法甚新颖，故能轰动一时。此种传记名为‘小说化了的传记’。其最早而得盛名者为 Andre Maurois's *Ariel*：*Life of Shelley*（安德鲁·莫洛亚的《阿里埃尔：雪莱传》），我与志摩皆爱读他。此君近年又出一部 *Disraeli*（《迪斯累里》），也很有名。近年学此体者，正多着呢。”（胡适：《日记》 94）

以上三种类型的传记，可以帮助读者了解某一位作家做了什么事，写了什么作品，他又是什么样的人。这就是我希望看到这样三种传记的原因，对鲁迅是如此，对其他作家也是如此。

当然，如果想深刻而又全面地了解一位作家，最主要的还是要阅读他的作品，有关的传记即便写得再好也只是辅助材料。作家的作品是作家最本质也最真实的体现，在作品中撒谎是瞒不过读者的眼睛的。别人为之写的传记，总或多或少打上了别人过滤甚至歪曲了的印记，尤其是怀有偏见的撰写，或者过分尊崇，或者过分贬损，这样写出来的传记都难免失真。

三

对于单纯的作家，我们为之写传相对来讲比较容易，最难的是为既是作家又是学者的大师级人物写传，这需要传记作者具备相当丰富的学识才行，否则就根本写不好甚至难以下笔。

在现代文化史上，胡适是一位重量级的人物，在文学、哲学、历史、教育、政治、外交诸方面、诸领域，都留下了深深的足迹。胡适首先倡导“文学革命”，与其他先行者们一起开辟了“五四”新文学历史时代。以他为首的“胡适学派”独树一帜，影响巨大。他担任过最高学府北京大学的校长和上海中国公学校长，晚年任台湾“中央研究院”院长，抗战时期又任驻美大使，政治方面胡适差一点当了中华民国“总统”。对于胡适的政治主张及其相关活动，有目共睹，不需要多加阐述。胡适在文学方面的业绩及其局限，对我们从事文学研究的人来说做出恰当的评价并不困难；教育者（大学老师）和受教育者（青年学生），对胡适的教育理念与举措，比如北大应注重提高向研究院发展、提倡选课制、大学开女禁、留学当以不留学为目的等，想来也并不陌生。问题或者说难点出在学术方面，如实验主义哲学、整理国故、中西文化比较、人生观的争论，等等。

胡适早年在美国哥伦比亚大学研究院师从实验主义哲学家杜威，成为实验主义哲学的忠实信徒，并把这一哲学体系率先引进到中国。据胡适自己说，他的所有政治活动、学术研究乃至考证中国古典小说，都是在进行实验主义的试验。胡适担任北大文学院长期间，还兼任哲学、英国文学、外国文学、中国文学、教育五个系的系主任，除了在国学门（相当于现在的中文系）讲课外，还同时在哲学门（系）讲课。他的很多著作是关于哲学的，如《中国古代哲学史》《中国中古思想史长编》《西洋哲学史大纲》《实验主义》（七讲）……安徽教育出版社出版的《胡适全集》中，收录哲学（包括宗教）方面的论著有五卷之多。要全面论述胡适，这些都是需要重点探讨的，绝对不应忽视，不可缺少。

哲学是我的短板，而写胡适的传记无论如何也避不开胡适所涉及的诸多哲学问题，我焉能写得了呢？近几年我出了几本关于胡适的书，但限于（或者说苦于）学识的欠缺，基本上都回避了“哲学”这一难点，因为它是我很难迈过去的门槛。坦率地说我根本写不了《胡适传》。

就以实验主义哲学为例。众所周知，实验主义是主观唯心主义哲学的一个变种，存在着许多根本性的谬误。实验主义者虽然也“注重真正的事实”，但在马克思主义看来，人的正确思想只能从生产斗争、阶级斗争和科学实验这三项实践中来，主张“通过实践而发现真理，又通过实践而证实真理和发展真理”（毛泽东：《实践论》 296），认为“在绝对的总的宇宙发展过程中，各个具体过程的发展都是相对的，因而在绝对真理的长河中，人们对于在各个一定发展阶段上的具体过程的认识只具有相对的真理性。无数相对的真理之总和，就是绝对的真理”（毛泽东：《实践论》 295）。一切真理（而非谬说）都具有实践性和客观性这两大特征，既非主观所能臆造，也不以人们的主观意志为转移。而实验主义则否认真理的客观性，片面夸大主观能动作用，把真理仅仅当作“实用”的“工具”，即所谓“有用即真理”，从而为剥削和压迫、侵略和扩张提供了“理论”依据。事实上，否认真理的客观性也就否定了真理的实践性，对真理客观性的否认和排斥必然会陷入“唯意志论”的泥坑。正如列宁所指出的那样：“把真理看作认识的工具，这就是在实际上已经转到不可知论方面，也就是离开唯物主义。在这一点上，以及在一切根本点上，实用主义者、马赫主义者、经验一元论者都是一丘之貉。”（罗森塔尔、尤金 639）实验主义者还反对用革命的手段对不合理的社会制度（包括经济基础及其上层建筑以及与它们相适应的意识形态）作根本性的变革，提倡一点一滴的改良，麻痹以致消解被压迫群众的革命斗争意志。胡适在这方面表现得尤为突出。

20 世纪 70 年代末，曾进行过一场关于真理问题的大辩论，“实践是检验真理的唯一标准”为拨乱反正、改革开放提供了理论根据。殊不知在这场大辩论之前，早在 1921 年胡适就站在实验主义立场上，提出过“一切学说与理想都须用实行来试验过；实验是真理的唯一试金石”（胡适：《杜威先生与中国》 361—362）。尽管措辞有所不同，但意思同“实践是检验真理的唯一标准”应该说基本上是一样的，这就给人们——至少是不懂哲学的我——出了一个难题：为什么水火不容的马克思主义和实验主义，在这个问题上却会有大致相同或相近的结论呢？莫非胡适说的“实验是真理的唯一试金石”，和马克思主义关于“实践是检验真理的唯一标准”性质截然相反，两者风马牛不相及，根本就不是一回事？

我知道过去鲁迅曾经讥讽胡适是“特种学者”（鲁迅：《且介亭杂文末编·〈出关〉的“关”》 423），说“杜威教授有他的实验主义，白璧德教授有他的人文主义，从他们那里零零碎碎贩运一点回来的就变成了中国的呵斥八极的学者”（鲁迅：《南腔北调集·大家降一级试试看》 417）。鲁迅的话虽然一针见血，但毕竟不是哲学批判，不能解决我在理论上的困惑。为此我请教了几位专门搞哲学的专家，哪知哲学家言有如云山雾罩，更让我摸不着头脑。我只好努力从马克思主义经典作家们的著作中寻求答案，包括通读列宁的《唯物主义与经验批判主义》，但我对有关问题的理解一定是肤浅的，因为我既不真正懂得马克思主义哲学，也不懂得实验主义哲学。不懂必然导致肤浅，肤浅是写不了胡适这个“庞然大物”的。

对郭沫若也是如此。周扬曾经将郭沫若和歌德相比，说“两个文化巨人确有相似之处。文思的敏捷和艺术的天才，百科全书式的渊博知识”（9）。首先在文学方面，郭沫若既是诗人，又是史剧作家，还写小说和散文，几乎无所不能，《郭沫若全集》文学编达二十卷之多。郭沫若还是历史学家，并且自成一派，如关于中国封建社会始于何时，范文澜等大多数历史学家认为自周朝开始，毛泽东在《中国革命与中国共产党》中采用的就是这一通常的观点，郭沫若则认为晚至战国时期中国方才进入封建社会。郭沫若在金文、甲骨文研究方面也取得了重大的、突破性的成就，受到过日本政坛元老西园寺公望的极口称誉。

郭沫若是一个绝顶聪明的人，他本来对金文、甲骨文一窍不通，除了断定拓片上有些白色的线纹是文字之外，几乎是两眼一抹黑，然而一旦找到了门径，差不多只有一两天工夫，他便完全了解了它的秘密。在流亡日本期间，郭沫若费了千辛万苦写成了《甲骨文字研究》，那时他们一家生活十分困难，虽然官办的中央研究院史语所所长傅斯年同意在中研院季刊上发表，以后再出版，付给作者优厚的稿酬，但“耻食周粟”的郭沫若还是拒绝了，1931 年《甲骨文字研究》和《殷周青铜器铭文研究》才由上海大东书局影印出版。从那时起，郭沫若这个文坛上的巨星，又在考古学和历史学领域持久不息地放射着耀眼的光辉。《郭沫若全集》收录的郭沫若的史学著作有八卷，考古方面的著作有十卷。所以，说郭沫若具有百科全书式的渊博知识并非溢美之词，像郭沫若这样的天才和巨匠是中华民族的骄傲而不是耻辱，国内外有些人大肆诋毁和贬损郭沫若实在是不自量力。王蒙先生就充分肯定郭沫若的成就，对诋毁和贬损郭沫若的言行嗤之以鼻。

《郭沫若传》出版过若干种，作者多数是学中文的，或在大学中文系任教，或在研究单位从事现当代文学研究。这些作者写的《郭沫若传》偏重于郭沫若的文学活动及其成就，对郭沫若在史学方面的成就论叙就显得薄弱，对郭沫若在考古方面的成就则基本未予涉及。学历史的人对郭沫若在史学方面的成就比较熟悉，他们写的《郭沫若传》具有史传的性质，但由于对郭沫若的文学创作缺乏艺术感悟力，谈不出多少门道出来。总之是各有所长，也各有所短，原因就在于这些作者的学识远不如郭沫若那么渊博。

我参与过《郭沫若全集》文学编的编辑工作，也写过关于郭沫若的书，本来我有撰写《郭沫若全传》的想法，但最终还是放弃了，原因就在于我的知识面不广，学识远远不够，对文学比较熟悉一点，对历史只略知一二，对于考古则全然无知。比起哲学来，考古更是我无法逾越的门槛，这样怎能写好《郭沫若全传》呢?

上面讲了那么多，无非是说明：为既是作家又是学者的大师级人物写传，需要传记作者具备相当丰富的学识。愿以此和从事传记写作的同行们共勉。

最后想说几句也许并非“题外”的话：我不大赞成年纪轻轻就为自己写传，如像某些影视明星和主持人那样。阅历尚浅，未经磨炼摔打，有什么可“传”可“记”的?王蒙先生就是在晚年才写自传的，在这之前不知有多少人为王蒙立传，但读者最想看的还是王蒙的自传——他说自己写总比别人“照猫画虎”或“隔帘观影”来得真切实在。须知创作是一种严肃的事业，作家是一种高尚的称谓，作家尤其是青年作家应当自尊自爱，在自己未悟透人生的真谛，创作尚不够成熟，远未能形成自己的独特风格之前，大可不必急着为自己树碑立传。如果有“好事者”找上门来，最好的“接待”方式就是像钱钟书先生那样将其拒之门外，因为这些人尤其是某些“娱记”无非是慕名求利而已。当然，中外都有英年早逝而卓有成就的作家，为他们写传不受此限。

注释【Notes】

①王蒙此次讲演内容未见诸文字，此处乃据作者记忆。

引用文献【Works Cited】

毛泽东：《实践论》，《毛泽东选集》第1卷。北京：人民出版社，1991年。

[Mao Zedong. "On Practice." *Selected Works of Mao Tse-tung*. Vol.I. Beijing: People's Publishing House, 1991.]

——：《新民主主义论》，《毛泽东选集》第2卷。北京：人民出版社，1991年。

[——. "On New Democracy." *Selected Works of Mao Tse-tung*. Vol.II. Beijing: People's Publishing House, 1991.]

胡适：《杜威先生与中国》，《胡适全集》第1卷。合肥：安徽教育出版社，2003年。

[Hu Shi. "Mr. Dewey and China." *Complete Works of Hu Shi*. Vol.1. Hefei: Anhui Education Press, 2003.]

——：《日记（1928—1930年）》，《胡适全集》第31卷。合肥：安徽教育出版社，2003年。

[——. "Diary (May 10, 1928)." *Complete Works of Hu Shi*. Vol.31. Hefei: Anhui Education Press, 2003.]

罗森塔尔、尤金主编：《简明哲学辞典》，中共中央马恩列斯著作编译局译。北京：人民出版社，1958年。

[Rosenthal, M., and P.Yudin. *A Concise Dictionary of Philosophy*. Trans. The Translation Bureau of CCCPC. Beijing: People's Publishing House, 1958.]

鲁迅：《且介亭杂文末编·〈出关〉的"关"》，《鲁迅全集》第6卷。北京：人民文学出版社，1985年。

[Lu Xun. "The 'Pass' in the Essay 'Out of Han Gu Pass' from 'Essays Written in the Backroom at Shanghai Semi-Concession'." *The Complete Works of Lu Xun*. Vol.6. Beijing: People's Literature Publishing House, 1985.]

——：《南腔北调集·大家降一级试试看》，《鲁迅全集》第4卷。北京：人民文学出版社，1985年。

[——. "If You Had Been Demoted' from Essays 'Mixed Dialects'." *Complete Works of Lu Xun*. Vol.4. Beijing: People's Literature Publishing House, 1985.]

周扬：《悲痛的怀念》，《悼念郭老》，新华月报资料室编。北京：生活·读书·新知三联书店，1979年。

[Zhou Yang. "The Mournful Commemoration." *In Memory of Mr. Guo*. Beijing: SDX Joint Publishing, 1979.]

上帝的归上帝，恺撒的归恺撒

——《花间词祖：温庭筠传》和我的传记生涯

李金山

内容提要：《温庭筠传》是“中国历史文化名人传”中的一本，它是我写作的第五部传记。我的写作从散文开始，以后逐步转向传记。所以，我的传记处处可见散文的影响：结构是散文化的，精神是写实的，语气则好比朋友谈心，促膝而坐，侃侃而谈。《温庭筠传》也有这样的特点。陈寅恪先生主张“了解之同情”，这是《温庭筠传》的一种基本态度，也是我写作传记的一种基本态度。好的传记不仅要够专业，还要够好读，既要保证真实性，还要有丰富的细节。历史的细节史料有记载最好，阙如时，须靠想象来补充。用想象来补充细节时，必须避免想象伤害到真实。真实与想象，各有各的边界，不可逾越。《温庭筠传》的做法是，但凡想象出来的细节，必定明确标出，以免读者混淆，所谓“上帝的归上帝，恺撒的归恺撒”。

关键词：李金山　传记　温庭筠　散文化　诗史互证

作者简介：李金山，1997年毕业于吉林大学哲学系，现供职山西省作家协会创作研究部。中国作协会员，中国传记文学学会理事。著有传记《司马光：自信不疑的保守派》(2009)、《李鸿章：“裱糊匠”的慷慨与悲凉》(2010)、《重说司马光》(2010)、《司马光传》(2015)、《温庭筠传》(2016)等。

Title:“Give to Caesar What Is Caesar's, and to God What Is God's”: *The Founding Father of Huajian Ci*: *Life of Wen Tingyun* and My Life Writing Career

Abstract: *Life of Wen Tingyun* is one of the book series Biographies of

Chinese Historical and Cultural Figures and my fifth biography. Starting from writing proses, my focus has gradually shifted to biographies, so the influence of prose-writing is ubiquitous in my life writing, especially on the structure. *Life of Wen Tingyun* is no exception. The sympathetic understanding advocated by the historian. Chen Yinque is the fundamental attitude guiding my practice, as reflected in *Life of Wen Tingyun*. A good biography should be professional and readable to ensure both truth and rich details. The gaps in historical documents should be filled with imagination and, in doing so, the biographer should prevent the imagination from impairing truth. Therefore, the boundaries of the truth and the imagination are definite and shall not be crossed. In *Life of Wen Tingyun*, all the imagined details are clearly labeled to "Give to Caesar what is Caesar's, and to God what is God's."

Keywords: Li Jinshan, biography, Wen Tingyun, influence of prose-writing, cross-proving of poems with history

Li Jinshan graduated in 1997 from Jilin University, China. He works at Office of Literature of Shanxi Writers Association. He is a member of China Writers Association and a director of the Biography Society of China. He is the biographer of *Sima Guang: A Confident Conservative* (2009), *Li Hongzhang: Generosity and Desolation of a Reformist* (2010), *A Reappraisal of Sima Guang* (2010), *A Biography of Sima Guang* (2015) and *A Biography of Wen Tingyun* (2016). E-mail: 739636144@qq.com.

这次，我的传主叫温庭筠，又作廷筠、庭云，字飞卿，本名岐，他生活在晚唐时代。

关于温庭筠在文学史上的地位，郑振铎在《中国文学史》中讲得极到位：晚唐时代的代表作家，无疑是温庭筠与李商隐，“其余诸作家，除杜牧等若干人外，殆皆依附于他们二人的左右者”（331）。关于晚唐时代的文学，则说：“这个时代的诗人们，其风起云涌的气势，大似开元、天宝的全盛时代。但其作风却大不相同。”（331）文学与国运盛衰，没什么直接关联，盛唐文学与晚唐文学，只有文学风格的不同，没有水平高下的差异。

郑振铎所讲的地位，主要指的是诗歌。温庭筠与李商隐，并称“温李”，他们是晚唐绮艳诗风的代表人物。此外，温庭筠又以“花间词祖”驰名，是晚唐五代香艳词风与词史上婉约词风的开拓者，与稍晚的韦庄并称“温韦”。

温庭筠是第一位大力填词的人，一生写了大量的词，流传至今的，就有七十首。而且，现存温庭筠的词作当中，所用曲调达十九种，其中多为温庭筠所创。调名常与词的内容相关，如此多样的曲调，为表现丰富的内容与情感提供了可能。温庭筠用他的大量作品，为词这种文学形式的独立奠定了稳固的基础。刘毓盘《词史》说："其所创各体……虽自五七言诗句法出，而渐与五七言诗句法离。所谓解其声故能制其调也，宜后人奉以为法矣。"（38）温庭筠精通音律，有能力"倚声制词"，词与诗因此分道扬镳。在词的发展过程中，温庭筠是个里程碑，词从此成为独立文体。

词在温庭筠的推动下勃然兴起，为宋词的兴盛奠定了基础。为什么承上启下的是温庭筠而不是其他人呢？我认为原因有三：首先，温庭筠生长江南。吴风越俗熏陶，他的情色启蒙早，而且异于中原。宋代词人柳永，也是生长江南，这个耐人寻味。其次，温庭筠郁郁不得志。他心向官场心无旁骛，可是偏偏累举不第，参加科举许多年，始终名在孙山外。不得志使他转身，背向官场面向青楼，他与歌妓们打成一片。他屡屡填词，既是为歌妓，也是为自己。歌妓演唱温词，演唱者和受众，又决定了词的艳。温庭筠的创作，是有规定情境的。最后，他有音乐方面的才华。倚曲填词非懂音律不行，而温庭筠恰是此中高手。

我写《温庭筠传》，是先做年表，年经事纬，传主一生事迹，能系于日的系于日，能系于月的系于月，能系于年的系于年，年表尽可能地细；然后，又把温庭筠置于晚唐的大背景下审视，以《资治通鉴·唐纪》设置底色，温庭筠的人生选择，都会找到合理的原因；年表做好以后，精心选取传主人生的关键节点，谋篇布局，安排章节，结构全书；此后，就是精心描绘，不吝笔墨，不惜精力。这是我写传记的方法。

现在我的作品以传记为主，但我的写作从散文开始。不是没有做过其他尝试，小说、诗歌、电影，等等，在写作的初期，我都曾涉猎，但一番比较之后，觉得散文这种文体更适合自己的才性。我的散文写作，可以分为三个阶段。第一个阶段对我影响最大的是金圣叹。2000 年左右，我在测绘局画地图，偶尔从旧书摊上，读到金圣叹的文章，文章的篇名记不起了，其中讲他惬意的那些时刻，比如盖了房子挂起画，自己坐在房子里，如此之类，这使我大为惊叹：原来文章可以这样有趣！所以“趣味”是我散文的一个特点，有人评价为“冷幽默”，寓诙谐于凝重的叙述当中，不是开怀大笑，而是会心一笑。这是我写散文的第一个阶段。十多年前，我流连“新散文”网站，既读帖也发帖，既是读者也是作者。当时的“新散文”网站，是一班写诗的朋友搞起来的，大概因为这个原因，“新散文”注重细节的呈现：时间慢下来，细节无限放大。受此影响，我的许多散文细节丰富。这是我写散文的第二个阶段。后来，我读到了韩石山先生的文章，他说散文作者应当先成为某方面的专家，然后其文可观。当时我恰好对宋代人物司马光感兴趣，所以就着手研究司马光，花了三年多的时间，写出一部《重说司马光》，韩先生欣然为之作序，由中国青年出版社出版，时间是在2010年。接着，我写了一批关于宋代吃喝的文章。这个阶段的散文注重知识性，可以为读者提供有趣的历史知识。这是我写散文的第三个阶段。从第三个阶段开始，我实际已转向传记写作，此后不怎么写散文了，传记倒是一本接一本地出。先后出版的传记有《司马光：自信不疑的保守派》（北京：中国发展出版社，2009年5月）、《李鸿章：“裱糊匠”的慷慨与悲凉》（北京：中国发展出版社，2010年1月）、《重说司马光》（北京：中国青年出版社，2010年12月）、《司马光传》（太原：北岳文艺出版社，2015年11月）等。

我的散文写作与传记写作，究竟有没有关系呢？如果有关系，又是种什么关系呢？我觉得它们肯定是有关系，散文写作为传记写作提供了经验。这种经验首先是文字方面的。散文是谈话的语气，就是说设置的情境是谈话，写散文犹如与读者交谈，虽然这位读者并非真的存在。因为是交谈不是宣讲，所以作者与读者是平视的，是平等的，是朋友的，是温和的，是敞开心扉的，是平易的，也是口语的，生僻的、书面的语言应尽量避免。这些也构成了我传记的特点，好比朋友谈心，促膝而坐，侃侃而谈。这一点与诗歌背景的作品有别：诗歌是独语的，像戏剧中的独白，设置的情境是与自己的对话，是讲给自己听的，是自言自语的，虽然观众也可以听到。比如吕新的小说，吕新早期写诗歌，所以他的小说，或多或少染上了诗歌的特色，某种程度上也是独语的，是自己讲给自己听的，尽管他也发表出来。其次是结构方面的。散文的结构是散的，形散而神聚，看似漫不经心，实际有一个主题。散文没有故事，没有情节，没有发生、发展、高潮和结局。我的传记结构上是散文化的，而非小说化的，这一点有别于小说家背景的传记作家作品，他们的传记结构是小说的，是故事的，是有起承转合的。比如刘小川的《品中国文人》系列，刘小川早期写小说，所以《品中国文人》或多或少染上了小说的特色，它是依托于故事的，是有起承转合的。最后，是精神方面的。散文是写实的，虽然也有人主张散文可以虚构，但整体的精神是写实的，寻求事物的本来面目，探究事件的来龙去脉。而小说的精神是虚构，追求虚构之美，真实不是它的终极目的，虚构才是终极目的。我的传记是散文的写实的，这一点有别于小说化的传记：它们有很多的虚构，有丰富的细节，但精神上与传记是冲突的。

关于我所作传记散文性的谈话语气，可以略举温词风格为例：王国维《人间词话》概括温词的风格说："'画屏金鹧鸪'，飞卿语也，其词品似之。"这里"画屏金鹧鸪"出自温词《更漏子》：

> 柳丝长，春雨细，花外漏声迢递。惊塞雁，起城乌，画屏金鹧鸪。
> 香雾薄，透帘幕，惆怅谢家池阁。红烛背，绣帘垂，梦长君不知。

考虑到读者是当代人，我对该词略作解释："迢递，悠远。谢家，即谢娘家，歌妓类人物的代称。红烛背，用屏、帐、帷等遮暗灯烛的亮光。"（李金山 3）这样的解释显然不够，我接下来这样谈：

> 温庭筠是状写妇人日常情态的高手。春雨似芒，柳丝如绦，更声远远传来。这更声惊着了北方飞来的雁和城楼上宿着的乌。女子面对画屏上的金色鹧鸪，黯然神伤：情郎沙场无消息。只好独自入眠，梦中好见情郎。温庭筠词中的女子，满腹心事，孤寂落寞，凄美，美得让人心痛。（李金山 3—4）

关于该词妙处，古来评价多多，我为读者介绍了晚清著名词家陈廷焯《白雨斋词话》，以及现代学者钱锺书《管锥编》的评价，并将二人的评价提炼为："温词蕴藉而含蓄，词写少妇思夫，但始终不道破，词有尽而意无穷。"（李金山 4）最后再与开头呼应，谈温词与温诗的关系。

正如举例所见，我所作传记设置的情境是谈话，写传记好比与朋友交谈，作者与读者是平等的，所以是平视的，尽量避免生僻的、书面的语言。

关于我所作传记的散文性形散神聚，可以举第四章《入蜀》为例。在叙述到温庭筠出蜀的经历时，我引入他的传奇小说《王诸》：

> 温庭筠正漫游蜀中，他的传奇小说《王诸》，讲了个蜀中故事。……《王诸》的故事是这样：大历（唐代宗李豫年号，766—779 年）间，邛州（治今四川省邛州市）刺史崔励，他的外甥王诸，家住在绵州（治今四川省绵阳市）。王诸经常往来秦蜀间，与仓部令史赵盈很投缘……与赵盈的外甥女，举行了仪式。故事先讲到这里。（李金山 45—46）

接下去，继续写温庭筠的出蜀经历：

> 温庭筠离开新津，不久到达巫山县（今重庆市巫山县），他为巫山神女写诗，《巫山神女庙》："黯黯闭宫殿，霏霏荫薜萝。晓峰眉上色，春水脸前波。古树芳菲尽，扁舟离恨多。一丛斑竹夜，环珮响如何？"（李金山 46）
>
> ……

叙述温庭筠出蜀经历，却又引入传奇小说《王诸》，形式上显得比较散，但实际是有一个主题，就是这个出蜀。这是散文的思维。我将经历与故事作为两条线索，纽结起来向前推进。这种叙述方式貌似漫不经心，旁逸斜出，但整个篇章的内容，逐渐丰富起来：本来只有一个主干，后来变得枝繁叶茂。

关于我所作传记散文性的写实，可以举第三章《江南》作例子。温庭筠祖籍山西太原，但出生与成长是在江南，具体在江南哪儿呢？在《花间鼻祖：温庭筠传》中，我从他的诗歌入手，来考证他的出生和生长地：

> 温庭筠有诗《送卢处士游吴越》，……卢处士游吴越，尚可见残梅，温庭筠很羡慕，自己不能归去。那么，温庭筠在江南的家，不是在吴就是在越。
>
> 我们还记得，《北梦琐言》卷二十说，温庭筠有个外甥名叫沈徽，吴兴人。吴兴即湖州……而温庭筠在江南的家，可能离舅舅家不远，可能就在湖州，或者距离湖州不远。（李金山 23—24）

接下去，我从温诗《卢氏池上遇雨赠同游者》，推知温庭筠在江南的家应在吴淞江流域；又用唐代佚名《玉泉子》的记载，推知温庭筠在江南的家应该就在江淮之间，或者距离江淮之间不远；再从温诗《寄卢生》，推知温庭筠在江南的家应在今江苏苏州附近，并且临近太湖；还有，再由温诗《吴苑行》，推知诗中的小苑应在吴苑之中，或者在吴苑附近，这小苑该是温庭筠在江南的家。最后我这样作结：

> 我们步步紧逼，逐渐接近目标，来总结一下：从温庭筠的诗中，我们先是推知，温庭筠在江南的家，在今浙江省湖州市，或者距此不远；而后我们更进一步，推知在今吴淞江流域；接着又推知，在今江苏苏州附近；继而又推知，在今苏州西南的太湖之滨。温庭筠在江南的家，就在今苏州西南的太湖之滨。（李金山 25）

如此例所见，我所作传记是写实的，这种写实源于散文。我用温庭筠的诗、相关记载作论据，来论证温庭筠在江南的家究竟是在江南的哪儿。

温庭筠到了京师，定居在京郊鄠县（今陕西省户县）。温庭筠不住长安却住在鄠县，这是为什么呢？传记属于史学的分支，史学就是史料学。传记作家的工作，首先在于获取材料。采访当事人及直接关系人，对于健在或者过世不久的传主，无疑是获取材料的好方法；即便对于数千年前的传主，实地走访也还是需要，山川形势古今变化不大，山还是那山，水还是那水，走访或有意外收获。刚才我们的问题，如果是针对为何不住在长安，原因很简单：长安消费太高。大诗人白居易初至长安，去拜访前辈诗人顾况，顾况打趣他：长安米贵，居不易也。温庭筠并不富裕，他不能住在长安，就好比今天生活在北京的人，购房的时候，不选三环以内，而愿意选择郊县。那么，长安下辖县份很多，为何偏偏选择鄠县呢？这个原因就要到当地去找。2013 年 10 月，我去到陕西户县渼陂。中国的北方通常缺水，而这里却有一片湖泊，天然的湖泊。空气一下子湿润起来，鱼戏莲叶间，舟荡碧波上，感觉像是到了江南。鄠县风物似江南。温庭筠生长在江南。我由此推断：该是环境的相似，使他选择住在这里。除非去户县实地走访，否则不可能做出这样的推论。这是实地走访的好处。

20 世纪 30 年代初，陈寅恪先生写《冯友兰中国哲学史上册审查报告》时，曾提出观察历史的一个基本态度，就是对历史中发生的一切事实和人物以及学说的产生，应具“了解之同情”。陈寅恪先生说：

> 凡著中国古代哲学史者，其对于古人之学说，应具了解之同情，方可下笔……而古代哲学家去今数千年，其时代之真相，极难推知。吾人今日可依据之材料，仅为当时所遗存最小之一部，欲藉此残余断片，以窥测其全部结构，必须备艺术家欣赏古代绘画雕刻之眼光及精神……与立说之古人，处于同一境界……表一种之同情，始能批评其学说之是非得失，而无隔阂肤廓之论。(281)

陈寅恪先生的判断主要基于两点：一是后人所能得到的史料不可能完全；二是后人极难对当时的历史事实和人物处境完全明了。所以“了解之同情”就极为重要。而要做到这一点，需努力与古人处于同一境界。虽然陈寅恪先生是就中国古代哲学史的研究发此感慨，但它对观察一切历史人物都具有启发意义。以此理解花间词祖温庭筠，正是《温庭筠传》的一种基本态度，也是我写作传记的一种基本态度。

温庭筠擅长诗赋，考场上八吟即成八韵，人送雅号“温八吟”，他是位“考试达人”。按照此种情形，他该是状元及第，仕途畅达，而实际情形却恰恰相反，温庭筠屡试不第，终生没有考中进士。那么，究竟是为什么呢？

这该与唐朝的科举制度有关。众所周知，科举制度肇始于隋朝，唐朝开国后继承下来，当时的科举尚不完备，人为的因素还很多。举个大诗人王维的例子，《唐才子传》卷二说：“王维，字摩诘，擅书法，通音律。”岐王喜欢与文士们交往，很看重他，考试前带着王维去见九公主。九公主听过王维的曲子，读过王维的诗作，喜欢得不得了，极力举荐他。开元九年（721 年），王维进士及第。王维的科举经历说明，权贵政要的举荐很重要，足以决定科举的结果。唐朝的科举制度不健全，权贵政要左右着科举结果，温庭筠屡试不第，根本原因在这里。

唐朝不健全的科举制度下，决定科举结果的不是才能，不是你的诗如何好赋如何好，而是与权贵政要的关系怎么样。不幸得很，温庭筠得罪了两个人：一个是宰相，一个是皇帝。有才自然容易骄傲，温庭筠恃才傲物。恃才傲物会受到嫉恨，嫉恨的人又位高权重，温庭筠的遭遇，可想而知。温庭筠坎坷终身，是注定了的。

清代顾予咸在《温庭筠诗解序》中说，温庭筠生性放纵，从不循规蹈矩，他才高八斗，卓尔不群，刚直不阿，“是则文人之才高乃穷，穷乃工，工乃传；传矣，久乃益新”（刘学锴 1311）。坎坷也不全是坏事，温庭筠坎坷终身，对他个人是悲剧，对后人却是财富，他留下了大量好作品，让人常读而常新。

《温庭筠全集校注》中收录的文章，颇多上某某启，这是写给权贵政要的书信：他希望得到权贵政要的举荐，以利中第。温庭筠的存世文章，很多都是这样的作品。这些书信用典丰富精致典雅，在当时都属于实用文体，写起来可能未必用心，但往往越是率性，越是好文章。这些书信奏效者稀。屡屡不奏效，只好接着写。温庭筠的这些文章，都是坎坷的产物。

晚唐知识分子的出路通常有两条：一条是科举，但当时科举选拔的人很少，这条路很窄；另一条就是依附政要，成为他们的幕僚。温庭筠一生足迹遍南北，目的基本只有一个，那就是寻求入幕。温庭筠有大量的羁旅行役诗，如《商山早行》《利州南渡》《送人东游》《过五丈原》《过陈琳墓》《赠知音》等，都是历代传诵的名篇。这些诗都是在旅途上写的，在寻求入幕的旅途上，寻求入幕是主要目的，羁旅行役诗是副产品。寻求入幕大多无果，却写出诸多诗歌名篇。

温庭筠生活的时代，藩镇割据，宦官骄横，朋党倾轧，危机四伏。温庭筠的远祖是初唐名相温彦博，祖先的荣耀规定了他的人生，修齐治平的儒家观念，早已深入他的骨髓，他渴望匡时济世，渴望有所作为。温庭筠在诗文中，一再写到他的理想，《过孔北海墓二十韵》："蕴策期干世，持权欲反经。"（刘学锴 576）《过陈琳墓》："词客有灵应识我，霸才无主始怜君。"（刘学锴 387）……可是温庭筠累举不第，他参加科举几十年，始终名在孙山外，历史没有给他施展抱负的机会。温庭筠的性格是不平则鸣，他不会忍耐更不会忘记，他将不满发泄在诗文里。温庭筠有很多的讽刺诗，如《晓仙谣》《鸡鸣埭歌》《春江花月夜词》《雉场歌》《达摩支曲》，等等。温庭筠批评历代的昏君，借以批评晚唐的昏君，他笔锋辛辣，敢想敢写，使晚唐批判现实的诗歌呈现出别具一格的风貌。唐代范摅《云溪友议》卷中说：唐穆宗时人平曾，恃才傲物，多犯忌讳，沉沦下僚，知己鸣不平，说他命不好，"后温庭筠为赋，亦警刺，少类于平曾，而谪方城……"（刘学锴 1300）温庭筠的赋尖锐，这些赋今已不传。温庭筠因为怀才不遇，为发泄而写尖锐的诗赋；反过来又因为这些诗赋，温庭筠更加怀才不遇。温庭筠批评性质的诗赋，同样也是坎坷的产物。

温庭筠现存诗歌有四百首，它们是我可凭借的材料。传主材料过多或过少，写作传记都会遭遇困难：材料过多难在选择，而过少则难在缺少凭借。这犹如历史研究，先秦史材料稀少，而明清民国材料繁多，两者都比较难于研究。所以传主材料，不多不少才好。温庭筠作为传主，材料既不过多，也不过少，可谓恰到好处：正史、笔记中的记载不多，而且语焉不详、颠三倒四、矛盾重重，可凭借的主要是诗歌，各种记载中的疑问，也可以从诗歌中解决。众所周知，陈寅恪主张“诗史互证”，将诗歌当作史料使用，大大扩展了史料的范围。就他的具体实践而言，在中古史研究方面，多取“以诗证史”，推明制度与文化；而在近代史研究方面，则多取“史以证诗”，探究人事与心史。温庭筠生当晚唐时代，本书的所作所为，可以归类为中古史研究；但传记这种文体，关注人事与心史。因此本书中对“诗史互证”的运用，既有“以诗证史”，也有“史以证诗”，但还是“以诗证史”居多：将温庭筠的诗歌作为史料，去探究温庭筠的心史，以及与传主有关的人事。

关于“以诗证史”，前文所举以温诗为材料，论证温庭筠在江南的家，在今苏州西南的太湖之滨，可以当作一个例子。关于“史以证诗”，我可以举第十九章《与鱼玄机》为例。温庭筠比鱼玄机大三十三四岁，他是她的文学启蒙老师。鱼玄机有倾城倾国貌，温庭筠别号“温钟馗”，两人的长相天上地下，看似绝不可能的事情，就在两人之间发生了，鱼玄机恋着温庭筠；但温庭筠似乎感情上有洁癖，他无法接受鱼玄机的感情。经温庭筠牵线，鱼玄机嫁给了状元李亿为妾，李亿年轻有功名，温庭筠完全出于好心。但李亿夫人悍妒，鱼玄机形同守活寡。李亿去鄂州做官，鱼玄机千里迢迢去追他，被相思煎熬着，鱼玄机的性格，爱就爱得深刻；到了鄂州，却不同李亿住在一起，因李亿跟妻子在一起，于是两人悄悄幽会。鄂州之后，鱼玄机又独自去了江陵（今湖北省荆州市荆州区），时令在秋天，她写诗《重阳阻雨》《江陵愁望寄子安》。鱼玄机为什么要从鄂州去江陵呢？为什么在江陵写下这两首诗呢？鄂州之行后她该返回长安，去江陵等于是南辕北辙。如果单独来看，鱼玄机的行踪不可解，两首诗也不可解；但若知道温庭筠的所在，就能明白鱼玄机的道理：此时温庭筠恰在江陵，她是去向他倾诉心中委屈，请他为自己出主意。温庭筠的所在是史，明白了这个史，就可以理解鱼玄机的诗，这算是“史以证诗”。

温庭筠累举不第，心情郁闷非常，于是狂狷放浪：他的交往圈子里，有不少的歌妓。温庭筠为歌妓们写下大量的词，这些词后来被收进《花间集》，他被尊为花间词祖。温庭筠的词还是坎坷的产物。

《唐摭言》卷十一《无官受黜》记载，开成年间，温庭筠名气很大，被贬为随州县尉，温庭筠赴任，“文士诗人争为辞送……”（刘学锴 1300）被贬官不是被提拔，文人送行肯定不是为了升官，那又是为了什么呢？除了为温庭筠的名声所倾倒，还有就是出于共鸣：温庭筠的人生遭遇，与多数文人的命运相似；温庭筠的倔强性格，受到多数文人的激赏。温庭筠是晚唐的代表作家，这个代表的前提，是共同的命运与遭际。

传记是历史的分支，是历史与文学的结合，史实须确凿，叙事须流畅，二者缺一不可。如果硬要分出哪个更重要，我认为真实更重要：如果一部传记不真实，即便它的文学性再强，那也是失败的，甚至不能称为传记；相反，如果传记是真实的，尽管文学性差些，它仍不失为一部传记。我写《重说司马光》时，曾对中国传记有个判断：中国的传记大致有两类：一类是专家写的，以大学教授居多，这样的传记非常专业，但也有缺点，就是晦涩难懂，属于专业论文；另一类是小说家写的，包括地方上的文史研究者，这样的传记非常好读，但真实性让人怀疑。好的传记不仅要专业，还要好读，既要保证真实性，还要有丰富的细节。历史的细节史料有记载最好，阙如时，须靠想象来补充。靠想象补充细节，这是退而求其次的办法，是不得已而为之。使用这种办法时，必须避免想象伤害到真实。真实与想象，各有各的边界，不可逾越。所以我的做法是，但凡想象出来的细节，必定明确标出，以免读者混淆，所谓“上帝的归上帝，恺撒的归恺撒”。

我在《温庭筠传》的后记中说：“三年多以来，我所思所想，无非温庭筠：我奔走在路上，开口闭口都是温庭筠；我埋首故纸堆，翻检史料，寻找他的蛛丝马迹；我读遍他的诗词文赋，一套全新的《温庭筠全集校注》，书脊被我翻秃……”（李金山 300）我花三年时间写下这部传记，它是我一段生命的结晶。

致谢【Acknowledgment】

本文受益于《现代传记研究》匿名评审人提出的修改意见，作者谨致谢忱！

I am grateful to the editor of *Modern Life Writing Studies* and anonymous reviewers for their suggestions and comments.

引用文献【Works Cited】

陈寅恪:《陈寅恪集·金明馆丛稿二编》。上海:生活·读书·新知三联书店,2001 年。

[Chen Yinque. *Works of Chen Yinque*: *Two Volumes of Manuscripts at Jinming Mansion*. Shanghai: SDX Joint Publishing Company, 2001.]

李金山:《花间词祖:温庭筠传》。北京:作家出版社,2016 年。

[Li Jinshan. *The Founding Father of Huajian Ci*: *Life of Wen Tingyun*. Beijing: Writers Publishing House, 2016.]

刘学锴:《温庭筠全集校注》。北京:中华书局,2007 年。

[Liu Xuekai. *Annotated Complete Works of Wen Tingyun*. Beijing: Zhonghua Book Company, 2007.]

刘毓盘:《词史》。上海:上海古籍出版社,2011 年。

[Liu Yupan. *A History of Ci Poetry*. Shanghai: Shanghai Classics Publishing House, 2011.]

郑振铎:《中国文学史》。西安:陕西师范大学出版社,2010 年。

[Zheng Zhenduo. *A History of Chinese Literature*. Xi'an: Shaanxi Normal University Press, 2010.]

稿　约

传记研究已进入当代人文社会科学研究的核心领域，为学术界日益重视。本刊是中国第一个传记专业学术刊物，办刊目的是拓展和丰富传记研究的内容，开展学术讨论，为国内外学者提供发表和交流的园地，吸引和培养本领域的学术新秀。

本刊立足学术前沿，以国际化为目标，发表中文和英文稿件。本刊倡导以现代眼光和方法研究中外传记的各种问题，设立【名家访谈】【比较传记】【理论研究】【传记史研究】【作品研究】【自传评论】【日记评论】【人物研究】【传记影视】【书评】【史料考订】【传记家言】等近20种栏目，以长篇论文为主，也欢迎言之有物、立意创新的短文。本刊尊重老学者，依靠中年学者，欢迎青年学者。

自2013年创刊以来，本刊得到了国内外学者的大力支持，上海交通大学也给予稳定的出版经费资助，刊物在国内外学界的影响不断扩大。2017年，本刊入选“中文社会科学引文索引”（CSSCI）来源集刊，也被一些国际著名大学列入“国际学术刊物”或将本刊所发论文收入传记“年度学术论著目录”。

为了进一步提升本刊质量和推进国际化，来稿请遵照以下要求。

1. 中英文来稿一般请勿超过10000字。本刊聘请国内外同行专家匿名审稿，在接到来稿3个月内，回复作者处理结果。本刊只接受原创性稿件，谢绝已发表过（包括用外文发表过）的文稿。作者应严守学术道德，文责自负。

2. 学术论文类稿件须遵循以下文本格式和规范：中（英）文标题、作者姓名、内容提要（200字左右）、关键词（3—5个）、作者简介（包括学位和学衔、工作单位、研究方向、近期代表性成果1—2种、电子邮箱等，不超过150字），与以上相对应的英（中）译文。正文字体一律用宋体或Times New Roman（5号）、1.5倍行距（提要与作者简介同此），引文超过4行应独立成段（整体左缩进两字符、上下各空一行，中文用楷体）。文中内容如另需注解、释义或补充说明性等文字应以注释（Notes）形式置于文末，即手动插入连续带圈、上标的阿拉伯数字编号，文末相应给出内容。文献的引注请参照MLA格式，即采用文中括号夹注并文末列出相应引用文献（Works Cited）的方式。引用文献按作者姓氏首字母排序（无作者按文献名首字母），非西文文献须给出相应的英译信息。注释和引用文献字体为小5号。如作者在执行此格式中确实存在困难，请联系编辑部，编务人员将协助予以解决。论文如受到项目资助或他人和组织等具体帮助的，可在文末单列致谢（中英文）。

3. 本刊只接受电子word格式来稿，稿件请寄编辑部信箱：sclw209@sina. com，勿寄私人。

来稿刊出后即付薄酬，并赠送样书2册。本刊在上海交通大学传记中心设立编辑部，负责编辑、出版方面的具体工作。欢迎作者和读者就本刊工作提出意见和建议。

Instructions to Contributors

Mission

Life writing studies have moved onto the central stage in the academia and gained ever more attention both in and outside China. As the first scholarly journal in the field of China, the biannual journal *Modern Life Writing Studies* intends to fill up the blank of life writing studies in China, provide a venue for scholars all over the world, attract and promote specialists in the field.

Aiming to keep abreast of the cutting edge of life writing research, Our journal seeks to, in modern views and perspectives, explore various topics of life writing in China and in the world, with almost 20 sections included, such as Interview, Comparative Biography, Theory Study, History of Life Writing, Text Study, Autobiography Study, Diary Study, Subject Study, Film Biography, Book Reviews, Life Writing Materials, From the Life Writer, etc.

Ever since its appearance in 2013, our journal has been well-received by scholars at home and abroad and funded by a steady grant from Shanghai Jiao Tong University. It is exerting increasingly greater influence in academia with a due wide positive response. In 2017, our journal was included in CSSCI(Chinese Social Science Citation Index), and listed in the international academic literature or included in the annual annotated bibliography by world prestigious universities.

Our journal accepts both Chinese and English submissions. All the articles will be subject to anonymous peer review.

Style

Submissions are welcome from both Chinese and international researchers. Simultaneous submissions are not accepted. English papers should be between 4,000 and 7,000 words of text in length (including notes), while English book reviews are about 2,500 words. Full-length articles take up most part of the journal, but short essays with originality and fresh ideas are also welcome.

Submission Guidelines

All written submissions should be formatted according to the eighth edition of *MLA Handbook for Writers of Research Papers*. All submissions should include a 100-word abstract both in Chinese and English, keywords (less than 5), a 70-word biographical statement, and works cited. Please adhere to the following requirements:

- Double spacing, Times New Roman, 12-point font
- One-inch margins
- Only Microsoft Word doc or docx files will be accepted
- Citations should be provided in parenthetical reference followed by "Works Cited".
- Endnotes are preferred if there are any.

Submissions should be emailed in Word format to the editor sclw209@sina.com. Each contributor will get two complimentary copies once his/her paper is published.

Our journal is based at SJTU Center for Life Writing. We welcome suggestions and proposals, from which we believe our journal will surely benefit.

编后记

本辑“名家访谈”的嘉宾穆兰（Joanny Anne Moulin）教授是一位法国传记理论家，也是出版过多部作品的传记家，他在本刊的采访中，结合自己的经验，对读者关心的传记写作和传记理论中的许多问题作了回答，让我们看到具有丰富哲学资源的当代法国学术界对传记的思考以及法国传记发展的现状。谢谢穆兰教授！

传记是一种古老的文类，但总不断有新形式出现，或者说旧形式复兴。本辑“理论研究”中的两篇论文都是对这一现象的探讨。传记以人物为对象，这是人们的共识，但是历来也不乏以物为对象的“传记”，20世纪末以来这又成为潮流，出现了“物传记”“江河传记”“建筑传记”，等等。芦坚强的论文研究“城市传记”，它是“与人物传记并列的一种传记类型，是隶属传记文学的一种类型化书写”，在对它进行历史梳理的基础上分析了其理论内涵与价值特点。芦坚强此文并不完全代表本刊编辑部的观点，我们发表它是为了表明对青年学者学术探索的支持。此文虽然多次修改，但仍存在一些问题，有待作者和学术界进一步研究。

魏莱民（Daniel Vuillermin）评介新近引起英美学界关注的一种传记文类“病患志”（pathography），即作者对自己或他人患病经过的记述，魏莱民追溯了这一文体的历史发展和代表作家，也介绍了当代的研究状况。他把“病患志”称为出于同情而帮助人的“传奇科学”（The Romantic Science of the Pathography），这是对其价值和意义的一种诗意的表述。

“比较传记”发表两篇论文。孙勇彬研究萨缪尔·约翰生多年，他发现约翰生所写的《弥尔顿传》中的传主形象同更早传记中的出现颇不相同，同弥尔顿有过直接接触的作者，把他写成一个有教养、慷慨、诙谐、温和、安静、喜欢交往的人，而在约翰生的笔下，他却是高傲自大，“没有多少朋友”“不太受人喜欢”，孙勇彬将这种差异称为“传记中文本主体的可变性”，不过约翰生为什么这样写，还是值得继续研究的论题。

刘萍的论文，是对毛彦文《往事》同柳溪《人生苦旅》的比较，刘萍指出，这两部传记都以普通女性的视角反映复杂、动荡的历史变迁，虽然叙事风格不尽相同，传主身份相距甚远，但都是通过婚姻和事业，展示出她们相似的隐忍与反抗兼具的品格，以及现代知识女性的成长历程。这一比较具有启发性，也可以提升阅读的兴趣。

本辑“作品研究”是对两部作家传记的研究。王尔德是英国著名作家，关于他的传记和影视作品已有多种，阿克罗伊德别树一帜，他以虚拟的王尔德日记的形式，写出一部实验性的、小说化的《王尔德别传》。“身份”是后现代批评的重要概念，吴轶群着重分析这部传记中王尔德对身份的追求，以及身份的剥离和重塑。这样就比较准确地把握了一部后现代传记的核心，有助于阅读这部作品和理解王尔德的一生。

卢婕介绍了艾米莉·狄金森的亲友所写的关于她的几部传记，这些作品中有大量的虚构的内容，包括矫饰、夸张、扭曲、变形，但是，他们共同塑造了一个神秘和超然的狄金森形象，极大地满足了读者对一位天才女性诗人的想象，推动和帮助了狄金森成为经典。传记所发挥的这种功能恐怕是教科书上没有的，它也丰富了我们对传记的认识。

“自传评论”发表三篇论文。高永研究的对象是一篇小说，即契科夫的名作《带小狗的女人》，但它又是契科夫的精神自传：契科夫将自己对爱情既向往又恐惧的心理透过变形镜投影到小说中。面对爱情，契诃夫似乎永远保持若即若离的姿态，他用这篇小说对自己的爱情观进行自嘲。毋庸置疑，文学作品常常具有自传性，但是研究者揭示时应当十分慎重，要避免穿凿附会和过度阐释，高永细致地探析契科夫同其小说之间的精神联系，为从小说中如何找出自传成分做出一种示范。

沈忱研究宋谭秀红的战时回忆录，称之为“独特的战争叙事”：她同民族主义疏离，从人性悲悯的视角关注战争；基于海外华人和女性作者的边缘身份，她将故土寻根和对家庭生活的渴望融入了战争反思。黄莉莉评论巴恩斯的自传《无可畏惧》，这部奇特的自传书写死亡，描写死亡恐惧，对死亡进行思考，探讨死亡与写作的关系；作者也在死亡书写中坚持自我意识和自己的身份以及文化渊源。这两篇评论都比较准确地把握了作品的特点。

本辑“口述历史研究”中的口述者都是被社会忽视的人物。第二次世界大战中，有超过100万的苏联女兵参战，她们付出巨大牺牲，为胜利做出重要贡献，但是她们却是一种沉默的存在，被淹没在男性的宏大历史叙事之中。白俄罗斯女作家阿列克西耶维奇打破禁锢，她的《我是女兵，也是女人》通过500多次采访，记录了战争中幸存的女兵们的声音，为她们“建造一座感情的圣殿”。朱研的论文探讨了这位诺贝尔文学奖得主在复调风格中刻画的女兵们流动的主体性，评价了这部口述历史社会的、历史的和审美的价值。

孙会的论文评介了中国特殊教育（即残疾人士的教育）第一位专家朴永馨的口述史，也希望更多的人来关注这一特殊教育领域和残疾人群体，改善其处境。传记是一种弘扬人道主义的文类，口述历史常常发挥特殊的作用。

“传记史研究”是一个需要加强的领域，本辑发表了胡燕对清末民初商务印书馆所出版的汉译传记的研究，阳清对刘孝标《世说新语注》中所征引的僧人别传的考订及对其学术价值的论析，虽然两篇论文所涉及的只是中国传记史中的细节，但对现有的研究成果也是重要的补充。

本辑“人物研究”的传主是英国16世纪著名的空想社会主义者《乌托邦》一书的作者托马斯·莫尔，他身居高位，才华出众，品质高尚，为世人仰慕，最后却死在亨利八世的断头台上。蔡青辰分析了造成莫尔死亡的复杂历史背景和实际原因，结论是他的死是“为信仰殉道”，使读者对这位伟大的空想社会主义者有了更深入的了解。

“传记影视”中的两篇论文都带有比较的性质，吴凑春对以革命家方志敏为传主的两部电影《血沃中华》和《可爱的中国》进行了比较，证明传记电影的即时性：无论传主形象的设计与呈现，其所作所为及其精神表征，与其说是历史还原的尝试，毋宁说是国家主流意识的需要，具有时效性特征。

刘涛对以爱因斯坦为主人公的10集影视剧《天才》，同其传记原著《爱因斯坦》进行了比较，指出前者把后者提供的素材改编成一个传奇故事，同时也将出身德国的犹太人爱因斯坦的形象进行美国式的阐释，使之符合美国精神，获得美国观众的认可，从而在保障了经济收益的同时又能达到意识形态言说的目的。两者之间的根本差异在于，原著强调传记书写的客观事实、注重“说什么”的问题，影视更加关注“怎么说”的问题；不过二者又是殊途同归，都在尝试通俗的爱因斯坦传记，只不过原著着重于将爱因斯坦的事迹视为一种知识结构，以平易的叙事和浅近描写将其通俗化，而影视则侧重于以主观叙事态度和戏剧性的情节讲述爱因斯坦富有趣味的人生故事。刘涛步步深入的分析，对两种不同媒介的爱因斯坦传记从不同的层次进行了充分的比较。

本刊关注中国当代传记的实践，本辑发表了两位传记家的心得。桑逢康谈他对作家传记的主张，他希望用传主自己的风格去写其传记。比如说用“京味小说”的风格写老舍；他希望对同一位传主能有“文学传记”“评传”和“传记小说”等不同类型的传记；他也呼吁为那些大师作传时，作者应该具备丰富的学识。这些观点虽然其他人可能也说过，但是出于一位资深的现代文学的研究者和传记家之口，分量自然不同，更值得传记作者注意。

李金山以自己的作品《温庭筠传》为例，谈写作经验，其中包括他选择传主的标准、散文化的写作方法和对材料的处理、对传记真实的理解，以及对陈寅恪的“了解之同情”的赞赏。传记形式繁复，不同的写作方法可以各擅胜场，李金山虽是一家之言，但也是长期实践的体验，同样可供传记作者参考。

编辑部

2018年6月

From the Editor

In this issue, Professor Joanny Anne Moulin, a renowned French practitioner of biography and the theory, answers with his own experience many questions of readers' concern in terms of biographical writing and theories, thus providing fresh information on the status quo of the development of French biography and the contemplation on biography from the contemporary French academia which is known to all for its rich philosophical rescources. We hereby express our heartfelt gratitude to him.

As a long-standing genre, life writing frequently features new forms or revives old forms. The two papers in the section of Theory Study explore this phenomenon. It is widely accepted that the subject in a biography is a person. But it is also noticeable that many lives focuse on objects, such as "a biography of a river," or "a biography of a building." It has been a trend since the end of the 20th century. Lu Jianqiang focuses on City Biography, elaborating on "a generic writing comparable to human biography in the broad category of life-writing literature." Lu analyzes the theoretical connotations and values of City Biography with a close examination of the genre in the ancient Chinese history. Though Lu's paper remains controversial in our editorial board, it manifests our support to young scholars' academic endeavor. It undertook several corrections, and there are still conspicuous problems to be solved by the author or scholars of biography study in further explorations.

Daniel Vuillermin discusses the genre of pathography, the narration of an illness of the biographer or others. Vuillermin traces the historical evolution of this genre, representative authors and the current situation of the research. Referring to the pathography as the Romantic Science of the Pathography, he provides us with a poetic representation of its values and signification.

Two papers fall into the category of Comparative Biography. Through many years of research on Samuel Johnson, Sun Yongbin discovers the image of John Milton depicted by Johnson is different from those in the earlier biographies. Those with direct contact with Milton described him as a good-mannered, generous, humorous, mild, calm and sociable person; according to Johnson's portrayal, however, he is arrogant and unpopular with few friends. Sun terms this difference as "changeability of textual subjects in biography," but Johnson's motivation needs further studies.

In Liu Ping's paper, Mao Yanwen's *The Past* and Liu Xi's *My Miserable Life* are compared to each other. Liu states that both works reflect the complex and turbulent history from the perspective of an ordinary female and, despite discrepancy in narrative styles and the subject's identity, demonstrate their character with endurance and rebellion by their own marriage and career, especially highlighting their growth as modern intellectual women. Her comparison is illuminating and stimulates the interest to read the two biographies.

Two biographies are examined in the section of Text Study. There are many Oscar Wilde biographies, printed, film or plays, of which Peter Ackroy stands out with his *Testament of Oscar Wilde* in the form of a pseudo diary. Wu Yiqun's paper studies Wilde's pursuit, removal and refashioning of identity, enabling readers to correctly understand this experimental biography and Wilde's life.

Lu Jie examines several biographies of Emily Dickinson by her friends or relatives. These works are fraught with fictions, such as affections, overstatements and distortions, but they help to construct a mysterious and detached image of the female poet, satiate readers' imagination of her, and contribute to the canonization of her. This function of biography is rarely taught in any textbook and broadens our understanding of it.

Three papers are included in Autobiography Study. Gao Yong explores Anton Chekhov's novel *The Lady with the Dog*. In a sense it is also an autobiography of Chekhov's inner world. Chekhov yarned for love and also feared love. He projected this psyche into the novel via a sort of distorting mirror. He seemed detached in front of love and used this novel to mock at his own love conception. Undoubtedly literary works tend to be autobiographical, but researchers should be prudent and prevent over-interpretation. Gao's scrupulous analysis of the inner connections between the novelist and the novel is a fine model of dissecting novels for autobiographical elements.

Shen Chen terms Tam Soong's refugee memoir as "war narrative." Shen Chen argues that Soong looked at the war from the perspective of humanity rather than nationalism. Her identity of a Chinese American and a woman enabled her to incorporate root-seeking and the desire for a family life into her war reflection. Huang Lili's comment on Julian Barnes's *Nothing To Be Frightened Of* centers on the writing of death, the fear for death, the contemplation on death and the relations between death and writing, revealing the author's advocation for self-consciousness and self-identity in the death writing and its cultural origins. Both papers get to the core of the works.

The interviewees in the section of Oral History Study are previously neglected by the society. More than one million Soviet females joined the army in WWII and made huge sacrifices for the eventual victory. Their stories, however, were drowned in the male-dominated grand narrative as a tacit existence. S.A. Alexievich, a female Belarusian writer, courageously speaks for the "unspeakable" through her *War's Unwomanly Face*, which documents in over 500 interviews the servicewomen surviving the war, their voices functioning as a *de facto* spiritual sanctuary. Zhu Yan's paper explores the fluid subjectivity of the veterans in the polyphonic style depicted by the Nobel prize winner and assesses the social, historical and aesthetic values of this oral history.

Sun Hui's paper comments on the oral history by Piao Yongxin, the first expert in China's special education(education for the disabled), calling more attention to the field of special education and the group of the disabled for the purpose of improving their situation. To the extent that life writing is a genre of enhancing humanism, oral history, the sub-genre, tends to exert a special influence.

History of biography is an area that more work should be done. In this issue, we feature Hu Yan's research on the Chinese translated biography published by the Commercial Press at the dawning of the 20th century and Yang Qing's study of Liu Xiaobiao's borrowing Monk Biographies for his *Annotations to A New Account of the Tales of the World* and analysis of its academic value. Though both papers focus on a specific detail in the history of Chinese biography, they are significant supplementary to the present scholarship.

The section of Subject Study welcomes a treatise on Thomas More, author of *Utopian* and the Utopian socialist of the sixteenth century. Assuming a high post, More was outstanding in both his talents and integrity and thus highly respected, but ended up on the chopping block as ordered by Henry VIII. Cai Qingchen analyzes the complex historical background and reasons of More's death to conclude that More was "a martyr to faith," thus enabling a better understanding of the great utopist.

The two papers under the rubric of Film Biography Study both conduct biography comparisons. Wu Couchun compares two films of Fang Zhiming, the Chinese revolutionary, *Shedding Blood for China* and *Lovely China*, to prove the historicality of film biography. He argues that not only the design and representation of the subject's image, but also the subject's deeds and spiritual representation are the product of the nation's mainstream ideology.

It is more than an endeavor to re-create the past.

Liu Tao compares the TV drama *Genius* and its original printed biography *Einstein: Life and the Universe* to discover that the materials in the latter are adapted into a legendary story in the former. He points out that the American interpretation also shaped the image of Einstein the German Jewish in conformity with the American spirit to make it acceptable to American audience. In doing so, the film both made profits and stated ideology. The fundamental difference between the two works lies in the emphasis on objective facts(what to speak) in the original and that on how to speak in the film. Both works, however, shared the common goal in attempting to produce a popular biography of Einstein. The book biography deemed the subject's deeds as an intellectual structure in an easy-going tone, while the film one put priority on telling his amusing life stories in subjective narration and dramatic plots. Liu's penetrating analysis compares the two biographies extensively at various levels.

Priority is put on China's contemporary life writing as well. Two biographers share their experiences with us in this issue. Sang Fengkang contends that a biography of a writer be written in this writer's unique artistic style. For example, a biography of Lao She, the distinguished Chinese novelist, should be written in the "Peking novel style." It would be desirable to produce various sub-genres of life writing for the same subject, such as "literary biography," "critical biography" and "biographical novel." In light of Sang's opinion, it is imperative for biographers to build on rich academic expertise to write a good biography for literary masters. As a senior literary researcher and biographer, Sang's views are insightful and worthy of attention.

Li Jinshan's writing experience is boiled down in the case study of his *Life of Wen Tingyun*, including his measurement of selecting biographical subjects, his adapting prose-writing style into life writing, his understanding of the biographical truth and his appreciation of Mr. Chen Yinque's adage "sympathetic understanding". There are a variety of effective ways in the craft of biography for the variety of biographical forms. Li's approaches, though they seem to stand alone, are equally valuable reference for biographers, since they derive from his years of practice.

June, 2018